Contents

100662130

HG
4015.
C43
2021

PART TWO   CORPORATION TAX

PART THREE   CAPITAL GAINS TAX

PART FOUR   VALUE-ADDED TAX

Chartered Accountants Ireland *Code of Ethics*

Chartered Accountants Ireland's *Code of Ethics* applies to all aspects of a Chartered Accountant's professional life, including dealing with income tax issues, corporation tax issues, capital gains tax issues, inheritance tax issues and stamp duty issues. The *Code of Ethics* outlines the principles that should guide a Chartered Accountant, namely:

- Integrity
- Objectivity
- Professional Competence and Due Care
- Confidentiality
- Professional Behaviour

As a Chartered Accountant, you will have to ensure that your dealings with the tax aspects of your professional life are in compliance with these fundamental principles. Set out in **Appendix 2** is further information regarding these principles and their importance in guiding you on how to deal with issues which may arise throughout your professional life, including giving tax advice and preparing tax computations.

Overview of the UK Tax System

Learning Objectives

After studying this chapter you will understand:

- The principal legislation governing income tax, corporation tax, capital gains tax and VAT.
- Government's taxation objectives in the context of economic, social and environmental issues.
- Who is assessable for income tax.
- The classification of income.
- The structure and operation of HM Revenue & Customs (HMRC).
- The administration procedures for tax assessment and collection.
- The difference between tax evasion and tax avoidance.

1.1 Introduction

The main taxes levied in the United Kingdom (UK) can be classified as **taxes on income** and **taxes on transactions**. The main taxes on **income** are income tax and corporation tax. Individuals (including partners in a partnership) pay income tax on their income, while companies pay corporation tax on the profits (and some chargeable gains) of the company. Taxes on **transactions** include value-added tax (VAT), customs and excise duties, stamp duty, stamp duty land tax (SDLT), capital gains tax (CGT) and inheritance tax (IHT).

The main taxes are sometimes categorised as 'revenue' or 'capital' taxes. Revenue taxes are charged on income and include income tax and corporation tax (on income profits of a company). Capital taxes include IHT and CGT. CGT is a tax on gains, i.e. the proceeds from selling (disposing) of an asset. The basic charge to CGT applies where there is a "chargeable disposal" of a "chargeable asset" by a "chargeable person" (which, for CGT, includes individuals and companies). Some chargeable gains of a company are, however, liable to corporation tax rather than to CGT.

In addition, the main taxes may be referred to as 'direct' and 'indirect' taxes. Direct taxes are collected directly from the taxpayer and are taxes on income and/or profits. Direct taxes include income tax, corporation tax, CGT and IHT. VAT and customs and excise duties are examples of an indirect tax as they are levied on goods and services rather than on income or profits. VAT is a tax on consumer spending and, as such, is sometimes referred to as a tax on turnover as opposed to profits. Indirect taxes are not collected directly from the taxpayer.

The objective of the Taxation 1 syllabus is to "equip students with the knowledge and skills to deal with most routine issues in personal income tax, corporation tax, capital gains tax and VAT".

Each of these taxes has its own set of rules around when it should be charged, the amount it should be charged on and the rate of tax used to calculate the tax payable. The purpose of this textbook is to enable the student to understand and apply the legislation, procedure and practice that governs each of these 'tax heads'. Personal income tax is dealt with in greater detail, while the chapters on corporation tax, CGT and VAT provide an introduction to these more complex areas of taxation.

From an income tax perspective, the calculation of a tax liability depends on the individual's type of income (such as employment, self-employment, interest and dividends – see **Section 1.4**) and whether they are employed or self-employed. Calculating income tax is a step-by-step process, which can be broadly outlined as:

1. determining an individual's exposure to UK income tax, especially their domicile and residence;
2. recognising the classification of the income in question;
3. computing the amount of taxable income;
4. applying the various reliefs, allowances and deductions that are available from the Government; and
5. computing the income tax payable.

1.2 Legislation and Guidance

The main sources of legislation for income tax, corporation tax, CGT and VAT are outlined in the table below.

Tax	Main source of legislation	Abbreviation
Income tax	Income and Corporation Taxes Act 1988	ICTA 1988
	Income Tax (Earnings and Pensions) Act 2003	ITEPA 2003
	Income Tax (Trading and Other Income) Act 2005	ITTOIA 2005
	Income Tax Act 2007	ITA 2007
	Capital Allowances Act 2001	CAA 2001
Corporation tax	Corporation Tax Act 2009	CTA 2009
	Corporation Tax Act 2010	CTA 2010
	Capital Allowances Act 2001	CAA 2001
CGT	Taxation of Chargeable Gains Act 1992	TCGA 1992
VAT	Value Added Tax Act 1994	VATA 1994

In addition, the annual **Finance Acts**, which are enacted after the Budget each year, amend the relevant legislation or create new legislative provisions. This textbook includes the provisions of Finance Act 2021, which is assessable for examinations undertaken in the summer and autumn of 2022.

Certain detailed tax rules relating to the legislation are set out in regulations that are issued by HM Revenue & Customs (HMRC) under powers conferred by the relevant tax legislation. Relevant tax case law, tax practice and HMRC guidance also play an important role in putting tax legislation into effect.

For tax purposes the United Kingdom includes Great Britain and Northern Ireland, including its territorial sea; it does not include the Isle of Man, the Channel Islands or the Republic of Ireland.

1.3   Income Tax – Classes of Taxpayer

Income tax is assessed on the following:

1. individuals, on their personal employment and/or self-employment income;
2. individuals in partnerships, i.e. each partner, on their share of the income from the partnership;
3. trustees, on the income from the trust; and
4. personal representatives of a deceased individual, on the income arising from the estate of the deceased person.

Married couples (including same-sex married couples since March 2014 in the UK and February 2020 in Northern Ireland) and civil partners are taxed as **individuals**, each entitled to their own personal allowances. (There is one exception to this rule: in certain circumstances the marriage allowance lets one spouse/civil partner transfer some of their own personal allowance to their spouse/ civil partner.)

Where married couples/civil partners hold money in a joint bank account, the interest earned on that account will be split between each spouse/partner and will be taxed individually in their respective income tax computations/returns. Similarly, where a property is held jointly and rental income is earned from that property, each spouse/civil partner will be taxed on their share of the rental profits.

If a parent gives income, or assets that generate income, to their child, then the income is still treated as the parent's if the child is less than 18 years of age and is unmarried. However, this rule does not apply if the income is £100 a year or less. Income derived from parental contributions to a child trust fund or Junior ISA does not count towards the £100 limit.

Income tax may be assessed by **self-assessment** (e.g. profits of a sole trader or a partner in a partnership) or by **deduction at source**, directly from an individual's income (i.e. employees under the PAYE system).

1.4   Classification of Income

The rules around the computation of income tax depend on the **source** of the income; different rules apply to different sources. For income tax purposes, income can be classified as:

- trading income;
- employment income;
- savings and investment income;
- property income; and
- miscellaneous income.

A broad distinction is also made between non-savings, savings and dividend income. This distinction is important as it determines the order in which income tax is charged – income tax is charged first on non-savings income, then on savings income and finally on dividend income. The table below shows the classifications of income.

Classification of Income	Type of Income
Trading income – profits of trades, professions and vocations (**Chapter 3**)	Non-savings
Employment income – income from employment, pensions and some social security benefits (**Chapter 5**)	Non-savings
Savings income – income from savings, including interest (**Chapter 6**)	Savings
Investment income – income from investments, including dividends (**Chapter 6**)	Dividend
Property income – profits of property businesses, e.g. rental income (**Chapter 7**)	Non-savings
Miscellaneous income – e.g. post cost cessation receipts, income from royalties	Non-savings

1.4.1 Exempt Income

Specific types of income are exempt from income tax, they include:

■ betting and gaming winnings;
■ certain tax-free investments, e.g. proceeds from National Savings Certificates and interest on Individual Savings Accounts (ISAs);
■ gifts of assets, including money (although these may be subject to inheritance tax, which is outside the scope of the CA Proficiency 1 syllabus); and
■ damages for personal injury.

1.5 The Scope of Income Tax

In tax law, the concepts of 'residence' and 'domicile' are important because they determine whether or not an individual is liable to UK income tax in respect of income they have earned in the tax year. Both concepts are used in making this determination so that individual can be either:

■ UK resident and UK domiciled;
■ UK resident and non-UK domiciled; or
■ Non-UK resident.

As well as the individual's residence and domicile status, the origin of the income itself is also important, i.e. whether the income arises in the UK, such as rental income from a UK property, or whether it arises overseas, e.g. rental income from a property in Spain.

1.5.1 Residence

The concept of residence is based on physical presence in a country. In the UK, the statutory residence test (SRT) is used to determine an individual's tax residence status. An individual is considered UK resident if they meet the criteria of the three components of the SRT: the automatic overseas test; the automatic UK test; and the sufficient ties test. The details of the SRT are beyond the scope of this textbook.

1.5.2   Domicile

The concept of domicile is one of general and common law, having evolved through the court system and not being legislatively defined. In broad terms, unlike residency, an individual can only ever have one domicile at any one time. There are three kinds of domicile: domicile of origin; domicile of choice; and domicile of dependency.

Domicile is distinct from nationality or residence. The following factors may be relevant when considering an individual's domicile: the individual's intentions; permanent residence; business interests; social and family interests; ownership of property; the form of any will made, burial arrangements and so on.

1.6   The Government's Taxation Objectives

In designing the UK taxation system, the government has two main considerations – efficiency and equity. Efficiency refers to the amount of tax revenue raised by the government in relation to the cost, to taxpayers and the government, of collecting it. The UK tax system requires taxpayers to pay taxes to the government, which affect the behaviour of consumers and suppliers/producers. It also places an administrative burden on taxpayers. An efficient tax system imposes minimum negative effects on behaviour and a smaller administrative burden on taxpayers. An equitable tax system is one where the burden of taxation is divided equally.

The policy of the government in power will affect the tax system in place. Every year the government passes the Finance Act(s), amending relevant tax legislation to implement its policy initiatives.

The UK government levies taxes for three main reasons:

1.   economic,
2.   social, and
3.   environmental.

1.6.1   Economic Reasons

The taxation system requires taxpayers to pay taxes to the government and the government, in turn, uses this money to run the country. For example, the money collected in taxes will be used to fund the public sector, education and health.

The government also uses taxation to encourage or discourage certain types of activity or behaviour. For example, tax-free savings accounts (i.e. Individual Savings Accounts) and income tax relief for paying money into a pension scheme are provided to incentivise individuals to save. Likewise, donations to charity are encouraged by income tax relief through the gift aid scheme or by the income tax calculation (see **Section 8.3.2**).

To discourage unwanted or undesirable activities, taxes can be increased, e.g. increasing the duty on tobacco products and alcohol discourages their use.

1.6.2   Social Reasons

Taxation policies can have the impact of redistributing income and wealth from the rich to the poor in society. Different taxes have different social impacts. For example, direct taxes (e.g. income tax and capital gains tax) tax those who have the resources. The more income an individual has or the more of a gain an individual makes, the higher their tax liability.

Indirect taxes (e.g. VAT) tax the consumer and so have the same impact on everybody, regardless of their income. The government may, for example, decide to reduce the standard rate of VAT or to zero-rate certain goods (see **Chapter 19**) to encourage individuals to spend.

1.6.3 Environmental Reasons

In the UK, taxation is also used to further the government's environmental policies. For example, the government annually increases the benefit-in-kind tax on cars provided to an employee (see **Section 5.4.3**) for cars with a higher level of CO_2 emissions. The introduction of new taxes, such as the climate change levy (which is paid by businesses depending on their energy consumption) and the levy on plastic bags, form part of the government's environmental measures. The government also provides tax incentives for businesses that invest in energy-efficient vehicles, in the form of capital allowances (see **Chapter 4**).

1.7   HM Revenue & Customs

Responsibility for the care and management of both direct taxes and indirect taxes rests with the Chair of the Board of Her Majesty's Revenue & Customs (HMRC). In simple terms this means that HMRC is responsible for the "collection and management" of tax. It has three strategic objectives:

- "maximise revenues due and bear down on avoidance and evasion
- transform tax and payments for our customers
- design and deliver a professional, efficient and engaged organisation".

The HMRC is a non-ministerial division within the Treasury Department, overall control of which rests with the Chancellor of the Exchequer. It consists of former high-ranking civil servants from various sections within HMRC, together with other non-executive personnel.

The role of the HMRC Board is to advise and challenge the management of HMRC, particularly focusing its attention on the performance of the department and its future strategic direction.

The HMRC's Executive Committee is the executive decision-making body. Following the strategic direction provided by the Board, it oversees the whole breadth of HMRC's work and is also responsible for driving forward continuous improvement and change agendas. It meets every month.

The UK is divided into various tax regions, each headed up by Inspectors, who are assisted by their colleagues and other Revenue Assistants.

The actual collection of taxes over the years has been centralised and, while the Board has overall responsibility, this has been delegated to collection offices. A specialised department, the Debt Management Unit, is responsible for following up amounts of unpaid tax referred to it from HMRC Accounts offices.

Interest, penalties and surcharges may be imposed to encourage the efficient collection of tax and to ensure that taxpayers comply in a timely fashion, e.g. daily penalties can be imposed where there is continued non-payment and/or requested information is not forthcoming.

1.8   Administration Procedures for Tax Assessment and Collection

HMRC operates a self-assessment system in the UK for income tax and VAT. For income tax, this system relies on individuals to register for income tax when they are required and to file their return and pay their tax on time. The self-assessment income tax return (SA100) must usually be filed by 31 October (if filed on paper) or 31 January (if filed electronically) following the end of the tax year. For example, for the 2021/22 tax year, if an individual files their SA100 online, the deadline for submission is 31 January 2023. Payments of self-assessed income tax should generally be made on 31 January and 31 July each year (see **Chapter 10** for further information).

It should be noted that many individuals receive a salary that has been taxed under the PAYE system only (see **Chapter 9**). Such individuals are not normally required to submit an income tax return under the self-assessment system unless they are a company director or have non-PAYE income (such as interest that cannot be adjusted for in their PAYE coding) in addition to their employment income.

For certain individuals (see below), HMRC can make a 'simple assessment' of their income tax without the individual first being required to complete a self-assessment tax return. HMRC will make the simple assessment based on information they already hold for the individual.

HMRC have, so far, removed the following individuals from the obligation to complete a self-assessment tax return:

- PAYE taxpayers who have underpaid tax but cannot have the underpayment collected via their tax code (see **Section 9.2.2**);
- State pensioners whose pension exceeds the personal allowance (see **Section 2.4**).

For VAT purposes, an individual needs to register for VAT when they breach the VAT registration thresholds (currently £85,000, see **Chapter 19**). A VAT-registered individual will usually account for VAT on a quarterly basis. VAT returns must be submitted online within one month and seven days of the relevant quarter end. For example, the VAT return for the quarter ended 30 June 2021 must be filed by 7 August 2021. Any VAT liability due should also be paid electronically by this date.

The self-assessment system is supported by a penalty regime that can apply to individuals who are not tax-compliant. Interest may also be charged by HMRC on the late payment of taxes. In addition, HMRC will randomly select individuals and businesses to enquire into on an ongoing basis. HMRC will undertake enquiries and make discovery assessments on individuals and businesses. HMRC will also undertake campaigns targeted at specific sectors that it believes may have tax-compliance issues.

1.8.1   The Appeals System

Disputes may arise between an individual taxpayer and HMRC in respect of a decision or view taken by HMRC about a taxpayer's affairs. Where agreement cannot be reached, the taxpayer can appeal the decision and the case may be heard by the appropriate tax tribunal.

In the UK there is a two-tier system for appeals, consisting of the First-tier Tribunal (Tax) and the Upper Tribunal (Tax and Chancery Chamber). The First-tier Tribunal is the starting point of the appeals process, after which appeals can be escalated to the Upper Tribunal then to the Court of Appeal and finally to the Supreme Court.

Timeframes to lodge an appeal, must be strictly adhered to. For example, for direct taxes an appeal must be lodged within 30 days of a review conclusion.

1.9   Tax Evasion, Tax Planning and Tax Avoidance

Tax evasion is illegal and is punishable by fines and/or imprisonment. For example, if a taxpayer deliberately provides false information to HMRC, such as reduced taxable profits, this would be regarded as tax evasion.

Tax planning involves a taxpayer organising their affairs in such a way so as to reduce their tax burden. For example, an individual deciding to open a tax-exempt Individual Savings Account (ISA) rather than an ordinary bank account is planning their tax affairs to minimise the tax paid and maximise their income. Tax planning is both legally and ethically acceptable.

Tax avoidance is often viewed as a grey area because it is regularly confused with tax planning. Tax avoidance is the use of loopholes within tax legislation to reduce the taxpayer's tax liability. HMRC defines tax avoidance as "exploiting the tax rules to gain an advantage that parliament never intended". HMRC has a multi-faceted approach to tackling tax avoidance. In addition to having targeted anti-avoidance rules (TAARs), in 2011 the General Anti-Abuse Rule (GAAR) was introduced in the UK. The primary objective of the GAAR is to deter taxpayers from entering into abusive arrangements. In summary, the GAAR enables HMRC to challenge tax advantages arising from arrangements that are put in place for the main purpose of avoiding tax or obtaining a tax advantage.

Appendix 3 discusses the issues of tax planning, tax avoidance and tax evasion in more detail.

Questions

Review Questions
(See Suggested Solutions to Review Questions at the end of this textbook.)

Question 1.1

(a) What is the deadline for filing a paper income tax return?
(b) What is the deadline for filing an electronic income tax return?
(c) When should self-assessed income tax be paid?

Question 1.2

Emma works in the tax department of a medium-sized practice. Yesterday she got a call from her friend, Jack. Jack is trying to buy a house at the moment and he is bidding against a local businessman. Jack knows that this businessman is a client of the practice where Emma works and he asks her to have a look at the businessman's tax file to see if he really does have the money to buy this house. Jack says to Emma, "Surely you have details of his income and bank balances." Jack tells Emma that he will owe her big time as this is the biggest investment decision he has ever made.

Requirement
What advice would you give to Emma about the request from Jack? You should make reference to Chartered Accountants Ireland's *Code of Ethics* (see **Appendix 2**).

Part One

Income Tax

2

Introduction to the Computation of Income Tax

Learning Objectives

After studying this chapter you will understand:

- The general terms and definitions used when computing income tax.
- The tax bands and the associated tax rates for 2021/22.
- The standard personal allowance and the restriction on same if income exceeds £100,000.
- The steps involved in calculating income tax.
- How to prepare a simple income tax computation.

Chartered Accountants Ireland's *Code of Ethics* applies to all aspects of a Chartered Accountant's professional life, including dealing with income tax issues. As outlined at the beginning of this book, further information regarding the principles in the *Code of Ethics* is set out in **Appendix 2**.

2.1 Introduction

Put simply, the purpose of the income tax computation is to enable us to calculate how much income tax an individual has to pay. The computation involves a number of stages and different calculations that follow in a logical sequence. In this chapter we will give an overview of each of the steps involved and introduce the basic terminology used.

In **Chapter 1, Section 1.4**, the important distinction between non-savings, savings and dividend income was noted, as was the classification of income depending on its source – trading income, employment income and so on. Each source of income has different rules and treatment for computing income tax, so recognising where an individual's income has come from is fundamental to the computation. For example, an individual's personal income tax computation may include:

- salary from employment;
- pension income;
- profits earned from a sole trade or partnership;
- rental profits;
- interest income from savings; and/or
- dividends from shares.

Before we look at the steps involved in assessing an individual's liability to income tax, it is important to be clear about the meaning of the key terms that you will encounter when studying income tax.

2.2   General Terminology and Definitions

The key terms and definitions that are used when discussing the computation of income tax include:

Income tax year – an individual's income tax computation brings together the income from all sources in a tax year. A tax year runs from 6 April to 5 April in the following year; so the 2021/22 tax year runs from 6 April 2021 to 5 April 2022.

Year of assessment – income tax is charged for a year of assessment.

Basis of assessment – refers to the way in which income is allocated to tax years for the purpose of assessing tax. There are a number of different types, for example: the cash basis (sometimes referred to as the receipts basis); the accruals basis or the current year basis. With the cash basis, income is assessable when it is received during the tax year; on the other hand, with the accruals basis assessable income includes amounts accrued during the tax year, regardless of whether it was actually received or not during the tax year. Under the current year basis, income earned in a tax year is assessable.

Self-assessment – this is the system by which taxpayers are responsible for self-assessing their own liability to income tax. They are responsible for reporting and paying the correct amount of income tax to HMRC.

The filing deadline for income tax self-assessment returns is 31 October for paper returns and, for returns filed online, it is 31 January following the end of the tax year. So, a paper tax return for 2021/22 must be filed by 31 October 2022, while an online return must be filed by 31 January 2023.

Taxable income – income that is liable to income tax after specified reliefs and allowances have been deducted (see **Section 2.5**).

Tax deducted at source – refers to tax that has already been deducted before an individual receives the income. Pay As You Earn (PAYE) is an example of tax deducted at source. PAYE may be deducted from gross employment earnings, for example, before it is received by an individual.

Tax relief – refers to an amount allowed as a deduction from an individual's total income. Examples of tax reliefs include: relief for trading losses (see **Chapter 4**); relief for pension contributions or relief for payments of eligible interest (see **Chapter 8**).

Allowances – most individuals are entitled to a certain amount of tax-free income each year. A number of different allowances may be available, including a personal allowance, the level of which depends on an individual's income level or the blind person's allowance.

PAYE – Refers to the system used to collect income tax and national insurance from employment earnings (see **Chapter 9**).

2.3   Income Tax Rates and Bands

UK income tax operates by using tax bands – ranges of taxable income – which correspond to different rates of income tax. Specific tax bands, or thresholds, and their corresponding tax rates apply to the three categories of income: non-savings, savings and dividend.

2.3.1 Non-savings Income

The table below shows the tax rates that apply to non-savings income.

	Income Band	**Tax Rate**
Personal Allowance	£0–£12,570	0%
Basic Rate	£12,571–£50,270	20%
Higher Rate	£50,271–£150,000	40%
Additional Rate	Over £150,001	45%

2.3.2 Savings Income

For savings income the same tax bands and rates apply as for non-savings income, except that there is a "starting limit" of £5,000 for which a 0% rate applies, but only if the individual's **taxable non-savings income** is less than £5,000. If taxable non-savings income is greater than £5,000, then the savings income is subject to the basic rate (20%) up to the basic rate limit (£37,700), the higher rate (40%) for savings income falling within the higher rate band (£50,001 to £150,000) and the additional rate (45%) for savings income above £150,000.

Therefore, it can also be said that in 2021/22, the starting rate for savings income will only apply where an individual has non-savings and savings income, before deducting the personal allowance (£12,570), of less than £17,570 (being the £12,570 personal allowance plus the £5,000 starting rate for savings band).

For example, if an individual has pension income, i.e. non-savings income, of £13,000 and savings income of £2,000, the individual's total income is £15,000. As this is less than £17,570 total income, the individual will be eligible for the starting rate for savings income. In order to arrive at taxable income, the personal allowance of £12,570 will be deducted from the pension income, i.e. £430 of taxable non-savings income. The starting rate for savings income applies to as much of the first £5,000 of taxable income that is savings income. In this example, the starting rate for savings income will apply to up to £4,570 of savings income. As the savings income is only £2,000, all of it will be 'taxed' at the 0% starting rate for savings income.

Personal Savings Allowance

A personal savings allowance is available for savings income earned from bank and building society accounts. This personal savings allowance allows up to £1,000 a year of a basic rate taxpayer's savings income to be tax-free; for higher rate taxpayers the annual threshold is £500. The personal savings allowance is not available to additional rate taxpayers.

The amount of personal savings allowance depends on an individual's adjusted net income (see **Section 2.5**).

The table below shows the amount of the personal savings allowance an individual is entitled to depending on whether they are a basic, higher or additional rate taxpayer.

Tax Rate	**Income Band (adjusted net income)**	**Personal Savings Allowance**
Basic: 20%	Up to £50,270 (£37,700 + £12,570)	Up to £1,000
Higher: 40%	£50,271–£150,000	Up to £500
Additional: 45%	Over £150,000	Nil

2.3.3 Dividend Income

For dividend income the same tax bands apply as for non-savings and savings income. However, the rates of tax applying to dividends are 7.5%, 32.5% and 38.1% (rather than 20%, 40% and 45%). A dividend allowance is also available.

Dividend Allowance

The dividend allowance allows up to £2,000 of income earned from dividends to be tax-free, regardless of the individual's level of income. Dividend income in excess of the allowance is taxed at the following rates: 7.5% (dividend ordinary rate); 32.5% (dividend upper rate); and 38.1% (dividend additional rate).

2.3.4 Summary

The 2021/22 tax bands and tax rates are summarised in the table below.

Tax Year	Income Type	Rate	Tax Rate	Tax Band/Threshold
2021/22	Non-savings	Basic rate	20%	£0–£37,700
		Higher rate	40%	£37,701–£150,000
		Additional rate	45%	Over £150,000
	Savings	Starter rate	0%	£0–£5,000*
		Basic rate	20%	£0–£37,700**
		Higher rate	40%	£37,701–£150,000**
		Additional rate	45%	Over £150,000
	Dividend	Dividend allowance	0%	£0–£2,000***
		Dividend ordinary rate	7.5%	£2,000–£37,700
		Dividend upper rate	32.5%	£37,701–£150,000
		Dividend additional rate	38.1%	Over £150,000

*   Provided non-savings income is not greater than £5,000.
**   Personal savings allowance available: £1,000 to basic rate taxpayers; £500 to higher rate taxpayers. There is no personal savings allowance for additional rate taxpayers.
*** When calculating how much of a personal savings allowance a taxpayer is entitled to, dividends that are covered by the dividend allowance are to be included in the individual's taxable income amount to establish if the individual is a higher rate taxpayer (and entitled to £500 personal savings allowance) or an additional rate taxpayer (and not entitled to any personal savings allowance).

2.4   Standard Personal Allowance

An individual may be entitled to a number of allowances that will help reduce the amount of their income that will be subject to income tax.

All individuals are entitled to the standard personal allowance, which is simply the amount of income, from any source, that income tax is not payable on. For 2021/22 the standard personal allowance is £12,570.

The standard personal allowance is reduced for individuals with an "adjusted net income" (see **Section 2.5**) that exceeds £100,000. For every £2 above the £100,000 threshold, the personal allowance is reduced by £1. This calculation will continue until the personal allowance is reduced to nil – in other words, if an individual has adjusted net income of £125,140 or more they lose their entitlement to the personal allowance.

The personal allowance is also modified by eligibility to claim the marriage allowance or the blind person's allowance. Further details of all the allowances available are discussed in **Chapter 8**.

2.5 Income Tax Computation

The tax legislation details how income tax should be calculated. The calculation steps are outlined below as an overview of the whole process. Details of the calculation of the different sources of income, and the rules and restrictions around the various reliefs, allowances and reductions, are dealt with in subsequent chapters.

STEP 1	Identify "total income" for each source ("component") of income: non-savings, savings income and dividend income. The **gross** income from each component is added up separately in the personal income tax computation.
STEP 2	Deduct from the components of "total income" any **specified reliefs** (see **Chapter 8**) that the taxpayer is entitled to, such as various trade loss reliefs. This gives "net income".
STEP 3	Deduct from the components of "net income" any **allowances** that the taxpayer is entitled to, such as personal allowance and blind person's allowance. The personal allowance is deducted from the non-savings component of income first, then savings income and finally dividend income. These may need to be restricted (e.g. if income is greater than £100,000). This amount is referred to as "taxable income".
STEP 4	For each component amount calculated in Step 3, calculate tax at the applicable rates. Before calculating the tax on the savings income component, the personal savings allowance must be considered. The amount of the personal savings allowance depends on whether the individual is a basic rate taxpayer (£1,000 taxed at 0%) or higher rate taxpayer (£500 taxed at 0%). When calculating the tax on the dividend component, the dividend allowance covering the first £2,000 of dividends is taxed at 0%.
STEP 5	Add together the component amounts calculated in Step 4.
STEP 6	From the total calculated at Step 5, deduct any tax reductions that the taxpayer may be entitled to, such as married couples allowance (see **Chapter 8**) or the basic rate tax reduction available for rented residential finance costs (see **Chapter 7**).
STEP 7	To the amount calculated at Step 6, add additional tax charges that may apply, such as the child benefit income tax charge (see **Chapter 5**).
STEP 8	Finally, income tax deducted at source (e.g. PAYE) is subtracted to get **tax payable**, which is the balance to be settled. The result is the taxpayer's income tax liability/(refund) – the income tax that is due to be paid or refunded for that particular tax year.

Steps 1–3

Steps 3–5

Steps 5–7

2.5.1 Pro Forma Income Tax Computation

A pro forma computation shows the layout of the calculation, indicating where the component amounts should be placed and systematically working through the computation.

	Non-savings Income £	Savings Income £	Dividend Income £	Total £
Gross income:				
Trading income	xx			xx
Property income	xx			xx
Employment/pension income	xx			xx
Savings and investment income:				
Bank/building society interest		xx		xx
National Savings & Investment a/c interest		xx		xx
UK dividends			xx	xx

		Non-savings Income £	Savings Income £	Dividend Income £	Total £
Step 1	**Total income**	xxx	xxx	xxx	xxx
	Less: specified reliefs	(xx)	(xx)	(xx)	(xx)
Step 2	Net income	xxx	xxx	xxx	xxx
Step 3	Taxable income	xxxx	xxxx	xxxx	xxxx

		£
Step 4	**Income tax:**	
	Non-savings income:	
	£ × 20%	xxxx
	£ × 40%	xxxx
	£ × 45%	xxxx
	Savings income:	
	£ × 0% (Starting limit for savings income and personal savings allowance, if available.)	0
	£ × 20%	xxxx
	£ × 40%	xxxx
	£ × 45%	xxxx
	Dividend income:	
	Up to £2,000 dividend allowance × 0%	0
	£ × 7.5%	xxxx
	£ × 32.5%	xxxx
	£ × 38.1%	xxxx
Step 5	**Total**	xxxx
Step 6	**Less: basic rate tax reduction for property finance costs**	(xxx)
Step 7	**Add: additional tax (e.g. child benefit income tax charge)**	xxx
Step 8	**Less: tax deducted at source**	(xxx)
Result	Income tax liability/(refund)	**xxx**

Having outlined the steps of the computation and the pro forma layout, let's now look at a simple worked example to illustrate the process.

Example 2.1

John is single, born 9 September 1962, and his sources of income for 2021/22 included income from employment of £16,420 (with PAYE deducted at source of £1,600), net commercial property income of £3,650, income from occasional lectures of £600 and bank interest of £100.

John's income tax liability for 2021/22 will be computed as follows.

John's Income Tax Computation for 2021/22

	£ Non-savings	£ Savings	£ Dividend	£ Total
Employment income	16,420			
UK land and property income	3,650			
Miscellaneous income	600			
Savings and investment income	_____	100	____	_____
Total income	20,670	100	0	20,770
Less: personal allowance	(12,570)	____	____	(12,570)
Taxable income	**8,100**	**100**	**0**	**8,200**

Income tax:

Non-savings income:	
£8,100 @ 20%	1,620
Savings income:	0
£100 × 0% (personal savings allowance)	
Income tax due	1,620
Less: tax deducted at source:	
PAYE	(1,600)
Total tax due	20

Questions

Review Questions

(See Suggested Solutions to Review Questions at the end of this textbook.)

Question 2.1

Pat's employment income in the 2021/22 tax year is £15,920 (gross). He is married to Una, who is not employed but has interest income in the period of £40,920. Pat has paid PAYE of £3,000.

Requirement

Compute both Pat and Una's income tax liabilities for the 2021/22 tax year.

Question 2.2

Paul and Jean are married. Paul had property income of £47,850 from a number of commercial units in Stranmillis in the 2021/22 tax year, as well as net employment income of £24,000 from his job with the council. PAYE suffered was £5,000. He also received interest income of £600 on a joint bank account he has with Jean.

Jean had self-employment income in the period of £41,850. Her neighbour also paid her £50 for cutting his grass when he was away for a week in the summer.

Requirement

Compute Paul and Jean's income tax liability for the 2021/22 tax year.

Question 2.3

M. Smyth lives alone. In 2021/22 he received commercial property income of £10,350, net employment income of £23,500 (PAYE suffered of £4,000), dividend income from a UK company of £6,000 and bank interest of £20,000.

Requirement

Compute M. Smyth's income tax liability for the 2021/22 tax year.

Trading Income

Learning Objectives

After studying this chapter you will be able to:

■ Explain the concepts of "badges of trade" (with specified case law examples) and determine whether or not a trade is being carried on by their application to the particular facts.
■ Compute tax-adjusted trading/professional profits.
■ Explain and apply the basis of assessment, including commencement, cessation and the impact of a change of accounting date.
■ Explain and compute the assessable profits using the cash basis of accounting and simplified expenses.
■ Compute the taxation liability of partners in a partnership, including allocation of losses to partners.

3.1 Introduction

Income tax is charged on profits or gains arising from any **trade**, **profession** or **vocation**. The tax treatment and computational rules of each are practically identical and are, therefore, considered together.

Individuals liable to income tax are sometimes referred to as being self-employed (as opposed to being an employee). Some examples of individuals who are liable to income tax include:

■ shopkeepers, manufacturers and farmers – as they are carrying on a trade;
■ doctors, solicitors, architects and accountants – as they are carrying on a profession; and
■ dramatists and jockeys – as they are carrying on a vocation.

It is important to establish whether an activity constitutes a trade, as specific rules apply to the taxation of trading income, the deductibility of expenses and, in particular, to the ways in which trading losses can be relieved. In some instances, a profit or sale may be taxed as capital income (as opposed to trading income) and be subject to capital gains tax (CGT) rules. For example, a gain on a one-off sale of an investment property will be treated as capital income and be subject to CGT and not income tax. CGT (see **Part Three**).

This chapter will begin by introducing you to the types of activities (trades, professions and vocations) that are subject to income tax. The specific tax rules for the commencement and cessation of a trade will be considered, in addition to the implications of a business changing its accounting date. The chapter will then discuss the rules for computing taxable trading income, including the simplified rules that have been recently introduced for smaller businesses. Finally, the chapter will discuss the specific tax rules that apply to partnerships and, in particular, to how a partnership's tax-adjusted profit/(losses) are calculated and apportioned.

3.1.1   Definition of "Trade", "Profession" and "Vocation"

Where the activity carried on by an individual falls within the definition of a trade, profession or vocation, then the income from that activity will be subject to income tax.

Trade

The term "trade" is not fully defined in tax legislation. Therefore, the interpretation of whether a trade exists or not is left largely to the courts. In the legislation, "trade" is taken to include "any venture in the nature of trade".

The question of whether or not a trade is carried on is a **question of fact** rather than a point of law.

Guidance as to what constitutes a trade can be taken from case law and this guidance is summarised in a collection of principles known as the "badges of trade". See **Section 3.1.2** below for further details on the badges of trade.

Profession

The term "profession" is not defined in tax legislation. Examples of individuals regarded as carrying on a profession include teachers, doctors, opticians, accountants and journalists.

Vocation

In tax case law the word "vocation" has been compared with a "calling". Judgments in various tax cases have held that a bookmaker, dramatist, jockey and an author are all vocations.

3.1.2   "Badges of Trade"

The "badges of trade" are a set of six rules drawn up in 1955 by the **UK Royal Commission on the Taxation of Profits and Income**. They are used to help decide whether or not a trade exists.

1.   "The subject matter of the realisation"

The general rule here is that an asset that does not give its owner an income or personal enjoyment merely by virtue of its ownership is more likely to have been acquired for the purpose of a trade. For example, an individual's principal private residence is more likely to have been bought for personal enjoyment rather than for the purposes of the individual's trade. A disposal of a residence, a disposal of shares and a disposal of a painting would all be capital transactions, and so any gain would not be subject to income tax. As noted above, gains from a capital transaction are subject to CGT.

In the case of *Rutledge v. CIR* (1929), in which 1,000,000 rolls of toilet paper were purchased in a single transaction and subsequently sold in a single transaction for a profit, it was held to be trading profit and not a capital gain; it was regarded as an "adventure in the nature of trade", there being no other justifiable reason to purchase such a large quantity of toilet rolls other than to sell them for a profit.

2. "The length of the period of ownership"

As a general rule, property acquired for a trading or dealing purpose is realised within a short time after acquisition. However, there may be many exceptions to this rule.

3. "The frequency or number of similar transactions by the same person"

If an individual completed a number of transactions involving the same type of asset in succession over a period of years, or if there had been several similar transactions around the same date, then a presumption arises that they were trading transactions.

In the case of *Martin v. Lowry* (1927), 34,000,000 yards of aircraft linen was sold. The size and frequency of the sales amounted to a trade. The subject matter, i.e. the aircraft linen, would not have been held as an investment asset and so on resale it gave rise to trading profits which would be subject to income tax.

In *Pickford v. Quirke* (1927), the individual purchased a mill and stripped and sold its assets in parcels. While this may be regarded as a capital transaction, where the individual repeated this exercise (i.e. the buying of a mill to strip and sell the assets) for a fourth time, he was viewed as carrying on a trade.

4. "Supplementary work on or in connection with the property realised"

If the asset is improved or developed in any way during the ownership so as to bring it into a more marketable condition, or if any special marketing efforts are made to find or attract purchasers, such as the opening of a sales office or a large-scale advertising campaign, then this would provide some evidence of trading. Where there is an organised effort to obtain profit, there is likely to be a source of taxable income. Likewise, if no work is done on or in connection with the property, the suggestion is that trading is not intended.

In *Cape Brandy Syndicate v. CIR* (1921), a group of accountants bought, blended and re-casked a quantity of brandy. They set up a phone line and information desk, and produced brochures in order to sell the product. As it was organised on a commercial basis, it was held that any profit on sale was trading profit.

5. "The circumstances that were responsible for the realisation"

This rule refers to possible circumstances that would eliminate the suggestion that the purchase was made deliberately for the purpose of a trade. For example, an asset may only be sold because of an emergency or "an opportunity calling for ready money".

Assets acquired by gift or inheritance are clearly not purchased with a trading motive, and so any future sale is unlikely to be trading.

6. "Motive"

Where a profit motive is evident, it is likely that the individual is trading. However, the absence of a profit motive will not necessarily be conclusive in establishing that a transaction is not trading.

When considering the "badges of trade", it is important to appreciate that the 'whole picture' needs to be taken into account, and that the weight given to the various factors may vary according to the circumstances. Furthermore, it should be recognised that any given factor may be present to a greater or lesser degree, and that the absence (or presence) of any single factor is unlikely to be conclusive in its own right.

Another rule not included in the "badges of trade", but one that can be of equal importance, is "intention". If the sale of an asset is clearly trading, then the individual's intentions are not relevant. However, it is possible that an individual could buy an asset for dual purposes. For example, an individual buys a premises intending to live on the ground floor and to convert the second and third floors into flats for resale. Therefore, the individual's intention for the second and third floors is to convert and sell the flats to make a profit. This intention is different to that of the ground floor of the premises, which will be kept as a capital asset.

Once it has been satisfactorily determined that an individual is carrying on a trade, profession or vocation and therefore has trading income, we then need to assess how much of this income is taxable and, importantly, when the tax is due to be paid.

3.2   Basis of Assessment of Trading Income

Each tax year runs from 6 April to 5 April; however, individuals who operate a trading business will not normally prepare their financial statements to 5 April each year. This would create a problem in terms of reporting income and hence the correct calculation of tax. To overcome this, a **basis period** is adopted to 'link' the "period of account" for a business (i.e. the accounting year/period end up to which the financial statements of the business are prepared) with the appropriate tax year. The basis period, for an ongoing trading business, will be **the 12-month period of account ending during the tax year**. Income, profits, etc. that fall in the basis period are considered when calculating income tax for the associated tax year.

Example 3.1

An individual running a trading business prepares the financial statements each year for the year ended 30 June.

What is the basic period for the tax year 2021/22? What would be the basis period for the tax year 2022/23?

For the 2021/22 tax year, the basis period will be the year ended 30 June 2021. For the 2022/23 tax year, the basis period will be the year ended 30 June 2022.

The basis period will be affected by the date of commencement (and cessation) of a trade and by any change in accounting date; each of these is subject to specific rules, which are outlined in **Sections 3.2.2–3.2.4**.

A summary of the key terms is outlined in the table below for easy reference.

Tax year or Year of assessment	6 April to 5 April
Period of account or Accounting year/ period end	Refers to the date to which the financial statements or accounts of a trading business are prepared, e.g. accounting year end 30 June 2021 refers to the accounts that show the business profits from 1 July 2020 to 30 June 2021.
Basis period	The period that links the tax year to the period of account. Usually the basis period is the period of account ending in the tax year, but the commencement, cessation and change in accounting date rules should be considered.

The effect of the rules for taxing trading profits using tax years often means that some profits are taxable more than once, due to the profits in one accounting period overlapping two tax years. These are known as "**overlap profits**".

3.2.1 Overlap Profits

"Overlap profit" is the amount of profit in an accounting period that is taxed in two successive tax years. Overlap profits can occur:

- in the opening years of a business (see **Section 3.2.2**); or
- on a change of basis period following a change of accounting date (see **Section 3.2.3**).

To ensure that the business is taxed over its life on the actual profits made, "**overlap relief**" is provided. Basically this means that overlap profits are not actually taxed twice. Overlap profits may arise more than once over the lifetime of a business so, to ensure that overlap relief is received, a record should be kept of both the amount of the overlap profit and its overlap period. (See **Section 3.2.5** for details on overlap relief.)

Where the accounting period of a business coincides with the tax year throughout the life of the business, overlaps will not occur. To avoid short overlap periods, accounting dates ending on 31 March or on 1, 2, 3, 4 or 5 April are treated as ending on 5 April, unless the individual elects otherwise.

3.2.2 Commencement of a Trade

The date of commencement of a trade determines the accounting period for the business, which in turn determines the basis period of assessment for the business.

There are special provisions for the first three years after the commencement of the business.

First Tax Year

The first tax year is the tax year during which the trade commences. The basis period for the first tax year is the **profit from the date of commencement of the trade to the end of the tax year** (i.e. the following 5 April). If the period of account of the business does not coincide with the tax year, then the assessable profit is arrived at by time apportionment.

Example 3.2

Mr Jones commenced to trade as a builder on 1 July 2021 and prepared accounts for 18 months to 31 December 2022.

The 2021/22 tax year is the tax year in which Mr Jones commenced to trade. He will therefore be assessed as a trader for 2021/22 on the basis of the profits from 1 July 2021 to 5 April 2022. These will be arrived at by time apportioning the 18 months' results to 31 December 2022, i.e. the amount assessed for 2021/22 will be 9/18ths of the total profits for the period.

If the calculation is performed using exact days, the time apportionment from 1 July 2021 to 5 April 2022 is 280/550 days. However, it is often more practical to apportion to the nearest month. Therefore, from 1 July 2021 to 5 April 2022 is nine months.

Second Tax Year

The basis period for the second tax year depends on the position in the second tax year. There are three possibilities:

1. If the accounting date falling in the second tax year is at least 12 months after the start of trading, the basis period is the **12 months to that accounting date**.
2. If the accounting date falling in the second tax year is less than 12 months after the start of trading, the basis period is **the first 12 months of trading**.

3. If there is **no** accounting date falling in the second tax year (because the first accounting period is a very long one that does not end until a date in the third tax year), the basis period **for the second tax year is the tax year itself (i.e. 6 April to the following 5 April)**.

Example 3.3: Accounting date ending in second year is at least 12 months after start date
Donna commences to trade on 1 January 2021. Accounts are prepared for the year ended 31 December 2021.

Taxable profits for year ended 31 December 2021 = £24,000
Accounts are prepared yearly to 31 December thereafter.

Tax Year	Period	Calculation	Profit
2020/21 (1st year)	01/01/21–05/04/21	£24,000 × 3/12	£6,000
2021/22 (2nd year)	01/01/21–31/12/21	£24,000	£24,000

Note: the three-month period from 1 January 2021 to 5 April 2021 is an "overlap period" where "overlap profits" of £6,000 have arisen. These will only be relieved on cessation of trade or on change of accounting date (see **Section 3.2.3**).

Example 3.4: Accounting date ending in second year is less than 12 months after start date
Lisa commences to trade on 1 October 2020. Accounts are prepared for the seven months ending 30 April 2021.

Taxable profits for the seven months ending 30 April 2021 = £35,000
Accounts are prepared yearly to end 30 April thereafter. Taxable profits for the year ending 30 April 2021 = £48,000.

Tax Year	Period	Calculation	Profit
2020/21 (1st year)	01/10/20–05/04/21	£35,000 × 6/7	£30,000
2021/22 (2nd year)	First 12 months:		
	01/10/20–30/04/21	£35,000	£35,000
	01/05/21–30/09/21	£48,000 × 5/12 = £20,000	£55,000

Note: the period 1 October 2020 to 5 April 2021 is an "overlap period" where "overlap profits" totalling £30,000 have arisen.

Example 3.5: No accounting date ending in second tax year
Rose commences to trade on 1 March 2021. Accounts are prepared for the 15 months ending 31 May 2022.

Taxable profits for the 15 months ending 31 May 2022 = £15,000
Accounts are prepared yearly to end 31 May thereafter.

Tax Year	Period	Calculation	Profit
2020/21 (1st year)	01/03/21–05/04/21	£15,000 × 1/15	£1,000
2021/22 (2nd year)	06/04/21–05/04/22	£15,000 × 12/15	£12,000

No accounting date

Third Year
The basis of assessment for the third tax year depends on whether an accounting date falls in the second tax year.

1. If the accounting date does fall in the second tax year, the basis period for the third tax year is the accounting period ending in the third tax year.
2. If the accounting date does not fall in the second tax year, the basis period for the third tax year is the 12 months to the accounting date ending in the third year.

Example 3.6: Accounting date does fall in second tax year
Wilma commences to trade on 1 August 2020. Accounts are prepared for 2021, 2022 and 2023 as follows:

	Profit
Accounts for 11 months to 30 June 2021	£44,000
Accounts for 12 months to 30 June 2022	£60,000
Accounts for 12 months to 30 June 2023	£30,000

Computation	**Assessment**
First Year of Assessment 2020/21	
Profit for period 01/08/2020–05/04/2021, i.e. £44,000 × 8/11	£32,000
Second Year of Assessment 2021/22	
First 12 months (01/08/2020–31/07/2021), i.e. £44,000 + (£60,000 × 1/12)	£49,000
Third Year of Assessment 2022/23	
12-month accounting period ending 30/06/2022	£60,000

Note:

	Overlap Profits
Overlap periods	
01/08/2020–05/04/2021 (assessed 2020/21 and 2021/22) (8 mths)	£32,000
01/07/2021–31/07/2021 (assessed 2021/22 and 2022/23) (1 mth)	£5,000
	£37,000

Overlap profit of £37,000 (9 mths).

Example 3.7: No accounting date ending in second tax year
Tanya commences to trade on 1 March 2021. Accounts are prepared for the 15 months ending 31 May 2022.

Taxable profits for the 15 months ending 31 May 2022 = £30,000.
Accounts are prepared yearly to end 31 May thereafter.

Tax Year	**Period**	**Calculation**	**Profit**
2020/21 (1st year)	01/03/2021–05/04/2021	£30,000 × 1/15	£2,000
2021/22 (2nd year)	06/04/2021–05/04/2022	£30,000 × 12/15	£24,000
No accounting date			
2022/23 (3rd year)	01/06/2021–31/05/2022	£30,000 × 12/15	£24,000

Note: the period from 1 June 2021 to 5 April 2022 an "overlap period" (10 mths) where "overlap profits" totalling £20,000 have arisen.

Fourth and Subsequent Years
For later tax years, apart from the year in which the trade ceases, the basis period for any particular tax year will be the accounting period ending during the tax year. This is known as the **current year basis of assessment**.

3.2.3 Change in Accounting Date

An individual may change the date to which they prepare the business accounts for a variety of commercial reasons: to align with the fiscal year-end; to align with the calendar year-end; to take account of seasonal variations and so on. On a change of accounting date, ending in that tax year, there may be either:

1. one set of accounts covering a period of less than 12 months; **or**
2. one set of accounts covering a period of more than 12 months; **or**
3. no accounts; **or**
4. two sets of accounts.

In the case of 1. and 2. above, the new basis period for the year will relate to the new accounting date. If the new basis period is less than 12 months, additional overlap profits may arise (see **Example 3.8** below). If the new basis period exceeds 12 months, a claim for overlap relief may be made (see **Example 3.9** overleaf).

Example 3.8: New accounting period less than 12 months
Ms Ryan commenced trading on 1 January 2017, preparing accounts to 31 December each year.
To coincide with a slack period, she changes her accounting year-end date to 30 June and prepares her first set of accounts to this date for the six months ending 30 June 2021. Her results were as follows.

	Profit
Year ended 31 December 2017	£12,000
Year ended 31 December 2018	£20,000
Year ended 31 December 2019	£32,000
Year ended 31 December 2020	£45,000
Six months ended 30 June 2021	£30,000

Computation	Assessment	Notes
2016/17 (01/01/2017–05/04/2017) = £12,000 × 3/12	£3,000	1
2017/18 (y/e 31/12/2017)	£12,000	1

Computation	Assessment	Notes
2018/19 (y/e 31/12/2018)	£20,000	
2019/20 (y/e 31/12/2019)	£32,000	
2020/21 (y/e 31/12/2020)	£45,000	
2021/22:		
12 months to new accounting date (01/07/2020–30/06/2021)		
= (£45,000 × 6/12) = £22,500		
= £22,500 + £30,000	£52,500	2

Notes:
1. Overlap period of three months (01/01/2017–05/04/2017). Therefore £12,000 × 3/12 = £3,000 taxed in 2016/17 **and** 2017/18.
2. Overlap period of six months (01/07/2020–31/12/2020). Therefore £45,000 × 6/12 = £22,500 taxed in 2020/21 **and** 2021/22.

Therefore the total overlap profits **to be relieved** in the future stand at £25,500 for the nine months involved: £3,000 in 2016/17 and £22,500 in 2021/22.

Example 3.9: New accounting period more than 12 months

Mrs Nelson commenced trading on 1 January 2018, preparing accounts to 31 December each year. To coincide with her VAT quarters, she changes her accounting year-end date to 31 January and prepares her first set of accounts to this date for the 13-month period ending 31 January 2022. Her results were as follows:

	Profit
Year ended 31 December 2018	£20,000
Year ended 31 December 2019	£32,000
Year ended 31 December 2020	£45,000
13 months ended 31 January 2022	£65,000

Computation	Assessment
2017/18 (01/01/2018–05/04/2018) = £20,000 × 3/12	£5,000
2018/19 (y/e 31/12/2018)	£20,000
2019/20 (y/e 31/12/2019)	£32,000
2020/21 (y/e 31/12/2020)	£45,000
2021/22:	
13 months to new accounting date of 31 January 2022:	
Profit for 13 months to 31/01/22	£65,000

See **Example 3.14** to see how overlap relief reduces this profit for income tax purposes.

If there is no accounting date in the tax year, the basis period is the 12 months to the date that will be the new permanent accounting date. In this situation, overlap profits are created.

Example 3.10: No accounting date in the tax year

Will's business has been trading for many years and he has always prepared his accounts to 31 December each year. There are no overlap profits forward. Will has now decided to change his accounting period end to 30 April. His recent results are as follows:

	Profit
Year ended 31 December 2020	£19,000
16-month period ended 30 April 2022	£75,000
Year ended 30 April 2023	£65,000

Computation

There is no accounting period ending in the 2021/22 tax year.

	Assessment
2020/21 (y/e 31/12/2020)	£19,000
2021/22:	
Period end deemed to be y/e 30 April 2021	
£19,000 × 8/12 + £75,000 × 4/16	£31,417

Overlap profits of £12,667 (£19,000 × 8/12) are created.

If there are two accounting dates in the tax year, the basis period for the year ends on the new accounting date. It begins immediately following the previous basis period. In this situation overlap relief is available for months exceeding 12 months.

Example 3.11: Two accounting dates in the tax year
Sam's business has been trading for many years and there are eight months' overlap profits forward of £16,000. Sam always prepared his accounts to 30 April each year. However, he has now decided to change his accounting period end to 31 August. His recent results are as follows:

	Profit
Year ended 30 April 2020	£18,750
Year ended 30 April 2021	£20,000
4-month period ended 31 August 2021	£8,750
Year ended 31 August 2022	£17,500

Computation
There are two accounting periods ending in the 2021/22 tax year: y/e 30/04/2021 and p/e 31/08/2021.

	Assessment
2020/21 (y/e 30/04/2020)	£18,750
2021/22:	
Period from 01/05/2020 to 31/08/21 (16 mths)	£28,750
Less: overlap profits for 4 months (Note 1)	(£8,000)
	£20,750

Note:
1. As only four months' overlap arises as a result of the accounting date change, only four months of the eight months of overlap profits carried forward can be utilised in 2021/22. Four months of overlap profits of £8,000 remain to be relieved in the future.

3.2.4 Cessation of a Trade

Final Year
The cessation of a trade results in the application of rules that override those outlined above.

1. If the trade commences and ceases in the same (first) tax year, the basis period for that year is from the date of commencement to the date of cessation, i.e. the whole lifespan of the trade.
2. If the trade ceases in the second tax year, then the basis period for that year runs from 6 April at the start of the second tax year up to the date of cessation.

Example 3.12
Jim Johnson is a qualified electrician and starts to trade from 1 June 2021. However, on 31 May 2022 he decides he is not making enough money and ceases the business from that date. His profit for the year ended 31 May 2022 was £12,000.

Computation
Tax year 2021/22 – from 1 June 2021 to 5 April 2022: 10/12 × £12,000 = £10,000
Tax year 2022/23 – from 6 April 2022 to 31 May 2022: 2/12 × £12,000 = £2,000

---

3. If the trade ceases in the third or later tax year, the basis period runs from the end of the basis period for the previous year to the date of cessation.

Example 3.13
J. Jones, who traded as a butcher for many years, retired on 30 June 2021. The results for the last few years of trading were as follows:

	Profit
Year ended 30/09/2019	£36,000
Year ended 30/09/2020	£48,000
Nine months to 30/06/2021	£45,000

Computation

Tax year 2019/20 (y/e 30/09/2019)	£36,000
Tax year 2020/21 (y/e 30/09/2020)	£48,000
Tax year 2021/22 **(period from 01/10/2020 to 30/06/2021)**	**£45,000**
Less: any relevant overlap relief (deducted in 2021/22 year)	(X)

3.2.5   Relief for Overlap Profits

As stated earlier, the overriding thrust of how trade profits are taxed is that the business should be taxed over its lifetime on the cumulative total of the profits it has generated. On occasion, some profits can fall to be taxed in two or more basis periods, resulting in overlap profits.

Overlap Profits Relief on a Change of Accounting Date
Relief for overlap profits may be given on a change of accounting date (provided the new date is closer to 31 March/5 April; if the new date is further from 31 March/5 April, additional overlap profits can arise). The additional overlap profits will then be available for relief at a future change in accounting date or on the cessation of the trade (see **Example 3.11** above).

Example 3.14: Relief for overlap profits where there is a change of accounting date
Following on from **Example 3.9** above, where Mrs Nelson changed her accounting year-end date to 31 January (previously 31 December) and prepared accounts for the 13-month period ending 31 January 2022, i.e. to her new accounting date. These accounts showed a profit of £65,000. Mrs Nelson also had incurred three months' overlap profits of £5,000 in her commencement years.

For 2021/22 her computation will include the 13 months to the new accounting date of 31 January 2022, but as the basis period exceeds 12 months, relief can be claimed for one month of the available overlap relief.

Profit for 13 months to 31/01/2022	£65,000
Less: one month's overlap relief: (£5,000 × 1/3)	£1,667
	£63,333

Two months of overlap profits remain **to be relieved** in the future, a running total of £3,333 (£5,000 – £1,667).

Overlap Profits on the Cessation of a Trade
On the cessation of a trade any overlap profits that remain unrelieved are deducted from the profit falling to be taxed in that tax year (or they are added to any loss). In these circumstances other "loss reliefs" may be available; we will look at these in **Chapter 4, Section 4.12**.

Example 3.15

Mr James commenced trading on 1 September 2017, preparing accounts to 31 August each year. He ceased trading on 31 December 2021 and his results were as follows:

	Profit
Year ended 31 August 2018	£6,000
Year ended 31 August 2019	£15,000
Year ended 31 August 2020	£34,000
16 months ended 31 December 2021	£25,000

Computation		Assessment	Notes
2017/18 (01/09/2017–05/04/2018) = £6,000 × 7/12		£3,500	1
2018/19 (y/e 31/08/2018)		£6,000	1
2019/20 (y/e 31/08/2019)		£15,000	
2020/21 (y/e 31/08/2020)		£34,000	
2021/22:			
Period from 01/09/2020 to cessation	£25,000		
Less: overlap profits not already relieved	(£3,500)	£21,500	

Note:

1. Overlap profits of seven months (01/09/2017–05/04/2018). Therefore £6,000 × 7/12 = £3,500 taxed in 2017/18 **and** 2018/19.

Total profits earned in period:

£6,000 + £15,000 + £34,000 + £25,000	£80,000

Total profits assessed:

£3,500 + £6,000 + £15,000 + £34,000 + £21,500	£80,000

Before we move on to the next stage, work through **Questions 3.1–3.6** at the end of this chapter.

3.3 Computation of Taxable Trading Income

3.3.1 Overview

An individual, carrying on a trade or profession, will prepare accounts based on commercial and accounting principles to arrive at their net profit/(loss) for a particular year. However, the net profit/(loss) per the statement of profit or loss (SOPL) in the accounts **is not the taxable profit** – the Taxes Acts have their own set of rules for determining the taxable profit of a person carrying on a trade, profession or vocation. Accordingly, the net profit/(loss) will inevitably need **adjustment (i.e. amounts will need to be added and deducted)** to arrive at "**tax-adjusted**" profits/(losses) for income tax purposes. A pro forma of the adjustment needed for the net profit/(loss) per the SOPL is shown in Figure 3.1 overleaf.

It is important to note some of the common terminology used in the adjustment process:

- Deductible expenditure can be referred to as "allowable expenditure" for tax purposes.
- Non-deductible expenditure can be referred to as "disallowable expenditure" for tax purposes.

The tax legislation provides that trading profits of a business are to be calculated in accordance with generally accepted accounting practice (GAAP). The majority of small and medium-sized businesses in the UK will apply FRS 102 (*The Financial Reporting Standard applicable in the UK and Republic of Ireland*) when preparing their annual financial statements.

FIGURE 3.1: PRO FORMA FOR TAX-ADJUSTED PROFITS

Net profit/(loss) per the SOPL

ADD

1. Expenses included in the SOPL that are not allowable for tax purposes
2. Income that is taxable trading profits that is not included in the SOPL

DEDUCT

1. Profit/income included in the SOPL that is not taxable as trading income
2. Expenses not included in the SOPL that are tax deductible
3. Capital allowances

EQUALS

Tax-adjusted trading profit/(loss)

for income tax purposes

3.3.2 The Adjustment of Profits – Allowable and Disallowable Items

When calculating tax-adjusted profit/(loss) for **income tax purposes**, there are two fundamental principles:

1. If an item is of a **capital** nature, it must be **disallowed**.
2. Even if an item is of a **revenue** nature, it may still be specifically disallowed by the legislation.

3.3.3 Capital versus Revenue Receipts

Capital receipts and expenditure (including profits and losses on the sale of non-current assets e.g. a property) are not subject to income tax as they are usually accountable under capital gains tax (CGT).

When deciding, for income tax purposes, whether a receipt is capital or revenue, the following general rules apply:

- **Capital receipt** The sale of fixed capital (i.e. assets that form part of the permanent structure of a business or assets that have an enduring benefit to the business) is a capital receipt. For example, income from the sale of land, buildings, machinery or motor vehicles would be treated as capital.
- **Revenue receipt** The sale of circulating capital (i.e. assets acquired in the ordinary course of a trade and sold) is a revenue receipt. For example, the groceries in a supermarket.

To further elaborate on the above rules, there are five basic principles:

1. Income from the sale of the **assets** of a business are, *prima facie*, **capital** receipts.
2. Income received as compensation for the destruction of the recipient's **profit-making apparatus** are capital receipts.
3. Income in lieu of **trading receipts** are of a revenue nature.
4. Income made in return for the imposition of substantial restrictions on the **activities** of a trader is a **capital** receipt.
5. Income of a **recurrent nature** is more likely to be treated as a **revenue** receipt.

Capital receipts (including income and gains) not taxable as trading income:

- **Profits on sale of fixed assets** Profits or gains on the disposal of fixed assets or investments are exempt from income tax, but can be subject to CGT. Where capital allowances have been claimed on the purchase of an asset, the receipt of disposal proceeds may give rise to a balancing allowance or charge (see **Chapter 4**).
- **Grants** Capital grants are exempt from income tax (but are taken into account for both capital allowances and CGT). Revenue grants are taxable.
- **Investment income** Bank interest, dividends and other investment income are not part of the trading profits and are taxed under the category of savings and investment income (see **Chapter 6**).
- **Rental income** Rental income is taxable as property income (see **Chapter 7**).

3.3.4 Capital versus Revenue Expenditure

Capital expenditure is **not** an allowable expense when calculating net trading profits/(losses) for income tax. Where capital expenditure or capital losses (e.g. loss on sale of fixed assets) have been included in the SOPL, they will be **disallowed** when arriving at taxable profits. Where the capital expenditure qualifies for capital allowances (see **Chapter 4**), the individual will receive tax relief for the expenditure by deducting the capital allowances for the period from the tax-adjusted profit.

The judicial statement of Lord Cave in the case of *Atherton v. British Insulated and Helsby Cables Ltd* (1925) is frequently used by the courts to assist them in resolving the problem of whether expenditure is of a revenue nature, and therefore allowable, or of a capital nature, and therefore disallowed:

> "When expenditure is made, not only once and for all, but with a view to bringing into existence an asset or an advantage for the enduring benefit of a trade . . . there is very good reason (in the absence of special circumstances leading to an opposite conclusion) for treating such an expenditure as properly attributed not to revenue but to capital."

The importance of the distinction is that, in the absence of a specific statutory disallowance (such as depreciation or political donations), revenue expenditure is an allowable expense of earning the profit, whereas capital expenditure is not. There are specific statutory provisions to allow some capital items to be deducted in arriving at tax-adjusted profit/(loss), e.g. the deduction of part of a short-lease premium spread over the term of the lease. Capital expenditure that does not qualify for capital allowances may form part of the allowable cost of an asset in arriving at the capital gain on a future disposal of the asset. However, on certain other assets (such as leases) the expenditure is deemed to waste away over the life of the assets and no tax relief is given.

Expenditure "wholly and exclusively" for the Trade

Unless it is covered by a specific statutory provision, expenditure is only allowable in computing profits if it is "wholly and exclusively" for the purposes of the trade. A payment that satisfies the general rule is not allowable if it is a criminal payment, such as a bribe or protection money to terrorists, or a payment made in response to threats, menaces, blackmail and other forms of extortion.

A distinction is also drawn between expenditure incurred in the capacity of a trader and the capacity of a taxpayer, the latter being an appropriation of profit (commonly called "drawings") and, therefore, not allowable.

Expenditure **not** wholly and exclusively laid out for the purposes of the trade includes the following:

- Any expenditure incurred on behalf of the trader or his or her family for private or domestic purposes.
- Rent of any dwelling house **not used** for the trade.
- Any sum expended **over and above** repairs to the premises, implements, utensils or articles employed for the purposes of the trade or profession.
- Any loss not connected with the trade.
- Any capital withdrawn from, or employed as capital in, the trade or profession or any capital employed in improvements to premises occupied by the trade or profession.
- Debts, other than the impairment of trade debts/receivables, or a **specific** estimation of an impairment loss.

Expenditure is, therefore, not tax deductible if it is not for trade purposes or if it reflects more than one purpose (duality of purpose). Note that any private proportions of expenses (e.g. light and heat, motor expenses, telephone, etc.) are not tax deductible. Relief is available for the business element of expenditure only. Note that where payments are to or on behalf of an employee, the full amounts are deductible, but the employee is taxed under the benefits-in-kind benefits code (see below).

3.3.5 Tax Treatment of Common Expenses

Expenses or Losses of a Capital Nature

Expenses or losses of a capital nature are disallowed and should be added to the net profit/(loss) per the SOPL. These costs include:

- depreciation;
- loss on sale of fixed assets;
- improvements to premises; and
- purchase of fixed assets.

Note: capital allowances may be claimed on certain qualifying assets (see **Chapter 4**).

Applications or Allocations of Profit

Applications or allocations of profit are disallowed and should be added to the net profit/(loss) per the SOPL:

- income tax;
- transfers to a general reserve; and
- drawings.

Payments from which Tax is Deducted

Payments from which tax is deducted are allowed if "wholly and exclusively" for trading purposes. For example, where an expense is incurred by a business in respect of patent royalties, the business should not have to add the expense back as long as it was incurred wholly and exclusively for the purposes of the trade.

Expenses not "wholly and exclusively" for the Business

Expenses not "wholly and exclusively" laid out for the purposes of the business are disallowed and therefore should be added to the net profit/(loss) per the SOPL. These will include:

- any private element of expenses;
- rental expenses;
- charitable (unless small and to local charities) and political donations and subscriptions (except where it can be shown that the political expenditure was incurred for the survival of the trade, in which case it may be deductible);
- life assurance premiums on the life of the individual or their spouse;
- fines and penalties (except parking fines for employees using their employer's car on business);
- subscriptions, unless professional or trade subscriptions.

Provisions

Once it has been decided that an item is revenue, it remains to be considered in which period it is to be relieved for tax purposes. International Accounting Standard 37 *Provisions, Contingent Liabilities and Contingent Assets* (IAS 37) sets out when such provisions should be made from an accounting perspective. HMRC has stated that, in the main, it will follow the treatment in the financial accounts if it is in accordance with IAS 37. Thus a provision will be deductible for tax if:

- it is a revenue amount;
- there is a present obligation (legal or constructive) as a result of a past event (the obligating event) and payment is probable (i.e. it is more likely than not); and
- it can be accurately quantified, i.e. it must be a specific provision and not a general provision.

Trade Debt Impairments (Bad Debt Provisions)

Trade debt impairments, i.e. the write-down in trade debtor balances that impact the SOPL, can be allowable or disallowable depending on their nature:

- an impairment loss is **allowable**, i.e. no adjustment required;
- a reversal of an impairment loss is **allowable**, i.e. no adjustment required;
- an increase in a specific impairment provision for bad debts is **allowable**, i.e. no adjustment required;
- a decrease in a specific impairment provision for bad debts is **allowable**, i.e. no adjustment required;
- an increase in a general impairment provision for bad debts is **disallowable**, i.e. it must be **added to the net profit/(loss)**; and
- a decrease in a general impairment provision for bad debts is **disallowable**, i.e. it must be **deducted from the net profit/(loss)**.

Write-off of Loans to an Employee

The write-off of a loan to an employee is generally tax deductible (so no adjustment needed) for the business and will be a benefit in kind for the employee.

Premiums on Short Leases

If an individual carries on a trade or profession in a premises leased for a period of less than 50 years, a proportion of any premium paid on the lease (as distinct from the assignment of a lease from one landlord to another) is allowable in computing the profits of a trade or profession. The applicable proportion is that part of the premium that is assessable on the landlord as additional rent, but spread over the period of the lease rather than as a single deduction.

The amount assessable on the landlord as additional rent is the total premium less 2% per annum for the number of years of the short lease, excluding the first year. The formula used is:

$$\text{Rental portion} = \text{premium} - \text{premium} \times \frac{(n-1)}{50}$$

where, n is the number of complete years of the lease.

The remainder will be subject to CGT (see **Part Three**).

Example 3.16

Joe Bloggs, a trader who has been in business for many years, makes up accounts to 30 September. He was granted a 21-year lease of business premises on 1 July 2021 at a premium of £105,000 and a rent of £25,000 per annum, payable quarterly in advance. Show the deductions to be made in respect of the lease in Joe Bloggs's accounts for the year to 30 September 2021.

Solution

	£
Premium payable 1 July 2021	105,000
Less: discount (2% × (21 – 1)) × £105,000	(42,000) (taxed under CGT)
Assessable on landlord as additional rent (property income)	63,000

Alternatively, the £63,000 can be calculated as follows:

£105,000 – (£105,000 × (21 – 1)/50)

Therefore the annual amount allowable to Joe Bloggs is £3,000, being the £63,000, spread over the duration of the lease. That is £63,000/21 = £3,000 per annum.

Thus in the year ended 30 September 2021, Joe Bloggs's deduction for the lease premium would be calculated on three months: 3/12 × £3,000.

	£
	750
Rent payable (one quarter) (£25,000 × 3/12)	6,250
Total	7,000

Entertainment Expenses

In general, entertainment expenses incurred are **completely disallowed** (this also applies to amounts reimbursed to employees for specific entertaining expenses, gifts and round-sum allowances which are exclusively for meeting such expenses). However, there are **exceptions to this rule**:

- Gifts carrying a conspicuous advertisement for the trader, not consisting of food, drink or tobacco and not exceeding £50 per person per annum.

■ Expenditure for the benefit of **staff**, e.g. staff entertainment, annual parties, etc. is allowable, provided the entertainment is open to all staff generally and is not excessive. This includes employees' guests.

■ Gifts to charities (except under gift aid), provided they are wholly and exclusively for the purposes of the trade – it is usually very difficult to show a trading motive for a gift to charity.

Legal Expenses

Certain legal expenses are **allowable**, meaning that **no adjustment is required**:

■ debt recovery;
■ renewal of a short lease of less than 50 years;
■ product liability claims and employee actions;
■ expenses incurred defending the individual's title to fixed assets; and
■ expenses connected with an action for breach of contract.

Other legal expenses are **disallowable** and must be **added to the net profit/(loss) per the statement or profit or loss**:

■ expenses associated with the acquisition of capital assets;
■ the drafting of an original grant of a lease; and
■ expenses associated with acquiring a new asset.

Repairs

Replacement or redecoration repairs not involving material improvements are allowable. Expenditure on improvements/extensions, new assets, etc. is not allowable. As a general rule, expenditure incurred on repairs to buildings is deductible. The concept of repair is that it brings an item back to its original condition, and in this respect the following points are critical:

■ The expenditure must have actually been incurred. However, provisions for work to be done in the future will be allowable for tax purposes if the conditions for IAS 37 are met (see **Provisions** above).

■ The term "repairs" does not include improvements and alterations to premises. In addition, it is not possible to claim a revenue deduction for the portion of the improvements or alterations that would represent the cost of repairs that could otherwise have been carried out.

■ The replacement of a capital asset or the "entirety" will not be treated as a repair. This would cover, for instance, the reconstruction of a trader's premises.

   The test to be applied is whether or not the repair entails the renewal of a component part or of the entirety. If it is the former, it will be regarded as a repair; if it is the latter, i.e. the renewal of an entirety, it will be treated as a capital expenditure.

   A separately identifiable portion of a building or structure may be regarded as an entirety in its own right and, accordingly, its replacement would be disallowed. A practical test is whether or not they are of sufficient size and importance to be regarded as an entirety. Examples of entireties from case law include the following:

   ● Replacement of a large chimney situated apart from other factory buildings (*O'Grady v. Bullcroft Main Collieries Ltd* (1932)).

   ● A ring in an auction mart (*Wynne-Jones (Inspector of Taxes) v. Bedale Auction Ltd* (1976)).

   ● A replacement of a stand in a football ground (*Brown v. Burnley Football & Athletic Ltd* (1980)).

   ● A barrier that protected a factory against the overflow from an adjoining canal (*Phillips v. Whieldon Sanitary Potteries Ltd* (1952)).

It appears that it is necessary to show that the item that has been replaced is ancillary to the complete building. In practice, the accounting treatment adopted and the total cost involved may also be important factors.

Repairs to Newly Acquired Assets

In *Odeon Associated Theatres Limited v. Jones* (1971), it was held that the expenditure on repairs to a newly acquired asset may be deductible, provided that:

■ the cost is properly charged to the revenue account in accordance with the correct principles of commercial accountancy; and
■ the repairs are not improvements; and
■ the expenditure is not incurred to make the asset commercially viable on its acquisition; and
■ the purchase price was not substantially less than it would have been if it had been in a proper state of repair at the time of purchase.

Leased Motor Vehicles

Where the CO_2 emissions of a leased motor car exceed 50g/km, 15% of the leasing costs are disallowed in calculating taxable profits. The threshold for leases entered into on or after 6 April 2018 but before 6 April 2021 was 110g/km (for companies, the threshold for leases entered into on or after 1 April 2008 but before 1 April 2021 was 110g/km). This 15% leasing cost restriction applies to operating and finance leases (see **Finance Leases** below).

Example 3.17

Joe, who is self-employed and prepares annual accounts to 30 September, leased a car on 20 April 2021. The car had CO_2 emissions of 65g/km. Lease charges of £6,000 are included in Joe's accounts for year-end 30 September 2021. Joe has agreed with HMRC that one-third of the usage is private.

Allowable lease cost is £6,000 × 85% = £5,100, less private element (1/3rd) = £3,400 for 2021/22.

Penalties and Interest on Late Payment of Tax

HMRC penalties and interest that have been incurred for late payment of income tax, VAT and most other tax heads are disallowed in computing tax-adjusted profits.

Intellectual Property

Any income or expenditure (excluding depreciation or amortisation) that is specifically associated with:

■ intellectual property (including patents, copyrights and know-how);
■ goodwill; and
■ other intangible assets (including agricultural quotas and brands),

is, in general, taxable/deductible as trading income. Therefore, no adjustment is needed to the net profit/(loss).

Redundancy Payments

Statutory redundancy payments are specifically allowable. Redundancy payments made when a trade ends are deductible on the earlier of either the day of payment or the last day of trading.

The deduction extends to additional payments of up to three times the amount of the statutory redundancy pay on cessation of trade. Compensation for loss of office and ex-gratia payments are deductible if for the benefit of the trade.

Renewal or Registration of Trademarks

Expenses on renewal or registration of trademarks are specifically allowable for trades only. Copyright arises automatically and so does not have to be registered.

Patent royalties and copyright royalties paid "wholly and exclusively" in connection with a trade are deductible as trading expenses. They are paid with deduction of basic rate tax, which is then collected through self-assessment. Generally, copyright royalties are paid gross.

Accountancy and Tax Advisor Fees

Normal accounting, auditing and taxation compliance costs are allowable. Accountancy fees arising out of an enquiry are only permitted if no additional tax charges arise (the special costs regarding Tribunal appeals would also potentially be allowable if the appeal were found in favour of the individual). If accountancy fees are in connection with non-trade income, i.e. investment income or CGT), they are not deductible.

Pre-trading Expenses

An allowance may be claimed in respect of pre-trading expenses in the case of a trade or profession, provided that the expenses:

- were incurred for the purpose of the trade or profession; and
- were incurred within seven years of commencement; and
- are not otherwise allowable in computing profits.

Where an allowance is granted for pre-trading expenses, it is treated as if the expenditure were incurred **on the date** on which the trade or profession **commenced**.

Examples of qualifying pre-trading expenses include accountancy fees, market research, feasibility studies, salaries, advertising, preparing business plans and rent.

Key Person Insurance

Key person insurance is insurance taken out by an employer in their own favour against the death, sickness or injury of an employee (the "key person") whose services are vital to the success of the employer's business.

In general, premiums paid under policies insuring against loss of profits, consequent on certain contingencies, **are deductible** for tax purposes in the period in which they are paid. Correspondingly, all **sums received** by an employer under such policies are treated as **trading receipts** in the period in which they are received. Key person insurance policies qualify for this treatment where the following conditions are satisfied:

- The sole relationship is that of employer and employee.
- The employee does not have a major shareholding.
- The insurance is intended to meet loss of profit resulting from the loss of the services of the employee, as distinct from the loss of goodwill or other capital loss.
- In the case of insurance against death, the policy is a short-term insurance providing only for a sum to be paid in the event of the death of the insured within a specified number of years.

When the conditions are not met, key person insurance premiums are disallowed and any sums received are consequently not taxable.

Finance Leases

Assets leased under finance leases may be included as fixed assets in the accounts, and interest and depreciation for such assets included in the statement of profit or loss.

For tax purposes, capital allowances **may not** be claimed in respect of such assets. Instead a deduction can be given for **gross lease payments** made, i.e. interest plus capital. The adjustments to be made to the accounting profits would then be as follows:

- add back interest and depreciation charged in respect of finance lease assets; **and**
- give a deduction for gross lease payments made.

Alternatively, in line with the thrust of HMRC accepting financial statements prepared using generally accepted accounting standards, the deduction for finance leases can follow the accounting treatment and comprise a mixture of the finance charge element and the accounting depreciation. In this way no adjustment is required for leased assets in these circumstances (except if there was any private use of the asset or if the finance lease related to a motor vehicle with CO_2 emissions of more than 50g/km, see **Leased Motor Vehicles**).

Unpaid Remuneration

If earnings for employees are charged in the accounts but are not paid within nine months of the end of the period of account, the cost is only deductible for the period of account in which the earnings are **paid**.

National Insurance Contributions

Only employer's national insurance contributions (NICs), i.e. its Class 1 secondary and Class 1A contributions, are tax deductible. A trader's self-employed Class 2 or Class 4 NICs are drawings and, as such, are not tax deductible. (See **Chapter 9** for full details on NICs.)

Incidental Costs of Obtaining Finance

Incidental costs of obtaining loan finance, or of attempting to obtain or redeem it, are deductible (e.g. bank fees/charges).

Pension Contributions

Ordinary annual contributions by an employer to a **Revenue-approved** pension scheme, for the benefit of employees, are **allowable** for tax purposes in the year in which they are **paid**. Thus, any **accruals** in respect of ordinary annual pension contributions due, which have been included in arriving at the accounts profit, will have to be disallowed.

Now that we have considered the allowable and disallowable items for tax purposes, let's look at a worked example to recap the calculation of tax-adjusted trading profits for income tax.

Example 3.18

Mr Bailey has operated a sports goods shop for 10 years. The statement of profit and loss for this business for the year ended 31 December 2021 is as follows:

Statement of Profit or Loss for the year ended 31 December 2021

	Notes	£	£
Sales			313,759
Less: cost of sales			(226,854)
Gross profit			86,905
Add:			
Bank interest received		1,300	
Profit on sale of equipment		580	1,880
			88,785
Less: expenses:			
Wages and NIC	1	45,000	
Rates	2	2,200	
Insurance	3	8,100	
Light and heat	2	850	
Telephone	4	970	
Repairs	5	3,400	
Motor and travel expenses	6	5,440	
General expenses	7	4,575	
Loan interest	2	9,000	
Bank interest and charges		3,260	
Depreciation		4,450	87,245
Net profit for the year			1,540

Notes:

1. Wages and NIC:

	£
Salary to self	20,000
Salary to wife	2,000
Own NICs	200
Bonus to staff	2,500

2. Rates, light and heat, loan interest

   In March 2008, Mr Bailey purchased, for £100,000, the shop premises in which the business had been carried on for the previous three years. Since 2008, the top floor, which is a self-contained flat, has been occupied free of charge by Mr Bailey's elderly father, who takes no part in the business. One-fifth of the rates, property insurance, light and heat relate to the flat, which represents one-tenth of the value of the whole property.

   The loan interest relates to interest paid on a loan taken out for the purchase of the premises.

3. Analysis of insurance charge

	£
Shopkeepers' all-in policy	1,400
Retirement annuity premiums for self	3,000
Permanent health insurance for self	2,400
Motor car insurance	800
Property insurance	500
	8,100

4. Telephone/home expenses

   Telephone costs include Mr Bailey's home telephone and 25% of the total charge is for personal use. Mrs Bailey carries out most of her bookkeeping duties at home and a special deduction of £156 is to be allowed for costs incurred in carrying out these duties at home. This item has not been reflected in the statement of profit or loss.

continued overleaf

5. Repairs charge:

	£
Purchase of display stand	500
Repairs to shop front	600
Plumbing repairs in shop	800

6. Analysis of motor and travel expenses

Included in the motor and travel expenses is the cost of a trip to London to a sports goods whole-sale exhibition. Mr Bailey attended the exhibition on two days and then spent a further five days visiting friends and relatives. Details of the expenses are as follows:

	£
Air fare	140
Hotel bill (for seven days)	400
Entertaining overseas exhibitor	100
	640

The remainder of the expenses relate to Mr Bailey's motor car, which had a market value of £25,000 and CO_2 emissions of 140g/km when first leased on 1 July 2019.

	£
Lease of car (12 payments × £240)	2,880
Running expenses	1,920
	4,800

Annual mileage:	
Personal mileage	6,000
Business mileage	12,000
Home to business mileage	2,000
Total mileage	20,000 miles

7. Analysis of general expenses

	£
Donation to church	405
Donation to church building fund (includes full-page advertisement in magazine – £200)	1,000
Subscriptions to trade association	350
Accountancy fee	1,100
Branded sponsorship of "open day" at local golf club	900
Entertainment – customers	520
Entertainment – staff Christmas party	300
	4,575

Computation of Tax-adjusted Profits

	Notes	£	£
Net profit per accounts			1,540
Add:			
Depreciation		4,450	
Wages and NIC	1	20,200	
Rates (1/5th)		440	
Insurance	2	5,500	
Light and heat (1/5th)		170	
Loan interest (1/10th)		900	
Telephone (25%)		242	
Repairs	3	500	
Motor and travel expenses	4	3,139	
General expenses	5	1,725	37,266
			38,806

continued overleaf

Deduct:		
Bank interest received	1,300	
Profit on sale of equipment	580	
Mrs Bailey's business telephone	156	(2,036)
Adjusted profits (prior to calculation in respect		
of capital allowances – see Chapter 4)		36,770

Notes:
1. Wages and NIC

	£
Salary to self	20,000
Own NIC	200
Disallowed, as these are drawings	20,200

2. Insurance

	£
Retirement annuity premiums for self	3,000
Permanent health insurance for self	2,400
Property insurance (1/5th)	100
Disallowed	5,500

The restriction in respect of the motor car insurance is included in Note 4.

3. Repairs
    Display stand is capital expenditure – disallowed.
4. Motor and travel

Leasing charges	£2,880
Running expenses	£1,920
Motor car insurance	£800
Cost per accounts	£5,600
Total mileage	20,000 miles
Personal mileage	(6,000)
Home to business	(2,000)
Business mileage	12,000 miles (60%)

Disallow – Car Restrictions:

(a) Lease restriction
     CO_2 emissions of car is 140g/km (therefore the 15% restriction applies. Lease signed on or after 6 April 2018 but before 6 April 2021 so 110g/km limit applies).

Payments £240 × 12 =	2,880
15% restriction	(432)
	2,448

     Lease hire restriction = £432
(b) Private car element
     Disallowable element: 40% × £2,448 = £979
(c) Private running expenses and motor car insurance
     Disallowable element: 40% × £2,720 = £1,088
(d) Air fare and hotel bill (none allowable because of

duality of purpose*)	£540
Business entertainment	£100
Motor and travel disallowed	£3,139

* The strict position is that because the expenditure was not incurred "wholly and exclusively" for the purpose of the trade, none of the expenditure is allowable. In practice, however, it would normally be acceptable to claim a deduction for a proportion of the total expenditure equal to the business element, e.g. 2/7ths.

continued overleaf

5. General expenses	
Donation to church	£405
Donation to church building fund (excluding magazine advertisement)	£800
Entertainment – customers	£520
Disallowable	£1,725

The sponsorship of the "open day" at the local golf club would be allowable as advertising.

The donations to church could potentially be allowable if it could be shown they were provided for the purposes of the trade, or if the business obtained a benefit from it (e.g. advertising in the church's newsletter). It has been assumed this is not the case here.

Before we move on to the next stage, try **Questions 3.7–3.11** at the end of this chapter.

3.3.6   Trading Allowance

A trading allowance of £1,000 is available to give income tax relief to small amounts of trading income. It applies to trades, professions and vocations, but not to businesses carried on in partnership. The allowance operates by reference to an individual's "relevant income". Generally, this is gross receipts (i.e. before deducting expenses).

Where an individual's relevant income for the tax year does not exceed the £1,000 trading allowance, there is no charge to tax.

Where an individual's relevant income exceeds the £1,000 allowance, the individual can elect to use an alternative method of calculating income. Under this method the charge to tax is on the excess of relevant income over £1,000.

3.3.7   Special Rules for Small Businesses: Cash Basis of Accounting and Simplified Expenses

Two measures are available when calculating tax-adjusted profits for small businesses: the cash basis of accounting and simplified expenses.

Cash Basis of Accounting

The cash basis of accounting is a simpler tax system designed for businesses that do not need, or want, to prepare accounts on an accruals basis. The cash basis of accounting allows small businesses to be taxed on their receipts (i.e. money received) less payments of allowable expenses, rather than having to make accounting adjustments and other calculations that are designed for larger or more complex businesses.

It is important to note that the cash basis scheme is only open to unincorporated businesses – companies must continue to prepare accounts on an accruals basis, regardless of their size.

The key aspects of the cash basis are as follows:

■   It is optional and must be elected into. In the case of a partnership, the election for the cash basis must be made by the person responsible for making the partnership's tax return (the "nominated partner"). If an election is made for the cash basis to apply, it applies for both income tax and NIC purposes (see **Chapter 9**).

■   Businesses can enter into the cash basis if their receipts for the year do not exceed the £150,000, or twice this limit (currently £300,000) for those in receipt of the Universal Tax Credit. In subsequent years businesses can continue to use the cash basis even though they exceed these limits, but once their receipts exceed £300,000 then, for the following tax year, the business must stop using the cash basis and return to using the accruals basis.

■ Businesses can leave the cash basis if their commercial circumstances change and it is no longer appropriate or desirable for them. Examples of such changes include a business that is expanding and wishes to claim more than £500 interest deductions (see later), a business that wishes to claim "sideways" loss relief or a business that decides to register for VAT.

■ Certain trades are excluded from using the cash basis, such as dealers in securities and waste disposal.

Electing into the cash basis has a number of tax implications. These include:

■ Expenses are only allowable when they are paid.

■ Allowable payments are those made "wholly and exclusively" for the purposes of the trade, subject to a small number of specific rules and exceptions.

■ Motoring expenses for motorcycles and goods vehicles may be calculated using either actual expenditure or the simplified expense mileage rates, i.e. rather than taking relief for actual expenditure, relief is claimed by multiplying business mileage in the period by the approved mileage rates (see **Section 5.4.2** and **Motoring Expenses** below).

■ The typical adjustment for trading stock taken for a trader's own use when calculating tax-adjusted profits is not applied to a business using the cash basis, i.e. when a trader takes items from the business for his or her own use, an adjustment is made to taxable trading profit to account for any profit that would have been recorded in the accounts had the sale been made to a third party. This adjustment is not required when using the cash basis. Under the cash basis, the stock can be accounted for at cost price.

■ Interest on cash borrowing is only allowable up to £500. It is not necessary to establish that the borrowing is financing capital employed in the business because it is not a condition of this deduction that the interest is "wholly and exclusively" for business purposes.

■ Capital expenditure (excluding cars) is an allowable deduction for the business (provided it would qualify for capital allowances).

■ As relief is given as a deduction from income for the cost of purchasing plant and machinery (other than cars), it follows that if the plant and machinery is sold while using the cash basis, then the proceeds must be included as trading income.

■ For a disposal of business assets while in the cash basis, the disposal does not give rise to a chargeable gain or allowable loss.

■ Business losses may be carried forward to set against the profits of future years but cannot be carried back or set off "sideways" against other sources of income (see **Chapter 4**).

Simplified Expenses
Certain items of expenditure, such as motoring expenses, often have both a business and a private element. Previously, in order to claim the relevant deduction, the taxpayer had to calculate the actual expenditure incurred and then apportion it between business and non-business use, supported by detailed records (e.g. appropriate mileage records). This was an administrative burden for the taxpayer, the business and the Government.

The simplified expenses measure is an alternative method to claim for particular items of business expenditure. It allows all **unincorporated businesses**, irrespective of size, to choose to use flat-rate expenses for particular items of business expenditure, namely:

■ business use of cars, motorcycles and goods vehicles;
■ business use of home; and
■ private use of business premises.

A separate claim can be made for each relevant category of expenditure, meaning that the taxpayer can claim using the flat-rate deduction (the simplified expenses measure) for one category and the apportionment method for another. For example, a business may decide to claim the flat-rate expense for motor expenses, while claiming relief on the business use of the home by apportioning actual expenses.

It is important to note that this measure only applies to unincorporated businesses. Companies must continue to prepare accounts on an accruals basis, regardless of their size.

Motoring Expenses

Car, van or motorcycle expenses can be calculated using a flat rate for mileage instead of the actual costs of buying and running the vehicle, e.g. insurance, repairs, servicing and fuel. The flat-rate amount depends on the type of vehicle and the level of business mileage.

Vehicle type	Rate	
	First 10,000 business miles	**Over 10,000 business miles**
Car	45p per mile	25p per mile
Goods vehicle		
Motorcycle	24p per mile	

Example 3.19

Michael uses his car for his business and he travelled 11,000 business miles in the year to 31 March 2022. In arriving at his taxable trading profits for the 2021/22 tax year, the allowable deduction for motor expense would be £4,750, where he claims the flat-rate mileage expense.

His £4,750 flat-rate expense claim is calculated as follows:

10,000 miles $\times$ 45p = £4,500

1,000 miles $\times$ 25p = £250

The rates are the same as the approved mileage rates for payments made to employees in respect of the business use of their own car (see **Chapter 5** on employment income).

There are a number of conditions to using the flat-rate deduction:

■ Once claimed, no other relief is allowed in respect of that vehicle. For example, no capital allowances (see **Chapter 4**) or lease rental payments deductions (see **Section 3.3.5**) can be claimed.
■ Once claimed, it must continue to be claimed for as long as the asset is used in the business. A trader cannot subsequently switch to claim the business element of the actual costs in a later accounting period.

In addition, the flat-rate deduction cannot be claimed for:

■ vehicles on which capital allowances (see **Chapter 4**) have already been claimed; and
■ goods vehicles or motorcycles where any expenditure incurred on acquiring the vehicle has been deducted in calculating the profits under the cash basis.

Business Use of a Home

A business owner, i.e. a sole trader or partner, can claim expenses, such as rent or mortgage interest and household utilities, for any time spent working at home. Prior to the introduction of the simplified expenses measure, the business proportion of such expenses had to be apportioned and verified to make a claim. The simplified expenses measure allows instead a simple monthly deduction based on the number of hours worked at home.

Number of hours worked at home	Rate
25–50 hours per month	£10 per month
51–100 hours per month	£18 per month
101 hours or more per month	£26 per month

Example 3.20

Angela is self-employed and she prepares her accounts to 31 March 2022. In the year ended 31 March 2022, she worked 40 hours from home for 10 months and 60 hours during two months.

In arriving at her taxable trading profits, the allowable deduction for tax purposes would be £136 (10 months × £10 + 2 months × £18 = £136).

The amount of hours per month relates to the hours spent working in the home "**wholly and exclusively**" for the purposes of the trade.

Unlike the flat-rate deduction for vehicle expenses, an individual can decide each tax year whether to claim the flat-rate deduction or to make a claim for the business proportion of actual expenses incurred.

Private Use of Business Premises

A business can only claim those expenses that relate solely to the running of the business. In circumstances where a business premises is also used for non-business purposes, the private expenditure must be excluded.

Rather than having to recognise and apportion the private-use element of the expenditure, the simplified expenses option allows businesses to claim relief for the full costs, i.e. business and non-business, with a flat-rate deduction to cover the private element.

The adjustment is made based on the number of occupants using the premises as a home each month.

Number of occupants	Reduction in claim
1	£350 per month
2	£500 per month
3 or more	£650 per month

Example 3.21

A husband and wife own a pub in which they also live. They incurred total expenses of £20,000 for the tax year and make a claim under the simplified expenses measure. The husband's aunt comes to stay with them for one month during the tax year.

In arriving at their taxable trading profits, the allowable deduction would be £13,850, being:

£20,000

Less: 11 months × £500 (when only husband and wife live in the pub)

Less: 1 month × £650 (when the aunt also stays, i.e. three occupants)

3.3.8 Partnerships

A partnership is regarded as a single unit for the purposes of determining tax-adjusted profits. However, for the purposes of tax assessment, each partner's share of the joint profits is treated as personal to that partner, as if they arose from a **separate trade or profession**. As a consequence, commencement and cessation rules apply to each partner **individually** when they enter or leave the partnership.

The Partnership Act 1890 defines partnership as **"the relationship which subsists between persons carrying on a business in common with a view of profit"**.

For taxation purposes, a partnership continues no matter how many partners are admitted or leave, provided one of the old partners continues after the change.

Once the partnership's profits for a period of account have been computed, they are shared between the partners according to the profit-sharing arrangements for that accounting period. Partners' salaries, commissions and interest on capital accounts are not deducted in arriving at taxable profits; they are treated instead as a prior share and are allocated to the partners concerned. The balance of profits is allocated in accordance with the profit-sharing ratios in operation. This allocation cannot create or increase a loss for a partner. Any "notional" loss calculated in this way must be re-allocated to the other partners.

The general approach is to calculate the partnership's profit, then to tax each partner as if they were a sole trader running a business equal to their share of the partnership (e.g. 50% of the partnership).

Example 3.22

Andrew and Charlotte are partners in AC Partnership. They agree to share profits equally after paying a salary of £8,000 to Andrew. The tax-adjusted trading profits for AC Partnership in respect of the year ended 31 December 2021 are £4,000.

What is the allocation of profits between Andrew and Charlotte for the year ended 31 December 2021?

	Andrew £	Charlotte £	Total £
Salary	8,000	–	8,000
Balance (split 50:50)	(2,000)	(2,000)	(4,000)
Partnership profit	6,000	(2,000)	4,000
Re-allocation of "notional loss"	(2,000)	2,000	–
Allocation of profits	4,000	Nil	4,000

A partnership may have **non-trading income**, such as dividends on shares or interest on a partnership bank account (see **Chapter 6**) or partnership rental income (see **Chapter 7**). Such items are kept separate from trading income, but they (and any associated tax credits) are shared between the partners in a similar fashion as trading income on the basis of the profit-sharing agreements. For income (excluding income taxed at source and dividends), the accounting period for trading profits is also applied to the source of income, and commencement and cessation rules equally apply. However, for income taxed at source, the basis period is the actual tax year (6 April–5 April).

A partnership **ceases** to exist when:

- the business ceases; or
- only one partner remains (i.e. the partnership becomes a sole trader); or
- a completely different set of partners takes over from the old partners.

The "nominated partner" is responsible for ensuring the partnership's tax return is prepared and submitted to the partnership's tax office.

Allocation of Partnership Profits/Losses

There are two steps in calculating each partner's share of the tax-adjusted trading profits/losses.

Step 1: allocate salaries, interest on capital, etc. to each partner first. (Note: pro rata for periods less than 12 months.)

Step 2: divide profit/losses between the partners according to profit-sharing ratio in the accounting period.

Example 3.23: No change in partnership members or profit-sharing ratios

John and Kate are in partnership. Trading profits (after tax adjustments) for the year to 31 October 2021 are £120,000. As per the profit-sharing agreement, profits will be shared in the ratio 70:30 between John and Kate, but this is after paying a salary of £7,000 per annum to John because he puts in longer hours each week into the partnership. Interest on capital of £3,000 per annum is paid to John and £5,000 per annum is paid to Kate (Kate has a higher capital account; therefore her interest on capital is higher).

During the year John drew £50,000 and Kate drew £48,000 on account of their profit shares. Partners' drawings are shown as a reduction in their capital account and will be reflected on the partnership statement of financial position.

Solution

Year ended 31 October 2021	Total (£)	John (£)	Kate (£)
Trading income	120,000		
Partner's salary	(7,000)	7,000	
Interest on capital	(8,000)	3,000	5,000
Residual profit	105,000		
Shared 70:30	(105,000)	73,500	31,500
		83,500	36,500

The information on drawings is irrelevant as far as the tax computations are concerned. When and how John and Kate draw these profits has no bearing on their tax liabilities. Drawings are simply the amount that partners draw on account in advance of their profit share being determined. (This is understandable, as partners do not know how much they have earned until the end of the accounting year, but they may not be able to afford to wait until the end of the accounting year to take money.)

The amount determined in relation to John and Kate will be entered into their respective tax returns (in this case for the tax year 2021/22).

Example 3.24: Change in partnership and in profit-sharing ratios
Mike and Phil are in partnership, sharing profits in the ratio 60:40. A salary of £10,000 per annum is paid to Mike.

Stephen is admitted to the partnership on 1 February 2021 and the profits are shared 40:40:20 between Mike, Phil and Stephen from that date. With effect from that date, Mike's salary is to be reduced to £8,000 per annum. Tax-adjusted profits for the year to 31 July 2021 are £130,000. The estimated profits for the year ended 31 July 2022 are £155,000.

Solution
When Stephen comes into the practice on 1 February 2021, the ratios will change. We need to approach the calculation by looking at the period up to the introduction of Stephen and then the period after he is admitted as a partner.

	Total (£)	Mike (£)	Phil (£)	Stephen (£)
1 August 2020 to 31 January 2021				
Adjusted profit (i.e. 6/12 × £130,000)	65,000			
Partner's salary (i.e. 6/12 × £10,000)	(5,000)	5,000		
Residual profit	60,000			
Shared 60:40	(60,000)	36,000	24,000	
1 February 2021 to 31 July 2021				
Adjusted profit (i.e. 6/12 × £130,000)	65,000			
Partner's salary (i.e. 6/12 × £8,000)	(4,000)	4,000		
Residual profit	61,000			
Shared 40:40:20	(61,000)	24,400	24,400	12,200
		69,400	48,400	12,200

These values will be entered into Mike, Phil and Stephen's tax returns. Note that Stephen will be subject to the trade commencement rules (see **Section 3.2.2**). Under the opening year rules, Stephen's profits will be taxed as follows:

2020/21: 1 February to 5 April 2021: 2/6 × £12,200 = £4,067
2021/22: First 12 months to 31 January 2022: £12,200 + 6/12 × (20% of (£155,000 – £8,000)) = £26,900
2022/23: Year ended 31 July 2022: £29,400 (i.e. 20% of (£155,000 – £8,000))

Stephen will have overlap profits of £18,767, being:

- the first two months (taxed in 2020/21 and 2021/22): £4,067; and
- the period from 1 August 2021 to 31 January 2022 (taxed in 2021/22 and 2022/23): 6/12 × £29,400 = £14,700.

As a check, the amounts taxed less overlap relief should match what Stephen will receive from the partnership for the periods ending 31 July 2021 and 31 July 2022 (i.e. £4,067 + £26,900 + £29,400 less £18,767 = £41,600, which is the same as £12,200 + £29,400).

Interest on Capital

Interest on capital is a distribution of profit and is, accordingly, a drawing. It is therefore a disallowable expense in computing the partnership's profits or losses for a period. Interest on capital must, however, be carefully distinguished from interest paid by the partnership in respect of a loan made to the partnership by an individual partner. Such interest, provided the funds borrowed have been used for the partnership business, will be an allowable trading deduction.

For periods of less than 12 months, interest on capital should be allocated to the respective partner on a pro rata basis.

Salaries

Salaries paid to a partner are treated in the same manner as drawings taken out of a business by a sole trader, i.e. they are disallowed for computation purposes. However, in reaching the residual profit share they must be included in the calculation. And again, for periods of less than 12 months, they should be allocated on a pro rata basis to the respective partner.

Rent Paid to a Partner

If a partner beneficially owns the premises from which the partnership is operated and lets the premises on an arm's length basis to the partnership, then the rent will be allowed as a deduction in computing the partnership profits and the landlord partner will be assessed personally on the net profit rents (see **Chapter 7** on property income for more details).

Change in Profit-sharing Ratios/Partnerships

Profits for an accounting period are allocated between the partners according to the profit-sharing agreement. If the salaries, interest on capital or profit-sharing ratio change during the accounting period, the profits are split in proportion to the periods before and after the change and allocated accordingly. The constituent elements are then added together to give each partner a share of profits for the period of account.

Limited Liability Partnerships

A limited liability partnership (LLP) is a special form of partnership in the UK. It is taxed on virtually the same basis as a normal partnership, but special rules apply for restricting loss relief to all the partners. The difference between an LLP and a normal partnership is that, in an LLP, the liability of the partners is limited to the capital they contributed. In practice, this structure gives commercial protection (similar to a limited liability company) to the partners of the business.

Apportionment of Tax-adjusted Profits

Partnerships prepare an annual profit and loss account, which is the basis of a tax-adjusted profits computation. Trading income rules regarding allowable and disallowable expenses are applied in arriving at the partnership's tax-adjusted profit or loss figure. The only unusual feature is that partners' **salaries/drawings/wages** are **not allowable** as they are an **appropriation of profit** (i.e. effectively the same as the **drawings** of a sole trader). Similarly, **interest paid on partners' capital accounts** is not an allowable deduction in arriving at the tax-adjusted profit.

The tax-adjusted profits of a partnership are divided among the partners in accordance with:

■ the specific terms of the partnership agreement regarding **guaranteed salaries and interest on capital**; and
■ the **profit-sharing ratio** that existed during the accounting period.

Capital Gains on the Disposal of Partnership Assets

Disposals of partnership assets are treated as disposals by the individual partners and not the partnership itself. Chargeable gains or allowable losses accruing on the disposal of partnership assets are apportioned among the partners in accordance with their capital profit-sharing ratio (see **Chapter 15.9**).

University of Ulster LIBRARY

Example 3.25

Smith and Jones are in partnership as engineers for many years, sharing profits 60:40. The statement of profit and loss for the year ended 30 April 2021 is as follows:

Statement of Profit or Loss for the year ended 30 April 2021

	Notes	£	£
Gross fees			200,000
Less:			
Overheads		50,000	
Salaries paid to partners	1	41,000	
Interest paid on partners			
Capital accounts	2	13,000	
Rent paid to Smith for partnership premises		35,000	
Entertainment expenses (all client related)		15,000	154,000
Net profit for the year			**46,000**

Notes:

1. Salaries	£
Smith	18,000
Jones	23,000
	41,000

2. Interest paid on capital accounts	£
Smith	6,000
Jones	7,000
	13,000

Computation of Taxable Profits

	£	£
Net profit per accounts		46,000
Add back:		
Salaries paid to partners	41,000	
Interest paid on partners' capital accounts	13,000	
Disallowed entertainment expenses	15,000	69,000
Assessable profit		**115,000**

Apportionment of Assessable Profit 2021/22	Total	Smith	Jones
	£	£	£
Salaries	41,000	18,000	23,000
Interest paid on capital accounts	13,000	6,000	7,000
Balance (apportioned 60 : 40)	61,000	36,600	24,400
Taxable profits	115,000	60,600	54,400

Now try **Questions 3.12** and **3.13** at the end of this chapter.

Questions

Review Questions

(See Suggested Solutions to Review Questions at the end of this textbook.)

Question 3.1

Ms Lola commenced trading on 1 June 2019 and makes up accounts to 31 May. Her trading results are as follows:

	£
01/06/2019–31/05/2020	48,000
01/06/2020–31/05/2021	39,000
01/06/2021–31/05/2022	37,200

Requirement

Calculate Ms Lola's taxable profits from her sole trade for the tax years 2020/21 to 2022/23, and any overlap profits arising.

Question 3.2

Mr Charlie commenced trading on 1 May 2020 and makes up accounts to 31 October. His trading results are as follows:

	£
01/05/2020–31/10/2020	44,800
01/11/2020–31/10/2021	54,400
01/11/2021–31/10/2022	53,600
01/11/2022–31/10/2023	46,400

He had no other income in each relevant tax year.

Requirement

Calculate Mr Charlie's taxable profits from his sole trade for the tax years 2020/21 to 2022/23, and any overlap profits arising.

Question 3.3

Jim commenced practice as a solicitor on 1 May 2020. Tax-adjusted profits for the opening years were as follows:

	£
1 May 2020 to 30 April 2021	48,000
Year ended 30 April 2022	60,000
Year ended 30 April 2023	9,600

Requirements

(a) Calculate Jim's taxable profits for the first four tax years, and any overlap profits arising.
(b) Do these taxable profits arise from a trade, profession or vocation?

Question 3.4

Donna Ross, a 32-year-old single parent, is a new client. She resigned from her job at Northern Bank on 31 March 2021 to sell children's clothing full time on eBay.

She tells you that she has traded on eBay part-time for a "few" years. She sold only household items or sale bargains picked up while shopping. She estimates that her sales were £5,000 in 2020/21 and her costs were minimal since the items sold were "lying about the house" and had been used by her family until they grew tired of them. She used the family computer and packed the items in her garage. In June 2021, she spotted a market opportunity when she bought a job lot of designer children's clothes for £10,000 and sold them on eBay individually for £20,000 in just one month! This prompted her to try to ramp up her selling on eBay from 1 September 2021. Her tax-adjusted profit for the year ended 31 August 2022 was £79,400.

Requirements

(a) Compute the income tax payable by Donna for 2021/22 and 2022/23, and any overlap profits arising. (Assume the same rates/allowances apply to 2022/23 as they do for 2021/22.)

(b) Write a letter to Donna explaining, with reasons, if her eBay activity for 2020/21 and 2021/22 is taxable, and how her overlap profits can be relieved.

Question 3.5

Ms Dora ceases trading on 31 December 2021. She made up her accounts annually to 31 May. Her trading results were as follows:

	£
Year ended 31/05/2020	72,000
Year ended 31/05/2021	9,600
Period ended 31/12/2021	12,000

She has unused overlap relief of £5,000.

Requirement

Calculate Ms Dora's taxable profits for the 2020/21 and 2021/22 tax years.

Question 3.6

In 2021, J. Cog changed his accounting date to 30 September, having previously always made up accounts for the year to 31 October. His tax-adjusted profits for recent periods were as follows:

	£
Year ended 31 October 2020	64,000
11 months to 30 September 2021	24,000

He had unrelieved overlap profits of £15,000.

Requirement

Calculate J. Cog's assessable profits for the 2020/21 and 2021/22 tax years, and overlap relief available going forward.

Question 3.7

Joseph Murphy is a trader. He prepares accounts annually to 31 December. His statement of profit or loss for the year ended 31 December 2021 was as follows:

Expenditure	Notes	£	Income	£
Salaries	1	61,864	Gross profit	112,500
Travelling	2	17,512	Discounts received	7,349
Commissions		7,236	Dividends from URNO Co.	2,813
Interest on late payment of VAT		1,121	Interest on National Loan Stock	2,250
Interest on late payment of PAYE		1,238	Deposit interest	170
Depreciation		13,793	Profit on sale of fixed assets	5,063
Bank interest		4,008		
Subscriptions	3	1,225		

continued overleaf

Repairs	4	6,480
Bad debts	5	2,475
Legal fees	6	1,069
Accountancy fees		2,250
Net profit		9,874
		130,145

130,145

Notes:

1. Salaries include salary to Mr Murphy of £7,500 and a salary paid to his wife of £5,000 for her work as secretary.
2. Travelling expenses include £1,000 for a holiday trip by Mr and Mrs Murphy.

3.
Subscriptions	£
Political party	75
Local football club	50
Traders' association	500
Trade papers	200
Old folks' home	150
Sports club	250
	1,225

4.
Repairs account	DR	CR
	£	£
Opening provision for repairs		855
Expenditure during period	2,335	
New extension to office	3,000	
Charge to profit and loss account		6,480
Closing provision	2,000	
	7,335	7,335

The opening and closing repairs provisions represent general provisions that do not conform with IAS 37.

5.
Bad debts account	DR	CR
	£	£
Opening provision – general		5,100
Bad debts recovered		2,675
Bad debts written off	2,275	
Charge to profit and loss account		2,475
Closing provision – general	7,975	
	10,250	10,250

6.
Legal fees	£
Bad debts recovery	60
Sale of freehold	1,009
	1,069

Requirement

Compute Joseph Murphy's taxable trading profits for 2021/22.

Question 3.8

Andy Reilly operates a consultancy business providing technical advice. He has been in business for many years and makes up annual accounts to 31 December. His profit and loss account for the year to 31 December 2021 is set out below.

	£	£
Fees charged		178,000
Less: Direct costs		
Technical salaries and employment expenses	64,000	
Stationery and printing	4,000	
Repairs to equipment	980	
Professional indemnity insurance	370	
Motor vehicle expenses (Note 1)	6,250	
Depreciation – Equipment	2,500	
– Motor vehicles	3,000	(81,100)
		96,900
Deduct: Overheads		
Rent, rates and property insurance	11,000	
Repairs to premises (Note 2)	6,500	
Light and heat	1,100	
Office salaries	7,200	
Telephone and postage	400	
Advertising	800	
Entertaining (Note 5)	390	
Bad debts (Note 3)	550	
Defalcations (theft) (Note 4)	6,000	
Successful claim by client not covered by insurance	2,500	
Andy Reilly's drawings	10,000	
Depreciation – office equipment and fittings	900	(47,340)
Net profit before taxation:		49,560

Notes:

1. £4,000 of the total motor vehicle expenses relate to the lease of Andy Reilly's car. The car cost £24,500 in January 2019, had CO_2 emissions of 189g/km and 40% of Andy's total mileage is business mileage. The other motor expenses relate to the lease of sales representatives' cars, all of which cost £19,000 when first leased in 2020 and have CO_2 emissions of 150g/km.
2. Repairs to premises include the charge for constructing two additional garages adjoining the firm's buildings for the sales representatives' cars. This amounted to £3,150.
3. The bad debts charge includes a credit for the recovery of a specific debt amounting to £350 and the creation of a general bad debt reserve amounting to £275.
4. The defalcations were traced to staff and were not covered by insurance.
5. The charge for entertainment comprises:

	£
Private holiday for Andy Reilly (June 2021)	120
Tickets for Andy Reilly and his friend to All-Ireland football final	30
Staff Christmas party	120
Business meals with customers	120
	390

Requirement

Compute Andy Reilly's taxable trading profits for 2021/22.

Question 3.9

Tony set up business as a car dealer/garage proprietor on 1 October 2020. His first accounts were made up for the 15-month period ended 31 December 2021 and subsequently to 31 December each year. The first two sets of accounts show the following results:

	15 months to 31/12/2021 £	Year ended 31/12/2022 £
Sales – cars	250,000	200,000
Sales – workshop	100,000	90,000
	350,000	290,000
Direct Costs		
Cost of cars sold	211,500	168,300
Salesman's salary and commission	15,000	13,000
Workshop labour and parts	62,500	66,000
	289,000	247,300
Gross profit	61,000	42,700
General and Administrative Costs		
Accountancy	1,500	1,250
Advertising	900	1,100
Bad debts (Note 1)	2,500	400
Depreciation	3,000	2,400
Drawings	15,000	12,000
Entertaining (Note 2)	1,500	700
Insurance	5,000	4,000
Interest (Note 3)	18,000	14,000
Legal fees (Note 4)	400	600
Light and heat	2,250	1,800
Office staff salaries	10,600	8,500
Postage, telephone and stationery	1,500	1,200
Sundries (Note 5)	1,250	650
Travel expenses (Note 6)	1,950	1,500
	65,350	50,100
Net loss	(4,350)	(7,400)

Notes:	15 months to 31/12/2021 £	Year ended 31/12/2022 £
1. Bad debts		
General provision	2,500	–
Bad debt written off	–	900
General provision no longer required	–	(500)
	2,500	400

continued overleaf

2. Entertaining   £

Hospitality for representatives of car
manufacturer during negotiations
for supply of cars   800   –
Entertaining customers   700   700
                                                         1,500   700

3. Interest

Interest on loan from car   9,500   7,000
manufacturer to buy stock
Interest on bank loan to establish business   8,500   7,000
                                                        18,000   14,000

4. Legal fees

Advice on supply agreement with   250   200
car manufacturer
Recovery of outstanding debts   –   200
Defending customer claim re. faulty car   150   200
                                                           400   600

5. Sundries

Security   500   300
Drinks at staff Christmas party   150   150
Subscription to trade association   200   200
Political donation   100   –
Charitable donation   50   –
Interest on late payment of VAT   250   –
                                                         1,250   650

6. Travel expenses   These expenses contain no disallowable element.

Requirements

(a) Compute the adjusted trading profits for the 15 months ended 31 December 2021 and the year
     ended 31 December 2022.
(b) Calculate Tony's taxable trading profits for the 2021/22 tax year.

Question 3.10

John Smith commenced trading on 1 May 2020. The statement of profit or loss for 1 May 2020 to
30 April 2021 shows the following information:

	Notes	£	£
Sales			201,230
Less: cost of sales			(140,560)
			60,670
Interest received	1		390
Gross profit			61,060

Expenses:

Wages	2	23,500	
Motor expenses	3	1,860	
Depreciation		1,250	
Rent and rates		12,800	
Leasing charges	4	4,300	
Repairs	5	3,900	
Telephone		800	
Bank interest and charges		3,800	
Sundry expenses	6	3,400	
Insurance	7	2,630	(58,240)
Profit for period			2,820

Notes:

	£
1. Interest received	390

	£
2. Included in wages charges are:	
Wage to Mrs Smith (wife), as bookkeeper	1,800
Wages to self	5,200
Accrued bonus for sales assistants	500
(paid on 1 July 2021)	
Own NICs	200

3. Motor expenses relate solely to Mr Smith's own motoring and include a £100 fine for careless driving; 60% of total mileage is for business purposes. Motor insurance has been included under the insurance charge.

	£
4. Analysis of leasing charges (all operating leases):	
Lease of till	300
Lease of shelving	1,200
Lease of Mr Smith's car	2,800
	4,300

The motor car had a market value of £25,000 and CO_2 emissions of 135g/km when first leased on 1 May 2019.

	£
5. Repairs:	
Painting outside of premises	1,000
Repairing shop front damaged in accident	1,300
Insurance claim re. above accident	(900)
Extension to shop	1,500
General provision for repairs	1,000
	3,900

	£
6. Sundry expenses:	
Trade subscriptions	250
Interest on the late payment of income tax	120
Donation to church	970
Christmas party for staff	560
Accountancy	1,500
	3,400

7. Insurance:

	£
Business 'all-in' policy	1,370
Motor car	300
Life assurance	460
Key person life assurance on salesman	500
	2,630

Requirement

Compute John Smith's tax-adjusted trading profits.

Question 3.11

Polly Styrene has been in business for many years manufacturing shoes, and she makes up her accounts to 31 December each year. Her statement of profit or loss for the year ended 31 December 2020 was as follows:

	£	£
Gross profit		170,000
Less:		
Wages and salaries (Note 1)	90,000	
Depreciation	20,000	
Light, heat and telephone (Note 2)	6,000	
Postage and stationery	500	
Repairs and renewals (Note 3)	5,000	
Legal and professional fees (Note 4)	3,000	
Bad debts (Note 5)	2,000	
Travel and entertainment (Note 6)	2,500	
Bank interest (Note 7)	3,500	
Royalties (Note 9)	25,000	
Insurance	3,000	
Freight	4,000	
Sundries (Note 8)	3,000	(167,500)
Net profit		2,500

Notes:

1. Wages and salaries – includes £8,000 for Polly Styrene.

2. Light, heat and telephone – includes £1,500 for light, heat and telephone at the residence of Polly Styrene. One-sixth is business-related.

3. Repairs and renewals

	£
Painting and decorating	1,600
Extension to shop	1,400
General provision for future repairs	2,000
	5,000

4. Legal and professional fees

	£
Debt collection	1,200
Accountancy	1,500
Surveyor's fees re. abortive purchase of premises	300
	3,000

5. Bad debts   £

	£
Trade debts written off	2,800
Bad debt recovered	(200)
Decrease in general reserve	(600)
	2,000

6. Travel and entertainment   £

	£
Car expenses (Note)	1,500
Christmas drinks for employees	400
Entertaining customers	600
	2,500

Note: the car cost £32,000, has CO_2 emissions of 100g/km and was bought in February 2019. Private use is one-third.

7. Bank interest   £

	£
Bank interest	1,500
Lease interest	2,000
	3,500

Polly leased plant and equipment through ACC Commercial Finance, under a three-year lease. The total repayments for the year were £18,600. Depreciation charged in the year on the asset was £15,000.

8. Sundries   £

	£
Advertising	1,051
Trade protection association	100
Political party subscription	1,000
Parking fines	49
Rubbish disposal	300
Donation to Cancer Focus (registered charity)	500
	3,000

9. Royalties – Polly pays royalties of £25,000 (gross) for the use of specialised equipment to manufacture her shoes.

Requirement
Calculate the trading taxable profits for 2021/22.

Question 3.12

A and B have traded as partners for many years, sharing profits equally. They prepare accounts each year to 30 September. On 1 October 2017, C was admitted as a partner and from that date profits are shared as follows:
A: 2/5ths
B: 2/5ths
C: 1/5th

Tax-adjusted trading profits were as follows:

	£
Year ended 30/09/2017	20,000
Year ended 30/09/2018	25,000
Year ended 30/09/2019	30,000
Year ended 30/09/2020	30,000
Year ended 30/09/2021	35,000

On 30 September 2019, A left the partnership. Since that date, B and C have shared profits and losses equally.

Requirement

Calculate the taxable trading profits for A, B and C for the years 2017/18 to 2021/22.

Question 3.13

Jack and John are in partnership as accountants for many years. Its statement of profit or loss for the year ended 30 April 2021 was as follows:

	£	£
Gross fees		200,000
Less: Overheads	100,000	
Jack's salary	20,000	
John's salary	21,000	
Jack's interest on capital	6,000	
John's interest on capital	7,000	154,000
		46,000

Disallowable expenses included in general overheads amount to £26,000. The profit-sharing ratio for year ending 30 April 2021 was 50:50.

Requirement

Adjust the trading profit for tax purposes and allocate the profits to the partners in the profit-sharing ratio.

Capital Allowances and Loss Relief

Learning Objectives

After studying this chapter you will be able to:

- Determine whether or not assets qualify for capital allowances.
- Compute the capital allowances available.
- Determine relief for losses, including losses on commencement and on cessation.

4.1   Capital Allowances: Introduction

In essence, income tax is a tax solely on income (revenue), which means that capital expenditure is not deductible for income tax purposes. This, therefore, denies the individual a tax deduction for depreciation or amortisation, which represents capital amounts written off in the accounts. In other words, when arriving at the tax-adjusted trading profits of a business, depreciation, for accounting purposes, is specifically disallowed and is added to the net profit/(loss) per the statement of profit or loss (SOPL). Instead, businesses can claim capital allowances on certain types of asset. The basic objective of capital allowances is to allow the business a **deduction** against tax-adjusted business profits for the **net cost of certain capital assets employed** for the purpose of the business.

The main types of capital allowance are:

- annual investment allowance (AIA)
- first year allowance (FYA)
- writing down allowance (WDA)
- balancing allowance/balancing charge.

Capital allowances are operated through the use of "pools". The cost of the asset is allocated to a specific "pool", depending on the nature of the asset. The "main pool" is where most assets meeting the definition of plant and machinery will be allocated.

The "special rate pool" is where specific assets, such as "integral features", will be allocated. A "single asset pool" may also be needed where assets are used partly for private purposes by the individual, e.g. the sole trader or the partner.

A business obtains relief for its capital expenditure by reducing the value of the pool in accordance with specific rates and rules. The reduction in the pool value (i.e. the capital allowance) is included as a deduction from taxable trading profits.

For unincorporated businesses (such as sole trades and partnerships), capital allowances are calculated for accounting periods.

This chapter will begin by looking at what assets can qualify for capital allowances. Once the type of assets that can qualify for capital allowances is understood, we will then move on to look at the main pool for capital allowances. It is into this pool that the vast majority of assets will fall. However, certain assets will fall into the special rate pool. The various types of capital allowance available on assets in the main and special rate pools will be discussed: the AIA, the FYA and the WDA. Special rules apply to assets that are used partly for private use and also assets that are categorised as "short-life assets".

4.2 Capital Allowances: Plant and Machinery

4.2.1 Meaning of "Plant"

Before we look at the capital allowances available for plant and machinery, we need to understand what is meant by "plant and machinery". There is no statutory definition of plant and machinery for the purposes of capital allowances. Therefore we must look to case law for various tests which must be satisfied if an item of expenditure is to qualify as "plant" for the purposes of capital allowances.

The question of whether an item is "plant" is considered a matter of fact and will be decided according to the circumstances of each particular case. The most quoted definition of the word "plant" is from *Yarmouth v. France* (1887), in which Lord Justice Lindley said:

> "There is no definition of plant in the Act, but in its ordinary sense, it includes whatever apparatus is used by a businessman for carrying on his business – not his stock-in-trade, which he buys or makes for sale; but all goods and chattels, fixed or moveable, live or dead, which he keeps for permanent employment in the business."

The principal test suggested by case law is whether the asset in question is **functional** to the operation of the business, as distinct from the **setting** in which the business is carried on. Other tests suggested by case law are:

- Is the expenditure incurred directly on the provision of plant and not, for instance, on the provision of finance, which is used to acquire plant?
- Does the expenditure replace an item previously regarded as plant?
- Is the expenditure related to an entire unit or is it merely expenditure on part of a larger, non-functional unit?

4.2.2 Expenditure on Buildings/Structures

The general rule is that expenditure on buildings/structures or on any asset that is incorporated into a building/structure, or that is of a kind normally incorporated into buildings/structures, does not qualify as expenditure on "plant". For example, expenditure on the walls and floors of a building would not be regarded as plant. Similarly, expenditure on a structure such as a bridge would not be regarded as plant.

However, over the years case law has made exceptions to this rule in certain instances. For example, the following have been ruled as qualifying expenditure on plant for capital allowance purposes:

- Cookers, washing machines, refrigeration or cooling equipment, sanitary ware and furniture and furnishings.
- Sound insulation provided mainly to meet the particular requirements of the trade.
- Computer, telecommunications and surveillance systems.
- Sprinkler equipment, fire alarm and burglar alarm systems.
- Partition walls, where moveable and intended to be moved.
- Dry docks and jetties.
- Silos provided for temporary storage and storage tanks, slurry pits and silage clamps.

This list is not exhaustive. All of the above items have been the subject of case law and are now enshrined in legislation at sections 21–23 Capital Allowances Act 2001, as Lists A, B and C (see **Appendix 4.1**).

Having identified what is and is not plant and machinery – and so what can and cannot be claimed as a capital allowance – we can now move on to look in detail at the main types of capital allowance.

4.3   Annual Investment Allowance

The annual investment allowance (AIA) is available to all businesses, and offers 100% capital allowances, up to a specified annual limit, on plant and machinery. It can be claimed against the main pool additions (see **Section 4.6**) and special rate pool additions (see **Section 4.7**).

There are some instances when the AIA cannot be claimed:

- cars;
- plant and machinery previously used for another purpose, e.g. a computer used at home and introduced into the business;
- plant and machinery gifted to the business;
- on a sale and leaseback where the leaseback is a long-funding lease; or
- expenditure incurred in the accounting period in which the business ceases.

For the period 1 January 2019 to 31 December 2021, the AIA limit is temporarily increased to £1,000,000, but from 1 January 2022 it will return to £200,000 (previously, from 1 January 2016 to 31 December 2018, it had been £200,000).

If the accounting period of the business is greater than or less than 12 months, the AIA is proportionately reduced or increased. For example, if the accounting period was for the six months to 31 December 2021, the AIA available would be £500,000 (i.e. £1,000,000 × 6/12).

4.3.1   AIA where Accountancy Period Straddles 31 December 2021

Where a business has an accounting period that straddles 31 December 2021, the following three steps are used to calculate the maximum AIA that can be claimed.

Step 1: Calculate the maximum **potential** AIA for the period. This will be the sum of:

The maximum AIA entitlement based on the £1,000,000 annual cap for the portion of the accounting period falling before 1 January 2022

PLUS

The maximum AIA entitlement based on the £200,000 cap for the portion of the accounting period falling on/after 1 January 2022

For example, if the accounting period ends 31 March, for 2022 the maximum potential AIA would be:

April 2021–December 2021: $9/12 \times £1,000,000$ + January 2022–March 2022: $3/12 \times £200,000 = £750,000 + £50,000 = £800,000$

Step 2: For capital expenditure incurred on or after 1 January 2022, the maximum AIA will be £200,000 multiplied by the number of months the accounting period falls on or after 1 January 2022.

Step 3: For capital expenditure incurred during the accounting period but before 1 January 2022, the maximum AIA will be the amount calculated in Step 1 minus the amount of any AIA claimed in Step 2.

Example 4.1

Michael runs a sole trade business and prepares his accounts to 31 March each year. In April 2021 he spent £500,000 on new machinery.

Step 1: Maximum potential AIA for year ended 31 March 2022 = $9/12 \times £1,000,000 + 3/12 \times £200,000 = £800,000$.

Step 2: Maximum AIA for last three months to 31 March 2022 is £50,000. As no capital expenditure incurred in this period, the AIA claimed is nil.

Step 3: Maximum AIA for first nine months to 31 December 2021 is £800,000 (from Step 1) less the amount of AIA claimed in Step 2, i.e. £800,000 – £Nil = £800,000. Therefore, all the £500,000 spent on machinery in April 2021 qualifies for AIA.

Total AIA for year ended 31 March 2022 = £Nil + £500,000 = £500,000.

Example 4.2

Sarah runs a sole trade business and prepares her accounts up to 31 March each year. In September 2021 Sarah bought new machinery for £100,000 and in February 2022 bought another machine for £70,000.

Step 1: Maximum potential AIA for year ended 31 March 2022 = $9/12 \times £1,000,000 + 3/12 \times £200,000 = £800,000$.

Step 2: Maximum AIA for last three months to 31 March 2022 is £50,000. So of the £70,000 spent on machinery (incurred on or after 1 January 2022), the maximum AIA that can be claimed is £50,000, meaning that £20,000 does not qualify for AIA.

Step 3: Maximum AIA for first nine months to 31 December 2021 is £750,000 (from Step 1) less the amount of AIA claimed in Step 2, i.e. £750,000 – £50,000 = £700,000.

Therefore, all of the £100,000 spent on machinery in September 2021 can qualify for AIA.

Total AIA for year ended 31 March 2022 = £50,000 + £100,000 = £150,000.

Example 4.3

Willy runs a sole trade business and prepares his accounts to 30 June each year. In November 2021 he spent £355,000 on new plant. He then spent £500,000 on new machinery in May 2022.

Step 1: Maximum potential AIA for year ended 30 June 2022 = $6/12 \times £1,000,000 + 6/12 \times £200,000 = £600,000$.

Step 2: Maximum AIA for last six months to 30 June 2022 is £100,000 (£200,000 × 6/12). So of the £500,000 spent on plant (incurred on or after 1 January 2022) the maximum AIA that can be claimed is £100,000, meaning that £400,000 does not qualify for AIA.

Step 3: Maximum AIA for first six months to 31 December 2021 is £600,000 (from Step 1) less the amount of AIA claimed in Step 2, i.e. £600,000 – £100,000 = £500,000. Therefore, all of the £355,000 spent on machinery in November 2021 can be claimed by AIA.

Total AIA for year ended 30 June 2022 = £100,000 + £355,000 = £455,000.

4.4   First Year Allowance

If an asset is purchased and it qualifies for the first year allowance (FYA), then the full cost of the asset can be deducted in arriving at the tax-adjusted trading profits of a business.

The **100%** FYA is available in relation to the following:

1.   New electric cars or zero-emission cars.
2.   New plant or machinery for an electric vehicle charging point installed solely for the purpose of charging electric vehicles.

The 100% FYA on electric/zero-emission cars is only available if these assets are acquired unused and are not second-hand.

Where the FYA is not claimed in full, the balance of expenditure is transferred to the main pool (see **Section 4.6**). An FYA is not reduced pro rata in a short period of account, unlike AIAs and annual writing down allowances (WDAs).

The AIA and the FYA **cannot** be claimed in respect of the same expenditure. Where both allowances are possible, the taxpayer can choose which, if any, to claim, with any excess being treated as noted above.

4.5   Research & Development Allowance and Structures and Buildings Allowance

4.5.1   Research & Development Allowance

A research and development allowance (RDA) of 100% is available on capital expenditure incurred on research and development (R&D) activities. R&D expenditure includes all expenditure incurred for carrying out, or providing facilities for carrying out, R&D. For example, RDAs are available for the cost of building or refurbishing R&D facilities and the cost of plant, machinery, fixtures or fittings to support R&D activities.

Expenditure on land and dwelling houses does not qualify for the RDA.

4.5.2   Structures and Buildings Allowance

The structures and buildings allowance (SBA) is available for eligible construction costs incurred on or after 29 October 2018, at an annual rate of 3% on astraight-line basis. Before 6 April 2020 (1 April 2020 for corporation taxpurposes), the annual rate was 2%.

The SBA is available once the building or structure has been brought into **qualifying use**. A building or structure is in qualifying use if it is in 'non-residential use' for the purposes of a qualifying activity. A **qualifying activity** includes a trade, profession or vocation. It also includes a UK property business (see **Chapter 7**).

SBA is given in respect of **qualifying expenditure** on the construction or purchase of a building or structure. Capital expenditure incurred on the renovation or conversion of a part of a building or structure may also be qualifying expenditure. If capital expenditure is incurred for the purposes of preparing land as a site for the construction of a building or structure, this counts as capital expenditure on the construction of the building or structure and the SBA will be available on this expenditure.

Expenditure incurred on the renovation or conversion of a part of a building or structure is treated as entirely separate from the original construction expenditure for the building or structure and may qualify for the SBA its own right.

The following expenditure is "**excluded expenditure**" for the purposes of the SBA:

■ Expenditure incurred on the acquisition of land or rights in or over land (including expenditure on fees, stamp taxes andother incidental costs attributable to the acquisition).

■ Expenditure incurred on the alteration of land, i.e. land reclamation, land remediation or land-scaping (other than so as to create a building or structure).

■ Expenditure incurred on, or in connection with, the seeking of planning permission (including fees and related costs).

■ Expenditure of a capital nature on the provision of plant or machinery.

■ Expenditure in excess of market value.

As noted above, with effect from 6 April 2020 (1 April 2020 for corporation tax purposes), the SBA for a chargeable period of one year is 3% of the qualifying expenditure. The allowance is given on a straight-line basis so that the qualifying expenditure is relieved in full over a 33 -year writing-down period. Previously, the rate was 2% of the qualifying expenditure and the writing-down period was 50 years. The change in rate applies to expenditure regardless of when it was incurred. The amount of the allowance is proportionately increased or reduced for chargeable periods of more than or less than one year.

For the purpose only of computing the SBA available for a chargeable period beginning before 6 April 2020 (1 April 2020 for corporation tax purposes) and ending on or after that date, the period is treated as if it were two separate chargeable periods, the first ending on 5April 2020 (31 March 2020 for corporation tax purposes) and the second ending at the end of the actual chargeable period.

Example 4.4

A sole trader has a 30 June year end. In the year ended 30 June 2019, qualifying SBA expenditure was incurred of £500,000. However, the building was not brought into qualifying use until 1 July 2019. The SBAs available are as follows:

Year ended 30 June 2019

No SBA as the building was not brought into qualifying use before the end of the period.

Year ended 30 June 2020

1 July 2019 to 5 April 2020	£500,000 × 2% × 9/127,500
6 April 2020 to 30 June 2020	£500,000 × 3% × 3/123,750
Total allowance	£11,250

Year ended 30 June 2021

SBA is £500,000 × 3% = £15,000

Assuming SBA continue to be available to the sole trader as the building is used for a qualifying activity, the SBA of £15,000 will continue to be available for each accounting period up to and including the year ended 30 June 2052. In the year ended 30 June 2053, any remaining tax written down value can be claimed.

4.6　The Main Pool

The majority of plant and machinery expenditure will fall into the main pool, which provides for relief at a rate of 18% per annum (see **Section 4.6.1**). The main pool comprises all items of plant and machinery, including cars with CO_2 emissions of 50g/km or less. The main pool does not include assets that should form part of the special rate pool (see **Section 4.7**), assets that are used for both business and personal use (see **Section 4.8**) and assets that have been elected as short-life assets (see **Section 4.9**).

When an individual buys assets that fall into the main pool, the additions will increase the size of the main pool. When assets are disposed of from the main pool, the value of the main pool is decreased.

4.6.1 Writing Down Allowance

The writing down allowance (WDA) is an annual allowance to reflect the wear and tear of plant and machinery (new or second-hand) in use for the purpose of a trade, profession or employment at the end of an accounting period. Unlike the AIA and the FYA, which are applied to the cost price of the equipment, WDAs are applied on a reducing balance basis. The WDA is calculated on the cost price of the plant and machinery **less any capital grants** received in the first period. The WDAs in subsequent periods are calculated based on the opening tax written down values (i.e. cost less previous WDA claimed) plus current period additions less current period disposals.

To qualify for WDA, an asset must be **owned** by the individual and in use "wholly and exclusively" for the purposes of the individual's trade, profession or employment.

Example 4.5
Regina, a sole trader in business for many years, prepares accounts to 5 April each year. During the year ended 5 April 2022 she bought the following assets:

		£
10/05/2021	Office equipment	1,000
01/04/2022	Printer	3,500

The tax written down value (TWDV) on the main pool at 6 April 2021 was £56,000.

Regina's capital allowances computation for the year ended 5 April 2022 is as follows:

	AIA/FYA Pool £	Main Pool £	Allowances Claimed £
TWDV b/fwd		56,000	
Additions		–	
Disposals		–	
Additions qualifying 100% AIA	4,500		
AIA	(4,500)		4,500
Remaining TWDV (transfer to main pool)	0	0	
		56,000	
Allowances @18%		(10,080)	10,080
TWDV c/fwd at 5 April 2022		45,920	
Total capital allowances claim			14,580

Businesses can claim a WDA of up to £1,000 in the case of either the main pool or the special rate pool (see **Section 4.7**) provided the unrelieved expenditure is £1,000 or less. If the maximum WDA is claimed, then the pool (main or special rate) will have a nil tax written down balance forward.

When plant is sold, the proceeds (limited to the original cost) are removed from the main pool. Where the trade is continuing, the pool balance remaining will continue to be written down on an annual basis by WDAs, even if there are no assets left.

Example 4.6

Rory, a sole trader in business for many years, prepares accounts to 5 April each year. During the year ended 5 April 2022 he did not buy any assets. However, he did dispose of a machine for £16,000 (it originally cost £15,000). The TWDV on the main pool at 6 April 2021 was £15,900.

Rory's capital allowances computation for the year ended 5 April 2022 is as follows:

	AIA/FYA Pool	Main Pool	Allowances Claimed
	£	£	£
TWDV b/fwd		15,900	
Additions		–	
Disposals (limited to cost)		(15,000)	
		900	
Allowances @ "small pool"		(900)	900
TWDV c/fwd at 5 April 2022		0	
Total capital allowances claim			900

For long or short periods of account, the WDA is pro-rated.

Example 4.7

A business had a tax written down value carried forward in its main pool of £12,000. The accounting period was for 10 months and there were no additions or disposals during this period.

The WDA claimed would be:

$$£12,000 \times 18\% \times 10/12 = £1,800$$

4.6.2 Balancing Allowances and Balancing Charges

Profits and losses on the disposal of non-current assets (such as property, plant and equipment) are **not included** in the tax-adjusted profits of a business. In order to adequately capture these profits and losses, the capital allowances system uses balancing charges and balancing allowances to reflect any profit or loss on the disposal (i.e. sale) of an asset.

A **balancing allowance** arises when the **sales proceeds of an asset are less than its tax written down value (a loss on disposal)**.

A **balancing charge** arises when the **sales proceeds of an asset are greater than its tax written down value (a profit on disposal)**. However, if the sales proceeds exceed the original cost, the sales proceeds in the capital allowances computation are restricted to the original cost.

Note that the tax-adjusted profit/(loss) will not be the same as the profit/(loss) on disposal in the accounts. This is due to the differing rates and rules between depreciation and capital allowances.

In essence, the aim is to ensure that the allowances potentially available to the taxpayer equate to the cost to them of the equipment.

Balancing allowances and charges can arise when one of the following occurs:

- the trade or profession ceases;
- the assets are no longer "in use" for the trade;
- an asset, on which capital allowances were previously claimed, is sold/scrapped; or
- an asset permanently ceases to be used for the purposes of the trade, profession or employment.

Where the sale proceeds are **not** at 'arm's length' (as they would be in a sale between unrelated parties) or where there are no sale proceeds (e.g. due to a takeover or to the gifting of a business asset for personal use), the market value is used to calculate the balancing allowance/charge.

Generally, on the disposal of an asset from the main pool or special rate pool, no balancing allowances or charges arise, except on the cessation of a trade. For this reason there is an option to treat certain assets as "short-life" assets. Short-life assets are kept in a separate asset pool, which means that relief will be obtained for any balancing allowances that may arise on the disposal of the asset (see **Example 4.9**).

Limitation of Balancing Charges

The balancing charge **cannot exceed** the aggregate of the capital allowances **already claimed** on the asset.

4.7   Special Rate Pool

The special rate pool contains capital expenditure on:

- thermal insulation;
- long-life assets (see **Section 4.7.1**);
- integral features of a building (see **Section 4.7.2**); and
- cars with CO_2 emissions greater than 110g/km (130g/km prior to 6 April 2018).

The WDA applied to the special rate pool is 6%.

The AIA can apply to all assets in the special rate pool except for cars. An individual can decide how to allocate the AIA in the most tax-efficient manner. For example, where there is **expenditure on assets in both pools in the period**, it will be **more tax-efficient to set the allowance against special rate pool expenditure (where the WDA is 6%) rather than to main pool expenditure (18% WDA rate)**. Expenditure in excess of the AIA is added to the special rate pool and will be eligible for WDA in the same period in which the expenditure is incurred.

Like the main pool, the 6% rate is per annum; therefore, a pro rata adjustment is required for long or short periods of account (see **Example 4.8**).

4.7.1   Long-life Assets

Long-life assets are assets with an expected working life of 25 years or more. In order for expenditure to fall within the long-life asset rules (and so be categorised as a special rate pool asset), total expenditure on assets with an expected working life of 25 years or more in a basis period must be more than £100,000.

If an individual spends less than £100,000 on long-life assets in a basis period, the long-life assets rules do not apply and the asset may fall into the main pool; if they spend more than £100,000 on long-life assets in a basis period, the long-life asset rules apply and all the expenditure falls into the special rate pool.

For shorter basis periods, the £100,000 should be reduced proportionately.

4.7.2   Integral Fixtures and Fittings

"Integral features" are certain features that are seen as essential to a building and which, in HMRC's view, have a longer average economic life than other plant and machinery and should therefore be written down using a lower capital allowance rate.

Expenditure on integral features therefore attracts a WDA rate of 6%. Integral features include:

- electrical systems (including lighting systems);
- hot and cold water systems;
- space-heating systems, powered systems of ventilation, air cooling or air purification, and any floor or ceiling comprised in such systems;
- lifts, escalators and moving walkways; and
- external solar shading.

Example 4.8

Danielle runs a bakery/café in the centre of Belfast. She makes up her accounts to 31 December each year. The TWDV of her main pool as at 1 January 2021 was £100,000. In the tax year 2021/22, Danielle had the following costs:

Date	Cost	General description
14 April 2021	£400,000	General plant and machinery, e.g. new shelving, new cooler machine, new refrigerators, etc.
19 August 2021	£50,000	New lighting system for the inside and outside of the shop/café
30 September 2021	£55,000	Lift installed
5 October 2021	£22,000	New car (CO_2 145 g/km) – 100% business use
5 November 2021	£12,000	New delivery van and signage

What is the maximum capital allowances claim that Danielle can make for the tax year 2021/22?

Y/e 31 December 2022	AIA	Main Pool	Special Rate Pool	Claim
	£	£	£	£
TWDV b/fwd		100,000		
Additions qualifying for AIA only:				
Lighting, lift, P&M, van	517,000			
AIA	(517,000)			517,000
T/f to main rate pool	0	0		
Additions not qualifying for AIA:				
Plant and machinery + van				
Car (>50g/km)			22,000	
Additions qualifying for WDA		100,000	22,000	
WDA @ 18%		(18,000)		18,000
WDA @ 6%			(1,320)	1,320
TWDV c/fwd		82,000	20,680	
Total capital allowance claim for period				536,320

Note: the AIA would first be set against the integral features (the lift and lighting system), leaving the remainder to be offset against the main pool additions. The maximum AIA for the period is £1,000,000.

Acquisition of Property that Includes Fixtures

Special rules apply where a business acquires a property that includes existing fixtures: part of the purchase price of the property will relate to the fixtures, and the purchaser may be able to make a capital allowances claim on these fixtures.

Since 6 April 2014, the purchaser can only claim capital allowances on fixtures where the seller has previously claimed either the FYA or the AIA on those fixtures, or where the cost of the fixtures has been allocated to a capital allowance pool. Basically, unless a capital allowance claim has been made by the seller, the new purchaser cannot make a claim.

4.8 Single Assets Pool: Private Use Assets

An asset that has mixed use and is used privately by a trader is dealt with in a **single asset pool** and the capital allowances are restricted. The allowance is calculated as normal and is then reduced by the private element. Only the business use proportion of the WDAs is allowed as a deduction from trading profits; however, the **full annual allowance is deducted** when arriving at the tax written down value at the end of each period. This restriction applies to the AIAs, FYAs, WDAs, balancing allowances and balancing charges.

An asset with some private use by an employee suffers no such private use restriction. The employee may be taxed on the benefit in kind (see **Chapter 5**) instead, so the business receives capital allowances on the full cost of the asset.

When an asset in a single asset pool is sold, a balancing allowance/charge arises, depending on the proceeds received. This differs from the disposal of an asset from the main rate or special rate pool where the tax written down value of the pool is reduced by the lower of the cost or the sale proceeds (thereby reducing the WDA available to claim in the future). (See **Examples 4.10** and **4.11**.)

4.8.1 Motor Cars: Recap

Cars are categorised in accordance with their CO_2 emissions:

1. CO_2 emissions over 50g/km – expenditure is added to the special rate pool (WDA at 6%).
2. CO_2 emissions of 50g/km or lower (but not zero) – expenditure is added to the main pool (WDA at 18%).
3. Electric or zero-emission cars – if the car is new, expenditure is eligible for 100% FYA.

Cars that have an element of private use by the taxpayer must be kept in **single asset pools**. The WDA on the special rate pool will be 18% if CO_2 emissions range from 50g/km or less (but not zero); and 6% if CO_2 emissions are over 50g/km.

Note, in the legislation, lorries, vans and trucks are not defined as cars. Cars do not qualify for AIA.

Example 4.9

Kieran started to trade Kieran's Kitchens on 1 October 2021, making up accounts to 31 March 2022 and each 31 March thereafter. On 1 November 2021 he bought a car for £19,000 with CO_2 emissions of 45g/km. The private-use proportion is 20%. The car was sold in October 2023 for £6,000.

Calculate the capital allowances, assuming:

1. the car was used by an employee; or

2. the car was used by Kieran.

Assumption 1

	Main Pool (18%)	Allowances
	£	£
Six months to 31 March 2022		
Purchase price	19,000	
WDA 18% × 6/12 × £19,000	(1,710)	1,710
	17,290	
Y/e 31 March 2023		
WDA 18% × £17,290	(3,112)	3,112
	14,178	
Y/e 31 March 2024		
WDA 18% × £14,178	(2,552)	2,552
	11,626	
Y/e 31 March 2025		
Proceeds	(6,000)	
Balancing allowance	**5,626**	5,626

The private use of the car by the employee has no effect on the capital allowances due to Kieran's Kitchens (see **Section 5.4.3** for details of the benefit in kind calculation for the employee's private use, which will be subject to income tax). The car would be included in the main pool and WDAs at 18% apply. The first accounting period was only six months in length; therefore, the WDA was reduced proportionately.

Assumption 2

	Single Asset Pool (WDA 18%)	Private Use (20%)	Allowances
	£	£	£
Six months to 31 March 2022			
Purchase price	19,000		
WDA 18% × 6/12 × £19,000	(1,710)	342	1,368
	17,290		
Y/e 31 March 2023			
WDA 18% × £17,290	(3,112)	622	2,490
	14,178		
Y/e 31 March 2024			
WDA 18% × £14,178	(2,552)	510	2,042
	11,626		
Y/e 31 March 2025			
Proceeds	(6,000)		
Balancing allowance	**5,626**	1,125	4,501

The private use is by the proprietor of Kieran's Kitchens, therefore only 80% of the WDAs and balancing allowance are available.

Example 4.10

Joe, who is self-employed and prepares annual accounts to 5 April, purchased a new car on 1 June 2021, which cost £20,000, with CO_2 emissions of 50g/km. His annual mileage is 20,000 miles, of which 5,000 are private.

Joe's sales director, Sarah, also has a business car, purchased on 30 September 2020 for £15,000, with CO_2 emissions of 50g/km. Sarah's mileage is 35,000 miles, of which 28,000 miles are business-related. Joe previously had a BMW, which he purchased for £20,000. The TWDV at 5 April 2021 was £11,000. Joe sold this car for £9,500 during the tax year 2020/21. Joe used this car 50% for business purposes. The TWDV of the main pool on 5 April 2021 was £10,000.

WDA	Pool	Joe's Car 1 (50% private use)	Joe's Car 2 (25% private use) (WDA 18%)	Private Use	Allowance
	£	£	£	£	£
TWDV @ 06/04/21	10,000	11,000			
Additions	15,000		20,000		
	25,000	11,000	20,000		
Disposal proceeds		(9,500)			
Balancing allowance		1,500		(750)	750
WDA @ 18%	(4,500)		(3,600)	900	7,200
TWDV @ 05/04/2022	20,500	nil	16,400		
Total capital allowance claim					7,950

Joe sold his previous car, which was included in a single asset pool. A balancing allowance arises of £1,500. However, as only 50% of use of the car was business use, its balancing allowance is restricted to 50%.

Joe's new car is included in a single asset pool under new rules because there is private use (25%). The WDAs are restricted by 25% private use. Sarah's car is included within the main pool as the CO_2 is 50g/km or less, and there is no private use element as Sarah is an employee. WDA at 18% applies. No AIA can be used as the additions relate to cars.

4.9 Short-life Assets

Where an asset is acquired and is likely to be disposed of within eight years from the end of the accounting period in which it was bought, it is considered a "short-life" asset. Provided an election is made to treat the asset in a single asset pool instead of the main pool, a balancing charge or allowance arises on its disposal.

If the asset is not disposed of within this time period, its tax written down value is added to the main pool at the end of that time.

The AIA and the FYA can be claimed for short-life assets. It will be more tax-efficient to set the AIA or FYA allowances against main pool expenditure in priority to short-life asset expenditure. The reason for this is that tax relief is more likely to be received quicker for assets elected to be short-life assets than for assets in the main pool where the writing down allowance is at a rate of 18% on a reducing balance method.

Short-life asset treatment cannot be claimed for motor cars or plant used partly for non-business purposes.

4.10   Disclaim of Capital Allowances

Where the capital allowances claim for a particular year of assessment exceeds the assessable profits from the trade or profession, it will give rise to a trade loss. In this situation an individual does not have to claim the full capital allowances to which they are entitled and can make a partial claim instead. This would reduce any trade loss and result in a higher tax written down value brought forward (increasing the WDA in future years).

A trader should therefore consider whether it is beneficial to claim capital allowances in the period and, if so, whether a full or partial claim should be made. Issues to consider include whether the individual has sufficient income in the period to utilise the trade loss without wasting their personal allowance (which is £12,570 for the 2021/22 tax year, see **Chapter 2**).

4.11   Treatment of Purchases, Capital Grants, Hire Purchase, Finance Leases, Lessors and VAT

4.11.1 Date of Purchase of Assets

For capital allowances purposes, expenditure is generally deemed to be incurred when the obligation to pay becomes unconditional (provided this is within four months). This will usually be the date of the contract, e.g. where payment is due a month after delivery, then the date of delivery is relevant.

However, if the amount is due more than four months after the obligation to pay becomes unconditional for capital allowance purposes, then the expenditure is instead deemed to be incurred when paid.

Assets acquired under a hire-purchase contract are deemed to be incurred at the time they are brought into use, i.e. the four-month rule does not apply.

4.11.2 Capital Grants

The qualifying cost for capital allowance purposes is the **net cost**, i.e. total cost minus grant receivable. Capital grants are increasingly rare in today's economic environment.

4.11.3 Hire Purchase

Capital allowances are available on assets acquired under hire-purchase (HP) agreements. The key features of capital allowances under HP agreements are:

- The appropriate allowance can be claimed in the period for which the asset is put into use.
- The qualifying cost for the purposes of computing the writing down allowance is limited to the cost of the asset, **exclusive** of hire-purchase charges, i.e. interest.
- The timing of the actual hire-purchase instalments is not relevant, provided the agreement is **executed** during the period.
- The individual will be able to claim the interest charges as a tax-deductible trading expense over the term of the contract.

4.11.4 Finance-leased Assets

Where an individual leases an asset on a finance lease, no capital allowances can be claimed on the capital expenditure. See **Chapter 3, Section 3.3.5** under **Finance Leases** for further information on how tax relief can be obtained.

4.11.5 Qualifying Cost and VAT

The qualifying cost of plant and equipment for capital allowance purposes is the **actual expenditure incurred** on the plant or equipment. This will be the cost of the plant or equipment **exclusive** of VAT, where the VAT paid on acquisition is recoverable by the individual because they are VAT registered. If, however, a business that is not registered for VAT acquires plant or equipment outright, then the VAT element of the purchase price represents a cost and the **total cost, including VAT**, could be claimed as a capital allowance.

4.12 Loss Relief

This section will discuss the tax implications of a tax-adjusted trading loss being incurred by an individual and how such a loss-suffering individual can use their trading loss to reduce their tax liability.

4.12.1 Introduction: Income Tax Loss Relief

As stated previously, businesses prepare accounts based on commercial and accounting principles to arrive at their net profit/(loss). This net profit/(loss) per the statement of profit or loss will then be adjusted in accordance with the tax legislation to arrive at the tax-adjusted profit/(loss) (see **Chapter 3**). It should be noted that a trading loss is computed in exactly the same way as a profit. When a tax-adjusted trading loss (hereafter referred to as a trading loss) is calculated for a business, which is traded by an individual alone or in a partnership, income tax relief may be available for trading losses in the following ways:

1. by offsetting the losses against other (general) income in the same year and/or the previous tax year. For losses incurred in the 2020/21 and 2021/22 tax years, a temporary extension to the carry back of trading losses from one year to three years was introduced for losses up to £2,000,000 per 12-month period;
2. by carrying forward the losses against subsequent (future) profits of the **same** trade;
3. where the losses occur in the early years of a trade, by carrying them back against other income from previous years;
4. by offsetting the losses against capital gains (which may arise on the sale of a property, for example) of the same or preceding tax year; or
5. by carry back in a "terminal loss" situation, i.e. where a trade ceases.

4.12.2 Effect of Capital Allowances

Capital allowances for a year of assessment may be used to create or augment (i.e. increase) a trading loss, provided that such allowances are **first** offset against any **balancing charges** arising in the tax year to which they relate and which are not covered by capital allowances brought forward.

This is a useful planning tool that individuals may utilise to try to preserve their personal allowance, for example. In addition, where the effective rate of tax for the individual is likely to be higher in future years, then it may be advisable from a tax point of view to defer claiming capital allowances to future years (i.e. by not claiming in the current tax year so that the balance carried forward to next year's capital allowances computation is higher).

4.12.3 Trade Loss Relief against General Income

Offsetting trade losses against other general income is provided for by section 64 of the Income Tax Act 2007 (ITA 2007), hence it is sometimes referred to as "section 64 relief". The trading loss is relieved by way of deduction from **any other income** chargeable to tax **in that tax year** or the prior tax year.

The loss is deducted from the **total income**, i.e. before deductions (personal allowances or other reliefs). The loss must be set-off first against non-savings income (i.e. trading income, employment income, property income and miscellaneous income), then from savings income and finally from dividend income.

One of the conditions of section 64 relief is that the business is conducted on a commercial basis with a view to the realisation of profits.

In addition, partial claims are not permitted under section 64. The relief must be for either the **full amount** of the loss available, or the total income, whichever is less. This means that by claiming the relief there could be a loss of personal allowances.

Example 4.11

Sandra is a self-employed beautician. She also works part time at a local spa and earns a gross salary of £15,000 annually. Sandra has incurred a lot of expenditure in her beautician business during the year ended 31 March 2022. As a result, she incurred a tax-adjusted trading loss of £28,000. Sandra had £5,000 of tax-adjusted trading profits for the year ended 31 March 2021.

In the 2021/22 tax year, Sandra's trade was loss-making. If Sandra claims to offset this trading loss in 2020/21 against her general income in 2021/22 and 2020/21, her position will be as follows:

	2020/21	2021/22
	£	£
Trading income	5,000	0
Employment income	15,000	15,000
Total income	20,000	15,000
Less: loss relief against general income	(13,000)	(15,000)
Net income	7,000	0
Less: personal allowance	(12,500)	(12,570)
Taxable income	0	0

As you can see, in the 2021/22 tax year, if Sandra claims to offset her trading loss against her employment income she will be fully wasting her personal allowance of £12,570. Similarly, if she carries the remaining trading losses back to 2020/21 for offset against general income, she will waste £5,500 of her 2020/21 personal allowance.

Sandra's options in respect of the 2021/22 trading loss are:

1. Set it against general income in 2021/22 only and carry forward the balance against same trade profits in future years (see **Section 4.12.4**).
2. Set it against general income in 2020/21 only and carry forward the balance against same trade profits in future years.
3. Set it against general income in 2021/22 and 2020/21 (as shown above).
4. Carry forward the loss against same trade profits in future years.

Where a trading loss is unrelieved, it will be carried forward to set against the first available profits of the same trade.

4.12.4 Extended Loss Carry Back for Losses Incurred in 2020/21 and 2021/22 – Temporary Measure

Finance Act 2021 introduced an extension to the existing trade loss relief against general income in section 64 of ITA 2007 (see **Section 4.12.3**). The temporary extended relief will apply **where a claim has been made under section 64** to set a trade loss for 2020/21 or 2021/22 against general income of the current year, the previous year, or both, **and relief for the loss cannot be fully given under that claim**. The extended relief applies to trades, professions and vocations.

If a claim under the temporary extended relief is not possible because there are no trading profits in earlier years against which to set a loss, any unrelieved loss will be carried forward and set against trading profits in future tax years.

Trading Losses Incurred in 2020/21

Where a section 64 claim has been made for set-off of a trade loss for 2020/21 against general income of 2020/21 only, a claim may also be made under the new provision to carry back unrelieved losses **against profits from the same trade** for 2019/20, 2018/19 and 2017/18.

Where a section 64 claim has been made for set-off of a trade loss for 2020/21 against general income of the previous year 2019/20 only, or for both 2020/21 and 2019/20, a claim may also be made under the new provision to carry back unrelieved losses against profits from the same trade in 2018/19 and 2017/18.

If relief for a loss for 2020/21 would be available under section 64 but a claim has not been made because the trader has no income to claim against for either 2020/21 or 2019/20, a claim may still be made under the new provision to carry back unrelieved losses against profits from the same trade in 2018/19 and 2017/18.

Losses carried back against profits of the trade in 2019/20, 2018/19 and 2017/18 (or only 2018/19 and 2017/18) will be set-off against the profits of the most recent year before earlier years.

Carry back of losses from 2020/21 to the previous year 2019/20 is uncapped against profits of the trade. Losses for 2020/21 carried back to set against profits of the trade in 2018/19 and 2017/18 are subject to a £2,000,000 cap.

The time limit for making a claim to the extended relief for a trade loss in tax year 2020/21 will be 31 January 2023.

Example 4.12

Sam runs a sole trade business. In 2020/21 he incurred a trading loss of £3,000,000 and he had property income of £50,000. His income for the previous three tax years is outlined below:

Tax year	Trading profit	Property income
2019/20	£500,000	£50,000
2018/19	£1,200,000	£50,000
2017/18	£1,200,000	£50,000

Sam claims under section 64 to set the 2020/21 loss against general income of both the 2020/21 tax year of loss (£50,000) and the previous tax year 2019/2020 (£550,000).

The remaining 2020/21 trading loss after the section 64 claims is £2,400,000 (£3,000,000 – £50,000 – £550,000). However, only up to a maximum of £2,000,000, is available to carry back to set against trading profits of 2018/2019 and 2017/2018 (in that order).

In respect of 2018/19, £1,200,000 trade profit will be offset by the 2020/21 trading loss.

In respect of 2017/18, a maximum of £800,000 of trading losses from 2020/21 can be offset against the trading profit of £1,200,000 for that year.

£400,000 of the 2020/21 loss remains available to be claimed to carry forward and set against trade profits in future years.

Trading Losses Incurred in 2021/22

Where a section 64 claim has been made for set-off of a trade loss for 2021/22 against general income of 2021/22 only, a claim may also be made under the new provision to carry back unrelieved losses against profits from the same trade for 2020/21, 2019/18 and 2018/19.

Where a section 64 claim has been made for set-off of a trade loss for 2021/22 against general income of the previous year 2020/21 only, or for both 2021/22 and 2020/21, a claim may also be made under the new provision to carry back unrelieved losses against profits from the same trade in 2019/20 and 2018/19.

If relief for a loss for 2021/22 would be available under section 64 but a claim has not been made because the trader has no income to claim against for either 2021/22 or 2020/21, a claim may still be made under the new provision to carry back unrelieved losses against profits from the same trade in 2019/20 and 2018/19.

Losses carried back against profits of the trade in 2020/21, 2019/20 and 2018/19 (or only 2019/20 and 2018/19) will be set-off against the profits of the most recent year before earlier years.

Carry back of losses from 2021/22 to the previous year 2020/21 is uncapped against profits of the trade. Losses for 2021/22 carried back to set against profits of the trade in 2019/20 and 2018/19 are subject to a £2,000,000 cap.

The time limit for making a claim to the extended relief for a trade loss in tax year 2021/22 will be 31 January 2024.

4.12.5 Carry Forward of Trading Losses

Any trading losses not relieved under section 64 can be carried forward and offset against profits (after deduction of capital allowances) of the same trade or profession in subsequent years (section 83 ITA 2007).

The loss must be set-off against the **first** subsequent year's trading profits, then against the second year's profits, and so on. Losses may be carried forward indefinitely, provided the trade that incurred the loss continues to be carried on.

Example 4.13

Alex has been trading as an accountant for a number of years and has his own accountancy practice, which is his only source of income. His tax-adjusted trading profits/(losses) for the last few years are:

Year to 31 July 2019	(£12,000)
Year to 31 July 2020	£9,000
Year to 31 July 2021	£15,000

In respect of the tax-adjusted loss of £12,000 incurred in the 2019/20 tax year, Alex claims carry-forward loss relief:

	2019/20	2020/21	2021/22
	£	£	£
Trading income	0	9,000	15,000
Less: carry-forward loss relief	0	(9,000)	(3,000)
Trading income after relief	0	0	12,000

4.12.6 Early Trade Loss Relief

Section 72 ITA 2007 provides for relief of trading losses that arise in the first four years of a trade. These losses may be offset against general income for the three tax years preceding the year of loss, taking the earliest year first. Thus a loss arising in 2021/22 may be offset against income from 2018/19, 2019/20 and 2020/21, in that order.

A single claim is required and the loss must be offset to the maximum extent possible against the income of all three years. In other words, an individual cannot choose a specific amount to relieve. However, the loss could be reduced by claiming less capital allowances for that tax year, which would also mean that higher capital allowances could be claimed in future years.

When considering early trade loss relief, care should be taken to ensure no double counting of loss relief where basis periods overlap. For loss relief purposes, a loss in the overlap period is treated as a loss in the earlier tax year (see **Example 4.14**).

Relief is not available unless the trade is operated on a commercial basis, in such a way that a profit could be expected within a "reasonable timeframe". In practice, this may be difficult to prove in the case of a new business and a viable business plan may be necessary to support a carry-back claim.

Example 4.14

John, a trader, started in business on 1 July 2019 and makes up annual accounts to 30 June. In the first and second years of trading, he incurred losses of £16,000 and £20,000 respectively. In the 2019/20, 2020/21 and 2021/22 tax years, John had taxable rental profits of £60,000.

What losses are available to John to carry back under section 72 ITA 2007?

As the losses available for offset under section 72 are less £50,000, the maximum amount of losses are available.

Tax year 2019/20
Loss: 01/07/2019–05/04/2020 = £16,000 × 9/12 = £12,000
This loss can be carried back and set against total income for the tax years 2016/17, then 2017/18 and then 2018/19.

Tax year 2020/21
Loss: year ended 30/06/2020 = £16,000 less amount assessed re. 2019/20 of £12,000 = £4,000
This loss can be carried back and set against total income for the tax years 2017/18, then 2018/19 and then 2019/20.

Tax year 2021/22
Loss: year ended 30/06/21 = £20,000
This loss can be carried back and set against total income for the tax years 2018/19, then 2019/20 and then 2020/21.

4.12.7 Offsetting Trade Losses against Capital Gains

Where an individual makes a claim for trading losses against general income in a tax year and some trading losses remain unrelieved, an individual can then make a further claim to have the unrelieved trading losses set against any capital gains in the year. (See **Part Three** for CGT.)

4.12.8 Terminal Loss Relief

Where a trade ceases, terminal loss relief can be claimed in respect of a loss incurred in the **final 12 months** of trading. This loss can be offset against trading profits in the tax year of cessation and **carried back** against profits for the previous **three tax years** (later years first).

The losses must be carried back against taxable trading profits of the same trade. The terminal loss for the final 12 months of trading must be calculated. It comprises:

1. The trading loss incurred from 6 April (at the beginning of the tax year of cessation) to the date of cessation (including any unrelieved overlap profits).
2. The trading loss for the 12 months prior to the date of cessation until the end of the penultimate tax year.

1. and 2. added together will give you the total terminal trading loss. However, it is important to note that if either 1. or 2. is a profit, then it is treated as zero for the purposes of adding 1. and 2. together to the total terminal trading loss.

Example 4.15

Andy has been trading as an architect for many years but he decides to cease trading on 31 May 2021 due to ill health. He has overlap profits from his years of commencement of £10,000. Until recently Andy had always made a profit. His tax-adjusted profits/(losses) for recent years are:

	£
Year to 30 June 2018	40,000
Year to 30 June 2019	16,000
Year to 30 June 2020	(7,000)
11 months to 31 May 2021	(33,000)

Andy has other non-savings income of £15,000 per year.

Andy ceases to trade in the 2020/21 tax year. His terminal loss for the last 12 months is:

Trading loss incurred from 6 April (beginning of the tax year of cessation) to the date of cessation (including any unrelieved overlap profits)	£33,000 × 2/11 + £10,000	£16,000
Trading loss for the 12 months prior to the date of cessation until the end of the penultimate tax year, i.e. 1 June 2020 to 5 April 2021	£7,000 × 1/12 + £33,000 × 9/11	£27,583
Terminal loss		£43,583

Andy can relieve this terminal loss as follows:

	2018/19	2019/20	2020/21	2021/22
	£	£	£	£
Adjusted profit	40,000	16,000	nil	nil
Less: terminal loss relief	(27,583)	(16,000)		
Total income	12,417	–	–	–
Other non-savings income	15,000	15,000	15,000	15,000
Total income	27,417	15,000	15,000	15,000

Special Relief where Trade is Ceasing because of Incorporation

If a business is transferred to a company, any unrelieved loss of the sole trader/partnership can be carried forward and set-off against the first available income received from the company by way of salary, dividends, interest, etc. The sequence is to offset the loss against non-savings income, savings income and then dividend income. The consideration for the transfer of the business must be wholly or mainly in the form of shares (at least 80%), which must be retained by the seller throughout any tax year in which the loss is relieved.

> **Practical tip:** an individual should choose whichever loss relief saves tax at the highest tax rate – but they need to be careful and consider the potential loss of other reliefs, such as personal allowances, etc.

Appendix 4.1: Capital Allowances – Lists A, B and C

Note: the versions of Lists A, B and C below have been modified for inclusion in this textbook.

List A (as per section 21 Capital Allowances Act 2001)

Buildings
Expenditure on the provision of plant or machinery does not include expenditure on the provision of a building. The provision of a building includes its construction or acquisition.
Assets treated as buildings:

1. Walls, floors, ceilings, doors, gates, shutters, windows and stairs.
2. Mains services, and systems, for water, electricity and gas.
3. Waste disposal systems.
4. Sewerage and drainage systems.
5. Shafts or other structures in which lifts, hoists, escalators and moving walkways are installed.
6. Fire safety systems.

The above is subject to List C below.

List B (as per section 22 Capital Allowances Act 2001)

Structures, assets and works
Expenditure on the provision of plant or machinery does not include expenditure on the provision of a structure or other asset in list B, or any works involving the alteration of land.
Excluded structures and other assets

1. A tunnel, bridge, viaduct, aqueduct, embankment or cutting.
2. A way, hard standing (such as a pavement), road, railway, tramway, a park for vehicles or containers, or an airstrip or runway.
3. An inland navigation, including a canal or basin or a navigable river.
4. A dam, reservoir or barrage, including any sluices, gates, generators and other equipment associated with the dam, reservoir or barrage.
5. A dock, harbour, wharf, pier, marina or jetty or any other structure in or at which vessels may be kept, or merchandise or passengers may be shipped or unshipped.
6. A dike, sea wall, weir or drainage ditch.

The above is subject to List C below.

List C (as per section 23 Capital Allowances Act 2001)

[Expenditure on any of the items on List C will be treated as expenditure on "plant" and will qualify for capital allowances. List C is a long list of specific items, most of which have been derived from case law.]
Expenditure unaffected by sections 21 and 22:

1. Machinery (including devices for providing motive power) not within any other item in this list.
2. Gas and sewerage systems provided mainly:
    (a) to meet the particular requirements of the qualifying activity, or
    (b) to serve particular plant or machinery used for the purposes of the qualifying activity.

3. [This item was withdrawn from List C as a result of Finance Act 2008.]
4. Manufacturing or processing equipment; storage equipment (including cold rooms); display equipment; and counters, checkouts and similar equipment.
5. Cookers, washing machines, dishwashers, refrigerators and similar equipment; washbasins, sinks, baths, showers, sanitary ware and similar equipment; and furniture and furnishings.
6. Hoists.
7. Sound insulation provided mainly to meet the particular requirements of the qualifying activity.
8. Computer, telecommunication and surveillance systems (including their wiring or other links).
9. Refrigeration or cooling equipment.
10. Fire alarm systems; sprinkler and other equipment for extinguishing or containing fires.
11. Burglar alarm systems.
12. Strong rooms in bank or building society premises; safes.
13. Partition walls, where moveable and intended to be moved in the course of the qualifying activity.
14. Decorative assets provided for the enjoyment of the public in hotel, restaurant or similar trades.
15. Advertising hoardings; signs, displays and similar assets.
16. Swimming pools (including diving boards, slides and structures on which such boards or slides are mounted).
17. Any glasshouse constructed so that the required environment (namely, air, heat, light, irrigation and temperature) for the growing of plants is provided automatically by means of devices forming an integral part of its structure.
18. Cold stores.
19. Caravans provided mainly for holiday lettings.
20. Buildings provided for testing aircraft engines run within the buildings.
21. Moveable buildings intended to be moved in the course of the qualifying activity.
22. The alteration of land for the purpose only of installing plant or machinery.
23. The provision of dry docks.
24. The provision of any jetty or similar structure provided mainly to carry plant or machinery.
25. The provision of pipelines or underground ducts or tunnels with a primary purpose of carrying utility conduits.
26. The provision of towers to support floodlights.
27. The provision of:
    (a) any reservoir incorporated into a water treatment works, or
    (b) any service reservoir of treated water for supply within any housing estate or other particular locality.
28. The provision of:
    (a) silos provided for temporary storage, or
    (b) storage tanks.
29. The provision of slurry pits or silage clamps.
30. The provision of fish tanks or fish ponds.
31. The provision of rails, sleepers and ballast for a railway or tramway.
32. The provision of structures and other assets for providing the setting for any ride at an amusement park or exhibition.
33. The provision of fixed zoo cages.

Questions

Review Questions
(See Suggested Solutions to Review Questions at the end of this textbook.)

Question 4.1

Barney Connor is a self-employed accountant who has been in business for many years and prepares accounts to 5 April each year. During the year ended 5 April 2022 he purchased the following assets:

		£	
29/12/2021	Computer	8,000	
30/12/2021	Car (CO_2 45g/km)	11,500	
08/03/2022	Desks	1,800	
20/03/2022	Filing cabinets	2,300	(not delivered until 15/04/2022 but paid for before 5 April 2022)
		23,720	

The tax written down value on the main pool at 6 April 2021 was £20,000.

Requirement
Prepare the capital allowances computation for the year ended 5 April 2022, and calculate the TWDV carried forward at 5 April 2022.

Question 4.2

Bobby Robson is a self-employed sports goods retailer who has been in business for many years and prepares accounts to 31 August each year. In the year ended 31 August 2021, he purchased the following assets:

		£
10/10/2020	Cash registers	7,000
31/12/2020	Air-conditioning unit	6,900
		13,900

The tax written down value on the main pool at 1 September 2020 was £100,000. In the same period he also purchased a car for use by an employee for £40,000 with CO_2 emissions of 165g/km, and a second car for use by another employee for £10,000 with CO_2 emissions of 45g/km.

Requirement
Prepare the capital allowances computation for the year ended 31 August 2021, and calculate the TWDV carried forward at 31 August 2021.

Question 4.3

Jim, a sole trader, has been in business for many years and prepares accounts to 31 August each year. The tax written down value on the main pool at 1 September 2020 was £120,000.

He bought a printing press, with an expected useful life of 50 years, on 30 September 2020 for £110,000. The following assets were also purchased in the period: a car for £20,000 (CO_2 emissions 45g/km) on 21 September 2020; a van for £15,000 (CO_2 emissions 135g/km) on 14 March 2021; and miscellaneous plant and machinery for £30,000 in May 2021.

Requirement

Prepare the capital allowances computation for the year ended 31 August 2021, and calculate the TWDV carried forward at 31 August 2021. The car is 100% for business purposes.

Question 4.4

Joan O'Reilly is a bookbinder who prepares accounts to 5 April each year. She made a profit on sale of some plant and machinery of £5,000 in the year to 5 April 2022. The net book value (NBV) of the assets sold was £10,000 (original cost £18,000). She also purchased machinery in June 2021 costing £10,000.

The tax written down value on the main pool at 6 April 2021 was £20,000.

Requirement

Prepare the capital allowances computation for the year ended 5 April 2022, and calculate the TWDV carried forward at 5 April 2022.

Question 4.5

Cormac Molloy, a self-employed farmer, has been in business for many years and prepares accounts to 31 December each year. His motor vehicle details are:

Motor car cost 01/06/2019	£26,000 (CO_2 emissions 155g/km)
Total estimated annual mileage	20,000 miles
Total estimated private mileage	5,000 miles (i.e. 3/4 of total mileage is business)

Requirement

Calculate the deductible capital allowances for the 2021/22 tax year and the TWDV carried forward at 31 December 2021. Assume no assets other than the motor car.

Question 4.6

Joseph Ryan is a shopkeeper who has been in business many years and prepares accounts to 5 April each year. On 10 November 2019 he bought a car for £13,000 with CO_2 emissions of 165g/km. The car qualifies for special rate pool allowances at a rate of 6% per annum on a reducing balance basis. The private use is one-third.

Requirement

Calculate the deductible capital allowances for the 2021/22 tax year and the TWDV carried forward at 6 April 2022. Assume no TWDV brought forward as of 6 April 2019.

Question 4.7

Louise Kenny is a clothes designer and commenced business as a sole trader on 1 January 2021. In the period ended 30 September 2021, she purchased the following assets:

	Cost £	Purchase date
Sewing machines	8,000	2 February 2021
Dummies	7,500	7 April 2021
Computer and laser printer	6,900	10 June 2021
Car (CO_2 emissions 47g/km)	11,000	10 June 2021

In the year ended 30 September 2022 she purchased the following assets:

	Cost £	Purchase date
Cutting table	2,000	18 August 2022
Cash register	1,500	21 September 2022

Requirement

What capital allowances will be deductible in calculating trading profits for the periods ended 30 September 2021 and 2022? Assume the same rates and allowances as for 2021/22 apply to the 2022/23 tax year.

Question 4.8

Joe is a butcher who prepares annual accounts to 5 April (he has traded for many years). He has a TWDV brought forward at 6 April 2021 on his main pool of £10,000. He sells plant in December 2021 with a net book value in his financial statements of £10,000 and realises a profit of £30,000. The plant had cost £35,000 originally. He did not purchase any assets in the year to 5 April 2022.

Requirement

Calculate the available capital allowances. What would the consequences be if Joe did not buy any plant in the year to 5 April 2023 but sold more plant for £3,000?

Question 4.9

Fitzroy runs a construction company in Northern Ireland. He has been in business for many years and prepares annual accounts to 31 December. During the year ended 31 December 2022 the following transactions took place:

1. Purchased an asset used in the business with a life of 28 years for £200,000.
2. Purchased a car for £11,000 (CO_2 emissions 50g/km).
3. Purchased a van for £14,000.
4. Purchased partition walls for his office for £5,000, toilets for £4,000, doors for £2,000 and a desk for £1,000. He also purchased a portacabin, which he used as an office when the head office was being refurbished, for £15,000. He purchased some portable toilets for £8,000 for use by employees on his various building sites in Northern Ireland.

Fitzroy has no other assets in respect of which capital allowances were claimed.

Requirement

Calculate the capital allowance available in the year to 31 December 2022.

Question 4.10

Joe Bloggs has operated a newsagent/tobacconist/confectionery shop for many years. He has previously dealt with his own income tax affairs and supplies the following details relating to his business for the year ended 31 March 2022:

	£	£
Gross profit	26,880	
Sale proceeds of old equipment	1,500	
Building society interest received	210	28,590
Wages to self	5,200	
Motor expenses	1,750	
Light and heat	1,200	
Wages to wife as bookkeeper and assistant	1,500	
Wages to other employees	7,600	
Advertising	270	
Christmas gifts to customers (bottles of whiskey)	300	
Depreciation:		
Motor car (CO_2 emissions 45g/km)	500	
Fixtures and equipment	400	
Rates	800	
Charitable donation	105	
Repairs to yard wall (June 2020)	200	
Painting of shop	450	
New cash register (purchased April 2020)	380	
Deposit on new shelving (paid July 2020)	1,000	
New display freezer (purchased August 2020)	600	
Insurance	375	
Insurance on contents of flat	100	
New shelving (purchased August 2020)	1,920	
Payment to self in lieu of rent	2,000	
Sundry expenses	2,250	(28,900)
Loss for year		(310)

Mr Bloggs owns the property, which consists of the shop and the flat above the shop where he and his wife live. He estimates that one-quarter of the heat and light costs relate to the living accommodation.

The motor car cost £8,960 on 1 January 2021. Mr Bloggs has advised you that business mileage accounts for three-quarters of his annual motoring.

TWDV brought forward in the main pool at 1 April 2021 is £12,750.

Requirement

Compute:

(a) Joe Bloggs's taxable trading income for 2021/22; and
(b) his capital allowance claim for 2021/22.

Question 4.11

Linda's income for 2021/22 is as follows:

	£
Trading loss y/e 30 September 2021	(50,000)
Salary for 2021/22 tax year	80,000

Requirement

Compute her assessable income for 2021/22.

Question 4.12

Mr Jones's income for 2021/22 is as follows:

	£
Trading profit (loss) y/e 30 June 2021	(30,000)
Salary	50,000
Interest on Government securities	25,000

Mr Jones has possessed the above sources of income for many years. He is single and was born in 1975.

Requirement

Compute his assessable income for 2021/22.

Question 4.13

Mr Fool, who has traded for many years, has the following profits and capital allowance:

	£
Profit y/e 31/12/2021	20,000
Capital allowance entitlement	(37,000)

He also had a balancing charge of £10,000 arising in the year.

Requirement

What is Mr Fool's taxable income (if any) for 2021/22?

Question 4.14

John has been in business for many years and prepares annual accounts to 30 September. He has the following sources of income:

	Tax Year		
	2019/20	**2020/21**	**2021/22**
	£	£	£
Rents	20,000	30,000	25,000
Interest (gross)	1,000	1,200	1,200
Trading profit/(loss)	30,000	(187,000)	45,000

Requirement

(a) What is John's net income in each period? (Assume he is claiming loss relief as soon as possible and that he had no taxable income in 2018/19 or 2019/20.)

(b) Prepare a loss memorandum.

Question 4.15

Jim's only source of income is his travel agency business, which he has carried on for many years. He prepares annual accounts to 30 June. Recent tax-adjusted results are as follows:

	£
Y/e 30/06/2019 tax-adjusted loss	(8,000)
Y/e 30/06/2020 tax-adjusted profit	7,000
Y/e 30/06/2021 tax-adjusted profit	30,000

Requirement

Calculate Jim's taxable income for all years.

Question 4.16

Basil Bond has the following income:

	Tax Year		
	2019/20	**2020/21**	**2021/22**
	£	£	£
Rents	20,000	30,000	25,000
Interest	1,000	1,200	1,200
Trading profit (loss) y/e 30/09 in tax year	80,000	(37,000)	45,000

Requirement

Calculate the assessable income for 2019/20 to 2021/22, claiming optimum relief for losses.

Employment Income

Learning Objectives

After studying this chapter you will be able to:

- Distinguish between employed and self-employed status.
- Explain the basis of assessment of employment income.
- Compute employment income to include taxation of round sum expense allowances, relief for employment related expenses and benefits in kind.

5.1 Introduction

In **Chapter 3** we saw how the taxable trading income of a self-employed individual is calculated. Important distinctions exist between the tax treatment of an individual who is an employee versus someone who is operating a business in a self-employed capacity. In this chapter we will look at the key differences and the guidance available to help decide whether an individual is an employee or not.

Employment earnings are generally understood in monetary terms, i.e. as salary or wages received on a weekly or monthly basis, but they can also include benefits or 'perks'. For income tax purposes, such non-monetary benefits must be converted to a cash equivalent. Any income tax computation must also take account of expenses incurred by an employee in the performance of their work and subsequently reimbursed by the employer – there are rules established to decide if such expenses are deductible from employment income. Each of these areas will be looked at in detail in this chapter.

However, first it is important to understand the meaning of general employment income (sometimes referred to as "general earnings").

General earnings are an individual's employment earnings plus the cash equivalent of any (taxable) non-monetary benefits. That is, "benefits in kind" or "perquisites" ('perks'). General earnings assessable for income tax include:

- salary/wages;
- directors' fees (i.e. income from office holders);
- bonuses and commission;
- non-monetary remuneration, i.e. benefits in kind and perquisites, such as:
  - use of a company vehicle;
  - provision of rent-free or subsidised accommodation to an employee;
  - holiday vouchers (say from a local travel agent to pay for employee's summer holiday);
  - preferential loans;

- round sum expense allowances, e.g. where an employer gives an employee £100 extra per month, in addition to their agreed salary, to cover personal expenditure that does not have to be employment related;
- payments on commencement of employment, e.g. inducement payments; and
- holiday pay.

Specific employment income includes payments on termination of employment and share-related income (which are beyond the scope of this textbook).

Throughout this chapter reference is made to "net taxable earnings" or "net earnings". The terms are interchangeable and are defined as employment income less any allowable expenses or deductions, e.g. statutory mileage allowances or contributions to registered occupational pension schemes.

The tax treatment of general earnings will be dealt with in greater detail as we work through the chapter, but first we need to understand the basis of assessment – what income is assessed, and when and how it is assessed.

5.2   Employment Status

The distinction between an **employee** and a **self-employed** person is not set out in tax legislation. Whether an individual is employed or self-employed is an important question for tax purposes as there are many differences in the way in which they are taxed.

Employees are taxed under the Pay As You Earn (PAYE) system with income tax and Class 1 national insurance contributions (NICs) being deducted from payments made to them. Class 1 NICs are also payable by their employers. By contrast, the self-employed pay income tax and Class 2 and 4 NICs directly to HMRC under self-assessment. (See **Chapter 9** in relation to the PAYE system generally, and **Section 9.5** for NICs.)

Some important consequences that arise from the above are:

1. the NIC liability of a self-employed individual is much lower than that of an employee (especially if the employer's liability is also taken into account);
2. the rules allowing tax relief for expenses are generally more relaxed for the self-employed – expenses incurred by the self-employed are allowable business expenses when they are incurred "wholly and exclusively" for the purposes of the trade, whereas employees can only obtain tax relief for expenses that are incurred "wholly, exclusively and necessarily" in the performance of their employment duties;
3. the self-employed have a cash-flow advantage in the timing of their payments compared with employees who are taxed at source (either weekly or monthly); and
4. if there has been an incorrect classification, the employer may find that he has additional income tax, NIC, penalties and interest to pay.

5.2.1   Contract of Service versus Contract for Service

As mentioned, there is no legislation to distinguish between employment and self-employment, but numerous cases decided in the courts provide guidance as to the indicating factors. Case law has determined that an employee is a person who has a **contract of service** with his employer; a self-employed person will provide services under a **contract for services**. A contract can be written, oral, implied or a combination of these.

Sometimes, the distinction between an employee and a self-employed person is not entirely clear, and accordingly the issue has been the subject of a number of cases. Initially, one should try to establish the terms and conditions of the engagement, which can normally be determined from the contract between the person and the client or employer. Next, any other relevant facts should be considered. No one single factor is decisive in itself; it is necessary to look at the circumstances as a whole. Where the evidence is evenly balanced, the intention of the parties may then decide the issue. HMRC provides an online tool, the Employment Status Indicator (ESI), to check the employment status of an individual or a group of workers (see www.gov.uk/guidance/employment-status-indicator). If used correctly, HMRC will now recognise the decision given by this online tool.

From case law, the main factors to be taken into account in determining whether a person is an employee or self-employed are:

1. **The terms of the contract** If, under the terms of the contract the individual providing the service is entitled to holiday pay, sick pay, pension entitlements, company car or other benefits, they are more likely to be an employee than self-employed. If the contract provides that the individual is required to work fixed hours on particular days, then they are more likely to be an employee, although this is not always the case.
2. **The degree of integration of the individual into the organisation to which their services are provided** The greater the degree of integration into the organisation, the more likely the person is to be regarded as an employee.
3. **Whether the individual can subcontract the work** If the individual is free to hire others to undertake the work, and under terms that they have set, this is more indicative of self-employed rather than employee status.
4. **Whether the individual provides his own equipment** If the individual provides their own equipment to carry out the work, this is also indicative of self-employed rather than employee status.
5. **The extent of control exercised over the individual** Generally, a self-employed person will have more control in terms of how, when and where the work is to be carried out than an employee would.
6. **The degree of responsibility for investment and management** A person who is responsible for running a business, who uses their own capital and who is responsible for determining the running and expansion of a business, is clearly a self-employed person.
7. **The degree of financial risk taken** Individuals who risk their own money (for example by buying assets, bearing their running costs, paying for overheads and large quantities of materials) are more likely to be self-employed. Financial risk could also take the form of quoting a fixed price for a job, with the consequent risk of bearing the additional costs of unforeseen circumstances. However, there must be a real risk of financial loss to be considered self-employed.
8. **Opportunity to profit from sound management** A person whose profit or loss depends on their capacity to reduce overheads and organise their work effectively is likely to be self-employed.

5.3 Basis of Assessment of Employment Income

5.3.1 General Employment Income

A **UK tax resident individual's general earnings**, excluding non-monetary remuneration (benefits in kind), are taxed in **the year of receipt, i.e. when the income is "received"**. Assessment is therefore on the "arising basis", i.e. in the tax year in which the income is earned; this is also sometimes referred to as the "receipts basis".

General earnings are treated as "received" on the earlier of:

- the date the payment is actually paid; or
- the date the employee becomes entitled to the payment.

For example, an individual is due to receive a cash bonus for their performance in 2021/22. If the bonus is paid on 20 May 2022 it will be treated as being received in 2022/23 for income tax purposes.

Directors' General Earnings

In the case of directors, general earnings are "received" on either the earlier of the dates as above, or on the earlier of:

- the date the director's remuneration is credited in the company's accounts; or
- the end of the accounting period during which the director's remuneration is determined; or
- the date the director's remuneration is determined, if that is after the end of the accounting period.

Benefits in Kind

Non-monetary remuneration, i.e. benefits in kind, is "received" in the **tax year in which it is provided to the employee**. However, as we will see shortly, a monetary value needs to be calculated. These rules will be considered later in this chapter.

Example 5.1

Sally is a director of Tully Ltd. In 2021/22 she receives a salary of £55,000. In addition, she is provided with a company car, the monetary value of this benefit in kind is £6,500. Due to her strong sales performance, the board of directors at a meeting on 1 April 2022 decide that Sally should receive a bonus of £12,000 for the year ended 31 January 2022. Sally's bonus was credited to the accounts of Tully Ltd on 2 April 2022, but she did not receive the bonus until 1 May 2022.

Sally's taxable employment income for 2021/22 is £73,500. Sally's bonus is determined by the board of directors on 1 April 2022 (i.e. in the 2021/22 tax year); hence it forms part of her taxable employment income for 2021/22.

The State Pension

An individual receiving the State pension is assessed on the total amount received (or accrued) in the tax year, irrespective of the date when the payment is received.

Having outlined the basic rules around what, when and how employment income is assessed for income tax purposes, we will now look at the computation of taxable employment income.

5.4   Computation of Taxable Employment Income

In simple terms, an individual's general earnings – the salary or wage they are paid, plus any bonus, commission or lump sum that they may have received – is subject to income tax on an arising/receipts basis, i.e. in the year it was received.

This general rule applies for most individuals in ordinary circumstances; however there are particular types of earnings or circumstances that require clarification on the terms of their treatment.

5.4.1   General Earnings: Tax Treatment of Lump Sum Payments

Lump sum payments fall under the "general earnings" category, and as such are taxed on the arising/receipts basis. There are a variety of lump sum payments, the terms of which need to be understood.

Restrictive Covenant Payment
A restrictive covenant is a lump sum payment made in return for an undertaking by an employee to restrict their conduct or activity in some way. For example, an employee may agree to not set up in competition for a certain length of time or to not behave in any manner that would be detrimental to the employer's (or former employer's) business. Such payments are fully taxable as general earnings.

Commencement or Inducement Payments
Payments made to an individual as an incentive to take up an employment, often known as 'golden hellos' or 'golden handcuffs', are generally treated as **advance pay** for future services of employment and are therefore taxable as general earnings.

A payment by one employer to induce an employee to take up employment with another employer is also taxable in full.

"Gardening Leave"
If a payment is made to an employee where notice has been given but not worked, the employee continues to be employed until the end of the notice period and the payment is taxable as general earnings.

5.4.2   General Earnings: Allowable Deductions from Employment Income

In order for an expense to be deductible from an employee's or director's employment income, it must be shown that it was incurred for "qualifying travel" or "wholly, exclusively and necessarily in performing the duties of the office or employment". The latter test is extremely difficult to satisfy in practice as:

1. the employee or director must be necessarily obliged to incur the expense;
2. the expense must be wholly, exclusively and necessarily incurred; and
3. the expense must be incurred in the actual performance of the duties.

It should be noted that all three criteria must be satisfied.

Qualifying Travel Expenses
Income tax relief is not available for an employee's normal commuting costs, i.e. those incurred in travelling between the workplace and home. However, employees are entitled to relief for travel

expenses, at full cost, incurred while travelling in the performance of their duties or to or from a place they have to attend in the performance of their duties (so long as their attendance at a particular workplace does not last, or is not expected to last, more than 24 months). Tax relief is available for travel accommodation and subsistence expenses incurred by an employee who is working at a temporary workplace on a secondment expected to last up to 24 months.

Other Allowable Deductions

Certain other expenditure is specifically deductible in computing net taxable earning:

- Contributions to registered occupational pension schemes.
- Subscriptions to professional bodies (HMRC-approved) if relevant to duties.
- Certain liability costs relating to the employment and insurance against them.
- Payroll giving, i.e. payments to charity through the payroll deductions scheme.
- Mileage allowance relief, i.e. where an employee uses his or her own car for business travel.

Mileage Allowance Relief

Where an employee uses their own private car for business purposes, the employer can pay approved mileage allowance payments (AMAPs) up to prescribed limits. The rates per mile that can be claimed are shown **Table 5.1**.

TABLE 5.1: MILEAGE ALLOWANCE RELIEF RATES

Vehicle	Flat rate per mile
Cars and goods vehicles: first 10,000 business miles	45p
Cars and goods vehicles: after 10,000 business miles	25p
Motorcycles	24p

Payments may be made tax-free by the employer and are not taxable in the hands of the employee. If the employer's policy is to pay less, the employee may claim tax relief up to that level. If employers pay in excess of these levels, the excess is a taxable benefit.

Round Sum Expense Allowance

In general, a round sum expense allowance advanced to an employee to be disbursed at their discretion is regarded as taxable general earnings. The employee can then make a claim for deduction against their general earnings in respect of actual expenses incurred in the performance of their duties, including capital allowances (for example, where an employee must buy a computer for the purpose of performing their employment duties, but the employer does not reimburse them for the cost of the computer.

Expenses not Reimbursed by Employer

If an employee incurs legitimate allowable expenses, i.e. those which were incurred wholly, exclusively and necessarily in the performance of their employment duties, for which they are not reimbursed by their employer, tax relief can still be available. Some examples of this may be fees and subscriptions to professional bodies, work-related books, allowable training and travel expenditure (see **Section 5.4.4** for further details).

5.4.3 General Earnings: Tax Treatment of Benefits in Kind

As noted previously, benefits in kind (BIK) are treated as received in the tax year in which they are provided.

General Rule

Some expense payments and benefits are treated as taxable remuneration. The main benefits that are taxable on all employees and directors include:

- non-exempt vouchers (e.g. gift vouchers, travel season tickets) – taxed on cost of providing;
- loans written off;
- living accommodation;
- costs charged to the employer's credit card for personal (i.e. non-business) expenditure;
- assets transferred by employer at below market value;
- gifts;
- payments made on the employee's behalf;
- payments made in respect of expenses payments other than those wholly for business purposes;
- cars/vans made available by the employer for private use;
- car fuel supplied for private motoring;
- private medical insurance;
- interest-free or low-interest loans;
- goods or services provided at less than their full cost;
- use of the employer's assets; and
- taxable excess mileage allowance.

Benefits provided to an individual (including his or her family or household members) are taxed on the cash equivalent of the benefit.

The cash equivalent is generally the cost to the employer of providing the benefit, less any amounts made good by the employee. Note, however, that there are special rules for valuing certain benefits, such as company cars, fuel for private use in company cars, living accommodation, etc.

If benefits are provided in-house, the value for tax purposes is generally the additional marginal cost to the employer.

Non-taxable payments and benefits include:

- Free car-parking facilities at or near the place of work.
- Mobile telephones (restricted to business mobile and only one per employee) and can include smartphones.
- Free canteen meals (provided they are open to all staff).
- Childcare facilities (if provided by employer). Specific details regarding the tax relief available under the Childcare Vouchers scheme and the Tax-Free Childcare scheme are given in **Section 5.4.4**.
- Sporting facilities provided in-house (must be offered to all employees).
- Bicycles or cycle safety equipment for travel to/from work (available to all employees).
- Gifts of goods from third parties not costing more than £250 (including VAT) per year from any one donor.
- Qualifying relocation/removal expenses and benefits up to £8,000 per annum.

- Job-related accommodation – living accommodation provided in the performance of employee's duties or due to a threat to the employee's security.
- Christmas and other parties, dinners, etc., provided the total cost to the employer for each person attending is not more than £150 per year, including VAT.
- Contributions by employer to an approved occupational scheme or to an employee's personal pension scheme.
- Non-cash long-service and suggestion scheme awards (conditions apply).
- Retraining expenses and courses to help an employee to find another post.
- Emergency vehicles for employees required to take vehicles home in order to respond quickly to emergencies when on-call.
- Vans provided by the employer for business travel, provided any private use is insignificant.
- Personal incidental expenses of employee while working away from home of up to £5 per night if in the UK (£10 per night if abroad).
- Certain other benefits (e.g. office supplies) provided for the employee's work, where private use is insignificant.
- Awards under staff suggestion schemes.
- A health screening assessment or medical check provided by an employer.
- Cheap loans that do not exceed £10,000 **at any time in** the tax year.
- Employer contributions towards additional household costs incurred by an employee who works partly at home. Payments up to £6 a week (£26 per month for employees paid monthly) may be made without supporting evidence.

Further details on some of the above taxable and non-taxable benefits are outlined below.

Provision of Living Accommodation

In general, if an employee is provided with free or subsidised living accommodation by their employer, the employee is liable to income tax to the value of the accommodation. The "value" of the accommodation depends on whether it is **owned** by the employer, or whether it is **rented** by the employer for use by the employee.

Where the accommodation is rented, the annual value charge is the **higher** of:

- the rent paid by the employer, or
- the annual value of the property (i.e. its rateable value),

less any sum paid by the employee.

Where the property is **owned by the employer**, the annual value charge is the rent that would have been payable if the premises had been let at an amount equal to its annual value.

An additional charge may also apply where the "cost of providing accommodation" exceeds £75,000. The "cost of providing" the accommodation is the aggregate of the purchase cost of the property and the cost of any improvements made **before** the start of the tax year. The additional charge is calculated as:

1. the excess cost of providing the accommodation over £75,000, multiplied by the official rate of interest (currently 2%), less
2. the amount by which any rent paid by the employee exceeds the annual value.

Example 5.2

Harry, a senior manager, is provided with a house by his employer by reason of his employment. He is required to pay a rental value of £1,500 per annum. The house cost his employer £175,000 in January 2015. The gross rating value of the property is £1,000 per annum. Harry occupies the property throughout the tax year 2021/22.

The benefit in kind assessable on Harry will be as follows:

No annual value charge arises because the annual rental value of £1,500 payable by Harry is more than the annual rating value of £1,000.

However, one must consider the potential additional charge as the cost of providing the accommodation exceeds £75,000.

	£
Cost of providing accommodation	175,000
Less	(75,000)
Excess	100,000
£100,000 × 2%	2,000
Less: (excess of rent paid over rating value)	(500)
Cash equivalent	1,500

The BIK value is £1,500

If the accommodation is not provided for the whole of the tax year, then the value (whether calculated on the rented or owned basis) is pro-rated.

If the property was acquired more than six years before being provided to the employee, then the cost of providing the accommodation is calculated on the "market value" when the accommodation is first provided, plus the cost of subsequent improvements made before the start of the tax year. The market value rule only applies if the actual cost of providing the accommodation (including only those improvements made before the start of the tax year) is in excess of £75,000.

Exemptions

There is an exemption to the benefit where the provision of accommodation is 'job-related' and one of the following applies:

1. it is necessary for the employee to reside in the accommodation (e.g. caretaker, clergy);
2. it is customary for the employee to be provided with accommodation (e.g. pub landlord); or
3. the accommodation is provided by reason of security (e.g. Government minister, police officer).

Provision of Accommodation: Related Expenses

In addition to the benefit of the accommodation itself, employees are also liable to income tax on the property's related expenses that are paid by the employer. Related expenses include:

- heating, lighting or cleaning the premises;
- repairing, maintaining or decorating the premises; and
- the provision of furniture (the annual value is 20% of the cost).

The full cost of such ancillary services (excluding structural repairs) is taxable as general earnings.

"Job-related" accommodation, although exempt from the cost of providing the accommodation itself, is still liable to tax on the ancillary services, although it is restricted to a maximum of 10% of the employee's "net earnings".

Provision of Company Vehicles

Company Cars

Where a company car is available for an employee's **private** use (which includes "normal commuting"), the employee is taxable on the value of the benefit.

The tax liability is calculated based on the car's CO_2 emissions, its list price when new and on whether the car was first registered before or after 6 April 2020. As the tables below show, the lower the car's CO_2 emissions, the lower the rate to be applied.

TABLE 5.2: COMPANY CAR TAX – CARS FIRST REGISTERED **BEFORE** 6 APRIL 2020

CO_2 emissions band	Electric range (miles)	Percentage of car's list price taxed
50g/km or less	>130	2%
50g/km or less	70–129	5%
50g/km or less	40–69	8%
50g/km or less	30–39	12%
50g/km or less	<30	14%
51–54g/km		15%
55–59g/km		16%
Above 60g/km		Additional 1% per every 5g/km over (rounded down to nearest multiple of five). Rate is capped at 37% of list price.

TABLE 5.3: COMPANY CAR TAX – CARS FIRST REGISTERED **AFTER** 6 APRIL 2020

CO_2 emissions band	Electric range (miles)	Percentage of car's list price taxed
50g/km or less	>130	1%
50g/km or less	70–129	4%
50g/km or less	40–69	7%
50g/km or less	30–39	11%
50g/km or less	<30	13%
51–54g/km		14%
55–59g/km		15%
Above 60g/km		Additional 1% per every 5g/km over (rounded down to nearest multiple of five). Rate is capped at 37% of list price.

There is a 4% supplement for all diesel cars (subject to the 37% cap). Cars that meet the Real Driving Emissions standard are exempt from the 4% diesel supplement.

The value of the benefit is calculated by reference to the "**cash equivalent**" of the company car, **less** amounts made good by the employee to the employer.

If the employee is provided with the car for only part of the particular tax year, the value of the benefit is proportionately reduced. This is also the case if the car is incapable of being used for a period of at least 30 days.

A car's list price is its retail price at first registration, **including** charges for delivery and standard accessories, **plus** the price (including fitting) of all optional accessories supplied when the car was **first provided** to the employee (excluding mobile phones and equipment needed by a disabled employee) plus the price (including fitting) of all optional accessories **fitted after** the car was provided to the employee and costing at least £100 each (excluding mobile phones and equipment needed by a disabled employee; replacement accessories are ignored.)

The list price is reduced by capital contributions made by the employee in that tax year and previous years for the same car up to a maximum of £5,000. These are payments in respect of the price of the car or car accessories.

The benefit in kind is reduced by any payment the user must make for the **private use** of the car. (Note, this is different from the capital contributions element, which reduces the list price of the car.) Also note that payments for insuring the car are ignored and are not taken into account.

Example 5.3

Niall was given a petrol company car by his employer on 1 January 2022. The car has a list price of £30,000 and was first registered in December 2021. Niall contributed £5,000 to the cost of the car. The CO_2 emissions of the car are 250g/km and Niall pays his employer £200 per month to be able to use the car for private journeys.

Niall's company car BIK (for three months in 2021/22) is calculated as follows:

List price of car	£30,000
Less: capital contribution (max.)	(£5,000)
	£25,000
£25,000 × 37% × 3/12	£2,313
Less: 3 months paid at £200/month	(£600)
2021/22 BIK	£1,713

Fuel Benefit Charge

The company car fuel charge is operated on the same basis as the car benefit charge. The same percentage rate, based on CO_2 emissions, is applied to a single set figure for all cars (currently £24,600; £24,500 in 2020/21) to arrive at the chargeable amount.

Fuel charges are reduced to nil if the employee is required (and actually does) make good all fuel provided for private use, including journeys between home and work (normal commuting). Note that all private fuel costs must be met in order to affect the benefit in kind. For example, if only half of private fuel is met by the employee, the full fuel benefit in kind charge is payable. Contrast this to payments made for private use of a car.

The fuel charge for private fuel provided with company cars is proportionately reduced where an employee stops receiving fuel partway through a year (unless he starts to receive fuel again in the same tax year, then the reduction does not apply). It is also proportionately reduced where a car is not available for any part of the year (provided this is at least 30 consecutive days).

Advisory fuel rates for company cars are produced by HMRC and periodically updated on 1 March, 1 June, 1 September and 1 December each year. These charges can be used by employers to calculate the payment/reimbursement due to employees in respect of business mileage where private fuel is not provided with the company car. The HMRC rates, per mile, from 1 June 2020 are as follows:

Engine Size	Petrol	LPG
1400cc or less	11p	8p
1401cc to 2000cc	13p	9p
Over 2000cc	19p	14p

Engine Size	Diesel
1600cc or less	9p
1601cc to 2000cc	11p
Over 2000cc	13p

Example 5.4

Tim was provided with a new company car costing £15,000 for 2021/22. It is a petrol vehicle with CO_2 emissions of 158 g/km and was first registered in February 2021. During the year Tim paid £270 for the private use of the car and £150 towards the fuel. His employer paid insurance of £800, repairs of £320, tax of £180 and all fuel costs. What is the taxable benefit to Tim?

CO_2 emissions of 158g/km, rounded down to 155g/km

Using Table 5.3 above, for cars first registered after 6 April 2020 the taxable percentage is calculated as:

(a) 155 – 55 = 100, and 100/5 = 20%; plus
(b) the base percentage for a car with CO_2 emissions of 55g/km, which is 15%.

Therefore, a car with CO_2 emission of 158g/km has a BIK percentage of 15% + 20% = 35%

Car: £15,000 × 35%	£5,250
Fuel: £24,600 × 35%	£8,610
	£13,860
Less: contributions for private use	(270)
	£13,590

Note: the £150 payment for fuel by Tim is ignored, as only payments for private use are taken into account. The insurance, repairs costs and motor tax are not treated as benefits. Therefore, Tim's BIK is £13,590.

Company Vans

Where a company van is made available to an employee for **private** use, the employee is taxable on a flat-rate benefit charge. The van benefit charge is currently £3,500 per annum (£3,490 for 2020/21). **For these purposes only, normal commuting is not treated as private use**. Normal commuting means the journey the employee takes between their home and permanent workplace. The van benefit charge covers insurance, servicing, etc. A van benefit charge exemption applies to zero-emission vans for 2021/22.

Note that an **additional** fuel charge of £669 will apply for fuel supplied for unrestricted private use.

The taxable amount is reduced by any payments made by the employee for private use (only if made during the relevant tax year) and is proportionately reduced if the van is not available throughout the whole of the tax year.

Example 5.5

On 6 October 2021, Denis was provided with a company van with CO_2 emissions of 120g/km. His employer also provides him with all fuel for the van.

Denis will have a BIK of:

Van benefit charge	£3,500
Fuel charge	£669
	£4,169
Van and fuel for six months	£2,085

Car and Van Pool Exemption

Where a company car or van is in a "pool", i.e. available for all employees generally, no benefit is assessed on any individual employee. A company car or van is treated as belonging to a pool where:

- it has been made available to, and actually used by, **more than one** employee and is not ordinarily used by any one of the employees to the exclusion of others; **and**
- any private use of the company vehicle by any employee is incidental to its business use; **and**
- it is not normally kept overnight at the home of any of the employees.

Provision of "Preferential Loans"

A "preferential loan" means a loan made by an employer to an employee, a former employee or a prospective employee, or their spouses, in respect of which no interest is payable, or that interest is payable at a rate **lower** than the "specified rate".

It does **not include** any loan made by an employer to an employee where:

- in the course of their trade, on an arm's length basis where normal commercial rates of interest are charged (e.g. a bank employee getting a loan from their employer at the same rate as any other customer); or
- if the total of all beneficial loans made to an individual employee did not exceed £10,000 at any time in the tax year.

The official rate of interest is set each year. The rate for 2021/22 is 2%.

Calculating the Taxable Benefit

The taxable benefit of a preferential loan is determined by considering the difference between the interest actually paid during the particular tax year and the amount of interest calculated at the official rate.

There are **two alternative ways** of calculating the taxable benefit: the 'average' method or the 'strict' method.

1. The **'average' method** averages the balances at the beginning and end of the tax year (or the dates on which the loan was made and discharged if it were not in existence throughout the tax year) and applies the official rate of interest to this average. If the loan was not in existence

throughout the tax year, only the number of complete tax months (from the 6th of the month) for which it existed are taken into account.

2. The **'strict' method** is to compute interest at the official rate (currently 2%) on the actual amount outstanding on a daily basis.

Example 5.6

Tom's employer loans him £17,000 interest-free on 8 June 2021 for personal use. He repays £2,000 on 1 December 2021. The remaining balance is still outstanding at 5 April 2022. What is the taxable benefit of the loan?

Average method
The maximum amount outstanding at commencement of the loan was £17,000.
The maximum amount outstanding at the end of the tax year was £15,000.
The average amount, therefore, is £16,000 ((£17,000 + £15,000)/2).
The number of whole months the loan is outstanding is nine. (Months run from the 6th to the 5th, so the loan was not outstanding for the whole month 6 June–5 July.)
Interest at official rate, i.e. taxable benefit, is £16,000 × 2% × 9/12 mths = £240

Strict method

Period	No. of days	Loan balance	Interest rate	Taxable benefit
8 June 2021 to 1 December 2021	177	£17,000	2%	£165
2 December 2021 to 5 April 2022	126	£15,000	2%	£104
Total				£269

As the strict method gives the higher figure, you would expect HMRC to apply that method.

Tax is charged on the amount written off any loans, whether or not the recipient is still employed and regardless of the amount of the loan written off.

5.4.4 General Earnings: Miscellaneous

Medical Insurance
Medical insurance provided by an employer is a taxable benefit, the taxable amount being the gross premium, i.e. the cost to the employer.

Employee's Subsistence Allowance
Where an employee performs the duties of their employment while temporarily away from their normal place of work or while working abroad on a foreign assignment, the employer may reimburse the employee for actual expenses incurred or, alternatively, may pay the employee a flat-rate subsistence allowance to cover costs incurred by the employee.

Where the employee pays all subsistence expenses and is reimbursed for these expenses by a flat-rate subsistence allowance in line with HMRC guidelines (civil service rates), then such an allowance may be paid **tax-free** by the employer and is not taxable in the hands of the employee, provided HMRC is satisfied that the allowance does no more than reimburse the costs incurred.

Removal/Relocation Expenses
An employer may pay or reimburse, free of tax, certain removal/relocation expenses incurred by an employee in moving house to take up employment. To qualify, the change of residence must satisfy a number of conditions, the most important being that the employee must change his or her only, or main, residence as a result of:

- starting a new employment;
- a change in the duties of the current employment; or
- changing the place where the duties are usually performed.

Expenses that can be reimbursed free of tax are those incurred **directly** as a result of the change of residence and include such items as:

- auctioneer's and solicitor's fees and stamp duty arising from moving house;
- removal of furniture and effects, and insurance on items in transit or in storage;
- storage charges;
- travelling expenses on removal;
- temporary subsistence while looking for accommodation at the new location; and
- temporary living accommodation.

The amount reimbursed or borne by the employer may not exceed expenditure **actually incurred**. There are no reporting requirements or income tax and NICs on amounts up to £8,000.

Canteen Meals
Where free or subsidised meals in staff canteens/or at the workplace are provided and **available to all employees**, a taxable benefit **does not** arise. If the facility is not available to all employees, the running costs of the canteen must be apportioned between those employees entitled to use the canteen and the apportioned costs are a taxable benefit for those employees.

Childcare Vouchers and the Tax-Free Childcare Scheme
A BIK exemption applies to the provision of qualifying childcare contracted by the employer, and on employer-provided childcare vouchers. An employee can receive vouchers for registered or approved childcare worth up to £55 per week free of income tax and NICs, provided certain conditions are met.

Higher rate and additional rate taxpayers receive the same tax relief as a basic rate taxpayer, i.e. up to £28 per week for higher rate taxpayers and up to £25 per week for additional rate taxpayers.

From October 2018, no new entrants will be able to join the Childcare Vouchers scheme.

Example 5.7

Emma is an employee and earns £600 (gross) per week. She is married with one child. Emma is a basic rate taxpayer (assuming this is her only income). If Emma was already a member of a childcare voucher scheme before October 2018, she could ask her employer to split her salary into cash and childcare vouchers.

That is, she could be taxed on £545 gross pay per week, plus £55 of childcare vouchers. On this basis, Emma would only pay income tax at 20% and NICs on £545. The childcare vouchers can be received free of income tax and NICs.

The Tax-Free Childcare scheme is available for parents with children under the age of 11 or parents who have a child with a disability who is under 17 years of age. Under the scheme, eligible parents can open a childcare account for each child. They pay 80% of their child's childcare costs, with the additional 20% topped up by the Government, up to a maximum of £2,000 per child per annum (£4,000 if the child has a disability).

Professional Subscriptions
Where an employer pays a subscription to a professional body on behalf of an employee, or reimburses the employee who has paid such a subscription, a taxable benefit **does not arise**, providing membership of that professional institute is **relevant** to the business of the employer. Membership of a professional body is regarded as relevant where:

- it is **necessary** for the performance of the employee's or director's present or prospective duties of the office or employment; or
- it **facilitates** the acquisition of knowledge, which is **necessary** for, or directly related to, the performance of the duties of the office or employment.

Course or Exam Fees
Where an employer pays or reimburses an employee for the cost of any course or exam fee that is relevant, necessary or directly related to the employee's duties (or prospective duties), this is not treated as a taxable benefit.

Staff Suggestion Schemes
Awards made under most staff suggestion schemes are tax-free. For example, financial rewards offered by an employer to encourage staff members to suggest ways to reduce costs, improve efficiency, add revenue and so on can be given tax-free. The scheme must be available to all employees and the maximum award is £5,000.

Long-service Awards
A taxable benefit will **not arise** in respect of long-service awards where the following conditions are satisfied:
- the award is made as a testimonial to mark long service of **not less** than 20 years;
- the award takes the form of a tangible article of reasonable cost;
- the cost does **not exceed £50 for each year of service**; and
- no similar award has been made to the recipient within the previous 10 years.

This treatment **does not apply** to awards made in cash or in the form of vouchers, bonds, etc. Such awards are fully taxable.

Use of Employer's Assets
Tax is chargeable on the annual rental value of land and for other assets (apart from those specifically excluded above) at **20% of the market value when they are first provided or the rental charge to the employer, if higher**. If provided for only part of a year, then there is a need to time-apportion. The benefit is reduced by any contributions made by the employee that are exempt BIK. There is a special rule for bicycles, which are exempt benefits.

Assets given to Employees
If the asset given is new, tax is chargeable on the cost to the employer (market value in the case of lower paid employees). If it is a used asset, tax is chargeable on the greater of:

(a) the market value at the date of transfer less the price paid by the employee; or
(b) the market value when first provided to the employee **less** amounts charged to tax previously.

5.4.5 General Earnings: State Pension and Child Benefit

The State pension is a taxable social security benefit, taxed as non-savings income.

Recipients of child benefit who have (or their partner has) "adjusted net income" of greater than £50,000 in a tax year, are liable to income tax on the child benefit income. That is, the child benefit income is included as general earnings when calculating the income tax liability. Adjusted net income is defined in the same way as the restriction of the personal allowance (see **Chapter 2**).

The tax liability depends on the actual income and is split into two bands:

1. Adjusted net income between £50,000 and £60,000 – the income tax rate is 1% of the child benefit award for each £100 of income greater than £50,000.
2. Adjusted net income greater than £60,000 – the income tax is a rate equal to the amount of child benefit received, i.e. the child benefit is effectively lost.

Example 5.8
An individual's adjusted net income is £55,000 and they are in receipt of child benefit of £400.

Income over £50,000 = £5,000
Income tax rate: £5,000/£100 = 50%
Income tax due: 50% × £400 = £200

If the individual's adjusted net income had been £70,000, the tax charge would have been equal to the child benefit and the child benefit would be lost in full.

If both the individual and their partner have adjusted net income greater than £50,000, then the partner with the higher income is the one liable.

Individuals claiming child benefit can decide not to receive the benefit if they (or their partner) do not wish to pay the income tax charge.

Questions

Review Questions
(See Suggested Solutions to Review Questions at the end of this textbook.)

Question 5.1

Dermot O'Donnell, a single man, is an employee of Super McBurgers, a fast-food restaurant chain. He retired on 1 October 2021. The following information is provided.

1. In the period from April 2021 to 30 September 2021, Dermot earned a gross salary and benefits in kind on his company car of £37,000. PAYE deducted was £9,500.
2. He was also provided with a mobile phone when he was employed by Super McBurgers. All calls on the phone were paid for by the company. The personal element of the calls cost £2,000 as his sister lived in Japan for a year.
3. He commenced new employment in Burger Palace on 1 November 2021 and his gross earnings in the period to March 2022 were £14,200 (PAYE deducted was £2,900). He also received a commencement incentive of £4,000 when he started this employment as a number of fast-food outlets were keen to have him as an employee.

Requirement
Calculate Dermot's final liability to income tax for the year 2021/22.

Question 5.2

Sid Harvey is an employee of General Services Ltd. His gross basic salary for 2021/22 amounted to £40,500. His employer also gives him £100 every month by way of a round sum expense allowance to meet incidental outlay. He is not obliged to provide his employer with receipts to account for this expenditure.

Sid is supplied with a company car (petrol), which was bought by General Services Ltd, second-hand, in July 2019, for £15,000. The car is a 2016 model and originally cost £36,000 (after 10% cash discount) when first registered. General Services Ltd pay all the outgoings in respect of the running of the car. However, Sid is required to reimburse the company for all private fuel used. The CO_2 emissions are 127g/km.

In recognition of the fact that he has the car available to him during leisure hours, Sid is also obliged to make a monthly contribution of £100 to his employer. This is deducted from his salary. Sid's total mileage in the tax year 2021/22 amounted to 25,000 miles, of which 16,500 miles were in the course of the performance of his duties. Sid spends approximately 50% of his working time away from the premises of General Services Limited.

General Services Ltd also provides a free apartment to Sid. The current market value of the apartment is estimated at £110,000. It was worth £80,000 when first made available to Sid in 2019. General Services Ltd pay the annual management charge and light and heat costs of the apartment, which, for 2021/22, amounted to £890. The apartment was purchased for £55,000 in 2006. The annual value of the apartment is £600.

Sid receives free meals in the staff canteen on the days he is located at his head office. The cost of providing these meals by his employer amounted to approximately £300. The staff canteen is available to all staff and all meals are provided free.

On 1 November 2017, General Services Ltd provided Sid with a £1,000 interest-free loan to enable him to go on his annual holidays. On 6 August 2021 the board of directors of General Services Ltd decided to waive repayment of the loan.

Sid is not married and paid £13,900 PAYE in the tax year 2021/22.

Requirement
Calculate Sid's taxable benefits assessable for 2020/21.

Question 5.3

Terry is considering an employment offer from Rich Bank plc, with a proposed start date of 6 April 2021. In addition to an attractive salary of £70,500, Rich Bank plc has offered to take over his mortgage loan of £125,000, which he used to purchase his first main residence in January 2008. The rate of interest payable on the loan is 2%. Such loans are not available to the public.

Rich Bank plc will also provide an interest-free loan of £4,000 to pay Terry's affiliation fees at the Posh Golf and Country Club, and will pay annual membership of £3,500 on his behalf.

He would also be provided with a new diesel VW Passat car, first registered in 2019 with a list price of £30,000 and CO_2 emissions of 127g/km. Rich Bank plc intends to pay all associated expenses. There is no business mileage.

Terry is married and will earn £75,500 with no benefits if he stays in his current job in 2021. He pays 5.5% on his mortgage and estimates that his car costs £10,500 per annum. He is not a member of any golf club and has no business mileage in his current job.

Requirement

(a) Calculate the taxable benefits assessable for 2021/22 from his new employer.
(b) Prepare income tax computations for both his current job and the new employment offer and advise which leaves him better off.

Question 5.4

Philip Stodge is employed as a commercial representative. Details of his income for the tax year 2021/22 are as follows:

	£
Gross salary	43,600
Sales commission	6,500
Pension contributions made by employer	10,000

The following additional information is available:

1. PAYE deducted amounted to £7,900.
2. The sales commission of £6,500 earned was paid directly to his wife.
3. He receives a monthly round sum expense allowance of £50 to meet routine incidental expenses, such as telephone calls, tips that he gives for food/beverages when travelling on business, etc. In addition, his employer pays his hotel accommodation costs directly. He is away on business in the UK 10 nights each month.
4. Philip runs an Audi A4 car (list price £27,000). He drove 10,000 business miles, but his fuel expenses are not reimbursed by his employer. CO_2 emissions are 150g/km.
5. He is provided with a free parking space in a public car park beside his work. This costs his employer £1,000 a year.
6. In addition to car expenses, the following expenses (vouched with receipts) are not reimbursed by his employer:

	£
Work-related telephone charges	180
Cost of new suit	450
Cost of advanced commercial correspondence course	150
Taxi/train fares while on business	130
	910

7. He pays a professional subscription of £400 per year.

Requirement

(a) Compute Philip Stodge's income tax liability for the tax year 2021/22.
(b) You are aware that Philip plays at the same golf course as your father and have heard that he made some money outside of his employment income in 2021/22. However, there is no mention of this in the information provided by Philip for his 2021/22 tax return. How should you approach this situation in line with ethical standards?

Question 5.5

Frank, a sales representative who is single, received a salary of £49,000 in 2021/22 and the following benefits in kind:

1. Company Ferrari (over 2000cc) with a list price of £120,000, first registered in 2018. CO_2 emissions are 300g/km. He had to pay £35,000 towards the cost of the car.
2. All fuel was paid for by the employer.
3. He paid professional subscriptions of £800.

Requirement

Calculate Frank's gross income tax liability (before credit for PAYE deducted) for the tax year 2021/22.

Savings and Investment Income

Learning Objectives

After studying this chapter you will be able to:

■ Explain the scope and basis of assessment of savings and investment income.
■ Determine the taxation of UK dividends.

6.1   Introduction

In the previous chapters we have learned how an individual's taxable trading income and/or taxable employment income are classified as non-savings income for the purpose of the overall income tax calculation. However, non-savings income is not the only type of income that an individual may earn in a tax year. For example, where an individual has money on deposit in a bank, savings income, i.e. interest, may be earned on the money invested. Similarly, an individual may have purchased shares in a company and if that company decides to pay a dividend to its shareholders, dividend income will have been earned and will need to be taxed accordingly.

Throughout this chapter you will be introduced to the various types of UK savings and dividend income and the various tax rates that apply to each. In this chapter we will consider a number of saving incentives available to encourage individuals to save to buy their first home or for their retirement. The various rules and regulations surrounding such savings incentives will be discussed.

6.1.1   Types of Savings and Investment Income

Savings Income

In simple terms, savings income is interest. It includes interest from:

■ a bank account;
■ a building society account;
■ a credit union account;
■ National Savings and Investment accounts;
■ gilt-edged securities – that is, British Government stock; and
■ debentures issued by companies (sometimes referred to as company loan stock).

Dividend Income

When an individual owns shares in a company, they may receive dividends from the company throughout the year. Such income is taxed as dividend income.

6.2 Basis of Assessment and Computation of Savings and Investment Income

6.2.1 General Rules

Generally, the amount of savings and investment income taxable for a tax year is the amount arising in that year. Income arises when it is paid or credited. Accrued income not yet paid or credited is ignored.

Savings and investment income is generally 'pure' income profit, i.e. it is unusual for there to be any deductions to be accounted for, e.g. expenses or costs. This makes the income tax computation of savings and dividend income a relatively straightforward calculation – in essence it is to determine the amount of taxable income and to then apply the necessary tax rate.

6.2.2 Savings Income

Personal Savings Allowance

In **Chapter 2, Section 2.3.2**, you were introduced to the personal savings allowance. The amount of personal savings allowance depends on an individual's "adjusted net income". Adjusted net income is total taxable income before deducting the personal allowance and after certain other tax reliefs, such as:

- trading losses (**Chapter 4**);
- donations made to charities through gift aid (**Chapter 8**);
- pension contributions paid gross, i.e. before tax relief (**Chapter 8**); and
- pension contributions where the pension provider has already given tax relief at the basic rate (**Chapter 8**).

Example 6.1

For the 2021/22 tax year, Maeve's total taxable income is £30,000, made up of £15,000 employment income, £5,000 bank interest and £10,000 of dividends. In 2021/22, Maeve also made a trading loss of £2,500.

Maeve's adjusted net income is £27,500 (£30,000 less £2,500).

The table below shows the amount of the personal savings allowance an individual is entitled to, depending on whether they are a basic, higher or additional rate taxpayer.

Tax Rate	Income Band (adjusted net income)	Personal Savings Allowance
Basic: 20%	Up to £50,270 (£37,700 + £12,570)	Up to £1,000
Higher: 40%	£50,271–£150,000	Up to £500
Additional: 45%	Over £150,001	Nil

There is an important interaction between the personal savings allowance and the new dividend allowance (**Section 6.2.3**). When determining the amount of the personal savings allowance, it is necessary to consider if the adjusted net income includes dividend income. If dividend income is included, that income is treated as if it is chargeable at the higher or additional rate, even if it is within the £2,000 dividend allowance, when calculating the personal savings allowance.

Example 6.2

Frank has the following income in 2021/22:

Employment income	£37,500
Savings income	£1,000
Dividend income	£12,000
	£50,500

Frank's adjusted net income is £50,500. His dividends will be taxed as the highest part of income with the first £2,000 of dividends being covered by the dividend allowance (**Section 6.2.3**), chargeable at 0%. Despite the fact that £2,000 of his dividends will be chargeable at 0%, for the purpose of considering the personal saving allowance the dividends are treated as if they are chargeable at the higher rate. Therefore, Frank's adjusted net income is £50,500, i.e. he is a higher rate taxpayer, and so will receive a personal savings allowance of £500.

Rates of Tax

As outlined in **Chapter 2** and in the table above, the same rates of tax that apply to non-savings income also apply to savings income. That is, the basic rate at 20%, the higher rate at 40% and the additional rate at 45%. In addition, a "starter rate" also applies to savings income only. The starter rate is 0% for savings income up to £5,000, i.e. it is tax-exempt. For the starter rate to apply, an individual's savings income must fall wholly or partly below the £5,000 limit and, importantly, the individual must not have non-savings income of £5,000 or more in the tax year. The table below outlines the rates of tax applicable to savings income.

	Rate	Taxable Income
Savings income starter rate*	0%	Up to £5,000
Basic rate	20%	Up to £37,700
Higher rate	40%	£37,701 to £150,000
Additional rate	45%	Over £150,001

*The personal savings allowance is available in addition to the savings income starter rate, increasing the amount of savings income that could be received tax-free to £6,000.

To illustrate how the different rates are applied, let's look at a few examples.

Example 6.3

Beth earns employment income of £15,000 in the 2021/22 tax year. She also earns £250 interest from her building society account.

Beth is a basic rate taxpayer. As Beth's savings income of £250 is covered by her personal savings allowance she will not pay any tax on her savings income.

Example 6.4
James has property income profits of £25,000 in 2021/22 and he also earns £1,500 in interest income.

James is a basic rate taxpayer. He will not pay income tax on £1,000 of his interest income as this is covered by his personal savings allowance. He will pay basic rate tax of 20% on the £500 interest over his personal savings allowance.

Example 6.5
Lisa earns employment income of £80,000 in 2021/22. She also earns £400 of interest income in 2021/22.

Lisa is a higher rate taxpayer. As Lisa's savings income of £400 is covered by her personal savings allowance (of £500), she will not pay any tax on her savings income.

Example 6.6
Edward has taxable trading profits of £60,000 in the 2021/22 tax year. He also earns £1,200 of interest income in 2021/22.

Edward is a higher rate taxpayer. He will not pay income tax on £500 of his interest income, as this is covered by his personal savings allowance. He will pay the higher rate tax of 40% on the £700 interest over his personal savings allowance.

Example 6.7
Jacqui has employment income of £170,000 in the 2021/22 tax year. She also earns £1,500 of interest income in 2021/22.

Jacqui is an additional rate taxpayer, and as such she is not entitled to the personal savings allowance. She will pay additional rate tax of 45% on the £1,500 interest income.

6.2.3 Dividend Income

Dividend Allowance
All individuals, regardless of their levels of earnings, are entitled to the tax-free dividend allowance, which means that no tax will be payable on the first £2,000 of dividend income.

Rates of Tax
An individual will pay the following rates of tax on dividends received over £2,000:

- 7.5% on dividend income within the basic rate band (£2,000–£37,700);
- 32.5% on dividend income within the higher rate band (£37,701–£150,000);
- 38.1% on dividend income within the additional rate band (over £150,001).

As noted above, dividend income covered by the dividend allowance will still count towards an individual's basic or higher rate bands, and will therefore affect the rate of tax that is payable on dividends received in excess of the £2,000 allowance.

Again, some examples will help to illustrate the application of the rates.

Example 6.8

Megan receives £1,000 of dividends in 2021/22.

She will not have to pay any tax on her dividends as they are covered by the dividend allowance.

Example 6.9

Ryan earns £7,920 employment income and £15,000 dividend income in 2021/22.

Ryan will be entitled to a personal allowance of £12,570, so £4,650 (i.e. £12,570 – £7,920) of his dividends will be covered by his remaining personal allowance. A further £2,000 comes within the dividend allowance, leaving tax to pay at the basic rate (7.5%) on £8,350.

Example 6.10

Nicole has taxable trading profits of £20,000 and £22,000 dividend income in 2021/22.

Nicole will be entitled to a personal allowance of £12,570, which will be fully used against her non-savings income. Nicole will not need to pay tax on the first £2,000 of dividends due to the dividend allowance, but will pay tax on £20,000 of dividends at the basic rate (7.5%) as her dividend income falls within the basic rate band.

Example 6.11

Anna has employment income of £42,420 and dividend income of £12,000 in 2021/22.

Of the £42,420 employment income, £12,570 is covered by her personal allowance, leaving £29,850 to be taxed at the basic rate. This leaves £7,850 of income that can be earned within the basic rate limit before the higher rate threshold is crossed.

The dividend allowance uses £2,000 of this £7,850 first, leaving £5,850 of the dividends to be taxed at 7.5%. The remaining £4,150 of dividends will all be taxed at the higher rate (32.5%).

6.2.4 Exempt Savings and Investment Income

Certain investment and savings income is exempt for investors resident and domiciled in the UK. Exempt income includes the following:

1. Interest and dividend income from individual savings accounts (ISAs). See below for more information.
2. Accumulated interest on National Savings Certificates issued by National Savings and Investments (NS&I).
3. Interest awarded as part of an award of damages for personal injury or death.
4. Betting and premium bond prizes.

Individual Savings Accounts

ISA savings can be held either as cash or as stocks and shares, or in combination of the two. Income earned in ISAs is exempt from income tax (and capital gains tax). Withdrawals can be made at any time.

Up to a maximum of £20,000 can be saved in an ISA in the 2021/22 tax year.

Questions

Review Questions
(See Suggested Solutions to Review Questions at the end of this textbook.)

Question 6.1

Mairead lives in London. In the 2021/22 tax year, she received rental income of £15,620, building society interest of £11,760.

Requirement
Compute Mairead's 2021/22 income tax liability.

Question 6.2

Jeremy is married and lives in Coleraine. In the 2021/22 tax year, he had trading profits of £30,630 and he received rental income of £750 and dividends of £115,100.

Requirement
Compute Jeremy's 2021/22 income tax liability.

Question 6.3

Giles lives in Newry. In the 2021/22 tax year, he had trading profits of £10,350 and he received debenture interest of £6,200, interest on an ISA of £1,240 and dividends of £14,000.

Requirement
Compute Giles' 2021/22 income tax liability.

Question 6.4

Maeve, who is widowed and 56 years of age, is in receipt of the following UK-source income in the 2021/22 tax year:

Dividend income received	£
Tyson Limited	17,520
Holyfield Manufacturing Limited	3,724
	21,244
Deposit interest received	
National Savings Bank account	6,800
Credit Union interest	1,550
Nationwide ISA interest	720
	9,070
Personal pension	7,800

Requirement

Compute Maeve's 2021/22 income tax liability.

Question 6.5

David Lee, a single person aged 44, works for a travel agency. In 2021/22 he had the following income and outgoings:

	£
Income	
Salary (gross)	42,500
Ordinary bank interest	625
Interest on Government loans	1,130
Ordinary building society interest	175
National Savings Certificates interest	100
Gift from neighbour for getting her shopping when she had a cold	30
Outgoings	
PAYE deducted	4,900
NIC deducted	2,255
Post Office (Note 1)	1,200

Notes:

1. David buys £100 worth of premium bonds each month. He received £10,000 from the bonds in the tax year.
2. David also won £40,000 on the National Lottery in January 2022.

Requirement

Calculate David Lee's income tax liability for the 2021/22 tax year, stating clearly the amount payable by, or refundable to, him.

Property Income

Learning Objectives

After studying this chapter you will be able to:

■ Explain the scope of rental income.
■ Explain the basis of assessment for rental income.
■ Determine the taxation consequences of receiving and paying premiums on short leases.
■ Determine relief for capital allowances and replacement furniture allowance.
■ Explain how rental losses can be utilised.
■ Explain the operation of the Rent a Room Scheme.

7.1 Introduction

Property income is a non-savings income. A taxpayer with UK property income is treated as if they are operating a UK property business, and as such the considerations and calculations for income tax purposes are broadly the same as for trading income (see **Chapter 3**). That is, all property/rental income (hereafter referred to as 'property income') and property expenses are consolidated to give a single profit or loss figure on which income tax is assessed. Property income, although similar to trading income, is subject to specific rules relating to the taxing of property income and to the property expenses allowable as deductions.

In this chapter, we will first look at the computation of taxable profits (or losses) for a property business, looking in detail at how the rental income amount in a tax year is established and the expenses that can be deducted, before looking in detail at the rent-a-room scheme.

7.2 Basis of Assessment of Property Income

7.2.1 UK Property Income

The profits of UK property income are computed for each tax year and each tax year's profit is taxed in that year. That is, for the 2021/22 tax year, property income profits from 6 April 2021 to 5 April 2022 are taxed.

7.3 Computation of Taxable Property Income

7.3.1 Property Allowance

A £1,000 property allowance, which is effectively an exemption from income tax, is available for individuals with gross receipts from property of £1,000 or less.

Where an individual's gross receipts from rent exceed £1,000, an election can be made to be taxed on the excess over £1,000. Where this election is claimed, no relief is then given for deductible expenses.

7.3.2 Computation of Profits

We have established that a landlord with property income is treated as if he or she is running a 'property business' and, as such, property income is essentially treated in the same way as trading income, with the calculation of profit or loss, i.e. income minus costs or expenses. Property income includes not only the agreed rents (whether weekly, monthly, quarterly or annual), but also the taxable portion of any premium paid (see **Section 7.3.3**). Many expenses are allowed as a deduction from property income, which will be covered in detail in **Section 7.3.4**.

Where property income receipts do not exceed £150,000, the cash basis is the default basis used to calculate the property income. The accruals basis (in accordance with generally accepted accounting practice) applies where rental receipts exceed £150,000. It is possible for an individual to make an election to disapply the cash basis.

If more than one property is being let, the income and expenses for each property are pooled together to calculate a total profit or loss for the tax year.

The pro forma computation overleaf shows the layout of the property income calculation. It does not include all potential expenses that are allowable as deductions against property income, but it does include the most common.

FIGURE 7.1: PRO FORMA PROPERTY INCOME COMPUTATION.

	£	£
Rental income	X	
Lease premium received	X	
		X
Less: expenses:		
Rent payable	X	
Rates/council tax	X	
Gas/electricity/waste disposal costs paid by landlord and not reimbursed by tenant	X	
Finance/mortgage interest costs (subject to restriction outlined in **Section 7.3.4**)	X	
Accountancy fees	X	
Legal fee re. lease renewal	X	
Travel costs to and from the property	X	
Replacement furniture relief (where a dwelling house is let)	X	
Capital allowances (where a commercial property is let)	X	(X)
Property income profit/(loss)		X

7.3.3 Premiums on Short Leases

As stated above, a landlord is taxed not only on the rents received but also on a proportion of the "premium" of the "short lease". A lease premium is a non-refundable lump sum payment made by the tenant to the landlord on the signing of a lease. A "short lease" is one that does not exceed 50 years.

The landlord is treated as receiving a proportion of the premium **by way of rent** (in addition to the actual rent received) and is also liable to income tax on this amount. It is calculated using the following formula:

$$\text{Premium} - \left(\text{Premium} \times \frac{(\text{Duration of lease}) - 1}{50} \right)$$

Note: the remainder of the premium is taxable as a capital gain.

Example 7.1

On 1 June 2021, Mr White rented premises to Mr Blake for 25 years at a rent of £2,000 per month (payable in advance on the first day of every month), subject to a premium of £20,000.

Taxable portion of premium:

	£
Premium	20,000
Less: £20,000 × $\dfrac{25 - 1}{50}$	(9,600)
Additional rent	10,400
2021/22	
Taxable portion of premium	10,400
Rent received (£2,000 × 11)*	22,000
Total property income assessable	**32,400**

* Rent received on 1 June 2021, 1 July 2021, 1 August 2021, 1 September 2021, 1 October 2021, 1 November 2021, 1 December 2021, 1 January 2022, 1 February 2022, 1 March 2022 and 1 April 2022.

Where a trader pays a premium for the lease of a premises that will be used for their trade, a deduction in respect of the premium is allowed against taxable trading profits for each year of the lease (see **Section 3.3.5**).

7.3.4 Allowable Deductions from Property Income

As property income rules broadly follow trading income rules, any qualifying costs incurred by the property business can be deducted to reduce the tax liability. The "wholly and exclusively" rule is the main rule applied to property income. The following costs are deductible from the gross rents received (assuming the default cash basis applies):

- Rent paid on the property. For example, where a landlord is renting a property and is in turn renting part of that property to others, i.e. subletting.
- Rates, council tax and ground rent paid on the property.
- The cost of goods or services that the landlord is obliged to provide and for which no separate consideration is received, e.g. gas, electricity, waste disposal.
- Cost of insurance, maintenance and management of the property.

■ For non-residential properties, the finance costs/mortgage interest on any loan associated with the purchase or renovation of the property is available as a deduction. Capital repayments in respect of loans are not deductible. See below for specific details regarding the amount of tax relief available for finance costs/mortgage interest on residential properties.

■ Accountancy fees paid in respect of drawing up rental accounts and keeping rental records.

■ Legal fees regarding the **renewal** of a short lease. A short lease is one lasting 50 years or less.

■ For **commercial** property, capital allowances may be claimed on plant and machinery (see **Chapter 4**).

■ Travel costs to and from let properties, unless the trip is partly for private purposes. The landlord may deduct actual motoring expenses or use approved mileage allowances (see **Section 5.4.2**).

■ Irrecoverable rent, i.e. bad debts, can be relieved as an impairment loss. This will only be relevant if the property income is assessed on the accruals basis.

■ Replacement furniture relief applies to the replacement of furnishings. The initial cost of furnishing a property is not allowable but, under the replacement furniture relief, landlords of all dwelling houses are able to claim a deduction for the capital cost of replacing furniture, furnishings, appliances and kitchenware provided for the tenant's use. This includes:
  ● movable furniture or furnishings, such as beds, sofas, etc.;
  ● televisions;
  ● fridges and freezers;
  ● carpets and floor coverings;
  ● curtains;
  ● linen; and
  ● crockery or cutlery.

The amount of replacement furniture relief available depends on the cost incurred in respect of the replacement item. If the replacement item is substantially the same as the old item, then its full cost can be claimed. If the replacement item is of a higher or improved quality, then the amount of relief is limited to the cost that would have been incurred if replacing 'like with like'.

■ Fixtures that are considered 'integral' to the property, i.e. those that would not normally be removed if the property were to be sold, are not allowable under replacement furniture relief, but can instead be claimed as a deductible expense as a repair to the property itself. They include items such as:
  ● baths, washbasins and toilets;
  ● boilers;
  ● fitted kitchen units; and
  ● repair of a windowpane, electric light fittings, door locks, etc.

Finance Costs/Mortgage Interest – UK Residential Property

A restriction applies to the amount of tax relief available for finance costs (mortgage interest on loans to acquire or renovate the rental property) in respect of UK residential property businesses. This restriction does not apply to commercial lettings.

The tax relief that landlords of residential properties receive on finance costs is restricted to the basic rate (20%) of income tax.

The basic rate tax reduction (which is deducted at Step 6 of the overall income tax calculation (**Section 2.5.1**)) is the lower of:

1. The finance costs in the tax year plus any finance costs brought forward.
2. The property business profits – the profits of the property business in the tax year (after using any brought-forward losses).
3. The individual's adjusted total income – the income (after losses and reliefs, and excluding savings and dividends income) that exceeds an individual's personal allowance.

The tax reduction cannot be used to create a tax refund. If the basic rate tax reduction is calculated using either points 2. or 3. above, then the difference between that figure and finance costs incurred is carried forward to calculate the basic rate tax reduction in the following years.

Example 7.2

In 2021/22, John has taxable trading income of £25,000 and rental income of £8,000 from a rented residential property. He pays finance costs of £9,000 on the mortgage he took out to acquire the rented residential property and also incurred repair expenses of £500 in 2021/22.

	£
Property income	
Rental income	8,000
Finance costs	–
Other allowable expenses	(500)
Property income profits	7,500
Income tax computation	
Trading income	25,000
Property income	7,500
Total/net income	32,500
Less: personal allowance	(12,570)
Taxable income	19,930
Income tax	
£19,930 × 20%	3,986
Less: 20% tax reduction (Note)	(1,500)
Income tax liability	2,486

Note:

Tax reduction is calculated as 20% of the lower of:
  (a) finance costs = £9,000
  (b) property profits = £7,500
  (c) adjusted total income (exceeding Personal Allowance) = £19,930.

The lowest amount is calculated at (b), therefore £1,500 (£7,500 × 20%) is the available tax reduction. The £1,500 finance costs (£9,000 – £7,500) that have not been used to calculate John's basic rate tax reduction are carried forward to calculate his basic rate tax reduction in the following year.

Pre-letting Expenses

Expenses incurred in the seven years prior to commencement of the property business (i.e. before the first lease is entered into) are treated as having been incurred on the first day of the business. Pre-letting expenses are subject to the same rules as allowable deductions, that is, they must be incurred wholly and exclusively for the property business and they must not be capital in nature. In addition, two other conditions must be met:

- the property was in a fit state to be rented (subject to furnishing, cleaning and the setting up of a tenancy agreement); and
- the landlord (taxpayer) was actively and genuinely trying to find tenants.

Common expenses that normally qualify as pre-letting expenses include:

- interest on any loan associated with the property, subject to the restrictions outlined above;
- costs of advertising for tenants; and
- telephone and travel expenses associated with tenant viewings.

Expenses between Lettings

During periods of vacancy, where the landlord is seeking to re-let the property, expenses incurred should still be tax deductible. HMRC normally accept a vacancy period of up to three years where the landlord was clearly trying to continue the property business

Typical expenses that can be claimed between lettings include:

- interest on a loan associated with purchasing or renovating the property (subject to the restrictions outlined above);
- management company fees;
- gas and electricity safety inspections and certificates;
- costs of advertising for new tenants;
- telephone and travel expenses associated with tenant viewings.

Now let's look at a worked example to recap the property income computation for income tax purposes.

Example 7.3

John Black has owned rental properties for several years. You are given the following information about the properties owned during the tax year 2021/22.

Property A	£
Rent receivable per annum (payable in advance on 1 July each year)	30,000
Expenditure incurred:	
Insurance (paid in 2021/22 for period 06/04/2021–05/04/2022)	1,200
Repairs (incurred and paid December 2021)	400
Interest paid on loan to acquire the commercial property	36,000

This commercial property is let on a 10-year lease, which commenced on 1 July 2021. A premium of £20,000 was paid on commencement of the lease. The property was acquired, with the intention of letting it out, on 6 April 2021 for £450,000 with a bank loan taken out on the same date.

Property B	£
Rent receivable per annum	9,600
Expenditure incurred and paid in 2021/22	
Insurance	280
Painting exterior	740
Repairs to door and alarm following burglary	1,250

Property B is a residential property that was let at £800 per month (to be received monthly on 15th of each month) on a two-year lease that commenced on 1 January 2021. The tenant left suddenly in December 2021, leaving rent owing for the month of November and December. Mr Black subsequently found out that the tenant had emigrated to Australia and has written-off the rent owing as a bad debt. The property was re-let to another tenant on 1 January 2022 at the same annual rent and payment deadlines.

Property C	£
Rent received for residential property	5,000
Expenditure incurred:	
Insurance	500
Construction of conservatory (May 2021)	12,400
Interest	22,500
Replacement furnishings	4,625

Property C had been let until 30 November 2021. It was vacant until re-let on a one-year lease from 1 March 2021.

Property D	£
Rent received	30,000

Mr Black acquired property D from his wife in 2010 for £450,000. Mrs Black had inherited the house from her mother in 2010. Mrs Black used funds from the sale of property D to Mr Black towards the cost of a new house purchased by Mr and Mrs Black as their principal private residence.

Rental Assessment	Prop. A	Prop. B	Prop. C	Prop. D
	£	£	£	£
Rent received/receivable (Note 1)	30,000	8,000	5,000	30,000
Income element of premium (Note 2)	16,400	0	0	0
Gross rent	46,400	8,000	5,000	30,000
Deduct:				
Insurance (Note 3)	1,200	280	500	0
Repairs/painting/replacement furnishings	400	1,990	4,625	0
Loan interest (Note 4)	36,000	0	0	0
Total deductions	37,600	2,270	5,125	0
Net profit/(loss)	8,800	5,730	(125)	30,000
Rental income assessable 2021/22 – total				**44,405**

Notes:
As rental income does not exceed £150,000, the cash basis of accounting will apply as John has not elected to disapply it.

1. *Property A*
   Using the default cash basis, the rental receipts taxable in 2021/22 are the £30,000 received on 1 July 2021.
   Property B
   The £800 per month was received for April 2021 to October 2021 inclusive (7 months) and then £800 per month for January–March 2022 inclusive (3 months).
2. *Property A*
   Taxable portion of premium: £20,000 – (£20,000 × 18%) = £16,400.
3. *Property A*
   Expenses incurred before first letting are allowed, provided incurred wholly and exclusively for the property business and are not capital in nature.
   Insurance allowed £1,200.
4. *Property A*
   Expenses incurred before first letting are allowed, provided incurred wholly and exclusively for the property business and are not capital in nature. As this is a commercial property, there is no restriction on the amount of finance costs claimed as a deduction against rental income.
   Property C
   As this is a residential letting, none of the mortgage interest on the loan to acquire/renovate the property (i.e. finance costs) is deductible from rental income. A basic rate tax reduction may be available in respect of the finance costs when calculating the income tax liability for the year. In addition, the interest incurred between lettings is allowable when calculating the basic rate tax reduction.
5. Transactions between Mr and Mrs Black on property D and subsequent purchase of principal private residence are not applicable to rental profits of property D.

7.3.5   Losses on Property Income

In general, losses from a UK property business can be carried forward indefinitely to be used against **future UK property profits** for the same property business. For a property business that has more than one property, the net profit or loss is computed for each one **separately** for the particular tax year. The profits/losses are then aggregated to arrive at the total UK profit/loss for the tax year.

Losses on favoured lettings, i.e. properties let at less than market value, are not allowed. Expenses are only permitted up to the level of income on such lettings. For example, if an individual lets an apartment to their friend for £1,000 per annum (whereas the market rent would be £5,000 per annum) and the management company fee for the apartment block is £1,500 per annum, as this is a favoured letting the £500 loss will not be permitted and the rental computation will be £1,000 of rental income less £1,000 of allowable expenses.

7.3.6   Rent a Room Scheme

Under the Rent a Room Scheme, where an individual rents out a furnished room (or rooms) in a "qualifying residence" and the **gross** income received, including an amount for food, laundry or similar goods and services, **does not exceed £7,500 per year**, this income is automatically **exempt** from income tax. Expenses and capital allowances are ignored under the scheme.

A "qualifying residence" is a residential premises occupied by the landlord as their sole or main residence during the year of assessment. If more than one person owns the residence, then the threshold is split accordingly.

If the £7,500 limit is exceeded, then the landlord has two options:

1. opt into the scheme and claim the £7,500 threshold as an allowance; or
2. ignore the scheme and be assessed in the normal way for a property business.

Under option 1, the landlord is taxed on gross receipts less £7,500 but with no deductions for expenses and capital allowances. An election to opt into the scheme remains in force until withdrawn or until a year when gross rents do not exceed the £7,500 limit.

Under option 2, the landlord can elect to ignore the exemption and claim expenses and capital allowances to generate a rental loss that can then be carried forward (see **Sections 7.3.4–7.3.5**). An election to ignore the exemption applies only for the current year.

Example 7.4

Clive rents out a spare room in his own home. The rent is £180 a week, which includes the cost of heating and electricity. Clive estimates that renting out a room means he pays an extra £80 in home insurance and his electricity and heating bills have increased by £400 per year.

If Clive were to claim the £7,500 as an allowance (Option 1), he would pay tax on:

Rental income	9,360
Less: expenses	(£7,500)
	1,860

If Clive were to use his actual profit (Option 2), he would pay tax on:

Property income	£9,360
Less: expenses	(£480)
	£8,880

It is therefore much more beneficial for Clive to claim rent-a-room relief and be taxed on £1,860.

Example 7.5

Matthew is a self-employed building contractor. He purchased a commercial premises a number of years ago, which has been let to a tenant since the purchase. He made a loss on his property income in 2020/21 of £10,000. During the 2021/22 tax year he invested in two new properties. Matthew has supplied you with the following information for the year to 5 April 2022.

Existing commercial premises

The premises was originally purchased for £1,500,000 in 2014, funded by a bank loan. Interest payable on the loan in the year ended 5 April 2022 was £65,000. The original tenant rented the property for £18,000 per month, but vacated the premises on 30 June 2021 when the lease ended. A new tenant rented the property from 1 August 2021 and the agreed rent was £210,000 per annum, payable annually in advance. During the period when the property was vacant, routine maintenance and decorating was carried out at a cost of £12,500. The insurance premium for the year ended 5 April 2022 was £2,200 and Matthew paid rates of £15,750 for the year.

New property 1

On 1 May 2021 Matthew bought a residential property for £550,000. Before letting, a small extension needed to be added to the property to make it rentable at a cost of £35,000, and £8,000 was spent on new furniture and appliances. The property was only available for letting, fully furnished, from 1 July 2021 at an annual rent of £48,000, payable on a monthly basis in advance. The following expenses were paid during the year ended 5 April 2022:

▦ Rates (from 1 May 2021 to 31 March 2022)	£1,985
▦ Insurance (from 1 May 2021 to 30 April 2022)	£640
▦ Legal fees to collect unpaid rent in January 2022	£440
▦ Repairs to broken toilet and boiler in November 2021	£3,577

New property 2

On 1 August 2021, Matthew purchased another residential property for £375,000, partially funded by a £300,000 bank loan with 4% interest payable annually. The property was immediately advertised for rent and new tenants moved in on 1 October 2021. The annual rent is £26,400, payable annually in advance. The property is let furnished and the following expenses were paid during the year ended 5 April 2022:

▦ Rates (from 1 August 2021 to 31 March 2022)	£3,300
▦ Insurance (from 1 August 2021 to 31 July 2022)	£470
▦ Legal fees for purchase of property	£2,100
▦ General repairs and maintenance	£330
▦ Replacement of a bed and fridge (similar standard)	£3,500

Matthew also lets a room in his own private residence to a tenant and in the 2021/22 tax year he received £9,000 and had £735 of allowable expenses.

Calculate Matthew's property business income for 2021/22.

As rental receipts exceed £150,000, the accruals basis of accounting will apply (not the cash basis).

	£	£
Commercial Property		
Rental income – original tenant (£18,000 × 3)		54,000
Rental income – new tenant (£210,000/12 × 8)		140,000
		194,000
Less: expenses:		
Loan interest (no restriction as commercial)	65,000	
Maintenance & decorating	12,500	
Insurance	2,200	
Rates	15,750	
Rental profit for commercial property		(95,450)
		98,550

continued overleaf

New Property 1

Rental income – new tenant (£48,000/12 × 9)		<u>36,000</u>
		36,000
Less: expenses:		
Extension & furniture (not allowable)	0	
Rates	1,985	
Insurance (£640/12 × 11)	587	
Legal fees re. unpaid rent	440	
Repairs	<u>3,577</u>	
	–	<u>(6,589)</u>
Rental profit for new property 1		29,411

New Property 2

Rental income – new tenant (£26,400/12 × 6)		<u>13,200</u>
		13,200
Less: expenses		
Loan interest (Note) (£300,000 × 4% × 8/12 × 25%)	2,000	
Rates	3,300	
Insurance (£470/12 × 8)	313	
Legal fees for purchase of property (not allowable)	0	
Repairs	330	
Replacement furniture relief	<u>3,500</u>	
		<u>(7443)</u>
Rental profit for new property 2		5757

Note: a basic rate tax reduction may be available in respect of 100% of the finance costs when calculating the income tax liability for the year.

Rent-a-room relief

Choice of being taxed on:

Option 1

Income	9,000
Less: exempt amount	<u>(7,500)</u>
Taxable profit	1,500

Or

Option 2

Income	9,000
Less: allowable expenses	<u>(735)</u>
Taxable profit	8,265

Matthew would choose to be taxed on the basis of rent-a-room relief (Option 1).

Total property income for 2021/22	135,218
Less: loss forward from 2020/21	<u>(10,000)</u>
Taxable property income for 2021/22	125,218

Questions

Review Questions
(See Suggested Solutions to Review Questions at the end of this textbook.)

Question 7.1

Mr O'Reilly owns five properties that he lets. Details of his income from these properties and the letting terms are as follows.

Property A (residential property) Acquired in November 2017 and let on a five-year lease, expiring in November 2022, at a monthly rent of £500, payable monthly in advance. Interest of £11,000 was incurred during the year on a bank loan taken out to acquire the property.

Property B (commercial property) Acquired on 1 April 2020 and let for the first time on 1 August 2021, on a 21-year lease at a full annual rent of £12,000, payable monthly in advance. A bank loan was raised to help purchase the property and interest of £3,600 was paid on 30 June 2021 and £3,600 on 31 December 2021. A premium of £10,000 was also received under the terms of the new lease.

Property C (residential property) Let at a full annual rent of £6,000 (payable on the 25th day of each month) under a seven-year lease, which expired on 30 April 2021. The property was vacant until 1 November 2021, when it was let again on a five-year lease at a full rent of £9,000 per annum (payable on the 25th day of each month).

Property D (residential property) Let to Mr O'Reilly's brother on a 21-year lease from 1 May 2008, at an annual rent of £52 (not a full rent).

The landlord is responsible for repairs on all properties, except for Property A, in respect of which there is a "tenants's repairing" lease. During the tax year 2020/21, the following additional expenses were incurred:

		£
Property B		
30 April	Dry rot repairs	950
30 June	Window broken by vandals	80
31 December	Storm damage	1,400
Property C		
20 May	Blocked drains	90
31 July	Painting	700
31 October	Advertising for tenant	130
Property D		
28 September	Roof repairs	1,600

Requirement
Compute Mr O'Reilly's UK property business income for the tax year 2020/21.

Question 7.2

Sonya, a widow aged 47, has recently brought you details of her property income, which will be needed to prepare schedules supporting her tax return. All properties are non-residential properties. Relevant information is as follows.

- Property 1 is let on a 10-year lease. The lease was granted in December 2019 at an annual rent of £160,000, payable monthly in arrears, subject to review every three years.
- Property 2 is let at a rent of £8,000 per annum, payable monthly in advance.
- Property 3 is let at a rent of £9,600 per annum, payable monthly in advance. The instalment of rent due on 1 December 2020 was never received. This property was first let some years ago.
- Property 4 was first let on a 15-year lease on 30 June 2021 and a rent of £9,000 per annum payable quarterly in arrears on 30 September, 31 December, 30 March and 30 June, subject to review every three years.
- Property 5 is let on a 15-year lease, expiring June 2022, at a nominal rent of £10 per month, payable annually in advance on 30 June. The tenant is Sonya's sister.

The expenses (all allowable) paid in 2021 by Sonya for each property were:

	£
Property 1	4,300
Property 2	1,200
Property 3	800
Property 4	NIL
Property 5	10

In addition, mortgage interest of £1,400 was paid on a loan to finance the purchase of Property 3.

Requirement
Prepare a schedule summarising Sonya's UK property business income assessable in 2021/22.

Question 7.3

In 2021/22, Josephine had taxable trading income of £40,000 from her retail business. She also received residential rental income of £14,375 during 2021/22. In December 2021, she incurred repair costs of £7,000 in respect of water damage due to a burst pipe in the rented residential property. She also paid finance costs of £22,500 on the mortgage she took out to acquire the rented residential property.

Requirement
Calculate Josephine's property rental profit and income tax liability for 2021/22.

Deductions on Income, Allowances and Reliefs

Learning Objectives

After studying this chapter you will be able to:

■ Compute the income tax payable by individuals.
■ Apply the income tax relief for contributions to registered pension schemes.
■ Apply the income tax relief for interest on loans.

8.1 Introduction

In **Chapter 2** the income tax computation pro forma was outlined, which provided an overview for the steps and calculations required to calculate income tax liability. In each of the subsequent chapters dealing with the specific types of income, the pro forma layout has been used first to determine "total income", then to calculate "taxable income" and finally to compute the income tax. In doing so we have encountered some of the more universal reliefs and allowances that are available to reduce a taxpayer's income tax liability. In this chapter we will consider all the various deductions, allowances and reliefs in greater detail.

To refresh, the pro forma income tax computation is shown overleaf (**Figure 8.1**). There are three areas of the computation that we will look at in turn:

1. "qualifying reliefs" – which are deducted from total income to give "net income";
2. "pension contributions and gift aid donations" – which are tax reliefs at the marginal rate; and
3. "personal allowances" – which are deducted from net income to give "taxable income".

FIGURE 8.1: PRO FORMA INCOME TAX COMPUTATION

	Non-savings Income £	Savings Income £	Dividend Income £	Total £
Gross income:				
Trading income	xx			xx
Property income	xx			xx
Employment/pension income	xx			xx
Savings and investment income:				
Bank/building society interest		xx		xx
NS & I account interest		xx		xx
UK dividends			xx	xx
Step 1 **Total income**	xxx	xxx	xxx	xxx
Less: specified reliefs	(xx)	(xx)	(xx)	(xx)
Step 2 **Net income**	xxx	xxx	xxx	xxx
Less: personal allowance	(max.12,570)			(max.12,570)
Step 3 **Taxable income**	xxxx	xxxx	xxxx	xxxx

	£
Step 4 **Income tax:**	
Non-savings income:	
£ × 20%	xxxx
£ × 40%	xxxx
£ × 45%	xxxx
Savings income:	
£ × 0% (starting limit for savings income and personal savings allowance, if available)	0
£ × 20%	xxxx
£ × 40%	xxxx
£ × 45%	xxxx
Dividend income:	£
Up to £2,000 dividend allowance × 0%	0
£ × 7.5%	xxxx
£ × 32.5%	xxxx
£ × 38.1%	xxxx
Step 5 **Total**	xxxx
Step 6 **Less: basic rate tax reduction for property finance costs**	(xxx)
Step 7 **Add: additional tax (e.g. child benefit income tax charge)**	xxx
Step 8 **Less: tax deducted at source**	(xxx)
Result Income tax liability/(refund)	xxx

8.2   Qualifying Reliefs

In the income tax computation, total income has qualifying reliefs deducted to arrive at "adjusted net income".

8.2.1   Relief for Eligible Interest

Interest charged on certain loans is eligible for income tax relief. As with the other qualifying reliefs, it operates by deducting the qualifying amount (the interest paid) from total income to give net income for a particular tax year (the tax year in which the interest has been **paid**).

The following loans are eligible for this relief:

- Loan to purchase an interest in a partnership.
- Loan to buy ordinary shares in, or to lend money to, a close company that the taxpayer manages, or in which they own more than 5% of the ordinary shares.
- Loan for the purchase of shares in an employee-controlled company, where the taxpayer is an employee.
- Loan to pay inheritance tax (allowable for a period of one year).

It is important to note from the list above that an eligible loan can be for business (trading) purposes, for investment purposes or, in the case of a loan to pay inheritance tax, for individual reasons. The purpose of the loan will determine from what class of income the interest paid should be deducted and, in some cases, on what basis it is assessed. For example, a taxpayer paying interest "wholly and exclusively" for business purposes can deduct interest against trading profits and it is tax deductible on an **accruals** basis, not on a **paid** basis.

Interest on an eligible loan is deducted from non-savings income first; then, if there is any interest amount remaining, it is deducted from savings income; and, lastly, any remaining amount will be deducted from dividend income.

Example 8.1

Janice has employment income of £50,570 and savings income of £5,000 in 2021/22. She also paid interest of £2,000 on a loan for the purchase of an interest in a partnership.

	Non-savings income	Savings income
	£	£
Income sources		
Employment income	50,570	
Savings income	_____	5,000
Total income	**50,570**	**5,000**
Less: qualifying reliefs	(2,000)	–
Net income	48,570	5,000
Less: personal allowances	(12,570)	_____
Taxable income	36,000	5,000

8.2.2   Gifts of Shares or Land to Charity

Gifts of qualifying investments to a UK charity are eligible for income tax relief as a qualifying relief. The following categories of investment qualify for the relief:

■ shares or securities that are listed on any recognised stock exchange, e.g. the London Stock Exchange and the New York Stock Exchange;

■ shares and securities dealt on any designated market in the UK, e.g. the Alternative Investment Market (AIM) of the London Stock Exchange; and

■ a qualifying interest in land.

As with the other qualifying reliefs, it operates by deducting the qualifying amount (the amount gifted) from total income to give net income for a particular tax year (the tax year in which the gift is made). The value of the gift of qualifying assets that is eligible for relief is deducted first from non-savings income; then, if there is any amount remaining, it is deducted from savings income; and lastly, any remaining amount will be deducted from dividend income.

8.3   Pension Contributions and Gift Aid Donations

Relief for pension contributions and gift aid donations are given at an individual's marginal rate of tax. An individual's marginal rate of tax is the highest rate of tax they pay.

8.3.1   Pension Contributions

Introduction

The Government aims to incentivise saving through pensions. It does this by offering tax relief to individuals who pay contributions to their pension schemes, allowing the pension schemes to grow tax-free. Each year an individual is limited on the amount that they can invest in a pension and a breach of these limits will mean that a tax charge will be incurred (see **Annual Allowance** section below). The size to which a pension fund can grow to be tax-free is also restricted (see **Lifetime Allowance** section below).

Where an individual is an employee, they will pay into their work/occupational pension scheme. Their employer will normally also contribute to the pension scheme on the employee's behalf. Auto-enrolment requires employers to automatically enrol most of their employees into a workplace pension scheme, although an employee may opt out of the auto-enrolment scheme. Legally, an employer is required to make minimum contributions to the workplace pension scheme. Where an individual is self-employed (or where an employee finds that their employer does not offer an occupational scheme), they can contribute to a personal pension scheme.

A pension scheme may be either a defined benefits scheme or a defined contribution scheme. In a defined benefits pension scheme (also known as a final salary scheme) the benefits payable to members are usually based on final salary (or career-average salary) and length of service. In a defined contribution scheme (also known as a money purchase scheme), the benefits payable to members are based on the size of the pension fund built up during a member's working life.

In addition, pension schemes can be either registered, i.e. formally approved by HMRC in accordance with tax legislation, or unregistered. Income tax relief is only available on registered pension schemes (see below for more details); unregistered schemes are liable to income tax.

Registered pension schemes include:

■ occupational pension schemes (including workplace pension schemes) – schemes set up by an employer for its employees;
■ public service pension schemes – schemes set up by Government, e.g. the civil service pension scheme; or
■ personal pension schemes – schemes set up by a financial institution for an individual's private contributions.

As already noted, registered pension schemes enjoy certain tax advantages. For example, they are exempt from income tax (and from CGT on capital gains arising on the disposal of investments). Tax relief is available in relation to contributions made by members and employers. Tax-free lump sums may be paid to members.

Income Tax Relief on Registered Pension Schemes

Income tax relief on an individual's contributions to a registered pension scheme is dependent on the rate of income tax paid by the individual: a basic rate taxpayer will receive relief at 20%; a higher rate taxpayer's relief will be 40%; and an additional rate taxpayer's relief will be at 45%.

Basic rate tax relief is generally deducted at source, i.e. net of tax; it is then 'repaid' by HMRC into the individual's pension scheme. Higher rate relief operates by increasing the upper limit of the basic rate tax band (£37,700) by the individual's **gross** contributions and applying the higher rate tax relief. The proportion of the relief applicable to the basic rate is deducted at source, i.e. net at 20% tax; the remaining relief, the higher rate, is claimed by the individual through their year-end tax return.

Example 8.2

Sara pays a personal pension contribution of £8,000 (net) to her private pension scheme. What is the position if Sara is:

1. a basic rate taxpayer?
2. A higher rate taxpayer?

1. The £8,000 contribution is net, the basic rate tax of 20% having been paid at source. Sara's gross contribution is £10,000 (100/80 × £8,000), so HMRC re-pays the 20% (£2,000) into the scheme on her behalf.
2. Sara's basic rate band is increased by the gross pension contribution: £37,500 + £10,000 = £47,500. Overall 40% income tax relief is available, 20% deducted at source (£2,000) and 20% through Sara's year-end tax return.

For occupational pension schemes only, an alternative method of administering the relief is available whereby the individual's (the employee's) gross contributions are deducted from their gross pay, i.e. before PAYE is deducted. This arrangement is referred to as a "net pay arrangement". The individual therefore obtains tax relief on the pension contributions at their marginal rate of tax without having to make a claim.

Example 8.3

Sara has an occupational pension scheme into which she pays £10,000 under a net pay arrangement. Her gross salary is £60,570.

Under the net pay arrangement the contribution to the pension fund is deducted from gross pay to give taxable pay of £50,570 on which PAYE is operated.

	£
Employment income	60,570
Less: pension contributions	(10,000)
Net income	50,570
Less: personal allowance	(12,570)
Taxable income	38,000
Income tax: non-savings income	
£37,700 × 20%	7,540
£300 × 40%	120
	7,660

Sara is therefore saving tax at the marginal rate (40%) as, instead of having £10,300 taxable at 40%, she has £300 only.

If Sara was a basic rate taxpayer, the relief would have been 20%. No separate claim would be required to obtain this relief (and there would be no need to extend the basic rate band).

Annual Allowance

The annual allowance is a 'ceiling' on the amount of pension contributions (an individual's and an employer's, if applicable) that can benefit from the tax relief. It does not restrict the amount of tax relief; instead it applies a charge, the **"annual allowance charge"**, when the annual allowance has been exceeded. In effect, the charge reverses the relief on the excess amount over the annual allowance. What this means is that if the amount paid into a pension exceeds the annual allowance, this does not mean that the relief is restricted to the annual allowance. Rather, the relief available is the greater of either:

- an individual's **"relevant UK earnings"** (subject to the annual allowance); or,
- if an individual does not have any relevant UK earnings in a tax year, £3,600.

"Relevant UK earnings" includes income from self-employment and employment. Investment and property income do not qualify as relevant earnings and therefore cannot increase a taxpayer's capacity to make pension contributions.

The annual allowance for 2021/22 is £40,000.

If an individual's gross contributions in a tax year (including any from an employer) exceed the annual allowance, the excess contributions are liable to income tax. This is known as the **annual allowance charge** and is calculated on the individual's marginal tax rate (i.e. top rate).

Example 8.4
Joseph had employment income of £190,000 in 2021/22. He made gross personal pension contributions of £60,000 in 2021/22.

Joseph's income tax position is as follows:

	£
Total income	190,000
Personal allowance	
(as adjusted net income over £125,140. See **Section 8.4**)	Nil
Taxable income	190,000
Income tax on savings income:	
£37,700 × 20%	7,540
£60,000 × 20%	12,000
£92,300 × 40%	36,920
£190,000	56,460
Add excess pension contribution	
£20,000 × 40% (Note 1)	8,000
	64,460

Note:
1. Excess pension contribution is £20,000 (£60,000 – £20,000 = £40,000 annual allowance amount).

Where the individual is an employee, if the **employer contributes to the pension scheme, these are exempt benefits**. There is no limit to the amount of the contributions that may be made by an employer, but they will count towards the individual's annual allowance (see above). An employer can contribute into an occupational scheme or into an individual's personal pension scheme but, in either case, the contributions will always be made **gross**. This is a tax-deductible expense for the employer if made **wholly and exclusively** for business purposes. On some occasions, the employer may have to **spread** the tax relief on large contributions over a number of accounting periods.

An individual may have more than one pension scheme at a time, e.g. an occupational scheme and a private pension; however, the maximum limit on contributions applies to all the pension contributions made, **not** to each of them separately.

Lifetime Allowance
There is no limit on the amount of benefits an individual can be paid from a pension scheme; however, the amount that can be received without suffering income tax is subject to the lifetime allowance. Like the annual allowance, the lifetime allowance operates by applying a charge (the **lifetime allowance charge**) for payments received that exceed the limit.

The lifetime allowance for the 2021/22 tax year is £1,073,100 (£1,073,100 in 2020/21).

The lifetime allowance is 'used' when a "benefit crystallisation event" occurs. The most common examples of such an event are the payment of a lump sum to a member or the commencement of pension benefits.

The value of the crystallised benefit is compared with the unused proportion of the lifetime allowance and any excess is charged to income tax. Whenever a benefit crystallisation event occurs, it is necessary to compare the value of the benefits that have crystallised with the proportion of the individual's lifetime allowance that remain unused after any previous such events. On the first occasion that a benefit crystallisation event occurs, the value of the benefits that have crystallised is compared with the lifetime allowance as it stands on the date of the event. On a subsequent event, the value of the crystallised benefits is compared with the proportion of the lifetime allowance (if any) that remains after previous events. However, this proportion is applied to the lifetime allowance as it stands on the date of the subsequent event.

The lifetime allowance charge is either 55% or 25% of the excess amount received, depending on whether it has been taken as a lump sum (55%) or as pension income (25%). The charge falls jointly upon the scheme administrator and the member concerned. In practice, it will usually be paid by the scheme administrator and then deducted from the benefits paid to the individual.

Example 8.5

Jeff is 60 years old in 2021/22 and decides to access his pension on retirement. His pension fund was valued at £1,855,000 on retirement. He receives a lump sum of £268,275 (i.e. a tax-free lump sum of pension pot, or lifetime allowance if pension pot exceeds £1,073,100 (£1,073,100 × 25%)) tax-free and buys an annuity for £804,825 to provide him with pension income. The remaining £781,900 over the lifetime allowance of £1,073,100 is taken as a lump sum.

Jeff will be subject to a lifetime allowance charge of £781,900 × 55% = £430,045.

Retirement Benefits

Unless retiring due to ill health, pensions will not normally be allowed to be paid out of a pension scheme until the individual member reaches normal pension age of 55 years.

All or part of the pension fund can be taken to provide pension benefits at any time from age 55 onwards. It is therefore possible to receive a pension and still continue to work.

As noted above, if the fund value exceeds the lifetime allowance, the excess is charged to income tax at differing rates, depending on how the excess is used, as explained above.

A tax-free lump sum payment of up to 25% of the lower of the fund value or the lifetime allowance can be paid out of the scheme; but a tax-free lump sum cannot be taken and recycled into future pension contributions to obtain double tax relief.

Defined Contributions Pension Schemes

Individuals with defined contribution pension savings have three main options when accessing their pension benefits. From age 55, individuals can choose any one option or a combination of them.

1. Individuals can purchase an annuity – a tax-free lump sum of 25% of the pension pot can be taken, with the remainder being used to purchase an annuity that will provide income for the rest of the person's life (subject to income tax on receipt).
2. Individuals can draw down funds – a tax-fee lump sum of 25% of the pension pot can be taken at the same time the funds are put into drawdown. The drawdown funds are invested and the individual can decide how much to take each year (taxed as income).
3. Individuals can take multiple lump sum payments from the pension pot – 25% of each lump sum will be tax-free, with the remainder being taxed as income. The lump sums are referred to as "uncrystallised funds pension lump sum" (UFPLS).

Defined Benefits Pension Scheme

The benefits from a defined benefit scheme depend upon length of service, pensionable earnings, etc. and are received in line with the rules set out by the scheme. Therefore individuals with defined benefit pension savings do not have the same options with regard to accessing their benefits. However, individuals can transfer from a defined benefit scheme to a defined contribution scheme to avail of the greater flexibility (although, traditionally, defined benefit schemes tend to provide valuable benefits and any transfer should be carefully considered).

Pension income is taxable as non-savings income. A pension provider will provide each pensioner with a Form P60 (see **Chapter 9**), showing details of their gross pension and the tax deducted at source.

8.3.2   Gift Aid Donations

Charitable donations made under gift aid are paid net of basic rate tax. This has the effect of giving basic rate tax relief when the payment is made.

Example 8.6

Nigel would like to give his local charity £1,000; to do so he need only donate £800. The charity can reclaim Nigel's tax relief on the £800 donation (20% = £200) from HMRC.

Gift aid donations attract relief at the donor's highest, or marginal, rate of tax. This is done by extending the taxpayer's basic rate band by the grossed-up amount for higher rate taxpayers; and by extending both the basic rate and higher rate bands if they are an additional rate taxpayer (i.e. similar to the way tax relief on pension contributions is given, see **Section 8.3.1**). No additional tax relief is due for basic rate taxpayers. As shown in the example, the charity will claim a basis rate taxpayer's tax relief.

Gifts can be once-off or part of a series of donations, and there is no minimum or maximum amount that can be donated. The donor must give an appropriate declaration to the charity concerned either in writing, by telephone, by fax or via the internet.

Example 8.7

Jean is 71 years old. In 2021/22 she receives income from property of £56,750. She makes a gift aid donation of £100. Calculate the tax payable by Jean.

Income Tax Computation 2021/22		£
Property income		56,750
Net income		56,750
Less: personal allowance		(12,570)
Taxable income		44,180
Income tax due:		
Basic rate:	£37,700 @ 20%	7,540
Extended basic rate (Note 1)	£125 @ 20%	25
Higher rate	£6,355 @ 40%	2,542
	£44,180	
Tax liability		10,107

Note:
1. The gift aid donation is paid net of £25 tax (£100 × 20/80) and higher rate tax relief is given by extending the basic rate band by the grossed-up donation.

Note: **sufficient tax must be paid by the donor to cover the basic rate repayment to the charity**. If a donor pays insufficient tax, it may be necessary to restrict their personal allowance or to raise an assessment to ensure that the tax paid to the charity has been paid by the individual.

Payroll Giving Scheme

Charitable donations may be deducted from gross employment earnings before tax is calculated. The employer must obtain HMRC approval to operate the scheme. The employer passes the donation on to the approved charity.

The donation made by an employee under a payroll giving scheme is an allowable deduction from the employee's earnings for income tax purposes. The tax relief is given at source as the employee will only pay tax on their salary, less the donations. Under the payroll giving scheme, if an individual is a basic rate taxpayer, and the individual authorises a monthly donation of £10 to charity, the individual will save £2 tax (20% of £10). Therefore, the actual cost of the donation to the individual is £8. If, for example, an individual is a higher rate taxpayer (i.e. 40%) and they authorise a monthly donation of £10 under the payroll giving scheme, they will save £4 tax (40% of £10) and the actual cost of the donation to the taxpayer is £6.

Example 8.8

Anne is a higher rate taxpayer, with employment income of £80,000 in 2021/22. Anne wishes to donate £50 via her employer's payroll giving scheme to her favourite charity. Anne's employer pays all the administration costs associated with running the payroll giving scheme.

Anne will have £50 deducted from her wages before tax. By having this amount deducted from her wages, her favourite charity will receive £50. Anne, as a higher rate taxpayer, will pay tax of £20 (£50 × 40%) as a result of making the donation. Therefore, the actual cost of the donation to her will be £30 (£50 donated from gross salary, i.e. a tax saving of £20).

8.4 Personal Allowances

When all an individual's income has been aggregated and the qualifying reliefs have been deducted, the result is the individual's net income from which personal allowances are deducted (see pro forma in **Section 8.1**).

8.4.1 Standard Personal Allowance

A personal allowance of £12,570 for 2021/22 can be claimed by any individual who is in receipt of any income and who is UK resident (whether UK domiciled or not); and by some non-UK residents, e.g. citizens from the European Economic Area (EEA), Isle of Man or Channel Islands. The personal allowance is deducted from net income, first from non-savings income, then from savings income and lastly from investment income (dividends).

In year of death, separation or divorce, full personal allowances are awarded. Therefore no apportionment is required.

Restriction on Standard Personal Allowance

The standard personal allowance is abated (reduced) where an individual's "adjusted net income" (see **Section 8.1**) is in excess of £100,000. For every £2 above £100,000, the standard personal allowance is reduced by £1. So, for example, adjusted net income of £110,000 would mean that the standard personal allowance would be reduced to £7,570 (£12,570 – £5,000). This restriction applies until the allowance is removed entirely; therefore, if your income is £125,140 or more, your personal allowance is zero.

It is for this reason that financial planning, such as pension contributions, is particularly important in reducing tax liability – by bringing adjusted net income below the £100,000 threshold, thus preserving personal allowances.

8.4.2   Blind Person's Allowance

If a taxpayer is registered as blind, the blind person's allowance can be claimed. This is in **addition** to the standard personal allowance and is £2,520 for 2021/22. A claim can also be made in the tax year before registration if blindness can be proved in that year.

The allowance is set against the taxpayer's net income and gives tax relief at the marginal rate (i.e. the highest rate at which the taxpayer pays tax). If all or part of the blind person's allowance cannot be fully used by one spouse/civil partner, then the unused portion can be transferred to the other spouse/civil partner, even if they are not a registered blind person.

8.4.3   Marriage Allowance

The marriage allowance lets an individual transfer £1,260 of his or her personal allowance to their husband/wife/civil partner. The marriage allowance can reduce an individual's tax by up to £252 (i.e. £1,260 × 20%) in the 2021/22 tax year.

For a couple to benefit from the marriage allowance, the lower earning spouse/civil partner must have an income of £12,570 or less. The higher earning spouse/civil partner must have income between £12,571 and £50,000 (i.e. they must be a basic rate taxpayer). In addition, both spouses/civil partners must be born on or after 6 April 1935 to be eligible for the marriage allowance.

8.4.4   Summary: Personal Allowances Rates and Thresholds

	2020/21 £	2021/22 £
Standard personal allowance	12,500	12,570
Income limit for personal allowances	100,000	100,000
Marriage allowance	1,250	1,260
Blind person's allowance	2,500	2,520

Questions

Review Questions
(See Suggested Solutions to Review Questions at the end of this textbook.)

Question 8.1

Jane and John are married. John was born in August 1948 and has income of £20,500 (pension) in the 2021/22 tax year. Jane was born in March 1946 and has no income.

Requirement
Calculate John's tax liability for the 2021/22 tax year.

Question 8.2

Mr Smith was born in January 1946 and is married. He has total taxable income before personal allowances of £34,400. His spouse has income of £15,000.

Requirement
Compute Mr Smith's tax liability for 2021/22.

Question 8.3

Joe has total income from his employment of £51,975 in 2021/22. He has taken out a loan of £40,000 to invest in 10% of the share capital of a close company run by his neighbour. Interest on the loan was £1,000 in the year.

He made a gift aid donation of £780 to a registered charity in the tax year.

Requirement
Compute Joe's tax liability for 2021/22.

Question 8.4

Rachel was born in March 1944. John was born in September 1947 and has no taxable income. Rachel's non-savings income was £60,500 in 2021/22, arising from a sole trade. She also received UK dividend income of £600.

Requirement
Compute Rachel's tax liability for 2021/22.

Question 8.5

Mr Frost is an employee of ABC Ltd and earned £30,500 in 2021/22. He suffered PAYE of £5,000.

He gave shares in BT Group plc, with a market value of £780, to Action Cancer, a registered charity, in the tax year.

He also gave £780 to his local Action Cancer shop's appeal. He has signed a gift aid declaration with Action Cancer.

Requirement
Compute Mr Frost's tax liability for 2021/22, and the amount of income tax reclaimable by Action Cancer.

Question 8.6

Compare and contrast the tax relief available on charitable donations made using gift aid and pay-roll giving donations.

Question 8.7

(a) Brian has no taxable income in 2021/22.
    What is his maximum pension contribution on which tax relief is available and why?

(b) Brian has employment income of £400,000 in 2021/22.
   What is his maximum pension contribution on which tax relief is available and why?
(c) Brian has employment income of £40,000 and property income of £10,000 in 2021/22.
   What is his maximum pension contribution on which tax relief is available and why?
(d) Brian has employment income of £50,000 and trading income of £60,000 in 2021/22.
   What is his maximum pension contribution on which tax relief is available and why?

Question 8.8

Sarah has trading income of £50,000 in 2021/22 and makes a gross pension contribution of £20,000 in the year. She also pays interest on a loan to buy into a qualifying partnership of £1,000.

Requirement
Compute Sarah's tax liability for 2021/22, and outline how the £20,000 will physically get into her pension fund.

Question 8.9

Irwin has gross employment income of £32,000, property income of £5,500 and dividend income of £9,000. PAYE of £7,000 was suffered. He also gifted £18,000 of quoted shares to a registered charity in 2021/22.

Requirement
Compute Irwin's income tax for 2021/22.

The PAYE System and National Insurance Contributions

Learning Objectives

After studying this chapter you will be able to:

- Explain the scope of the PAYE system, including the operation of Real Time Information (RTI).
- Calculate liability under the PAYE system given an individual's details regarding remuneration and benefits in kind.
- Determine and calculate the national insurance contributions (NICs) payable for Classes 1, 1A, 2, 3 and 4.
- Consider the NICs payable by a taxpayer who is both employed and self-employed in the same tax year.

The Chartered Accountants Ireland *Code of Ethics* applies to all aspects of a Chartered Accountant's professional life, including dealing with PAYE issues. As outlined at the beginning of this book, further information regarding the principles in the *Code of Ethics* is set out in **Appendix 2**.

9.1 Introduction

Pay As You Earn (PAYE) is the method used by HMRC to collect income tax and national insurance contributions (NICs) on most **employment** income and pensions. Broadly speaking, it obliges an employer to deduct income tax and NICs from wages, salaries and other payments made to employees, such as bonuses, commission, vouchers exchangeable for cash, etc., **when the remuneration is actually paid**.

The PAYE system is a good example of the principle of deduction of **tax at source**, whereby the **payer** (the employer), and **not** the **recipient** (the employee) of the income is liable to account for the income tax and other deductions to HMRC. It is the employer that must account to HMRC for the tax/NICs deducted. Under PAYE, tax and other deductions are paid on a **cumulative basis**, i.e. each time the employee is paid. In this way much of the administrative cost involved in collecting income tax is, in effect, imposed on the employer. In recent years, the operation of PAYE has been significantly altered with the introduction of Real Time Information (RTI).

Although PAYE is most frequently used to collect income tax and NICs, it is also the mechanism used by HMRC to collect student loan repayments and CIS deductions (see **Chapter 11**).

In this chapter we will look in detail at how the PAYE system operates on a cumulative basis throughout the year, and the method by which HMRC allocates tax codes and how they are calculated. The operation of RTI is discussed, as well as the numerous payment methods available and the penalties that employers are exposed to if they do not operate correctly within the filing and payment deadlines. Finally, we will look at the national insurance contribution categories that currently exist.

9.2 Calculating Income Tax through PAYE and Tax Codes

9.2.1 Calculating Income Tax through PAYE

PAYE is designed to collect tax from employees on a cumulative basis. To calculate income tax on a cumulative basis, specific steps need to be followed.

1 **Step 1** Calculate gross pay to date.

2 **Step 2** Deduct employee's allowances to date.

3 **Step 3** Calculate income tax due to date.

4 **Step 4** Deduct tax already paid.

5 **Step 5** Finally, calculate tax due for the month/week.

Example 9.1

Pamela earned £4,400 in the months to 5 May 2021, 5 June 2021 and 5 July 2021, and paid PAYE of £700 each month. In the month to 5 August 2021, she earned £4,500. She is entitled to a personal allowance of £12,500 for 2021/22.

What PAYE will be deducted from Pamela's salary in the month to 5 August 2021?

		£
1.	Cumulative pay to date £4,400 × 3 + £4,500	17,700
2.	Personal allowances to date are £12,570 × 4/12	(4,190)
	Taxable pay	13,510
3.	Income tax due to date	
	£37,700 × 4/12 = £12,567 @ 20%	2,513
	£13,510 − £12,567 = £943 @ 40%	377
	Tax liability for year to date	2,890
4.	Less: tax paid to date £700 × 3	(2,100)
5.	Tax due in month to 5 August 2021	790

9.2.2 Tax Codes

Essentially a tax code is a shorthand 'instruction' from HMRC to an employer to explain how an employee's income should be taxed. All employees are assigned a tax code by HMRC.

When determining tax codes, the amount of the personal allowance is reduced by benefits in kind (BIKs) (see **Section 5.4.3**). If BIK exceeds the personal allowance, then a K code applies. This is a negative code, which is added to (rather than deducted from) pay. The K code is subject to a regulatory upper limit of up to 50% of gross pay.

Tax codes consist of numbers and/or letters. For example, the tax code for an individual who is entitled to the standard personal allowance is 1257L, being £12,570 divided by 10.

A D0 code means that all the employee's pay should be taxed at the higher rate; and a D1 code means that the additional rate of tax should be applied to an employee's pay.

A K code followed by one to four numbers means that additional tax for benefits is to be deducted (total allowances are less than total deductions). For example, an individual with the tax code K200 effectively has a negative tax code of £2,000. They are deemed to have taxable income of £2,000 that will increase their tax liability for the year. Such negative tax codes may arise as a result of a benefit in kind received and/or underpayments from previous years.

Some tax codes have letters only. For example:

BR = all of the employee's pay should be taxed at the basic rate, i.e. no tax-free allowances.

NT = no tax is to be deducted.

An employee's tax code may have a 'W1' or 'M1' at the end. W1 (week 1) and M1 (month 1) are **emergency tax codes** and appear at the end of an employee's tax code. Where a W1 or M1 is present, the employee's tax should be calculated only on what they are paid in the current pay period, not the whole year.

Tax codes generally change each tax year due to changes to the personal allowance. For 2020/21 the personal allowance was £12,500. A change in an employee's circumstances will also affect their tax code.

HMRC will collect an underpayment of tax (on amounts up to £3,000) by reducing an individual's tax code for the next tax year. For example, if an individual is a higher rate taxpayer and had £1,000 of underpaid tax in 2020/21, then their tax code for 2021/22 would be 1007L (i.e. £12,570 personal allowance less £2,500 (i.e. £1,000/40%) underpayment equates to £10,070, and divided by 10 = 1,007)

An employer **must not alter** an employee's tax code unless HMRC notifies them to do so.

9.3 The Administration of PAYE: Real Time Information (RTI)

The PAYE system was transformed with the implementation of Real Time Information (RTI), which was introduced to improve its operation, as well as to support the introduction of the Universal Tax Credit. Essentially, RTI collects information on PAYE deductions each time an employer pays an employee. The information is provided by the employer and must be submitted electronically to HMRC on or before the day the employee is paid.

9.3.1 Operation of RTI

The information submitted to RTI is generated by the employer's payroll software or payroll provider. There are a number of different submissions that can be made, the two main ones being:

1. a Full Payment Submission; and
2. an Employer Payment Summary.

A Full Payment Submission (FPS) is made each time an employer makes a payment to an employee, provided that the payment is greater than the "lower earnings limit". The lower earnings limit (LEL) is £120 per week (see **Section 9.5.1**).

An FPS includes details of:

- the amount of total pay to the employee(s) that is taxable, including any BIKs;
- deductions, such as income tax and NICs; and
- if applicable, starting and leaving dates of employees (see below).

An Employer Payment Summary (EPS) is submitted when no payments have been made during a pay period, or no payment has exceeded the LEL. An EPS is also used to notify HMRC of any reductions to payments already submitted. An EPS must be submitted within 14 days of the end of the pay period, i.e. by the 19th of the following month.

In some cases, where there is a reduction in the amount being paid to HMRC, employers may submit an EPS as well as an FPS. This may occur if they need to reduce the amount of PAYE or NICs they pay to HMRC to recover statutory payments (such as maternity pay), Construction Industry Scheme deductions (see **Chapter 11**) and NICs "employment allowance" (see **Section 9.5.1**).

Starting and Leaving Employment

RTI has simplified the administrative burden of reporting and registering the details of employees who commence or leave employment. All the details pertaining to the individual, whether leaving or starting, are provided to HMRC by the employer's FPS.

On leaving an employment, the employer must provide the leaver with their P45. The P45 details the income tax and NICs the individual has paid so far in the tax year.

On commencing employment, the employer must obtain and record certain information that must be submitted on the FPS when the new employee is first paid. The information required is the employee's name, gender, address, date of birth and national insurance number. If the employee has been previously employed and has a P45 from their last employment then this should be given to the new employer. If the new employee does not have a P45, the employer must ask the new employee to declare their previous employment situation in the tax year. For example, have they been receiving any benefits or pensions since the start of the tax year?

The declaration effects the employee's designated tax code (see **Section 9.2.2**) and how much tax the employer must deduct. Depending on the employee's circumstances, they may be entitled to benefit from the personal allowance, they may be taxed on an emergency basis or the employer may have to deduct tax at the basic rate.

An employer is required to keep a written record of the new employee's answers and to include it on their FPS.

9.3.2   Aspects of PAYE Not Affected by RTI

The basics of the PAYE system, such as deductions from payments to employees and the frequency of payments to HMRC, were unchanged with the move to RTI. As noted above, employers still have to provide a P45 to an employee who is leaving, and they must also still provide each employee with a P60 (which indicates how much tax has been paid in the tax year) if applicable. Employees' expenses and benefits in kind (and the associated national insurance contributions) are also still reported on form P11D.

In terms of the administration required for expense payments being made to employees, an exemption system is in place for certain expenses (e.g. business travel, phone bills, business entertainment expenses, uniforms and tools for work) paid to employees and also for reimbursed expenses. To qualify for an exemption, the employer must be either:

1. paying a flat rate to an employee as part of their earnings – this must be either a benchmark rate or a special ('bespoke') rate approved by HMRC; or
2. paying back the employee's actual costs.

There is no need to apply for an exemption if the employer is paying HMRC's benchmark rates for allowable expenses. An exemption only needs to be applied for if an employer wants to pay bespoke rates to employees.

9.3.3   Payment of PAYE

As noted above, PAYE is used to collect income tax, NICs, student loan deductions and the CIS withheld from subcontractors. It is the employer's responsibility to ensure that payments are remitted to HMRC correctly and on time. Payment can be made either:

- electronically through a bank – cleared payment for the full amount due must reach HMRC by the 22nd of the month (payment options include online/telephone banking, debit/credit card, CHAPS, BACS or direct debit); or
- by cheque (if not required to pay electronically) – payment must be processed by HMRC no later than the 19th of the month.

If an employer's average monthly total for PAYE is less than £1,500, they can choose to pay quarterly, i.e. tax quarters ending 5 July, 5 October, 5 January and 5 April. Cleared electronic payments are due by the 22nd of the month in which the quarter ends or, if paid by cheque, by the earlier date of the 19th of that month.

Large employers, which are those who have 250 or more employees, must make their monthly payments **electronically**.

9.4   Penalties under RTI

There are two main penalties under RTI:

1. in-year late filing penalties; and
2. in-year late payment penalties.

In-year penalties are penalties levied during the tax year rather than after the end of it.

9.4.1   Late Filing Penalties

An employer will incur an in-year late filing penalty for failing to file an FPS on or before payment to the employee (although HMRC have announced that penalties would not be imposed where the delay in filing is three days or less).

In addition, a late filing penalty may be issued where:

- the employer did not send the expected number of FPSs; or
- the employer did not submit an EPS when it should have.

The first instance where an employer fails to file an FPS on time will not incur a penalty; but the penalty will be applied if there is a repeat occurrence at any time in the future.

The amount of the late filing penalty depends on the number of employees within the PAYE scheme (see **Table 9.1**).

TABLE 9.1: PAYE LATE FILING PENALTIES

Number of employees	Amount of monthly penalty
1–9	£100
10–49	£200
50–249	£300
250 or more	£400

Ordinarily, HMRC will send employers a filing penalty notice quarterly (in July, October, January and April) where appropriate. These penalty notices show the amount of the filing penalty for each tax month identified in that quarter. For example, a penalty notice in July will show any filing penalties arising in the first quarter of the tax year – that is, month 1 (6 April–5 May), month 2 (6 May–5 June) and month 3 (6 June–5 July).

Penalties are due for payment 30 days following the date of the penalty notice. Penalties not paid on time will attract interest on a daily basis at a rate of 2.60% per annum (from 7 April 2020).

Additional Penalties – Late Filing

Where a return is late for three months or more and the information that it would have contained has not been provided on a later return, a further penalty may be charged. This additional penalty is set at 5% of the tax/NICs that should have been shown on the late return. This will be used for the most serious and persistent failures.

Again, the penalty payment is due 30 days from the date of the penalty notice; and late payment attracts interest.

9.4.2   Late Payment Penalties

The penalty for late payment depends on the number of late payments in a tax year and the total amount that is paid late. The penalty is calculated as a percentage of the total amount that is late in the relevant tax month (ignoring the first late payment in the tax year) depending on the number of defaults (see **Table 9.2**).

TABLE 9.2: PAYE LATE PAYMENT PENALTIES

Number of defaults in a tax year	Penalty %	Amount to which penalty percentages apply
1–3	1%	
4–6	2%	The total amount that is late in the relevant tax month (ignoring the first late payment in the tax
7–9	3%	year, unless it is more than six months late).
10 or more	4%	

For example, if an employer paid months 2 to 6 late, the first late payment (month 2) is not counted as a default. This means that a penalty of 1% will be charged on the amount paid late for month 3. A penalty of 1% of the months 4 and 5 amounts, and 2% of the month 6 amount (because by month 6, there have been four defaults in the tax year) of PAYE paid late will be charged.

Late payment penalties are usually issued after each quarter. In which case, using the example above, the penalty for the defaults for months 4, 5 and 6 would generally be issued together on one notice from HMRC.

Late payment penalties are not issued automatically; instead they are reviewed and issued on a "risk assessed" basis (i.e. HMRC will review on a case by case basis).

Additional Penalties – Late Payment

If an employer has still not paid a monthly or quarterly amount in full after six months, an additional penalty of 5% of the amounts unpaid is incurred. A further penalty of 5% will be charged if they have not paid the amount after 12 months.

These penalties may be charged in addition to the penalties for monthly and quarterly payments described in the previous section and apply even where only one payment in the tax year is late.

If PAYE has been underpaid, i.e. the amount paid is less than the FPS or EPS declares for the corresponding period, and if the underpayment is not significant, then no penalty is applied. However, daily interest will continue to accrue on all unpaid amounts from the due and payable date to the date of payment.

9.5   National Insurance Contributions

Individuals and employers pay national insurance contributions (NICs). NICs are paid to provide for the State retirement pension, unemployment and sickness benefits; they are collected by HMRC.

NICs are based on an individual's "earnings". "Earnings", from an NIC perspective, comprises gross pay, excluding benefits that cannot be turned into cash by surrender (e.g. holidays). It includes readily convertible assets given to employees (e.g. quoted shares). No deduction is made for employee pension contributions. An employer's contribution to an approved pension scheme is not "earnings" for an employee; however, NICs are due on employer contributions to an unapproved pension scheme.

In general, income and NIC exemptions mirror each other, e.g. a company-provided mobile phone is not "earnings" for tax (see **Section 5.4.3**) or NICs.

In general, non-cash vouchers are subject to NICs. However, the following are exempt:

- Childcare vouchers up to £55 per week or £28 (higher rate taxpayer) and £25 (additional rate taxpayer). The exemption only applies to individuals who joined a childcare voucher scheme on or before 4 October 2018.
- Vouchers for the use of sports and recreational facilities (where tax-exempt).
- Any other voucher that is exempt from income tax.

National insurance is categorised into 'classes' depending on employment status – essentially whether the taxpayer is employed or self-employed and the level of earnings. The principal national insurance classes are:

- Class 1 – an employee's earnings. This includes company directors, although they are subject to slightly different rules.
- Class 1A – an employee's expenses or benefits in kind.
- Class 2 – self-employed earnings above £6,515 per annum.
- Class 3 – voluntary contributions.
- Class 4 – self-employed earnings above £9,568 per annum.

Different rules regarding the calculation and the frequency and timing of payments apply to each class.

9.5.1 Class 1 and Class 1A NICs

Class 1 NICs apply to an employee's earnings, i.e. their gross pay, and are calculated for the employee's pay period, which can be weekly, monthly, quarterly or annually. This differs from income tax, which is always calculated on an annual basis. Company directors, however, are an exception and their NICs are calculated on an annual basis regardless of their pay period.

Individuals who have more than one employment are liable to Class 1 NICs in respect of each employment. Each employer will operate PAYE (including NICs) as they would for an employee with only one employer. If an employee with two employments pays too much in NICs over the two employments, a refund can be claimed after the end of the tax year from HMRC. To make a claim, the employee should write to HMRC attaching their two P60s.

Class 1 Primary NICs

Primary Class 1 NICs are those **paid by the employee**. That is, the employee's take home pay will be reduced by the amount of primary Class 1 NICs paid. The rates of primary Class 1 NICs are 0%, 2% and 12%. **Table 9.3** shows the weekly, monthly and annual limits and thresholds that impact on the percentage of primary Class 1 NICs paid.

TABLE 9.3: RATES OF CLASS 1 PRIMARY NICS

	Weekly £	Monthly £	Annual £	Employee Class 1 (Primary) %
Up to the lower earnings limit (LEL)	0–120	0–520	0–6,240	0
From the LEL to the primary earnings threshold (PT)	120–184	520–797	6,240–9,568	0
From the PT to the upper earnings limit (UEL)	184–967	797–4,189	9,568–50,270	12
Above UEL	Above 967	Above 4,189	Above 50,270	2

Employees over the national pension age, currently 66, are not required to pay primary Class 1 NICs.

Example 9.2

Matthew earns £52,000 gross employment income in the 2021/22 tax year and is paid weekly (£1,000 per week).

What are the Class 1 primary NICs due in respect of Matthew's pay?

Class 1 primary NICs are paid by Matthew on his earnings, calculated on the basis of the pay period (weekly in this case), as follows:

£184	× 0%	
(£967 − £184)	× 12%	= £93.96 per week
(£1,000 − £967)	× 2%	= £ 0.66
Total NICs		£94.62

Matthew's Class 1 primary NICs are therefore £94.62 per week. His employer will deduct this amount from his weekly salary and will pay it to HMRC.

Class 1 Secondary NICs

Secondary Class 1 NICs are **paid by the employer**. The rates of secondary Class 1 NICs are 0% and 13.8%. There is no upper limit for secondary NICs. **Table 9.4** shows the weekly, monthly and annual limits and threshold that impact on the percentage of secondary Class 1 NICs paid.

TABLE 9.4: RATES OF CLASS 1 SECONDARY NICS

	Weekly **£**	**Monthly** **£**	**Annual** **£**	**Employer Class 1** **(Secondary)** **%**
Up to the secondary threshold (ST)	0–170	0–737	0–8,840	0
From the ST to the upper earnings limit (UEL)	170–967	737–4,189	8,840–50,270	13.8
Above UEL	Above 967	Above 4,189	Above 50,270	13.8

Special rules apply to employers with employees under 21 years of age. In such cases the employer does not have to pay Class 1 secondary NICs on earnings up to the "upper secondary threshold" (UST) for those employees. The UST is equivalent to the UEL (£967 per week).

As mentioned above, no primary Class 1 NICs are payable once an employee reaches State pension age (currently 66); however, the employer's secondary Class 1 NICs remain payable.

Example 9.3

Matthew earns £52,000 gross employment income in the 2021/22 tax year and is paid weekly (£1,000 per week).

What are the Class 1 secondary NICs due in respect of Matthew's pay?

Class 1 secondary NICs are payable by Matthew's employer, calculated on the basis of the pay period, i.e. weekly, as follows:

(£1,000 − £170) = £830 × 13.8% = £114.54

Employment Allowance

An "employment allowance" is available to most businesses to reduce their Class 1 secondary NIC liability. The allowance is intended to encourage business growth and to help small businesses in particular with the costs of employment. It can be claimed through the Employment Payment Summary (EPS) on RTI (see **Section 9.3.1**). The employment allowance can only be claimed if the business had total Class 1 secondary NICs liability below £100,000 in the previous tax year.

For 2021/22, the employment allowance is £4,000 (2020/21: £4,000), and can only be offset against Class 1 NICs (not against Class 1A NICs). It is offset in full against the first monthly payment of the employer's Class 1 secondary NICs, provided this is equal to or greater than £4,000. Any unused allowance is carried forward until the next payment period. For example, if an employer's Class 1 secondary NICs are £2,400 each month, then £2,400 of the allowance would be offset to the first month's payment, and £1,600 would be offset to the next month.

Class 1A NICs

Class 1A NICs apply to an employee's expenses and benefits in kind (see **Section 5.4.3**). They are collected from the employer only, on an annual basis, at a rate of 13.8%. Employee contributions are not charged on BIKs. Class 1A NICs are calculated on the amount of the BIK.

Example 9.4

Matthew's employer also pays his private medical insurance. The cost to his employer is £2,500 per annum.

What are the Class 1A NICs due in respect of Matthew's BIK?

Class 1A NICs will be calculated on an annual basis, as follows:

Total BIK	£2,500
Class 1A NIC =	£2,500 × 13.8% = £345

Class 1A NICs are due for payment by 22 July (19 July if paying by post) following the tax year.

Example 9.5

Melissa works for Sharp Tech Ltd and earns £42,000 gross employment income in the 2021/22 tax year. She is paid £3,500 monthly and is provided with a company car and a fuel allowance. The taxable value of the car's BIK is £3,960 and the taxable value of the fuel's BIK is £5,302.

What are the Class 1 primary and secondary NICs and the Class 1A NICs due in respect of Melissa's pay and benefits?

Class 1 Primary NICs

Class 1 primary NICs are paid by Melissa on her earnings, calculated on the basis of the pay period (monthly in this case), as follows:

(£3,500 − £797) × 12% = £324.36 per month

Melissa's Class 1 primary NICs are therefore £324.36 per month. Her employer will deduct this amount from Melissa's monthly salary and will pay it to HMRC.

Class 1 Secondary NICs

Class 1 secondary NICs are payable by Melissa's employer, calculated on the basis of the pay period, i.e. monthly, as follows:

(£3,500 − £737) × 13.8% = £381.29 per month

Sharp Tech Ltd will pay the monthly Class 1 secondary NICs of all employees, including Melissa, to HMRC by the 22nd of each month. Sharp Tech Ltd can claim up to £4,000 relief per annum from its Class 1 secondary NIC liability.

Class 1A NICs

Class 1A NICs are paid by employers on the provision of most BIKs (unless the BIK is equivalent to cash, in which case Class 1 primary and secondary NICs are due, or the BIK is exempt from NICs). Employees do not pay Class 1A NICs.

Class 1A NICs will be calculated on an annual basis as follows:

Car BIK:	£3,960
Fuel BIK:	£5,302
Total BIK	£9,262

Class 1A NIC = £9,262 × 13.8% = £1,278.16

Sharp Tech Ltd will pay this amount to HMRC by 22 July 2021.

Example 9.6

Taking **Example 9.5**, Melissa receives a bonus in July 2021 of £2,000. How does this affect her Class 1 primary and secondary NICs?

Class 1 Primary NIC

Class 1 primary NIC in respect of July 2021:

(£4,189 − £797) × 12% = £407.04
(£5,500 − £4,189) × 2% = £26.22

Melissa's Class 1 primary NIC liability in respect of July 2020 will be £433.26.

Class 1 Secondary NIC

Class 1 secondary NIC in respect of July 2021:

(£5,500 − £737) × 13.8% = £657.29

Melissa's Class 1 secondary NIC liability in respect of July 2021 will be £657.29.

Example 9.7

What difference would it make if Melissa was a director rather than an employee (assuming Melissa receives her bonus in July 2021)?

If Melissa was a director, Class 1 primary and secondary NICs would be calculated using the annual NIC thresholds for the 2021/22 tax year. Her annual salary is £3,500 × 12 + £2,000 = £44,000.

Class 1 Primary NIC

(£44,000 − £9,568) × 12% = £4,131.84

Total Class 1 primary NIC payable by Melissa is £4,131.84.

Class 1 Secondary NIC

(£44,000 − £8,840) × 13.8% = £4,852.08

A comparison of the Class 1 NICs payable by Melissa as an employee versus those payable as a director is set out below:

	Employee	Director
	£	£
Class 1 primary: (£324.36 × 11) + £433.26	4,001.22	4,131.84
Class 1 secondary: (£381.29 × 11) + £657.29	4,851.48	4,852.08
Class 1A	1,278.16	1,278.16
Total	**10,130.86**	**10,262.08**

The difference in Class 1 primary NIC of £131 (£4,132 – £4,001) is due to the fact that more of the bonus payment is charged at 2% when NICs are calculated monthly (£5,500 – £4,189 = £1,311 × 10% = £131) rather than 12% on an annual basis.

9.5.2   Class 2 and Class 4 NICs

Self-employed taxpayers pay Class 2 and Class 4 NICs. Class 2 NICs are payable at a flat rate. Class 4 NICs are paid at two different rates and the amount of Class 4 NICs due depends on the level of the taxpayer's trading profits. We will now look at each NIC class separately.

Class 2 NICs

Class 2 NICs are assessed on **self-employed** persons at £3.05 per week, if earnings exceed the small earnings exception (SEE) of £6,515. Therefore, if a taxpayer has trading profits of over £6,515 for 2021/22, then the amount of Class 2 NICs due will be 52 weeks at £3.05 per week. That is, £158.60.

Payments may be made voluntarily, if earnings are below this amount, so as to maintain a full contributions record for social security purposes. A Class 2 contribution record is very important as it goes towards State pension and social security benefits for the self-employed.

The amount of Class 2 NICs due is calculated based on the number of weeks of self-employment in the tax year and is, in most cases, determined when the taxpayer completes their self-assessment return and the Class 2 NICs are paid alongside their income tax (see **Chapter 10**) and Class 4 NICs (see below).

However, there are a number of cases where Class 2 NICs are not collected through self-assessment. For example, if the taxpayer is working abroad.

Where Class 2 NICs are not collected through self-assessment, HMRC will send a bill by the end of October each tax year instructing the amount of Class 2 NICs to be paid. Payment can then be made electronically or by post.

Class 4 NICs

Class 4 NICs are assessed on trading profits. The amount collected is 9% of profits from all trades in the tax year between the lower profits limit of £9,568 and the upper profits limit of £50,270. Class 4 NICs of 2% are collected on profits above the upper profits limits. Therefore, a taxpayer with trading profits of £55,000 will pay Class 4 NICs of £3,758. That is, £40,702 (£50,270 – £9,568) at 9% and £4,730 (£55,000 – £50,270) at 2%.

Class 4 NICs are paid by taxpayers at the same time as their associated income tax liability under self-assessment (see **Chapter 10**). Trading losses can be taken into consideration to reduce profit for Class 4 NICs, as well as for income tax. If income tax relief is claimed for a loss against non-trading income or against capital gains, the loss can still be set against future trading income for Class 4 NIC purposes.

Example 9.8: Class 2 and Class 4 NICs
Roberta runs her own business as a dance instructor. She earns trading profits of £80,000 in the 2021/22 tax year. Calculate her NICs in respect of the 2021/22 tax year.

Class 2 NIC
Weekly Class 2 NICs are due at a rate of £3.05 per week.
Roberta's Class 2 NIC liability will be £158.60 (£3.05 × 52 weeks).

Class 4 NIC
Class 4 NICs are calculated on the basis of trading profit as follows:

(£50,270 − £9,568) × 9% = £3,663.18
(£80,000 − £50,270) × 2% = £594.60

Roberta's total Class 4 NIC liability is £4,257.78.

9.5.3 Class 3 NICs

Class 3 NICs are **voluntary** contributions that can be paid by individuals who have a 'gap' in their NIC record, i.e. periods when they were not paying any NICs. Gaps can occur where:

■ an employee's earnings were below the "lower earnings limit", i.e. £120 per week;
■ the individual was unemployed and not claiming social security benefits;

- if self-employed, the individual's earnings were less than the £6,475 small earnings exception; or
- the individual was living abroad.

Gaps in an NIC record are important to consider as they may affect future eligibility to receive the full State pension. Class 3 contributions therefore allow an individual to maintain a full contribution record.

9.5.4   NICs Payable by a Taxpayer who is both Employed and Self-employed

If a taxpayer is both employed and self-employed, they are liable to Class 1 NICs as an employee, and to Class 2 and Class 4 NICs with regard to their self-employment income.

How much NICs need to be paid depends on the taxpayer's combined income from employment and self-employment. There is a maximum figure above which contributions will be refunded; however, the calculation of this figure is very complicated and has up to nine stages. The maximum figure is not a fixed amount and will vary according to the mix of employment/self-employment and the amounts earned.

Questions

Review Questions
(See Suggested Solutions to Review Questions at the end of this textbook.)

Question 9.1

Mary is 50 years old. She earns £30,000 from her employer in 2021/22 and also receives BIKs worth £400.

Requirement
What is Mary's tax code for 2021/22?

Question 9.2

Andrew earns £20,000 in 2021/22. He has anticipated BIKs of £750. He has no other income.

Requirement
What is Andrew's tax code for 2021/22?

Question 9.3

Sean, a married man of 50, is employed by NEW Ltd. He is allowed unrestricted private use of a company van in the 2021/22 tax year and doesn't pay for any fuel. He earns £30,000 a year.
    Sean has an underpayment of PAYE from 2020/21 of £1,000.

Requirement
What is Sean's tax code for 2021/22? Explain what this means.

Question 9.4

Alison, aged 45, is married to Sean. She earns £60,000 a year and is provided with a company mobile phone for which the company picks up the bill (private calls were £750) and medical insurance for which the premium is £500.

She has an overpayment of PAYE from 2020/21 of £150.

Requirement
What is Alison's tax code for 2021/22?

Question 9.5

Paul earned £2,500 in the month to 5 May 2021 and paid PAYE of £500. He is paid on a commission basis and earned £4,433 in the month to 5 June 2021. His tax code is 360L.

Requirement
What PAYE will be deducted from Paul's salary in the month to 5 June 2021?

Question 9.6

David has earned £17,000 in the tax year so far, and paid PAYE of £3,600. He earns £3,000 in the month to 5 October 2021. His tax code is K120.

Requirement
(a) What PAYE will be deducted from David's salary in the month to 5 October 2021?
(b) How would the answer be different if PAYE deducted had been £2,900 instead of £3,600?

Question 9.7

Brian is an employee with gross monthly earnings of £50,000 in September 2021.

Requirement
What NICs will Brian pay on this wage?

Question 9.8

Jonathan is 67 years old. He earned £4,000 in August 2021.

Requirement
What NICs will Jonathan pay on this wage?

Question 9.9

Sarah is 27 years old. She earned £12,000 in 2021/22, paid in equal instalments of £1,000 per month. Sarah was also self-employed in 2021/22, preparing accounts to 5 April. Her profits for the year ended 5 April 2021 were £22,000.

Requirement
What NICs will Sarah pay for 2021/22?

Question 9.10

Frank is a company director who earns an annual gross salary of £50,000 in 2021/22 and also receives the following benefits in kind:

1. Company car (over 2,000cc) with a list price of £20,000 (first registered in January 2020) and CO_2 emissions of 300g/km. He had to pay £5,000 towards the cost of the car.
2. All fuel is paid for by the employer.
3. His employer pays his annual golf subscription of £800.

Requirement
What Class 1A NICs are payable for 2021/22?

Administration and Procedures

Learning Objectives

After studying this chapter you will be able to:

■ Explain the operation of the self-assessment system, including interest and late filing penalties.

The Chartered Accountants Ireland *Code of Ethics* applies to all aspects of a Chartered Accountant's professional life, including dealing with various aspects of the tax system. As outlined at the beginning of this book, further information regarding the principles in the *Code of Ethics* is set out in **Appendix 2**.

10.1 Introduction

As we saw in **Chapter 1**, residency and domicile are key factors in determining if an individual is liable to income tax. However, it is important to note that income tax is payable by the following types of taxpayer:

■ adults, on their own income and on their share of the income of a partnership;
■ children, if they have sufficient income to pay tax; and
■ trustees (on the income of a trust or settlement) and personal representatives of the estate of a deceased person (not within the scope of the CA Proficiency 1 Competency Statement).

This chapter will look at the overall system for the administration of tax in the UK. The chapter will begin by looking at the self-assessment system for tax, whereby an annual tax return is filed. It is worth noting that not all taxpayers have to operate within the self-assessment system. For example, an individual who is only a PAYE worker (see **Chapter 9**) will not be obliged to operate within the self-assessment system, as all of their income tax and national insurance contributions should be collected through the PAYE system.

For taxpayers within the self-assessment regime, the payment of tax to HMRC follows automatically from the self-assessment return and this chapter will look at the various dates, rules and regulations in this regard. In order for HMRC to encourage the correct operation of the self-assessment system in the UK, a penalty regime is in place for late filing and HMRC will also charge interest on late payments.

A new income tax self-assessment penalty regime will replace the existing penalties currently in place for 2021/22 and 2022/23. This new regime will be introduced on a phased basis and will initially apply to certain taxpayers for accounting periods beginning on or after 6 April 2023.

10.2   Self-assessment

The term 'self-assessment' refers to the system under which the taxpayer is responsible for calculating their own tax liability, reporting it to HMRC on their tax return and also making payment of their income tax based on the information contained in their tax return. The self-assessment system places the responsibility on the taxpayer to calculate their income tax liability, allowing HMRC to devote more resources to checking the accuracy of the submissions and offering advice to taxpayers. Given the complexities of the tax system in the UK, many taxpayers will engage a tax agent, tax advisor or accountant to help with the calculation of their tax and the submission of their income tax return (see **Section 10.2.3**).

10.2.1   Registration for Self-assessment

Self-employed individuals, i.e. sole traders, must be registered as such with HMRC; registration means they will automatically be treated under self-assessment and will be liable for Class 2 self-employed NICs. All self-assessment registrations must be carried out online by completing Form CWF1. The '**Government Gateway**' is an online central registration service for many of the different Government services, including self-assessment tax registrations and agent services (see **Section 10.2.3**).

When an individual commences self-employment, or anticipates starting to trade within the next 28 days, they must submit Form CWF1. HMRC also state that an individual should register no later than 5 October following the end of the tax year for which they need to send a tax return. Late registrations will not incur a penalty (see **Section 10.4.1**) where the required tax is paid by the self-assessment deadline (see below).

When an individual registers for self-assessment, they will automatically receive a Unique Taxpayer Reference (UTR). This UTR will then be quoted on all tax returns they submit as a self-employed individual.

10.2.2   Tax Returns

A tax return is a taxpayer's declaration of their income in any particular tax year. Currently, a taxpayer that is registered for self-assessment is sent a tax return or, if registered for online filing (see below), a notice to file online. Generally these are sent by HMRC in April/May each year.

HMRC's ambition is to become one of the most digitally advanced tax administrations in the world. In pursuit of this goal, its Making Tax Digital (MTD) initiative proposes that the self-assessment tax return will be replaced by five new reporting obligations made during and after the tax year. This MTD measure is not anticipated to commence until April 2023.

The current self-assessment tax return consists of a basic eight-page form, form **SA100**, plus a number of supplementary pages, each dealing with a different type of income, e.g. income from employment is SA102, self-employment is SA103 and property income is SA105. Taxpayers are sent only those supplementary pages that are thought to be relevant to their circumstances, but they can request further supplementary pages if needed. If a taxpayer is filing their tax return online, they can complete whichever supplementary pages they need.

Partnerships must file a separate return, form **SA800**, which includes a partnership statement declaring the firm's profit, losses, tax suffered, tax credits, the division between partners, etc. in the tax year. Each partner must then declare their share of partnership profits on their personal tax return.

The tax return includes details of all income and claims for allowances. A four-page **short tax return** (form SA200) may be issued to taxpayers with simpler tax affairs. For example, a short tax return can be used where a taxpayer was a paid employee or had taxable benefits, where a taxpayer was self-employed with an annual turnover of less than £85,000, or where a taxpayer had property income of less than £85,000 from rents or letting a room in their own home.　　.

A taxpayer has the right to insist on completing a tax return where they feel the need to submit a self-assessment tax return.

In situations where a taxpayer is liable to income tax under self-assessment (for example, if they were in receipt of miscellaneous or property income, or they received interest income), but they have not been issued with a tax return, they must **notify** HMRC within six months of the end of the tax year in question, i.e. by 5 October. Failure to do so results in a penalty. Taxpayers can authorise someone else to complete their tax return, whether it be a family member, friend or a tax professional. However, the taxpayer is responsible for the information being submitted and they must sign the completed return.

Online Filing

Taxpayers (and their agents) are encouraged to file tax returns online using the self-assessment online service. The online service allows most individuals to file their tax returns this way; likewise, agents and tax practitioners can file clients' tax returns using the Self Assessment for Agents online service (see **Section 10.2.3** for more detail).

To file tax returns online, the taxpayer (or agent) must register to do so – this is a separate registration process from registering for self-assessment. The self-assessment online service is accessed through the Government Gateway portal. On registering, an 'Activation Code' is sent, within 10 working days, by post to the address held. The activation code is a 12-character security code that the taxpayer can then use to access online services.

Tax Return Filing Deadlines

A **paper tax return** must be completed and submitted to HMRC by the "filing date", which is:

- 31 October following the end of the tax year; or
- if the tax return was issued after 31 October following the end of the tax year, three months after it was issued.

If the paper return is received before 31 October, HMRC will calculate the taxpayer's income tax liability and notify them before 31 January.

An **online return** must be submitted by 31 January following the end of the tax year. So, if a taxpayer misses the paper return deadline, they can file online without incurring a late filing penalty charge (providing they allow sufficient time to complete the registration process). If the first notice to file a return is issued to the taxpayer after 31 October, then the latest filing deadline is the end of three months following the notice.

For taxpayers who would like HMRC to collect any income tax they owe through their wages or pension, the tax return must be filed online by 30 December. For example, for the 2020/21 tax year, a taxpayer must file online by 30 December 2021 if they want HMRC to collect their income tax liability through the PAYE system.

Amending Tax Returns

The taxpayer can **amend** their tax return within 12 months after the filing date. This facility enables a taxpayer to deal with an error/omission discovered after the income tax return has been submitted. The taxpayer's income tax bill will be updated based on the amendments made and any extra tax due as a result of the amendment will need to be paid to HMRC immediately. If a refund arises as a result of the amendment, the refund should issue once HMRC have dealt with the amendment.

HMRC may amend a return for obvious errors or mistakes, e.g. simple arithmetical errors, or entries that the HMRC officer has reason to believe are incorrect in light of information available. HMRC have until nine months after the date the return is filed to amend in this manner.

Accounting Information

If declaring trading income and expenses, the tax return requires that the figures are presented in a "standard format", i.e. certain boxes on the tax return need to be completed. There is no requirement to submit accounts with the tax return.

Records

All taxpayers are expected to make, and keep, sufficient records for them to provide a complete and accurate return. HMRC's view is that it is reasonable to expect a person who does not understand a tax issue to take care to check the correct tax treatment, or to seek suitable advice from HMRC or a tax professional.

All individuals who carry on a business (e.g. a self-employed individual) are obliged to keep records of:

- all receipts and expenses;
- all goods purchased and sold; and
- all supporting documents relating to the transactions of the business, such as accounts, books, contracts, vouchers and receipts.

These records must be kept for five years after 31 January following the tax year.

Other taxpayers should keep evidence of income received for one year after 31 January following the tax year.

HMRC can inspect "in year" records, i.e. before a tax return is submitted to HMRC, if it believes it is reasonably required to check a tax position.

Simple Assessments

HMRC have announced that they are removing the following groups of taxpayer from the obligation to complete a self-assessment tax return:

- PAYE taxpayers who have underpaid tax but cannot have the underpayment collected via their tax code; and
- new/existing State pensioners whose pension exceeds the personal allowance.

Taxpayers removed from self-assessment will instead be sent a simple assessment. HMRC can make a 'simple assessment' of an individual's income tax liability without the taxpayer first being required to complete a self-assessment tax return. The simple assessment will be made on the basis of information already held by HMRC, whether it was received from the taxpayer or a third party.

HMRC can make more than one simple assessment on a person for any tax year. An appeal can be made against a simple assessment but only after the person assessed has raised a query about the assessment and has been given a final response to that query.

Personal Tax Accounts

HMRC provides personal tax accounts to help taxpayers manage their records with HMRC online. A taxpayer can use their HMRC personal tax account to:

- check income tax estimates and tax codes;
- complete, send and view a personal tax return;
- claim a tax refund;
- check and manage tax credits;
- update personal address details.

10.2.3 Tax Agents, Tax Advisors and Accountants

As previously noted, if a taxpayer authorises someone else to complete the tax return, it is still the taxpayer who is responsible for the information submitted. If a tax professional has been engaged to complete the tax return and it is a paper return, the taxpayer is required to sign and the date the return for submission.

If the tax agent is submitting the return online, they must be registered with the Self Assessment for Agents online service. When online filing, agents should still make a copy (either a softcopy or a photocopy) of the completed return for their client to sign (an electronic signature is valid) and approve.

10.3 Payment of Self-assessed Income Tax and National Insurance Contributions

Where a taxpayer pays their taxes under the self-assessment system, they may have to make up to three payments of income tax and NICs a year. In general, due dates of "payments on account" of **income tax and Class 4 NICs** are as follows:

- first payment on account by 31 January in the tax year;
- second payment on account by 31 July following the end of the tax year; and
- balancing, or final, payment by 31 January following the end of the tax year.

Self-assessed taxpayers are expected to know when they need to make their payments on account. If they are registered online with HMRC for filing their returns, then the HMRC's online system will remind taxpayers of their payment deadlines.

The first and second payments on account each equal **50% of the prior tax year's income tax and Class 4 NICs liability, i.e. less tax deducted at source**, such as PAYE. This is called the "relevant amount".

Payments on account are not required if:

- the relevant amount is less than £1,000; or
- if more than 80% of the income tax liability for the previous year was paid through PAYE.

At any time before 31 January following the tax year, a taxpayer can **claim to reduce** their payments on account. Such a claim can only be made if the tax payable for the current year is expected to be less than the payments on account, i.e. less than the tax payable for the previous tax year. An incorrect claim can lead to interest and penalties.

Class 2 NICs are to be paid along with the balancing payment on 31 January following the end of the tax year. Class 2 NICs are not payable on account in the way that income tax and Class 4 NICs are.

Example 10.1

David has taxable trading profits of £74,074 for the tax year 2021/22. He also earned dividend income of £5,027. He paid £78 per month into a private pension scheme. David made payments on account in respect of income tax and Class 4 NICs for the tax year 2021/22 of £7,396.68 each in January and July 2022.

Calculate the tax payable by David on 31 January 2023 and the payment on account due on 31 July 2023.

David – Income Tax Computation 2021/22

	Non-savings	Dividends	Total
	£	£	£
Trading income	74,074		74,074
Dividends	———	5,027	5,027
Total income	74,074	5,027	79,101
Less: personal allowance	(12,570)	–	(12,570)
Taxable income	61,504	5,027	66,531

Income tax due:		
On non-savings income		£
Basic rate band:	£37,700 @ 20%	7,540.00
Extended basic rate band: Non-savings	£1,170 @ 20%	234.00
Higher rate band: Non-savings	£22,634 @ 40%	9,053.60
Higher rate band: Dividends (after £2,000 dividend allowance)	£3,027 @ 32.5%	983.78
		17,811.38
Tax liability		17,811.38
Class 4 NICs: £50,270 – £9,568 @ 9%		3,663.18
£74,074 – £50,270 @ 2%		476.08
		21,950.64

Payments on account:	Jan 2021	7,396.68	
	July 2021	7,396.68	(14,793.36)
Balance by 31 January 2023			7,157.28
Payments on account due for 31 January 2023 (£21,950.64/2)			10,975.32
Total income tax and Class 4 NICs due at 31 January 2023			18,132.60
Add: Class 2 NICs			158.60
Total payment due on 31 January 2023			18,291.20

Taxpayers have numerous methods by which they can pay their income tax. For example, HMRC can accept payment by online or telephone banking, CHAPS, by debit or credit card or by direct debit.

10.3.1 Underpayment of Income Tax and NICs

An underpayment of income tax or NICs will be subject to penalties and interest. See **Section 10.4** for more details in respect of the penalties for late payment of tax and also the interest charged on late paid tax.

10.3.2 Overpayment of Income Tax and NICs

Where an assessment to tax is excessive due to error or mistake in the return, the taxpayer can claim back the amount overpaid. The claim must be made by the taxpayer not more than four years after the end of the year of assessment.

A claim cannot be made where the tax liability was in accordance with the tax rules and practice prevailing at the time the return was made.

Interest on Overpayments of Tax/NICs

Interest, or repayment supplement, is paid by HMRC on an overpayment from the original date of payment. Tax deducted at source is assumed to have been paid on 31 January following the tax year. The interest rate of repayment supplements is 0.5%.

10.3.3 Arrangements for Payment of Tax

Budget Payment Plan

A taxpayer can decide to make regular tax payments in advance under a budget payment plan. Such a plan allows a taxpayer to decide how much to pay each week or month and they can stop paying into the plan for up to six months. To set up a plan, a taxpayer must register online and must pay by direct debit. Where the total payments made by the taxpayer during the year do not cover their full tax bill, the difference should be paid by the normal payment deadline.

Time to Pay Arrangements

Where a taxpayer fails to pay an amount of tax, and before liability to a penalty arises, i.e. within the 30-day grace period, they can request a "time to pay arrangement". If HMRC agrees, then any penalty due will be suspended. The suspension will stop, however, if the taxpayer breaks the agreement and HMRC serves notice of the penalty. A time to pay arrangement is a negotiated agreement with HMRC to allow the taxpayer to settle their tax liabilities by regular instalments. The arrangement will take into full account the taxpayer's circumstances, such as illness, unemployment, unforeseen short-term business difficulties, etc.

Such an arrangement is normally subject to adequate provision being made to settle future liabilities on time. Interest will arise as normal by reference to the original due date and not the instalment date. Penalties, however, may be avoided where a time to pay arrangement is in force. Such arrangements must be paid by direct debit.

10.4 Penalties for Late Filing and Late Payment

In an attempt to encourage taxpayers to pay their income tax and file their income tax returns on time, a penalty regime is in place that penalises taxpayers for non-payment of tax and non-submission of tax returns.

10.4.1 Late Filing Penalties

A fixed penalty system for the late filing of returns was introduced by Finance Act 2009. Under these provisions, the penalties for late filing of a tax return are:

1. Initial penalty of £100 for failure to submit the return on time.
2. After three months, HMRC can impose a daily penalty of up to £10 for a maximum of 90 days.
3. After six months, the penalty will be the greater of £300 or 5% of the tax due.
4. After 12 months, the penalty will again be the greater of £300 or 5% of the liability. If the taxpayer withholds requested information, the penalty can rise to 100% if the withholding is deliberate and concealed, and 70% if just deliberate. The 100% and 70% thresholds may be reduced by voluntary disclosures under the new penalty regime for errors (see below).
5. Separate provisions have been included for the Construction Industry Scheme (CIS) (see **Chapter 11**).

A late filing penalty can be appealed if the taxpayer has a "reasonable excuse". A reasonable excuse is considered as "something unexpected" or outside the taxpayer's control that prevented them from filing on time. HMRC suggest the following would be considered a reasonable excuse:

- a partner or close relative died shortly before the filing date;
- a serious illness or an unexpected stay in hospital;
- a computer or software failure;
- a technical fault with the HMRC online service;
- destruction of records through fire, flood or theft; or
- an industrial dispute in the post office **after** the return was posted.

10.4.2 Late Payment Penalties

Similar to the late filing penalty, a fixed penalty system is in place if **full payment** of tax due is not received by HMRC by the required date. There is a 'grace period' of 30 days from the due date where no penalty is imposed; thereafter:

1. Any tax due that is outstanding more than 30 days after the due date, an initial penalty of 5% of the unpaid tax.
2. Any tax outstanding more than five months after the first penalty is charged (i.e. six months after the due date), a second penalty of 5% of the unpaid tax.
3. Any tax outstanding more than 11 months after the first penalty is charged (i.e. 12 months after the due date), a third penalty of 5% of the unpaid tax.

The above penalty regime will only apply where the tax liability is not discharged in full by 31 January following the tax year. For example, for the 2021/22 tax year, a penalty will only be incurred if payment has not been received by 31 January 2023. As noted previously, a taxpayer may have to make payments on account in respect of their tax liability, e.g. payments on account for the 2021/22 tax year will be due on 31 January 2022 and 31 July 2022. The late payment penalty regime outlined above does not apply to payments on account that are paid late.

Late payment penalties are due for payment within 30 days of their imposition. If the penalty is not paid in that time, interest at 2.60% (from 7 April 2020) per annum will accrue on it from the date the payment is due.

Interest on Late Payments
In addition to the fixed penalties above, late payments can incur interest charges on the amount of tax due. Interest, at 2.60% per annum is accrued from the due date to the day before payment is received.

For payments on account that are received late, interest would accrue for a maximum period from 31 January in the tax year to 31 July following the end of that tax year. Interest on late payment of a balancing payment would accrue from the later of:

- 31 January following the tax year; or
- three months after the tax return was issued.

Questions

Review Questions
(See Suggested Solutions to Review Questions at the end of this textbook.)

Question 10.1

The senior partner of your firm has come to you with a letter from one of the firm's clients, John Murphy, who was previously an employee and has set up his own business on 1 July 2021. Mr Murphy will prepare accounts annually to 31 January. Mr Murphy is very worried about the self-assessment system.

Requirement
Write a brief letter to Mr Murphy describing the self-assessment system, including details on the self-assessment system for each of the following:

(a) income tax returns and penalties; and
(b) payment of tax liabilities.

Question 10.2

Cian Connors is a single man, born in March 1972. His accounts for the year ended 31 October 2021 show a tax-adjusted profit of £48,000. £920 interest was received on gilts, i.e. UK Government stock (see **Chapter 6**).

Requirement
Compute the income tax and NICs due for 2021/22. What payments on account will be due, and when, for 2022/23?

Question 10.3

Mark Johnston is a single man, born in June 1969. He has employment income of £50,000 in 2021/22 and income from gilts of £10,500. PAYE deducted at source was £11,000.

Requirement
Will Mark have to make payments on account for 2022/23? Explain why.

Question 10.4

You are Tom, a newly qualified Chartered Accountant and you have recently joined the tax department of a medium-sized practice. The partner in the practice has asked you to help draw up an aggressive tax planning scheme that will enable clients to reduce their tax liabilities to nil by undertaking a number of artificial transactions. Although you do not fully understand the steps in the tax scheme and the tax legislation involved, you are asked to ring your 10 biggest clients to try to get them to buy into the scheme.

Requirement

Provide the partner with your comments in respect of the above situation. You should highlight the fundamental principles within the Chartered Accountants Ireland *Code of Ethics* that may be compromised.

The Construction Industry Scheme

Learning Objectives

After studying this chapter you will be able to explain the scope and implications of Construction Industry Scheme (CIS) taxes.

11.1 Introduction

The Construction Industry Scheme (CIS) was introduced with the main objective of reducing the level of tax evasion by subcontractors in the construction industry. The construction industry has such a large number of mobile, self-employed workers that the risk of tax evasion was significant. Therefore, the CIS is a special system designed around construction workers to help ensure tax compliance within the industry.

The current CIS operates on a HMRC centralised database of contractor and subcontractor information. It places an onus on the contractor to operate the scheme correctly by deducting the correct amount of tax from payments to subcontractors (where necessary) and to file monthly returns recording specific subcontractor information.

HMRC's *Construction Industry Scheme: Guide for contractors and subcontractors* (CIS340) provides guidance on the operation of the current regime.

11.1.1 General Scheme

In simple terms, the CIS requires that where a "construction contract" is in place, that the "contractor" deduct tax from payments made to a "subcontractor", and that the amount deducted is then paid to HMRC. In essence it works on the same principle as tax deducted at source: it places the burden of tax collection on the contractor.

Deductions made by a contractor are either at the standard rate (20%) or the higher rate (30%) of the payment to the subcontractor, excluding the cost of materials.

In certain cases, where strict criteria are met, the CIS deductions can be waived, i.e. payments to a subcontractor can be "gross payments" (see **Section 11.2.4**).

The mechanics of the CIS are set out below, but before we look at the detail of how it works we must understand the very specific definitions contained in the legislation.

11.1.2 Definitions

"Contractor"

Under CIS legislation, "contractor" has a special, broader meaning that includes:

- any person carrying on a business that includes "construction operations" in the UK (these are referred to as "mainstream contractors");
- local authorities, NHS trusts, housing associations and a number of other specified public bodies that have spent, on average, at least £1,000,000 a year on construction operations over the last three years ending with their last accounting date; and
- persons not carrying on a construction business, but whose business has spent, on average, at least £1,000,000 a year on construction operations over the last three years ending with their last accounting date, e.g. retailers, banks, manufacturing entities, etc.

The last two categories in the list are referred to as "deemed contractors".

"Subcontractor"

A "subcontractor" is a person, partnership (including a limited liability partnership (LLP)) or company that is employed to carry out, or provide labour for, "construction operations", or who is responsible for such operations being carried out by others.

"Payment"

Under the CIS, a "payment" is an amount paid out by the "contractor" to the "subcontractor" under a "construction contract". It includes cash, cheques or credit. An advance or a loan is credit and, as such, must be treated as a payment, and applies regardless of whether the payment was made directly to the subcontractor or not.

"Construction Contract"

A "construction contract" is a contract relating to "construction operations". The CIS scheme operates only in the UK (and its territorial waters), but it also includes non-UK businesses carrying on construction operations in the UK.

Some construction contracts may include a non-construction component, such as the delivery of materials. In such cases, the CIS applies to **all** operations under the whole contract, even if shown on separate invoices. However, if a contract exists solely for the delivery of materials, for example, it will fall completely outside the CIS.

"Construction Operations"

As a general rule, the CIS includes work done to a permanent building, a temporary structure and civil engineering work/installation. Examples of "construction operations" include:

- preparing the site, e.g. laying foundations and providing access works;
- demolition and dismantling;
- building work;
- alterations, repairs and decorating;
- installing systems for heating, lighting, power, water and ventilation;
- cleaning the inside of buildings after construction work.

Examples of works that are specifically **excluded** from the definition of construction operations include:

- architecture and surveying;
- scaffolding hire (with no labour);

■ carpet fitting;
■ making materials used in construction, including plant and machinery;
■ delivery of materials.

11.1.3 Exceptions to the Scheme

HMRC recognises specific circumstances where the CIS need not apply. So, **deemed contractors** do not need to apply the scheme to expenditure that relates to property used for the purposes of its own business, or if the business is a company used within the same corporate group (greater than 50% shareholding relationship). This extends to offices, warehouses and nursing homes used for the business. This exclusion does not apply to property let out, held as an investment or up for sale/let.

HMRC can also authorise deemed contractors not to operate the scheme for construction operations that amount to less than £1,000 (excluding the cost of materials).

11.2   Mechanics of the CIS

The operation of the CIS is based on a centralised database of contractors and subcontractors. The information held in the database includes the contractor's/subcontractor's name, their unique tax reference (UTR) and their national insurance number (NINO) if an individual or partnership, or the company tax reference and company registration number if a company.

The mechanics of the CIS relies upon:

1. registration – contractors must register for the CIS; subcontractors' registration is optional;
2. verification of a subcontractor's "payment status" by the CIS; and
3. monthly returns and payments to HMRC by the contractor.

11.2.1 Registration for the CIS

Subcontractors
Subcontractors are not required to register for the CIS, but by doing so they qualify for the lower, standard rate of deductions (20%); unregistered subcontractors pay the higher rate of 30%. The rate that is applied is referred to as the subcontractor's "payment status".

Subcontractors can register using **Form CIS301**, or by telephoning HMRC with details of name, trading name, address, telephone number, UTR and NINO.

If a subcontractor fails to register with HMRC before a payment from the contractor is received, then the contractor is obliged to deduct the higher rate of 30% from the payment. HMRC may refuse payment under deduction of 20% if a subcontractor has a bad tax compliance record. In such cases a 30% deduction will apply.

If they meet certain conditions, subcontractors can also apply for "gross payment status", meaning that the contractor is permitted to pay the subcontractor in full with no deductions (see **Section 11.2.4**).

Registration or non-registration for the CIS does not affect a subcontractor's other tax obligations, that is they must still be registered for self-assessment income tax and Class 2 NICs (see **Chapter 9**).

Contractors
Contractors are **obliged** to register with HMRC before they 'take on' their first subcontractor, regardless of the "payment status" of that subcontractor. HMRC compile separate lists of contractors

and subcontractors; therefore, if a business is a contractor **and** a subcontractor, two registrations are required. In regard to this, it is important to note that when a business is acting as a contractor, it must follow the compliance rules for contractors; likewise, when acting as a subcontractor it must follow the compliance rules for subcontractors.

Registration permits contractors to verify the payment status of a subcontractor. It also obliges the contractor to make monthly CIS returns and monthly CIS remittances.

Status of Relationship

The CIS operates only where the relationship is contractor–subcontractor; it does not operate where the relationship is employer–employee. The correct identification of the relationship is very important at the outset, and should be reviewed throughout the arrangement (see **Section 5.2**). Where there is a contract of employment, payments do not fall within the CIS – instead PAYE and NIC (Class 1) deductions should be operated (see **Chapter 9**).

HMRC emphasises that employment (i.e. employee) or self-employment (i.e. subcontractor) status is determined from the facts and from the terms of each engagement. If a worker who has been treated as self-employed is re-categorised by HMRC as an employee, the employer (i.e. previously the contractor) is exposed to PAYE, NICs, interest and penalty liabilities.

11.2.2 Verification by the CIS

Once a contractor is registered for the CIS, they can verify the "payment status" of the subcontractor, i.e. whether the standard rate of 20% or higher 30% rate should be deducted from payments, by phone or online.

The verification process consists of three simple steps:

1. The contractor provides their own name, unique tax reference (UTR), accounts office reference and employer reference.
2. The contractor provides the subcontractor's name, UTR and NINO for individuals and partnerships, or the company tax reference and company registration number for companies.
3. HMRC advises the contractor of the "verification number", which must be retained and included on the monthly return.

If the subcontractor has been included on the contractor's CIS monthly return for the current tax year or the previous two tax years, then verification of the subcontractor is **not** required and, in this instance, the contractor applies the same payment status as the last time the contractor paid the subcontractor, unless HMRC has notified the contractor of a change in payment status.

Example 11.1

Date contractor engages subcontractor A:	September 2021
Date contractor last paid subcontractor A:	Never
Date contractor proposes to pay subcontractor:	30 November 2021

Verification details: the contractor **must** verify this subcontractor before they can pay them under CIS on 30 November 2021. HMRC will tell the contractor whether a deduction should be made from this and all future payments to the subcontractor.

Example 11.2

Date contractor engages subcontractor B:	September 2021
Date contractor last paid subcontractor B:	February 2018
Details of last payment return:	Contractor made last payment return for the subcontractor in tax year 2017/18.

Verification details: as the period of the last payment return is not within the last two tax years before the tax year in which payment is now being made (2021/22), the contractor must verify this subcontractor with HMRC before they can pay them under CIS. HMRC will tell the contractor whether a deduction should be made from this and all future payments to the subcontractor.

11.2.3 CIS Returns and Payments

When a registered contractor has made a payment to a subcontractor, they are obliged to submit a CIS return, form CIS300, and remittance of the amount deducted from the payment to HMRC **within 14 days of the end of the tax month** (the payment deadline is extended to 17 days if payment is made electronically). For example, the return for 6 December 2021–5 January 2022 should be filed, along with any CIS payments, with HMRC by 19 January 2022 (payments can be made by 22 January 2022 if paying electronically). If a contractor has not made any payments to subcontractors in a tax month, they are not required to submit a return for that month, although they can submit a 'nil' return if they wish. In practice, it is advisable to submit a nil return to avoid HMRC assuming that a return has been missed or is late.

Online filing of all CIS returns is mandatory (except for those unable to access online resources by reason of age, disability, remote location or religious objection).

Where the average monthly payments of PAYE, NIC, CIS and student loan deductions are less than £1,500, i.e. "small" payers, the contractor can choose to pay quarterly instead – but monthly CIS returns are still required.

Monthly CIS returns are pre-populated with details of subcontractors previously returned or verified within the last three months and are sent by HMRC to the contractor each month. The returns must be filed online or via some commercial CIS software.

The CIS return (CIS300) should include the following information on all "construction contracts" during that month:

- contractor's details such as – name, UTR, or company tax reference number;
- Subcontractor's details;
- the verification number as provided by HMRC;
- details of **all payments** made to subcontractors, including to those with "gross payment status";
- cost of materials paid to the subcontractor in the month.

In addition, as part of the monthly return the contractor must declare that the employment status of each individual has been considered and that payments have not been made under contracts of employment.

Deductible Costs

CIS deductions are withheld from the gross payment to a subcontractor, excluding deductible costs. Deductible costs are costs incurred by the subcontractor and include:

- materials (the VAT-exclusive cost of materials, i.e. the price before VAT);
- plant hire;

- fuel (except fuel for travelling to and from the work site); and
- cost of manufacture or prefabrication of materials.

From 1 March 2021, VAT-registered subcontractors, where certain conditions are met, will not charge VAT on their invoices as the domestic reverse charge will apply (see **Section 19.9.6**). Therefore, the need to exclude VAT when working out the amount of CIS deductions will not be an issue.

The contractor can ask the subcontractor for evidence of the direct cost of materials. If this information is not provided, then the contractor must make a fair estimate of the material costs involved.

Example 11.3

A subcontractor, registered for VAT, agrees to paint the interior of a building and to supply the materials. The painter pays £240 for the materials (including VAT of £40). The total cost to the contractor is £600 (excluding VAT). The subcontractor has a poor compliance record and therefore suffers 30% deductions.

It is confirmed that the CIS domestic reverse charge should apply to the invoice from the painter to the contractor.

Subcontractor invoice issued August 2021:

	£	
Labour charge	400	
Materials	200	
	600	
VAT (CIS reverse charge applies)	0	
Amount due (invoice amount)	600	

Calculation of CIS deduction:

Total payment	600	
Less: cost of materials (exc. VAT)	(200)	
Amount liable to CIS deduction	400	
Amount deducted @ 30%	(120)	
Net payment to subcontractor	480	[£600 – £120]

Entries on the contractor's monthly return:

Total payment	480
Direct cost of materials used	200
Amount deducted	120

Contractor's Obligations to a Subcontractor

The contractor **must** issue a "**payment and deduction statement**" to subcontractors within 14 days of the end of the tax month that a payment has been made. A statement can be issued to a subcontractor each month; or for each payment if they are paid more often. This statement may be used by subcontractors to work out their income tax liability for the tax year or they may prepare their own payment analysis statements including the same information.

The contractor, if an employer in addition to having subcontractors, is still obliged to file a full payment submission under Real Time Information (RTI) and should include on the full payment submission (FPS) the total amount of CIS deductions due to be paid so that HMRC can reconcile the total payments made during the tax year.

CIS Deductions and Income Tax

From the subcontractor's perspective, the payment and deduction statement received from the contractor is evidence of tax withheld under CIS payments. As such it is an important document for the subcontractor as the sums withheld are included on the their income tax return for the tax year and credited against any income tax and Class 4 NIC liability due for that year.

Subcontractors who are companies may offset CIS deductions from the company's income against its PAYE liability or against CIS deductions withheld from other subcontractors in the same tax year. Subcontractors that are partnerships or self-employed cannot offset their CIS deductions in this manner.

11.2.4 Registration for "Gross Payment Status"

A subcontractor can apply to HMRC to be classed as "gross payment status" status, meaning that the contractor is permitted to pay the subcontractor in full without any CIS deductions. There are three criteria, all of which must be met, for the 12 months prior to application (the "qualifying period") in order to qualify for gross payment status:

- the business test;
- the turnover test; and
- the compliance test.

The Business Test

The business test requires that the subcontractor provide evidence that they carry out construction work in the UK or provide labour for construction work in the UK and that this business is substantially operated through a business bank account. HMRC will require evidence of business contact details and business activities, e.g. copies of invoices, bank statements, construction contracts, details of payments for construction work, the books and accounts of the business, etc.

The Turnover Test

HMRC will look at the subcontractor's net turnover from "construction operations" for the 12 months prior to application, ignoring the cost of materials and VAT. Depending on whether the subcontractor is an individual, a partnership or a company, turnover must be at least:

- Individual – £30,000 from labour on construction operations only.
- Partnership – £30,000 for each partner in a partnership, or at least £100,000 for the whole partnership.
- Company – £30,000 for each director of a company, or at least £100,000 for the whole company. If a company is controlled by five people or fewer, there must be an annual turnover of £30,000 for each of them.

The Compliance Test

Subcontractors (including all partners/directors/participators if a partnership or company) must have met all of their tax compliance obligations during the previous 12 months. This includes filing and paying all business taxes, PAYE, CIS and VAT on time, as well as filing and paying all personal taxes on time.

Withdrawal of Gross Payment Status

A subcontractor's gross payment status is reviewed annually by HMRC. A subcontractor must file tax returns and make payments in a timely manner to retain gross payment status. However, HMRC will allow a subcontractor a small amount of late payments or returns before deeming them to fail the annual review. If a subcontractor fails the review, HMRC will remove the availability of gross payment status.

The withdrawal of gross payment status is first notified to the subcontractor in question, who has a right to disagree with HMRC. In which case the subcontractor should write to HMRC outlining the reasons/explanations why gross payment status should not be removed. If HMRC accept the subcontractor's explanations, gross payment status will not be removed. If HMRC is not contacted by the subcontractor or they do not accept the subcontractor's explanations, it will inform the subcontractor that they are withdrawing gross payment status in 90 days. Contractors are then notified of the change of status of a subcontractor.

11.3   Penalties under the CIS

A penalty regime is in place to encourage contractors to file their CIS returns on time. The following penalties apply where a CIS return is submitted late:

How late the return is	Penalty
1 day late	£100
2 months late	£200
6 months late	£300 or 5% of the CIS deductions on the return, whichever is higher
12 months late	£300 or 5% of the CIS deductions on the return, whichever is higher

For returns submitted more than 12 months late, an additional penalty may be incurred of up to £3,000 or 100% of the CIS deductions on the return, whichever is the higher.

Questions

Review Questions
(See Suggested Solutions to Review Questions at the end of this textbook.)

Question 11.1

A subcontractor, who is not a taxable person for VAT, agrees to plaster part of the interior of a building and to supply the materials for a total cost of £4,600. The plasterer pays £900 for the materials, which includes VAT of £150. The plasterer provides an invoice to the contractor as follows:

	£
Labour charge	3,700
Materials	900
Amount due (invoice total)	4,600

The plasterer is registered and verified by HMRC for standard rate CIS deductions.

Requirement
Calculate the CIS deduction to be made by the contractor and the payment made to the subcontractor.

Question 11.2

A contractor contracts three new subcontractors, for the month ended 5 February 2022, to assist in the construction of an office block for a developer client. The CIS reverse charge applies. The invoices received from the subcontractors for the period are as follows:

	Subcontractor A	Subcontractor B	Subcontractor C
	£	£	£
Labour	5,000	10,000	2,000
Materials	3,500	2,000	1,500
VAT*	—	—	—
Total due	8,500	12,000	3,500

* CIS reverse charge applies.

The contractor has verified the status of the subcontractors with HMRC, which has advised as follows:

Subcontractor A – Gross payment status
Subcontractor B – Standard rate deduction
Subcontractor C – 30% deduction due to poor tax compliance record

The contractor and subcontractors are registered for VAT.

Requirement
Calculate the CIS deductions to be made by the contractor and declared in the CIS return for the period ended 5 February 2022. What are the payments made to each of the subcontractors?

Part Two
Corporation Tax

Introduction and General Principles of Corporation Tax

Learning Objectives

After studying this chapter you will understand:

- The operation of the self-assessment system, including payment of tax, penalties, interest and the filing of returns.
- How to determine the appropriate rate of corporation tax.
- How to determine the amount of property income assessable.
- How to apply relief for expenses against property income.
- How to tax premiums on short leases.
- The treatment of property losses.
- The Loan Relationship Provision.
- How to treat trading and non-trading loan relationships.
- How to apply the appropriate treatment of capital gains within the context of corporation tax.

Chartered Accountants Ireland's *Code of Ethics* applies to all aspects of a Chartered Accountant's professional life, including dealing with corporation tax issues. As outlined at the beginning of this book, further information regarding the principles in the *Code of Ethics* is set out in **Appendix 2**.

In addition, **Appendix 3** examines the distinction between tax planning, tax avoidance and tax evasion, which can arise in relation to all taxes, including corporation tax.

12.1 The UK Corporation Tax Regime

Corporation tax chargeable is calculated by applying the relevant corporation tax rate to the company's taxable total profits (TTP). The financial year (FY) for corporation tax commences on 1 April every year, so the FY 2021 commenced on 1 April 2021. The main rate of corporation tax for the FY 2021 is 19% (FY 2020: 19%). It is worth noting that Finance Act 2021 has introduced significant reforms to the rate of corporation tax which will apply from 1 April 2023. From this date, the main rate of corporation tax will increase to 25% for profits in excess of £250,000. From the same date, a "small profits rate" of 19% will apply to profits up to £50,000. For businesses with profits between £50,000 and £250,000, corporation tax will be charged at the main rate, subject to marginal relief provisions which will provide a gradual increase in the effective corporation tax rate. However, for FY 2021 and FY 2022, the corporation tax rate remains at 19%.

Payment of corporation tax depends on the size of the company.

- ■ A small or medium-sized company's corporation tax is due and payable nine months and one day after the end of the accounting period.
- ■ "Large" companies and "very large" companies are required to pay their corporation tax liabilities in instalments. See **Section 12.5**.

12.2 Overview – Application and Accounting Periods

A company is defined as "any body corporate or unincorporated association". Therefore, unincorporated societies, trade and voluntary associations, members' clubs and certain charities will find themselves within the corporation tax regime. Partnerships are specifically excluded from the definition of a "body corporate".

Corporation tax is levied on the profits of companies, as defined, and is payable by the company. For companies, all transactions should be included in the financial statements. Therefore, the computation of corporation tax requires the analysis of those profits between the various sources of income and chargeable gains. The types of profit that are chargeable to corporation tax consist of trading income, chargeable gains, property income, miscellaneous income, profits from non-trading intangible assets and surplus non-trade loan relationship credits. A dividend payment is not an expense of the company and therefore does not attract tax relief per se. A company's income and gains are generally calculated using income tax and CGT principles and the rules for the various types of income apply, in the main, to the UK corporation tax regime.

The FY for corporation tax purposes commences on 1 April and ends on the following 31 March with corporation tax rates fixed for financial years.

Directors of UK companies are required to prepare and file statutory accounts with Companies Registry (or Companies House) for every 12-month accounting period. At the end of an accounting period, HM Revenue & Customs (HMRC) will issue a notice (Form CT603) specifying the 12-month period for which HMRC consider that a corporation tax return (Form CT600) is due. While the corporation tax accounting period would normally follow the statutory accounting period, there are specific rules that determine the date of commencement and cessation of a corporation tax accounting period.

12.2.1 Accounting Periods

Corporation tax is assessed on the profits arising in the company's accounting period. The term "accounting period" is given a special meaning for corporation tax purposes. Ordinarily it is the period for which the company makes up its accounts ("period of account"), **but an accounting period cannot exceed 12 months**.

12.2.2 The Beginning of the Accounting Period

For corporation tax purposes, the first accounting period of a company begins whenever the company comes within the charge to corporation tax. A company may come within the charge to corporation tax in one of several ways:

1. A new company may be created and acquire a source of income.
2. An unincorporated partnership or sole trade may become incorporated.
3. A company may acquire for the first time a source of income chargeable to corporation tax. For example, a non-resident company may start to trade in the UK through a permanent establishment (such as a branch or agency), at which point an accounting period will start.

12.2.3 The End of the Accounting Period

An accounting period runs for a maximum of 12 months from its start. It will end earlier if the company's own accounting date (i.e. its period of account) falls within the 12 months. A new accounting period starts immediately at the end of an accounting period, unless the accounting period ended because the company ceased altogether to be within the charge to corporation tax.

An accounting period ends when any one of the following happens:

- the expiry of 12 months from the beginning of the accounting period;
- the accounting date of the company, that is the date to which it makes up its accounts;
- the end of a period for which a company does not make up accounts;
- the company begins to trade;
- the company comes within the charge to corporation tax in respect of its trade or, if it carries on more than one trade, of all its trades;
- the company ceases to trade;
- the company ceases to be within the charge to corporation tax in respect of its trade or, if it carries on more than one trade, of all its trades;
- the company ceases to be within the charge to corporation tax; or
- the commencement of the winding up of the company.

Example 12.1

Start Ltd was incorporated on 1 June 2021. The money subscribed for share capital was put on deposit. The company commenced to trade on 1 September 2021. It prepared its first set of financial statements for the period ended 31 December 2021 and intends to prepare annual financial statements to 31 December each year thereafter.

As Start Ltd acquired a source of income on 1 June, an accounting period commenced. As it commenced to trade on 1 September, an accounting period is deemed to end, even though no actual set of financial statements are prepared. Therefore, Start Ltd has an accounting period of three months, ending on 31 August 2021. Its next accounting period is from 1 September to 31 December 2021. Thereafter it will have accounting periods ending on 31 December each year.

12.2.4 Companies that Prepare Accounts for a Period of Less Than 12 Months

For accounting periods of less than 12 months that have resulted from a change in the normal annual accounting date of the company, HMRC has no special powers. For example, if a company has prepared a 12-month set of accounts to 31 December 2020, then an eight-month set of accounts to 31 August 2021 followed by a 12-month set of accounts to 31 August 2021, corporation tax is simply payable for each of the three accounting periods. However, when seeking to amend the accounting periods of a company, the relevant company law conditions must be met. Broadly, a company may not extend accounting periods more than once in five years unless it falls into some very specific categories.

12.2.5 Companies that Prepare Accounts for a Period Exceeding 12 Months

As the maximum length of an accounting period is 12 months, where a company prepares a set of accounts for a period exceeding 12 months, this "period of account" must be broken down into tranches, each a maximum of 12 months long.

Example 12.2

X Ltd prepared a set of accounts for 18 months ending on 30 June 2022. In these circumstances corporation tax is payable for the following "accounting periods":

1. 12-month accounting period to 31 December 2021.

2. Six-month accounting period to 30 June 2022 (remember an accounting period is terminated automatically by reference to the date to which a set of accounts is prepared).

As you can see from this example, **if the period of account is longer than 12 months, the first accounting period will always be at least 12 months long**.

In the above example, the statement of profit or loss was 18 months long, meaning a tax-adjusted profits computation would have to be prepared. This would involve adjusting for the various normal add-backs and deductions to produce a tax-adjusted profits computation (ignoring capital allowances for the moment) corresponding to an 18-month period. One would then **time-apportion** the tax-adjusted trading profits for this 18-month period to arrive at the relevant trading income for each of the accounting periods mentioned above.

It should be particularly noted that, as a general rule, the profits should be apportioned on a time basis according to the number of days in the accounting period. However, HMRC reserves the right to divide and apportion profits in a different fashion if they believe, and can demonstrate, that it was a "more accurate and fairer estimate". Notwithstanding this, chargeable gains are always allocated to the period in which they occurred. For example, if there was only one capital disposal in the 18-month period, say on 1 May 2022, then the adjusted chargeable gain would be assessed and brought into the computation for the six-month accounting period ending on 30 June 2022. In addition, qualifying charitable donations (see **Chapter 13**) are split between the two chargeable accounting periods, based on the date that the donation is actually paid. Finally, dividends that represent franked investment income are split between the two chargeable accounting periods, based on the date of receipt of the dividend (rather than being time-apportioned).

In the above example, the capital allowances would have to be computed separately for each of the two accounting periods. Therefore, in this situation, capital allowances are not allowed as a trading expense until after the trading income has been time-apportioned.

Each of the split periods will require the preparation of a separate company tax return, and have separate due dates for the payment of corporation tax. There is only one filing deadline, however, which is normally 12 months after the end of the second period of account.

12.2.6 Corporation Tax Self-assessment

As each company has its own accounting year end, the law relates payment of tax and filing of returns to that year end, split if necessary, as discussed above. Companies report their liability to corporation tax to HMRC via the self-assessment procedures and each company must calculate its own liability. Thus companies are required to prepare a corporation tax computation, setting out the liability due, and submit this to HMRC in conjunction with the corporation tax return (Form CT600) and a copy of their statutory accounts (in iXBRL format), which are the accounts the company must file at Companies House or that the organisation must prepare under its constitution. They include directors' and auditors' reports. However, if the company files abbreviated accounts at Companies House, it **must** file full accounts as part of its company tax return. Accounts can be prepared under International Financial Reporting Standards (IFRS) or UK GAAP. See **Section 12.10** for more on corporation tax self-assessment.

12.2.7 UK GAAP

For the avoidance of doubt, UK GAAP includes accounts of companies prepared under International Accounting Standards, International Financial Reporting Standards and under Financial Reporting Standards, including FRS 102 *The Financial Reporting Standard applicable in the UK and Republic of Ireland*.

12.3   The Charge to Corporation Tax

Corporation tax is assessed on the profits of companies for accounting periods. Accordingly the concept of basis periods in the income tax code is not carried into the corporation tax system.

The question of whether, and how, a company is to be charged to corporation tax depends on whether or not it is resident in the UK. In the case of a **company resident in the UK**, the charge to corporation tax is imposed on **all its income** wherever arising and **its chargeable gains** wherever the assets were situated, irrespective of whether or not they are remitted to the UK.

12.4   Rates of Corporation Tax

The rates of corporation tax applicable for single companies with a full 12-month accounting period are given in the table below.

Rate	Name	As From	Taxable total profits (TTP)
19%	Main rate	1 April 2020	All profits, irrespective of size
19%	Main rate	1 April 2021	All profits, irrespective of size
19%	Main rate	1 April 2022	All profits, irrespective of size

12.4.1 Main Rate of Corporation Tax

The main rate of corporation tax for the 2021 financial year, i.e. the FY that commenced on 1 April 2021, is 19%. The main rate for the 2020 financial year was 19%.

A separate corporation tax regime has been proposed to come into operation in Northern Ireland at a currently undetermined date. Under this proposed special corporation tax regime for Northern Ireland, qualifying profits of certain qualifying companies may be subject to a 12.5% rate of corporation tax. The detailed provisions of this regime are beyond the scope of this textbook.

Example 12.3

Mary Ltd had taxable total profits (TTP) from selling clothes of £200,000 in the year ended 31 March 2022.

Corporation tax payable by Mary Ltd is £38,000 (£200,000 × 19%).

12.4.2 Short Accounting Periods

If a company produces accounts for a period of less than 12 months, taxable total profits are still taxed at the main rate applicable to the relevant financial year(s).

12.4.3 Accounting Period Straddles Two Financial Years

Where a company's accounting period straddles two financial years, and the rate of corporation tax for each year is not the same, its taxable total profits must be apportioned on a time basis for each of the two financial years and then charged to corporation tax at the rates applicable for each financial year.

HMRC reserve the right to amend this general rule if a more accurate and fairer estimate can be applied to the split between the financial years.

12.5 Dates of Payment of Corporation Tax

12.5.1 Overview

A small or medium-sized company's corporation tax is due and payable nine months and one day after the end of the accounting period. However, "large" companies are required to pay their corporation tax liabilities in up to four quarterly instalments. The number of quarterly instalment payments a company needs to make depends on the length of the accounting period and the number of related 51% group companies at the end of the prior period. A company is deemed to be "large" if its augmented profits exceed the upper relevant maximum amount, currently £1,500,000, as adjusted for the number of related 51% group companies. However, the company will not be required to pay by instalments in an accounting period where the "augmented profits" for that period do not exceed £10 million **and** it was not "large" in the previous period. Also, a company is not treated as "large" for an accounting period if its corporation tax liability does not exceed £10,000.

Augmented profits are taxable total profits (TTP) plus non-group franked investment income (FII). FII is any dividend received irrespective of location of the paying company. Only non-group FII is included, i.e. dividends received from shareholdings less than 51%.

However, while augmented profits are measured against the above limits to establish if instalment payments are required, the actual instalment payments are only calculated on the basis of TTP. This is because, often, any non-group FII received will meet one of the dividend exemptions outlined in **Chapter 13**.

12.5.2 Related 51% Group Companies

The above limits (of £10 million, £1.5 million and £10,000) are reduced where the company has related 51% group companies and where the accounting period is less than 12 months. The number of related 51% group companies to be taken into account for the purpose of these limits are those in existence **on the last day of the previous accounting period**.

For the purpose of the corporation tax instalment payment rules, a company is classed as a related 51% group company if it is a member of a 51% group. A "group" of companies, for this purpose, means a group headed by a company. So if, for example, an individual shareholder and their family were to directly own the shares in a number of companies, the companies would not be related 51% group companies.

If, instead, an individual shareholder and their family were to own a company, which in turn owned at least 51% of the share capital of three subsidiaries, then the four companies would be related 51% group companies.

Each company's profits are looked at separately when determining whether or not it must pay corporation tax in instalments. In the situation above where a 51% group relationship does exist, the profit limit would be divided by four in determining whether each company was or was not liable to pay corporation tax in instalments.

A related 51% holding is either a holding of at least 51% of the issued share capital or voting power or being entitled to at least 51% of the distributable income or net assets on a winding up.

The residence of a company is irrelevant.

Importantly, companies that have only been related 51% group companies for part of any accounting period are deemed to have been related 51% group companies for the whole of the accounting period for the purposes of determining if the augmented profit limits for instalment payments has been exceeded.

However, a related 51% group company is ignored for these purposes if it has not carried on any trade or business at any time in the accounting period (or for the part of the period during which it was a related 51% group company); generally this applies to dormant companies.

Finally, a holding company is considered as not carrying on a trade or business (and thus is not included in the number of related 51% group companies for the purposes of the instalment payment rules) provided that:

1.   its only assets are shares in subsidiaries;
2.   it is not entitled to deduct any outgoings as charges or management expenses; and
3.   its only profits are dividends from subsidiaries and these are distributed in full to its shareholders.

All of the above conditions must be satisfied.

The related 51% group company rules therefore play an important part in determining if a company is required to pay corporation tax in instalments.

Example 12.4

A Ltd (which prepares accounts to March each year) has five related 51% group companies (all wholly-owned subsidiaries) at the end of the year ended 31 March 2021. A Ltd then acquires a new subsidiary in September 2021, but also disposes of two of its subsidiaries in September 2021. A Ltd has augmented profits for the accounting period ended 31 March 2022 of £425,000. A Ltd was not "large" in 2021.

To determine if the company was "large" in 2022, the number of related 51% group companies at the end of the previous accounting period is used. Therefore, £1.5 million would be divided by six – being five related 51% group companies plus the company itself. The threshold would be £250,000. Having established that the company is "large" in 2022 (because it has profits of £425,000, which is clearly in excess of £250,000) we then need to determine if it is subject to the quarterly instalment regime.

As A Ltd was not "large" in the prior year (i.e. in 2021), the £10 million threshold is used for the purposes of assessing whether instalments are required in the 2022 period. We divide this by the number of related 51% group companies at the end of the 2021 period (i.e. six – being five related 51% group companies plus the company itself).

The limit for A Ltd is thus £1,666,667 (£10,000,000/6). Therefore A Ltd will not pay in instalments and its corporation tax will fall due on 1 January 2023. The acquisition of a new subsidiary in 2022 and the disposal of two of the existing subsidiaries does not impact on the number of related 51% group companies in the 2022 accounting period – because it is the number of related 51% group companies at the end of the previous accounting period, for both the £1,500,000 and £10,000,000 limits, that is used.

However, when assessing whether instalments will be required in 2023, the number of related 51% group companies will be six (and the limits will be divided by seven, being A Ltd plus six related 51% group companies). The acquisition is counted, but the two disposals are not – because a company is treated as a related 51% group company for the whole period if it is one even for a single day.

12.5.3 Due Date and Calculation of Instalments

The first of the maximum four quarterly instalments falls due six months and 13 days after the start of the accounting period, the second after a further three months, the third after a further three months with the fourth and final instalment due three months and 14 days after the end of the accounting period. In essence, for a company with a 12-month accounting period, the instalments are due on the 14th day of the seventh and tenth months during the accounting period and the first and fourth months after the end of the accounting period.

Where the accounting period is less than 12 months, the **final instalment remains due on the normal date, three months and 14 days after the end of the accounting period**. In this scenario, earlier instalments only fall due if their due date is prior to the date of the final instalment.

The liability due at each instalment is calculated using the following formula:

$$\frac{3 \times \text{company's total liability}}{\text{No. of months in accounting period}}$$

For example, for an eight-month period, the first instalment would be 3/8ths of the total tax liability, then the second instalment would be another 3/8ths, and a final instalment of 2/8ths of the total tax liability for the period. Interest is charged on instalments paid late at the late instalment rate as set by HMRC (2.75% from 30 March 2020 to 6 April 2020 and 2.60% from 7 April 2020).

Example 12.5

Trust Limited is a large company with an accounting year end of 31 December. Its instalments of corporation tax will fall due for payment on:

(a) 14 July and 14 October in the accounting period; and
(b) 14 January and 14 April after the accounting period.

Example 12.6

Syracuse Ltd had a corporation liability for the year ended 31 March 2022 of £1,000,000. The amount of each instalment is 3 × £1,000,000/12 = £250,000 and these payments will fall due on: 14 October 2021, 14 January 2022, 14 April 2022 and 14 July 2022.

Example 12.7

Andes Ltd has a corporation tax liability of £990,000 for the nine-month period ended 31 October 2021. The company is large due to the number of related 51% group companies. The instalment amount is calculated initially by applying the above formula, i.e. £330,000 (3 × £990,000/9). The instalments and due dates are thus:

■ £330,000 on 14 August 2021;
■ £330,000 on 14 November 2021; and
■ £330,000 on 14 February 2022.

The first instalment is always due six months and 13 days after the first day of the accounting period, i.e. 14 August 2021 which is six months and 13 days after 1 February 2021. The final instalment is always due three months and 14 days after the end of the accounting period.

As noted above, the instalments are based on the estimated corporation tax liability for the current period. Thus it is very important that companies accurately forecast their potential corporation tax liabilities to avoid incurring significant interest charges. This will invariably entail the company reviewing its estimates each quarter and adjusting payments already made and still to be made accordingly.

12.5.4 Very Large Companies

"Very large" companies are required to make their corporation tax payments earlier. A very large company is one whose augmented profits exceed £20 million. This threshold is adjusted for the number of related 51% group companies at the end of the previous accounting period and if the company has an accounting period less than 12 months.

When a company is first classed as very large, no grace period is given, i.e. the earlier due dates will immediately apply to that accounting period.

Where the accounting period is 12 months, the first payment will be due two months and 13 days after the beginning of the accounting period. The second, third and fourth payments will be due three months after the previous payment, i.e. the second payment three months after the first, the third three months after the second and so on. This will be the 14th day of months three, six, nine and 12 of the accounting period.

Where the accounting period is less than 12 months, the final instalment will remain due on the normal date, i.e. on the 14th day of the last month of the accounting period. Once again, earlier instalments only fall due if their due date is prior to the date of the final instalment.

The calculation of each instalment is unchanged.

Example 12.8

Design Ltd has a 12-month accounting period ended 31 March 2022. It is a "very large" company with a projected corporation tax liability of £5,000,000.

Each corporation tax instalment is:

$$\frac{3 \times £5,000,000}{12} = £1,250,000$$

The due date of each instalment is:

1. First instalment: £1,250,000 due 14 June 2021 (two months and 13 days from the beginning of the accounting period).
2. Second instalment: £1,250,000 due 14 September 2021 (three months after the first instalment).
3. Third instalment: £1,250,000 due 14 December 2021 (three months after the second instalment).
4. Fourth instalment: £1,250,000 due 14 March 2022 (three months after the third).

Design Ltd will therefore pay its entire corporation tax liability for 2022 before the end of the period.

Example 12.9

Tidal Ltd has an eight-month accounting period ended 30 November 2021. It is a "very large" company under the instalment payment rules with a projected liability of £6,000,000.

Each corporation tax instalment is:

$$\frac{3 \times £6,000,000}{8} = £2,250,000$$

The due date of each is as follows:

1. First instalment: £2,250,000 due 14 June 2021 (two months and 13 days from the beginning of the accounting period).
2. Second instalment: £2,250,000 due 14 September 2021 (three months after the first instalment).
3. Third instalment: £1,500,000 due 14 November 2021 (on the 14th day of the final month of the period).

Again, the company will have paid its entire corporation tax liability for the accounting period in question before the period has ended.

12.5.5 Interest

If a company pays its corporation tax liability after the due date, then it will be charged late payment interest, calculated from the day after the normal due date until the effective date of payment. For companies required to pay in instalments, the position is considered after the due date for each instalment (where applicable) on a cumulative basis and the interest position is calculated by HMRC after the company submits its corporation tax return.

If a company has overpaid corporation tax, it may make a repayment claim and it will also be entitled to interest on the repayment. The repayment interest runs from the "material date" to the date when the repayment was issued. Interest paid/received on late payments or overpayments of corporation tax are treated as interest paid/received on a non-trading loan relationship and included in the calculation of the net loan relationship debit or credit. The effect of this is that interest paid is deductible for corporation tax and any interest received is taxable.

Example 12.10
Wright Ltd, a large company, has always prepared accounts to 31 March. It had paid the following instalments in respect of the accounting period ending 31 March 2022:

- £2.5 million on 14 October 2021;
- £6.5 million on 14 January 2022;
- £3 million on 14 April 2022; and
- £3 million on 14 July 2022.

A total of £15 million.

On submission of its corporation tax return, the company's tax liability was actually £16 million, and the balance of £1 million was paid on 1 January 2023. Thus the £16 million should have been paid in instalments of £4 million each (3 × (£16 million/12)) and the schedule below sets out the under-/overpayments:

Date	Paid	Actually Due	Under/(over)	Cumulative
	£	£	£	£
14 October 2021	2.5m	4.0m	1.5m	1.5m
14 January 2022	6.5m	4.0m	(2.5m)	(1.0m)
14 April 2022	3.0m	4.0m	1.0m	Nil
14 July 2022	3.0m	4.0m	1.0m	1.0m

Interest would thus be charged/(received) as follows:

- Charged on £1.5 million from 14 October 2021 until 13 January 2022.
- Received on £1 million from 14 January 2022 until 13 April 2022.
- Charged on £1 million from 14 July 2022 until 31 December 2022.

12.5.6 Penalties

In order to dissuade companies from deliberately understating their instalments, HMRC reserve the right to impose penalties (on top of the above interest charges) where they find no justifiable reasons for inadequate instalment payments. This would normally involve consideration of the contemporaneous records of the company and a request for the company's explanation of why their estimates were incorrect.

A penalty can arise where:

- a company, or person acting on its behalf, deliberately or recklessly fails to pay the right amount on a particular instalment date; or
- a company, or person acting on its behalf, fraudulently or negligently makes a claim for repayment under the Instalment Regulations.

The penalty is an amount not exceeding twice the amount of interest charged on any unpaid amount in respect of the total liability of the company for its accounting period. Any penalties paid are not deductible for corporation tax purposes.

12.6   Computation of Income

The basic rule for the calculation of taxable income is that, apart from certain special provisions relevant only to companies, it is computed in accordance with income tax principles.

The income tax scheme of capital allowances and balancing charges is brought into the corporation tax system. However, **capital allowances** due to trading companies are **treated as trading expenses** for corporation tax purposes and not as a deduction from the assessable income as in the case of income tax. Similarly, balancing charges are treated for corporation purposes as trading receipts.

For the purposes of computing the tax-adjusted profits of a company from its statement of profit or loss for an accounting period, the following particular points of difference should be noted:

- Bona fide directors' salaries, fees, benefits payable for directors, etc. are deductible, unlike the drawings/salary of a self-employed person.
- Where a director has a company car available for private use, there is no adjustment for "personal element" for corporation tax purposes, unlike the personal element of a self-employed person.

Example 12.11

Joe and Ann jointly own Deduction Ltd and are both directors on the board of the company. Deduction Ltd pays all the motor expenses incurred in running Joe's car. Only 75% of the expenses are incurred in respect of the business. The balance of 25% is personal.

Deduction Ltd will be entitled to a full deduction for all the motor expenses, even though some of the expense is personal; however Joe will be liable to income tax on the benefit in kind arising on the personal motor expenses paid by the company.

- Dividend payments by a company are not deductible as they are treated as appropriations of profit.
- Interest on borrowings, which are used for trading purposes (e.g. financing of stock, debtors and fixed assets used for the purpose of the trade), are fully allowable on the **accruals** basis. If, on the other hand, a company has borrowed money and applies the funds for non-trading purposes, say, for the purchase of shares in a subsidiary or as other investments, then such interest charges are not deductible against trading income. However, these would generally qualify as non-trade deficits under the loan relationship rules (see **Section 12.8**).

A pro forma corporation tax computation, together with notes on important adjustments, is set out in **Chapter 13**.

12.7 Computation of Property Income

12.7.1 Property Income (Income from Land and Buildings)

Companies are charged corporation tax on income arising from the letting of land and property, wherever situated. Income generated from land and property in the UK is aggregated into one "UK property business". Income from all land and property outside the UK is combined into the company's "overseas property business".

Property business profits/(losses) are computed in accordance with generally accepted accounting principles and the types of income assessable under this schedule would include payments for a licence to occupy, exercise or use of a right over land, income from furnished lettings, ground rents and other annual payments in respect of land and so forth.

While capital allowances are available for plant used in a letting business, they are not available for plant let for use in a residential property.

Landlords of residential property can deduct only the actual costs incurred on replacing furnishings in the company's accounting period. This relief is available for domestic items, including furnishings, appliances and kitchenware provided for the use of a lessee in a dwelling-house. Fixtures are excluded. The old item must no longer be available for use in the dwelling-house. The expenditure must be of a capital nature and incurred "wholly and exclusively" for the purposes of the property business.

The deductibility of property expenses generally follows the income tax principles which were set out in **Chapter 7**. However, for a company, **interest is excluded** from a property income computation and is dealt with as a non-trading "debit" under the loan relationship rules (see **Section 12.8**).

Basis of Assessment

Tax is charged on the income arising during the accounting period. The rent taken into account is the amount receivable, whether or not it is actually received, i.e. on an accruals rather than a cash basis. The cash basis for property income that applies to individuals and partners does not apply to companies.

12.7.2 Premiums on Short Leases

Where a company receives a premium on the creation of a short lease (i.e. one that does not exceed 50 years), the premium will be treated partly as a disposal for CGT purposes (outside the scope of this text) and partly as income.

The latter is treated as property income in the year in which the lease is granted (in addition to any actual rent for that period), and is computed using the same formula explained in **Section 7.3.3**, namely:

$$\text{Premium} - \left(\text{Premium} \times \frac{\text{Duration of lease} - 1}{50} \right)$$

12.7.3 Allowable Deductions in Calculating Property Income

The following amounts may be deducted from the gross rents:

1. Rent payable.
2. Rates (if any), property insurance, etc.
3. Cost of goods or services which the landlord is obliged to provide and for which he receives no separate consideration, e.g. gas, electricity, waste disposal.
4. Cost of repairs (excluding improvements and items treated as capital expenditure).

Examples of common repairs that are normally deductible in computing rental business profits include:

- exterior and interior painting and decorating;
- stone cleaning;
- damp and rot treatment;
- mending broken windows, doors, furniture and machines such as cookers or lifts;
- re-pointing; and
- replacing roof slates, flashing and gutters.

5. Accountancy fees incurred in drawing up rental accounts and keeping rental records.
6. Company landlords of residential property can deduct the actual cost incurred on replacing furnishings in the company's accounting period – see **Section 12.7.1**.
7. Legal fees of a revenue nature wholly and exclusively incurred in connection with the rental business. Legal costs involved with the first letting of a property for more than one year are deemed to be of a capital nature and are not allowable. However, legal and professional costs incurred in respect of the renewal of short-term leases (a lease of less than 50 years) are allowable, though not the payment of a premium. Finally, legal costs incurred in acquiring or adding to a property and those involved with the change of use of a property in vacant periods between lets are disallowable.

Allowable expenses are normally deducted on an accruals basis rather than on a paid basis. Expenses incurred in respect of a property before a lease commences in respect of that property are, in the main, not deductible. In the case of interest and rent, no deduction is allowed for either interest or rent payable in respect of a period before the property is first **occupied** by a lessee. However, relief may be available under the legislative provisions for pre-trading expenditure.

Expenses incurred after the termination of a lease are not deductible. However, expenses incurred after the termination of one lease and before the commencement of another lease of the property are deductible, provided the following three conditions are satisfied:

1. the expenses would otherwise be deductible;
2. the person who was the lessor of the property does not occupy the premises during the period when the property is not let; and
3. the property is let by the same lessor at the end of the period.

Example 12.12

A company purchased a rental property on 1 April 2021. Between the date of purchase and 31 May 2021 the company spent £25,000 refurbishing the property. On 1 June 2021 the property was leased for £800 per month payable in advance.

The following expenses were incurred up to 31 May 2021:

	£
Auctioneers/advertising fees for first tenants	800
Repairs and maintenance	600
Light and heat	300
Security and insurance	500
Interest on loan	1,200

continued overleaf

The following expenses were incurred in the period 1 June 2021 to 31 March 2022:

	£
Water charges	600
Light and heat	350
Security	400
Interest	2,250
Repairs/maintenance of a revenue nature	870

Calculate the taxable rental profits for the year ended 31 March 2022.

Solution

	£	£
Gross rents receivable (£800 × 10)		8,000
Less: qualifying expenses		
Auctioneers/advertising for first tenants	800	
Water charges	600	
Light and heat	350	
Security	400	
Repairs/maintenance income	870	(3,020)
Property income		4,980

Note: expenses incurred prior to letting the property are not allowable, save for auctioneers or advertising for first tenants. The interest incurred on the property loan is not a property-deductible expense. Instead, this is an allowable non-trade loan relationship deficit (see **Section 12.8**).

12.7.4 Property Income Losses

If a property company, carried on commercially, incurs losses in an accounting period on its rental business, these losses can be set against the company's total profits for the same accounting period. The treatment of property income losses is dealt with in more detail in **Chapter 14**.

12.7.5 Letting of Surplus Accommodation

The letting of surplus business accommodation (not land held as trading stock and not part of a building of which another part is used to carry on the trade) on a short-term basis is taxed as trading income rather than as property income.

Accommodation is deemed to be surplus to requirements only if it has been used in the last three years to carry on the trade (or was acquired in the last three years) and the trader intends to use it for the trade at a later date and the letting is for a term of not more than three years.

12.8 Loan Relationships

12.8.1 General

A loan relationship arises when a company lends or borrows money, including issuing or investing in debentures or buying gilts. This can be either:

1. a creditor relationship (where the company lends or invests money); or
2. a debtor relationship (where the company borrows money or issues securities).

The following types of debt (not exhaustive) have always been included within loan relationships: bank loans and deposits, advances, mortgages, overdrafts, debentures and government stock.

A normal trade debt is however not a loan relationship, nor are, *inter alia*, finance leases, hire-purchase agreements or loan guarantees.

From a corporation tax standpoint, it is imperative to distinguish whether a loan relationship is trading or non-trading.

12.8.2 Treatment of Trading Loan Relationships

In making any distinction between trade or non-trade loan relationships, accounts must have been prepared in accordance with the appropriate accounting standards and methods. This approach means that all credits and debits (both capital and revenue) have been brought into account in the corporation tax computation under the accruals basis.

In essence, where a company either owes or is due monies for the purposes of its trade (other than those items mentioned above), then it is within the trading loan relationship rules. In this situation, any resultant credits and debits are included as trading receipts and expenses within the trading income computation and no adjustments are required.

When the company is the lender, it is very difficult for it to fall within the "trading loan relationship" regime unless the loans were entered into in the course of activities forming an integral part of its trade. This is only likely to be the case for companies in the financial sector.

12.8.3 Treatment of Non-trading Loan Relationships

If a loan relationship does not relate to a trading purpose it will be a non-trading loan relationship, in which case all credits and debits must be pooled together, i.e. non-trading loan relationship debits and credits are combined to result in a net deficit or surplus. If a surplus results, the surplus is taxable as "surplus non-trade loan relationship credits". If a deficit results, relief may be available (see **Section 12.8.4**). For many companies, their only source of non-trading income will be bank interest receivable from investment of surplus funds.

The property business of a company is not deemed to be a trade for the loan relationship rules. So for example, a property rental business that has interest payable will not get a deduction for the interest payable as a property rental expense or as a trading expense (because property rental does not constitute a trade), but may be able to obtain relief for the interest as a non-trading loan relationship debit. Such interest and related costs would therefore be added back, firstly in the adjustment of trading profits computation.

Some examples of non-trade loan relationships are:

■ interest and other costs on monies borrowed for a property generating property income;
■ interest and other costs on monies borrowed to lend to or invest in another company.

12.8.4 Relief for Non-trading Deficits

The company has a choice about how it uses the surplus net deficit on non-trading loan relationships arising from the loan relationship pooling exercise. Relief can be given by:

1. set-off against total profits of the company of the same accounting period, before QCDs and in preference to trading and property losses (a partial current-year claim can be made, i.e. the in-year set-off does not have to be automatically and fully applied);
2. carry back against surplus non-trading loan relationship credits (if any) for the previous 12 months (an 'all or nothing' claim, and can be carried back even if a current-year claim has not been made); or
3. carry forward and set against total profits in future accounting periods of the company. This is subject to the loss restriction rule that applies only to losses carried forward (see **Chapter 14, Section 14.1.1**).

The company must make a claim to utilise the surplus deficit within two years of the end of the accounting period.

12.9 Computation of Chargeable Gains

Where a chargeable gain accrues to a company in an accounting period, the chargeable gain is included in the company's taxable total profits. The gain calculated is after deducting both allowable capital losses in the current accounting period and those brought forward from previous years.

Since company chargeable gains are included within the company's taxable total profits, they will fall to be taxed at the same rate as trading profits and other income. Note that companies are not liable to CGT, but instead pay corporation tax on their chargeable gains.

12.9.1 Disposals

It is important to note that the disposal of intangible assets may come within the intangible assets regime, while the disposal of loan stock is dealt with under the loan relationship rules. Thus the main category of disposals that will be relevant to companies will be the disposal of land and property, goodwill (acquired or created before 1 April 2002) and shareholdings, i.e. assets which give rise to chargeable gains or losses.

The basic calculation is broadly computed in accordance with normal CGT principles (see **Chapter 15**), with a few important exceptions. Unlike the situation for individuals, a company does not have any annual exemption. Companies are also able to avail of the indexation allowance up to 31 December 2017 (or the date of disposal, if earlier).

12.9.2 Basic Computation

The basic chargeable gains computation considers the difference between the net selling price of the asset being disposed of, compared with its original cost (or March 1982 value, if relevant and higher) coupled with any further allowable items of expenditure. As money values are being compared over different time periods, HMRC allows companies to apply indexation to the historical costs of the item being disposed of, but only up to December 2017 for disposals on or after 1 January 2018.

The gross sales proceeds are reduced by the incidental costs of sale, which could include such items as legal fees, estate agent fees, valuation fees, etc. The costs associated with the purchase are added to the actual purchase cost (or March 1982 valuation) and these items will attract indexation from the relevant date up to 31 December 2017, at the latest.

The indexation factor is calculated by taking the movement in the Retail Price Index (RPI) between the date of acquisition of the asset and the date of sale.

The indexation factor is computed using the following formula:

$$\frac{\text{RPI at sale} - \text{RPI at acquisition}}{\text{RPI at acquisition}}$$

The result is rounded to three decimal places and is then applied to the relevant cost items to arrive at the indexation allowance. This is deducted in the computation.

Indexation allowance can reduce a chargeable gain down to nil; however, indexation allowance can neither create nor increase a capital loss. In the final CA Proficiency 1 examination you are provided with these figures (see also **Appendix 1**).

12.9.3 Capital Losses

The above basic calculation could result in a capital loss, although note that the indexation allowance cannot create or increase a loss. If the company has other chargeable gains in the same period, this loss is first set against such chargeable gains. If unutilised, the capital loss is carried forward to set against future chargeable gains of subsequent accounting periods.

There are no provisions for the carry back of capital losses by a company.

If a company has an **accounting period exceeding 12 months**, the chargeable gains are allocated to the period in which the **disposal took place** and are not time-apportioned.See **Chapter 14, Section 14.7** for further discussion on capital losses.

Example 12.13

X Ltd prepares accounts to 31 March. In the year ended 31 March 2022, the tax-adjusted trading profit was £20,000. On 30 November 2021 the company sold a chargeable asset for £16,000, incurring incidental costs of sale of £1,000. It had purchased the asset for £10,000 a number of years previously and the indexation factor was 0.107.

X Ltd – Year ended 31 March 2022

	£
Trading income	20,000
Chargeable gain (Note)	3,930
	23,930
Corporation tax due: £23,930 @ 19%	4,547

Note – chargeable gain

	£
Gross sales proceeds	16,000
Less: incidental costs of sale	(1,000)
	15,000
Purchase cost	(10,000)
	5,000
Indexation allowance: £10,000 × 0.107	(1,070)
Indexed chargeable gain	3,930

Example 12.14

Lauren Ltd prepares accounts to 31 March each year.

In February 2003 the company bought an asset for £12.6 million. The costs of acquisition were £0.7 million. In April 2004, enhancement capital expenditure of £1.8 million was incurred on this asset. Lauren Ltd disposed of this asset in July 2021 for £37.9 million, having incurred £1.1 million on incidental costs of sale.

Set out the chargeable gain to be included within the corporation tax computation of the above company for the year ended 31 March 2022.

Assume the following Retail Price Index (RPI) figures:

December 2017	278.1
February 2003	179.3
April 2004	185.7

Solution

	£000	£000
Gross sales proceeds		37,900
Less: incidental costs of sale		(1,100)
Net sales proceeds		36,800
Acquisition costs	12,600	
Incidental costs of acquisition	700	
Enhancement expenditure	1,800	(15,100)
Unindexed gain		21,700
Indexation allowance:		
Acquisition cost (£12.6m × 0.551)	6,943	
Incidental costs of acquisition (£0.7m × 0.551)	386	
Enhancement (£1.8m × 0.498)	896	(8,225)
Chargeable gain		13,475

Indexation factors

Cost	(278.1 − 179.3)/179.3 = 0.551
Enhancement	(278.1 − 185.7)/185.7 = 0.498

Notes

In the corporation tax computation, the chargeable gain amount is included immediately after the total income has been ascertained, as follows:

	£
Trading income	X
Surplus from non-trade loan relationship credits	X
Miscellaneous income	X
Property income	X
Chargeable gains	X
Total profits (TP)	X

12.10 Self-assessment and Administration

12.10.1 Filing of Company Tax Return

Companies are obliged to notify and report their liability to corporation tax to HMRC through the Corporation Tax Self-Assessment (CTSA) procedures.

The resultant company tax return must include a declaration by the person making the return that, to the best of their knowledge and belief, the return is correct and complete.

A complete company tax return should include:

1. completed form CT600;
2. any appropriate supplementary pages;
3. a copy of the relevant statutory accounts, generally including the statement of profit or loss provided in iXBRL format;
4. a tax computation showing how the figures on the CT600 have been derived from the statutory accounts.

If the company files abbreviated accounts at Companies House, it must file full accounts as part of its company tax return. A company tax return is due for filing online with HMRC by the due date (in response to a "notice to deliver" sent by HMRC on form CT603). The due date is the last day of whichever of the following periods is the last to end:

1. Within 12 months of the end of the accounting period.
2. If the company's statutory accounting period lies between 12 and 18 months, then 12 months from the end of the accounting period.
3. If the company's statutory accounts are for a period longer than 18 months, then 30 months from the beginning of that period.
4. Within three months of receiving a notice to deliver (where the notice has been forwarded late to the company).

All companies and organisations are required to file their company tax return online in iXBRL format. This means that data within the accounts and computations must be XBRL tagged. XBRL (Extensible Business Reporting Language) is an XML-based computer language for the electronic transmission of business and financial data. Companies and organisations are also required to pay any corporation tax and related payments due electronically (for example, by direct debit).

It is always the responsibility of the company to inform HMRC, in writing, within three months from when it comes within the charge to corporation tax; this is normally satisfied by completing and submitting form CT41G. However, in many cases, Companies Registry will have informed HMRC of the formation of the new company. HMRC would then write to the company (sending them form CT41G) requesting all the relevant information and details relating to the new company.

While HMRC will generally write to the new company (provided they have been supplied with the relevant details), the responsibility for notification always rests with the company. If a company fails to notify HMRC, then it will assume that the first accounting period will run for 12 months from the date of incorporation, which may or may not be the actual position. It is therefore imperative that the company keep HMRC appraised of any relevant changes in the company's details (address, accounting period, directors, etc.).

Penalties for failure to notify are contained within UK taxes legislation and are applicable to most taxes. However, in respect of corporation tax, these generally mean that a company that has not received a company tax return or notice to file must inform HMRC if it becomes chargeable to tax within 12 months from the end of the relevant accounting period.

Different companies can have different accounting dates, so the time limit for notifying HMRC will differ accordingly. If a company's accounting date is 30 June 2021 and it is liable to corporation tax for that period, notification of chargeability must be given to HMRC by 30 June 2022.

Penalties for failure to notify are calculated based on the potential lost revenue to HMRC that could have arisen due to failure to notify (so this could be calculated on the basis of the corporation tax liability in the first accounting period).

The level of penalty will depend on how the failure to notify arose, and how HMRC became aware of it (see **Table 12.1**). No penalty will be charged if the company has a reasonable excuse for failure to notify.

TABLE 12.1: HMRC PENALTIES – FAILURE TO NOTIFY

Type of failure to notify	Unprompted disclosure	Prompted disclosure
Non-deliberate – notified within 12 months	0%–30%	10%–30%
Non-deliberate – notified after 12 months	10%–30%	20%–30%
Deliberate but not concealed	20%–70%	35%–70%
Deliberate and concealed	30%–100%	50%–100%

Example 12.15

The following scenario would be an example of "deliberate and concealed" failure to notify.

Ferdinand Ltd has never submitted tax returns. The company bought a property in 2012 from which it has been receiving rental income. When questioned by HMRC about the source of funds to purchase the property, Ferdinand, the sole shareholder and director, says the money was lent to the company by overseas family members. HMRC later find that Ferdinand Ltd owned a number of rental properties prior to 2012 and that the money actually came from the sale of one of those properties.

For the earlier years, when asked to explain the source of the company's funds, Ferdinand took active steps to conceal the company's liability. For those years the failure is deliberate and concealed. There may also be a failure to notify penalty on the company for the chargeable gain on the sale of the property.

The act of concealment can include:

■ creating false stock records;
■ creating false evidence of a non-taxable source to explain undisclosed taxable income;
■ creating false invoices to support inaccurate figures of turnover;
■ back-dating or post-dating invoices or contracts;
■ deliberately destroying records so that they are no longer available;
■ creating sales records that deliberately understate the value of the goods sold.

12.10.2 Company Records

A company must keep all business records and accounts, including contracts and receipts, until the latest of:

1. **six** years from the end of the relevant accounting period;
2. the date that any enquiries are completed; or
3. the date after which enquiries may not be commenced.

If a return is demanded more than six years after the end of the accounting period, any records that the company still has must be retained until the later of the end of the enquiry or the expiry of the right to start an enquiry.

The maximum penalty for failing to preserve records is £3,000 per chargeable accounting period. However, there is no penalty for failing to keep or preserve records which might have been needed only for the purposes of claims, elections or notices not included in the return.

12.10.3 Company Tax Return and Amendments

Directors of UK companies are required to file statutory accounts with Companies House for every 12-month accounting period. In general, the corporation tax accounting period follows the statutory accounting period but, for corporation tax purposes, there are specific dates at which an accounting period will begin or end and, as discussed earlier, these can differ from those for the statutory accounts.

If the statutory period of account is greater than 12 months, it is divided for corporation tax purposes into 12-month tranches and a residue period. For example, if A Ltd prepared accounts for the 18-month period ending 31 December 2022, it would be required to submit company tax returns for the 12 months ended 30 June 2022 and for the six-month period ended 31 December 2022. The filing date for both returns is 31 December 2022, being 12 months after the end of the period of accounts. However, there will be two deadlines for payment of corporation tax, providing the instalment payment rules do not apply.

A company can amend its return at any time within 12 months of the return's filing deadline. This time limit is not extended if a return is delivered late. If a return is delivered more than 12 months late, no amendment to the return can be made.

Penalties

If the company's tax return is not filed within three months of the due date, it will incur a flat rate penalty of £100. The penalty rises to £200 after this and is increased to £500 and £1,000 where the failure occurs for a third successive time.

While the above penalties are not tax-related, if a company fails to deliver a return within 18 months of the end of an accounting period (or a later filing date, if applicable), then the penalty becomes 10% of the unpaid tax at that date if it remains undelivered within two years of the due date, rising to 20% thereafter. The latter tax-related penalties are in addition to the flat rate penalties above.

Questions

Review Questions
(See Suggested Solutions to Review Questions at the end of this textbook.)

Question 12.1

Venus Ltd
Venus Ltd prepares accounts to 31 December each year. It owns shares in the following companies:

Company	% shareholding*	Date acquired
Solar Ltd	59	31/03/2008
Saturn Ltd	40	15/08/2012
Mars Ltd	71	29/12/2014
Neptune Ltd	60	01/03/2022

* The remaining shares are held by entirely unconnected third parties.

Taxable profits of the company in the year ended 31 December 2021 are £550,000. Projected taxable profits are £425,000 for 31 December 2022. The company also expects to receive a dividend from Saturn Ltd of £80,000 in the 31 December 2022 accounting period. No dividend was received in 2021.

Energy Ltd
Energy Ltd has no related 51% group companies. Recently it changed its accounting date from 31 March to 31 December.

Recent results of the company are as follows:

	£
Year ended 31 March 2022	1,200,000
Nine months ended 31 December 2022 (projected)	1,200,000

Requirement
Explain whether Venus Ltd and Energy Ltd are required to pay their corporation tax liability in instalments for the accounting period ended 31 December 2022. If instalment payments are required, you are **not** required to calculate these.

Venus Ltd and Energy Ltd are entirely unconnected companies.

Question 12.2

During the year ended 31 December 2021, Venus Ltd had the following loan relationship transactions:

- Interest received from a bank deposit account: £15,000.
- A bank loan of £75,000, which at the bank's instigation of an early repayment agreement, was fully settled for £55,000 by 31 December 2021.

Legal fees of £1,500 were incurred in connection with the above bank loan settlement.

Requirement
Calculate Venus Ltd's net non-trading loan relationship credit/deficit for the year ended 31 December 2021.

Question 12.3

Special rules apply to a company's loan relationships for corporation tax purposes.

(a) Explain the term "loan relationship".
(b) Give examples of loan relationships.
(c) Briefly explain how the amount to be included in the corporation tax computation is calculated.

Question 12.4

During the year ended 31 March 2022, a manufacturing company had the following transactions in interest receivable and payable:

	£
Interest receivable:	
Customers charged interest for paying late	724
Bank deposit interest	6,233
Bond held with local council	775
Interest payable:	
Bank overdraft	4,210
Mortgage on rental property	3,178
Bank loan for purchase of trading equipment	7,500
Bank loan to acquire shares in unconnected companies	555

Requirement

Calculate the amount of interest that should be included under non-trading loan relationships in the company's corporation tax computation for the 31 March 2022 accounting period end.

Question 12.5

Cleanoff Ltd is an office cleaning company. During the year ended 31 March 2022, the following transactions took place:

- The company paid interest of £475 to HMRC in respect of corporation tax paid late.
- The company took out a loan to finance the purchase of new equipment. Loan interest paid during the year totalled £2,000, with a further £200 owed at 31 March 2022.
- The company arranged a mortgage to purchase new office premises. The interest payable on this mortgage in the period to 31 March 2022 was £4,500, all of which was paid during the period.

Requirement

Explain how the above interest expenditure should be treated in the corporation tax computation of the company for the year ended 31 March 2022.

Question 12.6

Graham Ltd paid and received the following amounts during the year ended 31 March 2022.

- Interest on a loan to buy a property in which two of the four floors are used in the trade of the company, the remaining two floors are rented to an unconnected company – £12,000.
- Incidental costs of obtaining the loan finance to purchase the above property – £2,500.
- Bank overdraft interest payable – £4,300.
- Debenture interest receivable – £7,000.

Requirement

Calculate the amount assessable as a non-trading loan relationship credit/(debit) for the year ended 31 March 2022.

Computation of Corporation Tax

Learning Objectives

After studying this chapter you will understand:

- The format of a corporation tax computation.
- How to compute tax-adjusted profits.
- Understand and apply the pension 'spreading' rules.
- Whether or not assets qualify for capital allowances and the computation of the capital allowances available.
- How to recognise the characteristics of qualifying charitable donations, and how to apply relief.
- How to recognise the characteristics of annual payments.
- How to describe the type of transactions regarded as distributions.

13.1 Pro Forma Corporation Tax Computation

COMPLEX COMPANY LIMITED
Corporation Tax Computation
for the 12-month accounting period to 31 March 2022

	Notes	£	£
***Trading income*:**			
Tax-adjusted trading profits	2	X	
Losses forward under section 45 CTA 2010		(X)	
			X
Property income	3		X
***Loan relationships*:**			
Surplus from non-trade loan relationship credits	4		X
Miscellaneous income	5		X
Chargeable gains	6		X

continued overleaf

Total profits		**X**
Deduct: surplus non-trade loan relationship debits	4	(X)
Deduct: qualifying charitable donations	7	(X)
Deduct: losses carried forward or carried back		(X)
Taxable total profits (TTP)		**X**

Notes

1. The computation should always have the name of the company at the top and an appropriate heading, i.e. "corporation tax computation for the 12-month accounting period to...".
    Remember: it is possible for a corporation tax accounting period to be less than 12 months but it can never exceed 12 months. This is discussed in detail in **Chapter 12**.
2. The tax-adjusted trading profits are arrived at after making a number of adjustments. It should be particularly noted that the tax-adjusted trading profits represent the final trading income figure **after** capital allowances have been deducted, but **before** relief for unutilised pre-1 April 2017 trading losses carried forward from **the same trade**. See **Section 13.2**.
3. The income to be included here is the income arising from the letting of land and property, wherever situated. See **Section 12.7**.
4. The income to be included includes interest relating to non-trading loan relationships. A company will have a non-trading loan relationship if it is not a party to that loan relationship for the purposes of its trade. Any debits and credits that are not brought into account as trading income and expenses are termed non-trading credits and debits. Non-trading credits and debits that have been deducted and added back in the adjustment of trading profits calculation are then pooled, i.e. added together, to arrive at the net amount to be brought into account. If the net amount is a debit this is deducted from total profits. See **Section 12.8**.
5. Miscellaneous income captures income received by the company that does not fall to be taxed under trading, property or loan relationships. It may include for example, patent income received by the company where the patent does not relate to the trading activities of the company.
6. A corporation tax computation also includes chargeable gains by companies. See **Section 12.9** for more information on computation of a chargeable gain.
7. Qualifying charitable donations (QCDs) made by a company are allowed as deductions from the company's total profits in calculating the corporation tax chargeable for an accounting period. See more on QCDs in **Section 13.4**.

13.2 Adjustments in Arriving at Trading Income

The starting point when calculating the adjusted trading profit/(loss) is always the profit/(loss) **before tax** as calculated in the statement of profit or loss. In arriving at "trading income" the following steps should always be considered:

1. Look out for receipts or income that are not taxable.
2. Deduct non-trading income and gains.
3. Add back any expenses not properly associated with the trading activities.

13.2.1 Add-back of Expenses not Properly Associated with Trading Activities

When an expense falls to be disallowed, it is added back in the adjustment of trading profits computation.

Summary of Expenses Commonly Disallowed

1. Expenses or losses of a capital nature:

   - Depreciation.
   - Loss on sale of fixed assets (if a chargeable asset, remember to compute the chargeable gain/loss position as discussed in **Chapter 12**).
   - Improvements to premises.
   - Purchase of fixed assets.
   - Losses on sale of non-trading intangibles.
   - Amortisation of goodwill acquired on or after 8 July 2015.
   - Amortisation of certain other intangibles.

2. Expenses not wholly and exclusively for the purposes of the trade or business:

   - Rental expenses (may be allowable against property income).
   - Political donations – never allowed.
   - Qualifying charitable donations should be added back and then allowed as a deduction from total profits.
   - Fines, defaults, surcharges, penalties and interest on tax (however, interest on late corporation tax is added back but later allowed as a non-trade debit to be deducted from non-trade loan relationship credits).

Treatment of Certain Specific Items

(a) Bad debts

Under UK generally accepted accounting principles (GAAP), a company may have general and specific bad debts provisions. Under general tax principles, general provisions are not deductible. Therefore, if there are any movements on the general bad debts provision account, an adjustment must be made, i.e.:

- Increase in a general provision for bad debts – not allowable; therefore, add this back.
- Decrease in a general provision for bad debts – not taxable; therefore, deduct this amount.

As there is no difference between the tax and accounting rules in relation to any other movements on bad debts, there is no adjustment required for the following items:

- Specific bad debts written off – deducted in the statement of profit or loss and also allowed for tax purposes.
- Specific bad debts recovered – credited to the statement of profit or loss and therefore taxable.
- Increase in a specific provision for bad debts – deducted in the statement of profit or loss and therefore allowed for tax purposes.
- Decrease in a specific provision for bad debts – credited to the statement of profit or loss and therefore taxable.

Under IFRS, the manner of calculating a provision for doubtful debts is more specific than under UK GAAP. As a result, increases in bad debt provisions are treated as deductible for tax purposes, provided that they are properly calculated in accordance with these standards.

(b) Entertainment Expenses

General entertainment expenses incurred are completely disallowed. Entertainment includes the provision of accommodation, food, drink or any other form of hospitality, including the provision of gifts.

Expenditure on bona fide staff entertainment is allowable, provided its provision is not incidental to the provision of entertainment to third parties (such as customers, suppliers or other business contacts). Entertaining for and gifts to employees are normally deductible for the company except for excessive amounts. Gifts to customers not costing more than £50 per donee per year are allowable if they carry a conspicuous advertisement for the business and are not food, drink or tobacco. In looking at whether the £50 limit has been breached it is necessary to take into account the cost of all such gifts carrying a conspicuous advertisement (excluding any gifts already disallowed) given to the same person in the same accounting period.

(c) Legal Expenses

- ▨ Debt recovery (if it relates to the company's trading income) – allowable.
- ▨ Acquisition of assets – not allowable, including any abortive expenditure.
- ▨ Renewal of short lease (defined as being less than 50 years) – allowable.
- ▨ Product liability claims and employee actions – allowable.
- ▨ Maintaining existing trading rights and assets – allowable.
- ▨ Fines or penalties for breaches in legislation, e.g. health and safety – not allowable.

(d) Repairs

Replacement of items, redecoration and repairs not involving material improvements – expenditure is allowable.

(e) Lease Payments for Assets

The accounting and tax treatment of finance lease assets is detailed in **Chapter 3, Section 3.3.5** under **Finance Leases**. In summary, where a finance-leased asset is capitalised in the statement of financial position the amounts expensed in the statement of profit or loss are the interest expense and depreciation. The lease payment is not expensed to the statement of profit or loss. Where the burden of the wear and tear of the asset is borne by the lessor, the lessee is not entitled to capital allowances. Rather, the accounts depreciation charge will be deductible for tax purposes, provided it is based on normal commercial accounting principles.

Chapter 3, Section 3.3.5, Leased Motor Vehicles introduced the 15% disallowance rule that can apply to the leasing costs associated with a leased car with CO_2 emissions exceeding 50g/km (the threshold for leases entered into on or after 1 April 2018 but before 1 April 2021 was 110g/km). The 15% disallowance can apply to a car leased under an operating lease or a finance lease.

Where a car is held on an operating lease and the company financial statements are not prepared under IFRS or FRS 101 (for UK companies that apply EU-adopted IFRS), the deduction available for the lease hire charges in the statement of profit or loss depends on the CO_2 emissions of the car. The 15% restriction does not apply to commercial vehicles. Any maintenance or insurance element included therein is fully allowable.

Example 13.1

A company, which prepares annual accounts under FRS 102 to 31 December, leased a new car under an operating lease on 1 June 2020. The car's CO_2 emissions are 143g/km.

In the annual accounts to 31 December 2021, lease hire charges of £10,000 were incurred and expensed in the statement of profit or loss.

Disallowable: £10,000 × 15% = **£1,500**

Where a car is leased under a finance lease, the amount of finance lease depreciation available as a tax deduction depends on the CO_2 emissions of the car.

Example 13.2

A company, which prepares annual accounts to 31 March, purchased a new car under finance lease for £26,775 on 1 October 2020. The car's CO_2 emissions are 120g/km.

In the annual accounts to 31 March 2021 depreciation of £2,678 has been charged.

Disallowable: £2,768 × 15% = £415

From 1 January 2019, companies reporting under IFRS or FRS 101 will be required to change the accounting treatment of operating leases when adopting the new standard IFRS 16 *Leases*. IFRS 16 removes the existing distinction between finance leases and operating leases for lessees. Leases dealt with under IFRS 16 are referred to for tax purposes as 'right-of-use leases'.

Broadly, in relation to a lessee, a right-to-use lease is treated for tax purposes as a finance lease. Therefore, under IFRS 16 operating lease rentals will no longer be charged to the company's statement of profit or loss. Instead, they will be reflected as both a depreciation charge and an interest charge in the statement of profit or loss. In line with the tax treatment for finance leases, tax relief will be available for the statement of profit or loss charges (that is, the interest and the depreciation charges).

As a result of the introduction of IFRS 16, there are a number of transitional changes to the tax treatment of such leases. These are beyond the scope of this textbook.

For companies reporting under FRS 102 (as opposed to IFRS or FRS 101), the distinction between operating leases and finance leases continues and therefore the tax treatment remains unchanged post-1 January 2019. That is, the operating lease rentals continue to be treated as revenue costs in the statement of profit or loss for the use of the asset over the period of the lease.

(f) Interest on Late Payment of Tax

Interest on late payment of any tax (including VAT, PAYE, etc.) is not allowed in computing tax-adjusted profits; neither are any penalties arising from VAT, PAYE or any other tax, including corporation tax. However, interest on late payment of corporation tax should be added back and then treated as a non-trade debit – meaning that it is allowable. Any interest received on overpaid corporation tax is thus taxable as a non-trading loan relationship credit.

(g) Accountancy/Taxation Fees

Normal routine accounting, auditing and taxation compliance costs are allowable. Special costs associated with Tribunal/Appeal hearings or HMRC enquiries or inspections are likely to be disallowed. However, if no additional tax results from the Tribunal/Appeal hearing, enquiry or inspection, there is a possible argument that the costs should be allowed.

Fee protection insurance charges to cover the risk of incurring additional costs are only allowable if the additional costs are of a revenue nature.

(h) Pre-trading Expenses

Pre-trading expenses, as their name indicates, are incurred before the trade has commenced. Relief for such expenses is given in the accounting period in which the trade commences in respect of those revenue items which satisfy the relevant test.

Qualifying expenses are those:

■ incurred in the seven years prior to the commencement, and
■ that would be allowed as a deduction in calculating trading profits if they had been incurred after trading commenced.

Examples of qualifying pre-trading expenses include: accountancy fees, market research, feasibility studies, salaries, advertising, preparing business plans and rent paid.

These pre-trading expenses are deductible against income of the trade if they were incurred in the seven-year period prior to commencement. If these expenses exceed the company's trading income, resulting in a loss, this loss **can** be offset against other profits of the company. It can also be carried forward against future income of the same trade. It cannot be carried back as the company was not trading in its previous period.

Qualifying charitable donations incurred before a trade commences are treated as paid when the trade commences, i.e. they are deductible from total profits as qualifying charitable donations in the first year of trading.

Any interest that a company incurs before trading commences is classified as a non-trade debit under the loan relationship rules.

Example 13.3

Ray Ltd commenced to trade on 1 July 2021. It incurred the following pre-trading expenditure:

		£
December 2013	Market research	8,000
December 2020	Director's salary	30,000
January 2021	Business entertainment	5,000
May 2021	Marketing expenditure	17,000

Notes:

- Market research expenditure is not deductible as it was not incurred within seven years before the trade commenced.
- Business entertainment expenditure is never allowable.
- Expenditure on the director's salary and marketing are allowable.

Therefore, Ray Ltd incurs deductible expenses of £47,000 on 1 July 2021. These are fully deductible in calculating trading income of the first accounting period. Should this expenditure exceed this income, the excess is available for offset against other profits, for group relief if applicable or against future income of this trade.

(i) Redundancy Payments

The following rules apply if a company, as an employer, makes a redundancy payment (statutory) or an approved contractual payment to an employee and the payment is in respect of the employee's employment in the employer's trade. An approved "contractual payment" means a payment which, under an agreement, an employer is liable to make to an employee on the termination of the employee's contract of employment.

Statutory redundancy payments are specifically allowable as are approved contractual payments up to the statutory limit. On cessation of the trade, a redundancy expense is not incurred "wholly and exclusively" for the purpose of the trade. However, UK tax legislation allows a deduction for statutory redundancy payments made to members of staff on cessation of trade. If the business wants to be more generous and pay amounts in excess of statutory redundancy levels, a deduction is available under section 79 ITTOIA 2005. However, **relief is limited to three times the statutory redundancy level**. Therefore when a business is ceasing, it can (in total) obtain a deduction for termination payments up to four times the statutory payment.

The deduction is allowed for the accounting period in which the payment is made unless the trade has permanently ceased in which case it is treated as made on the last day of the trade.

(j) Subscriptions

Political subscriptions and donations are not allowable. Subscriptions to a relevant professional body or to trade magazines are generally allowable.

(k) Pension Contributions

"Wholly and exclusively" Rule

Where an employer's payments to a pension scheme meet the "wholly and exclusively for the purposes of the trade" test and are of a revenue nature, they will be an allowable deduction from profits on a **paid** basis. This rule applies to employer contributions only. Given the large number of owner-managed companies, HMRC would be anxious to establish that contributions in respect of controlling directors (or the wider family circle) meet the "wholly and exclusively for the purposes of the trade" test. HMRC is also likely to enquire into the deductibility of the pension contributions paid in connection with the sale or transfer of shares, or shortly before such a transaction. Thus, the amount included within the statement of profit or loss may well require adjustment in the trading income computation if it includes accrued employer contributions. Accrued contributions deducted from the salary of employees are not subject to the 'paid' rule or the "wholly and exclusively" rule and are allowable even if accrued.

Thus, ordinary annual contributions by an employer to a registered pension scheme for the benefit of his employees are generally allowable for tax purposes in the year in which they are paid if the company is carrying on a trade.

'Spreading' Provisions

Pension contributions, although allowable, may have to be spread forward where they exceed certain limits. An initial comparison is made with the **contributions** of the previous chargeable period, where the current year contributions are greater than 210% of the previous period spreading may have to take place. This rule does not apply to the first accounting period in which employer contributions are made, as there is no previous year to compare to.

In this situation, HMRC considers the excess of the current year's payment over 110% of the previous year. Where this excess is:

- less than £500,000 there is no forward spreading of the contributions;
- between £500,000 and less than £1 million, half of the excess is spread into the following year;
- between £1 million and £2 million, one-third of the excess is spread into each of the next two accounting periods;
- £2 million or more, one-quarter of the excess is spread over the next three accounting periods.

If spreading of the payments is required, a deferred tax implication arises, as the timing of relief for the payment differs to the actual timing of the payment itself in the accounts.

Example 13.4

An employer makes the following pension contributions for the two years ended 31 December 2021:

	£
31 December 2020	200,000
31 December 2021	1,420,000

As the 2021 contribution is greater than 210% of that of 2020, HMRC will calculate the potential amount, if any, to be spread forward.

The excess is found by comparing the current year (2021) contribution with 110% of that of the previous period, namely £220,000. The resultant excess is thus £1,200,000. Since this figure lies between £1 million and £2 million, one-third of the excess is spread over each of the next two accounting periods. The £220,000 not treated as excess is fully deductible in 2021, in addition to £400,000 of the £1,200,000 excess. Therefore £800,000 would be added back in 2021.

Relief would thus be available to the company as follows:

	£
31 December 2021	620,000
31 December 2022	400,000
31 December 2023	400,000

(l) Key Person Insurance

Generally premiums paid under loss of profits insurance policies are tax deductible, therefore any sums received from the insurance company are taxable as trading receipts.

Policies which provide indemnity for loss or damage to fixed or intangible assets, trading stock and trade debts are allowable if they are deemed to be wholly and exclusively for the purpose of the trade.

Key person insurance is insurance taken out by a company in its own favour against the death or critical illness of key employees whose services are vital to the success of the employer's business. Such premiums are, generally, allowable and the proceeds of any such policies are taxable as trading receipts. However, there is a potential argument that, if the key person is also the sole or majority shareholder, HMRC may seek to argue that there is a dual purpose to the premiums, i.e. that they seek to protect the value of the shares of the company and thus that there is also a private benefit to the payment of the premiums. This could result in the premiums not being allowable for tax but, potentially, if the policy did pay out it may still seek to argue for taxing the pay-out.

(m) Royalty Payments to a Related Party

A special rule applies where a royalty is:

- payable by a company to, or for the benefit of, a 'related party' and is accrued in the accounting period; and
- it is not paid within 12 months of the end of the accounting period in which it is accrued; and
- its receipt is not at some time fully taxable on the recipient.

In such circumstances, the royalty will only count as deductible when it is actually paid and should therefore be added back in the corporation tax computation for the period in which it is accrued.

13.2.2 Deduction of Non-trading Income and Gains

Deduct	Then tax instead as follows:
Interest received	Generally taxed under the loan relationship rules.
Rents	Property income, deduct related expenses and any expenditure incurred on replacing furnishings in residential property. See **Chapter 12, Section 12.7.1**.
UK dividends	Tax-free. See **Section 13.6.2**.
Foreign dividends	Should be tax-free provided one of the exemptions is met. See **Section 13.6.2**.
Profits on disposal of assets	If a chargeable asset, then compute chargeable gain as described in **Chapter 12, Section 12.9**.

13.2.3 Provisions made under IAS 37 and FRS 102

Provisions made under IAS 37 *Provisions, Contingent Liabilities and Contingent Assets* or FRS 102 are generally allowable for tax purposes, provided that the provision would be allowable under general rules if it were an expense, e.g. a provision in relation to a capital item would not be deductible.

13.2.4 Interest

Interest, and any related expenditure, is deductible on an accruals basis if it is **trade-related**. That is, it is treated the same as in the financial statements and, therefore, no adjustment is required. This is the case even if the money is borrowed to buy capital assets. However, such capital assets must be used in the trade for the interest expense to be allowed as a trading deduction.

Other interest, which is not trade-related, must be disallowed in calculating trading income and may then be relievable as a non-trade debit (see **Chapter 12, Section 12.8**).

13.2.5 Payments to Directors and Other Employees

Bona fide directors' salaries, fees, and benefits payable for directors, etc. are deductible for corporation tax purposes. Such income is, of course, assessable in the hands of the individual director as employment income. Where a director has a company car available for private use, there is no disallowance for the inevitable "personal element" for corporation tax purposes. Again, a director with the use of a company car for private purposes will, of course, suffer tax under the benefit in kind regime (see **Chapter 5, Section 5.4.3**).

13.3 Capital Allowances

The amount of capital allowances available to a trading company must be deducted from trading income to arrive at tax-adjusted trading profit/loss. The computation of capital allowances is dealt with in detail in **Chapter 4**. Broadly, the same capital allowance rules and reliefs that apply to an unincorporated trade (sole trade or partnership) also apply to an incorporated business operating via a company (see **Chapter 4**). However, Finance Act 2021 introduced some enhanced allowances for companies from 1 April 2021 until 31 March 2023.

13.3.1 Super-deduction

A super-deduction was introduced allowing companies to benefit from a 130% first-year allowance for capital expenditure on qualifying new plant and machinery assets. The super-deduction will apply to expenditure on new main pool plant and machinery that normally qualifies for the 18% main pool rate of writing down allowances (see **Chapter 4, Section 4.6**).

Certain general exclusions apply. For example, expenditure on cars and plant or machinery for leasing are not eligible.

13.3.2 Special Rate Allowance

A temporary first-year allowance of 50%, the special rate allowance (known as the 'SR allowance'), will apply to companies investing in new plant and machinery qualifying for special rate pool plant and machinery. This will include qualifying expenditure on integral features in a building and long-life assets that normally qualify for 6% writing down allowances (see **Chapter 4, Section 4.7**).

The super-deduction and the SR allowance will not apply to qualifying expenditure on "second hand" or "used" plant and machinery and will not apply to expenditure incurred in respect of a contract entered into prior to 3 March 2021. In addition, when an asset which qualified for the super-deduction or the SR allowance is sold, the disposal receipts will be treated as balancing charges rather than an adjustment to the plant and machinery pools. Adjustments will be required if only part of the expenditure has been claimed as part of the temporary allowance.

13.4 Qualifying Charitable Donations

A payment made to a charity by a company may be a qualifying charitable donation (QCD) if certain conditions are met (these conditions are beyond the scope of this textbook). QCDs include:

- cash donations to charity (these are always paid gross by a company);
- gifts of shares quoted on a recognised stock exchange (including the AIM) to a charity,
- gifts of UK land or buildings to charity.

QCDs incurred before a trade commences are treated as paid when the trade commences, i.e. they are deductible from total profits as qualifying charitable donations in the first year of trading.

For cash donations, the amount paid to charity is first added back in the adjustment of trading profits and then deducted from total profits in arriving at taxable total profits for the chargeable accounting period in which the donation is made.

For gifts of shares or UK land/buildings, it is the market value at the date of the gift (plus any costs of transfer) that is treated as a QCD. Again, these are first added back and then deducted as a QCD.

Under section 1300(5) CTA 2009, QCDs made by a company are deducted from the company's total profits for the period **after** any other relief from corporation tax, other than group relief (group relief is covered at CA Proficiency 2 level).

The amount of the deduction is limited to the amount that reduces the company's taxable total profits for the period to nil. Reliefs, such as trading losses carried back, are given **prior** to any deduction of QCDs. This may result in the company's QCDs being wasted as it is not possible to choose how much of a loss is to be carried back and partial claims are not possible. Any surplus is not available to carry forward and relief is effectively lost, e.g. if a company has a trading loss or no total profits, it will not receive any relief for QCDs.

In addition, where the company has a long period of account, QCDs are split between the two chargeable accounting periods, based on the date that the donation is actually paid (see **Chapter 12, Section 12.2.5**).

13.5 Annual Payments

13.5.1 Relevant Payments

A company must deduct 20% basic rate income tax when making certain relevant payments. These payments include:

- Patent royalties, where the recipient is not a UK company or where payment is to an individual.
- Annual interest and other annual payments, where the recipient is not a UK company or where payment is to an individual.
- Rents paid to non-residents in respect of property in the UK.
- Royalties paid to non-residents.

The following annual interest may be paid without deduction of tax:

- Interest paid to a bank or building society in the UK and to other UK companies that carry on a trade of lending that satisfy certain conditions.
- Interest paid to a resident of a country with which the UK has a tax treaty that provides that withholding tax is to be reduced to nil, provided that clearance has been received from HMRC to make such gross payments.
- Annual payments made by a member of the group to another member of the same group.
- Interest on loans for fixed periods of less than one year.

Royalties Paid to Non-residents

Additional obligations to deduct income tax at source from royalties paid to non-resident persons apply. These rules were introduced to ensure UK tax of at least 20% is deducted and paid to HMRC in respect of royalty payments classed as contrived arrangements used by groups (typically large multinational enterprises) that result in erosion of the UK tax base. Detailed knowledge of these rules are beyond the scope of this textbook.

13.5.2 Payment of Tax Deducted from Annual Payments

Banks, building societies, etc. are not required to deduct income tax from interest paid, hence this source of income is paid gross.

Income tax at the basic rate of 20% must be deducted from relevant annual payments and paid over to HMRC. Any amounts so deducted must be paid online using form CT61.

13.5.3 Credit for Tax Suffered on Annual Payments Received

Where, in an accounting period, a company receives a payment from which UK income tax has been deducted, the grossed-up amount is included within the company's corporation tax computation. For example, if patent royalties used in the company's trade were paid net of tax, the grossed-up figure would be included within the trading income computation.

Where a company both makes and receives payments from which it deducted income tax and had it deducted, respectively, then as well as completing the relevant CT61 form for the period in which the various payments were made, the company must also consider the net income tax position at the end of the accounting period. If the tax suffered on income exceeds the tax deducted from amounts paid net, then this excess is reclaimed by subtracting it from the company's corporation tax liability.

13.6 Distributions

13.6.1 Distributions Paid by UK Companies

For corporation tax purposes, no deduction is allowed in computing income from any source for dividends or other distributions paid by a company. When doing a computation for a trading company, always start with 'profit (or loss) before taxation' so that there is no need to adjust for dividends as they will, generally, not have been deducted at that stage.

Dividends paid on preference shares are treated, for accounting purposes, as "share interest" and will already have been deducted from the profit or loss before tax, so must always be added back.

For corporation tax purposes, the distribution rules also apply whenever cash or assets are passed to the company's members. However, where the payment relates to a member who is an employee or director of a close company, the payment is taxed as employment income and is thus deductible for corporation tax (see **Chapter 5, Section 5.4.3**).

Distributions can take a variety of forms and include:

1. Dividends paid by a company, including a capital dividend.
2. Redemption of bonus securities or redeemable shares.
3. Any distribution out of assets in respect of shares (except any part of which represents a repayment of capital).
4. A bonus issue subsequent to a repayment of share capital (other than fully paid preference shares).

5. Certain payments made by a close company including interest payments in excess of a normal commercial rate of return and the provision of benefits by a close company to certain individuals who do not work for the company. The detailed definitions and rules regarding close companies are covered at CA Proficiency 2.

13.6.2 Distributions Received by UK Companies

The rules on the taxation of dividends and other distributions **received** by UK companies follow the **basic principle** that all dividends and other income distributions received by UK companies are **taxable**, regardless of the residence of the payer of the dividend.

However, due to a wide range of exemptions, in practice both UK and non-UK dividends received are **exempt** from corporation tax.

Note that this means dividends received from non-group companies (whether resident in the UK or not) are franked investment income (FII). The concept of FII is only relevant when calculating augmented profits for the purpose of the instalment payment rules for corporation tax (see **Chapter 12**).

The dividend exemption rules, and how they work, depend on whether the recipient company is a "small company" (section 931B CTA 2009) or a "large company".

Small Company
The definition of a "small company", for the purpose of the dividend exemption rules, is that the company receiving the dividend:

- has no more than 50 employees; and
- has an annual turnover of less than €10 million; or
- gross assets of less than €10 million.

All companies that are not small companies are "large companies" for the purposes of the dividend exemption.

The small company exemption applies to dividends received where:

- the payer is resident in the UK or a qualifying territory. These are countries with which the UK has a comprehensive double taxation treaty that contains a non-discrimination clause;
- the dividend is not interest that has been re-categorised as a distribution;
- the dividend has not been allowed as a deduction from taxable profits outside the UK; and
- the general anti-avoidance rule is met, i.e. that the distribution is not part of a scheme of tax avoidance.

Large Company
The large company exemption applies to dividends that fall into one of five classes, is not re-categorised interest and where no deduction is allowed outside the UK. The five classes of exempt dividend are:

1. Where the recipient controls the payer – section 931E CTA 2009.
2. Distributions in respect of non-redeemable ordinary shares – section 931F CTA 2009.
3. Distributions in respect of portfolio holdings (broadly, where the recipient controls less than 10% of the payer) – section 931G CTA 2009.
4. Distributions from transactions not designed to reduce tax – section 931H CTA 2009.
5. Dividends from shares accounted for as liabilities – section 931I CTA 2009.

13.6.3 Exempt Distributions

Some transactions, mainly dealing with situations where a company is being reorganised or wound up, are treated as exempt distributions.

Questions

Review Questions
(See Suggested Solutions to Review Questions at the end of this textbook.)

Question 13.1

Telestar Ltd, a company which commenced to trade many years ago, makes up its accounts each year to 31 March. It has no related 51% group companies.

The statement of profit or loss to 31 March 2022 is as follows:

	£	£
Gross profit		239,800
Grant for extension of premises		10,000
Employment grant		1,000
Patent royalty received from individual (net of 20%) (Note 1)		1,600
Discount received		3,300
Dividends from a UK company received on 10 May 2021		
(UK company qualifies as small)		1,300
Profit on sale of van (Note 2)		1,000
Profit on sale of shares (Note 3)		3,000
Bank deposit interest (paid gross)		600
		261,600
Less: Discount given	3,000	
Goods stolen	3,000	
Business overdraft interest	5,800	
Depreciation	15,389	
Van expense	3,400	
Motor expenses	2,400	
Bad debts	2,300	
Obsolete stock – written off	2,600	
Salaries and wages	100,000	
Telephone	311	
Entertainment (Note 4)	2,700	
Depreciation on finance leases (Note 5)	1,300	
Legal fees (Note 6)	2,400	(144,600)
Profit before tax		117,000

Notes

1. The patent royalty was received in December 2021 and relates to the company's non-trading activities. The patent was granted in 2002.
2. Profit on sale of van – the van was acquired second-hand on 03/02/2008 for £12,000. It was sold on 05/05/2021 for £4,000. The net book value of the van at 31/03/2021 was £3,000. To date, capital allowances of £12,000 have been obtained thereon.
3. Profit on sale of shares – these shares in Video Plc were acquired on 31/03/2008 for £3,000 and sold on 30/04/2021 for £6,000. Indexation factor up to 31 December 2018 is 0.456. The shares represented 0.25% of Video Plc's share capital and the company owns no other shares in Video Plc.
4. The charge for entertainment is made up as follows:

	£
Prizes for top salespersons of the year	900
Christmas party for staff	750
Christmas gifts for suppliers (hampers)	150
Reimbursement of managing director for costs incurred entertaining customers at home	350
General customer entertainment	550
	2,700

5. Finance lease depreciation – this relates to a machine leased in 2018, the cost of which is capitalised in the company's accounts.
6. The legal fees relate to the extension of the premises.
7. Capital allowances for the year are £7,272.

Requirement

Calculate the corporation tax liability for the year ended 31 March 2022 and show the dates on which the tax is payable.

Question 13.2

Zaco Ltd has no related 51% group companies. The statement of profit or loss of Zaco Ltd for the year ended 30 September 2021 is as follows:

STATEMENT OF PROFIT OR LOSS

	£		£
Salaries and wages	62,500	Gross profit	489,250
Rent and rates	5,400	Dividends (Note 6)	3,600
Repairs (Note 1)	16,100	Bad debts	300
Insurance	1,720	Profit on sale of assets (Note 7)	15,200
Professional fees (Note 2)	1,600	Bank interest receivable	1,200
Depreciation	13,000	Property income	4,300
Audit fees	1,000		

continued overleaf

Subscriptions (Note 3)	2,400		
Entertainment (Note 4)	600		
Staff award (Note 5)	1,000		
Discount allowed	320		
Bank interest	7,060		
Light and heat	21,250		
Profit	379,900		
	513,850		513,850

Notes

1. Repairs – includes improvements to offices of £5,200.
2. Professional fees – includes debt collection fees of £200, architect's fees re. office improvements of £300.
3. Subscriptions – includes political donations of £750 and staff race sponsorship of £1,000.
4. Entertainment – this is made up as follows:

	£
Customer entertainment	450
Supplier entertainment	150
	600

5. Staff award – a special award of £1,000 was made to an employee who achieved first place in Ireland in his engineering examinations during the year.
6. Dividends – foreign dividends received on 31 August 2021 and meet one of the dividend exemptions.
7. Profit on sale of building – indexation factor 0.035:

	£
Cost June 2010	200,000
Proceeds July 2018	215,200
Profit on sale	15,200

8. The capital allowances (including balancing allowances and charges) are £9,846.
9. There are capital losses brought forward of £10,000.

Requirement

Calculate the company's corporation tax liability for the year.

Question 13.3

From the following information you are required to calculate the corporation tax liability of Alpha Ltd for the year ended 31 March 2022. Alpha Ltd has two wholly-owned subsidiaries.

STATEMENT OF PROFIT OR LOSS

	£		£
Salaries and wages (Note 1)	71,300	Gross profit	600,000
Rent and rates	7,600	UK dividends (Note 13)	7,000
Repairs (Note 2)	18,500	Gain on sale of fixed assets (Note 14)	1,000
Insurance (Note 3)	1,350	Amortisation of grant (Note 15)	240
Loss on sale of investments (Note 4)	600	Interest on corporation tax overpaid	475
Legal expenses (Note 5)	2,700		
Commissions	9,209	Rent received	6,000
Depreciation	13,260	Deposit interest	1,500
Audit fees	1,550	Bad debts recovered	50
Subscriptions (Note 6)	3,400		
Discounts allowed	900		
Bank interest (Note 7)	3,300		
Other interest (Note 8)	7,000		
Light and heat	11,234		
Motor expenses (Note 9)	33,126		
Sundry (Note 10)	3,740		
Entertainment expenses (Note 11)	1,191		
Finance lease depreciation (Note 12)	1,700		
Net profit	424,605		
	616,265		616,265

Notes
1. Salaries and wages include £25,000 in respect of staff bonuses relating to the year ended 31 March 2022 which were paid in full by 31 March 2022.
2. Repairs include an amount of £15,000 for an extension to the factory premises.
3. Insurance includes an amount of £350 relating to the let premises.
4. Loss on sale of investments (2% shareholding):

UK shares purchased 2005	£
Cost	10,000
Proceeds (01/07/2021)	(9,400)
	600

5. Legal expenses:

	£
Debt collection	700
Extension to factory	2,000
	2,700

6. Subscriptions:

	£
Chamber of Commerce	450
Trade association	1,135
Political	1,815
	3,400

7. Bank interest – bank interest includes an amount of £1,500 relating to borrowings taken out to finance the extension to the factory premises.
8. Other interest is deemed to be from a trading loan relationship £7,000.
9. Motor expenses – the company leased six new motor cars on 1 April 2019. The retail price of each, at the time the lease contracts were entered into, was £26,000. All of the cars had CO_2 emissions of 145g/km.
   The motor expenses can be analysed as follows:

	£
Leasing charges on leased cars	21,126
Running costs of leased cars	12,000
	33,126

10. Sundry:

	£
Interest on late payments of VAT	1,630
Health and safety fines	30
Christmas party	500
Gifts to customers (hampers)	541
General office expenses	1,039
	3,740

11. Entertainment includes an amount of £1,191 for hotel and accommodation for overseas customers
12. Finance lease depreciation relates to new machinery leased in 2008, the cost of which is capitalised in the company's accounts.
13. UK dividends:

	£
Dividend on Bank of Ireland shares received 1 December 2021	1,800
Dividend from subsidiary received 1 April 2021	5,200
	7,000

14. Sale of fixed asset:

	£
Cost (July 2008)	4,000
Proceeds (January 2021)	5,000
Profit on sale	1,000

The asset is not a chargeable asset for capital gains tax.
15. A grant of £1,200 was received on 2 April 2021 in respect of the factory extension. This is being amortised over a five-year period.
16. Capital allowances for the accounting period are £46,006.
17. There is a capital loss carried forward of £189 from year ended 31 March 2021.

Question 13.4

Paul Morrisey, a relatively new client of your practice, called you in early February for some advice in relation to his company, Classic Engineering Consultancy Ltd, which provides consultancy services to local engineering businesses. The company is not a client of your practice and the tax compliance work is carried out by a small 'one man band' in the local area who is not a Chartered Accountant.

It is now early July 2023 and only yesterday Paul received a letter from HMRC informing him it had opened an enquiry into the company tax return for 31 March 2022, which had been filed online by the local accountant on 10 June 2023. The HMRC Inspector has asked for detailed analysis of a number of items. The computation filed for that period is reproduced below.

CLASSIC ENGINEERING CONSULTANCY LTD
Corporation tax computation for the accounting period ended 31 March 2022

Trading Profits

	Notes	£	£
Net profit per accounts			1,610,622
Add: Profit on sale of machine		11,400	
Disallowed repairs and renewals	1	–	
Disallowed advertising and promotion	2	1,450	
Disallowed legal fees	3	–	
Depreciation	4	22,900	
Disallowed motor expenses	5	–	
Disallowed travel expenses	6	–	
Disallowed donation	7	500	
Disallowed entertainment	8	1,200	(37,450)
Adjusted profit			1,648,072
Less: capital allowances			(49,744)
Tax-adjusted trading profits			1,598,328
Corporation tax payable @ 18%*			287,699

*Paid in full on 1 January 2023.

Taxable profits in 2021 were noted as £1,423,333.
Net profit per company accounts (agreed to final company accounts) = £1,610,622.

Notes:

1. Repairs and renewals (reviewed and all allowable) comprises:

	£
Painting the exterior of the existing workshop	12,750
Repairs and maintenance of equipment	11,267
Extension to workshop	<u>50,400</u>
Total	74,417

2. Advertising and promotion comprises:

	£
Christmas gifts to regular customers (gourmet hampers – disallowed)	1,450
Promotional literature	12,000
Business advertising in newspaper and trade magazines	<u>9,200</u>
Total	22,650

3. Legal fees (reviewed and all allowable) comprises:

	£
Planning appeal costs for planning application denied for workshop in new location	13,225
Renewal of lease on parts store for another 10 years	<u>2,500</u>
Total	15,725

4. Depreciation comprises:

	£
Depreciation on motor vehicles	6,744
Depreciation on building	2,000
Depreciation on machinery: hire purchase*	28,289
non-hire purchase	<u>14,156</u>
Total	51,189

* Treated as an allowable deduction in the computation.

5. Motor expenses (reviewed and all allowable) comprises:

	£
Fuel, road tax and insurance	5,222
Parking fines incurred by staff visiting other sites	240
Speeding fines	400
Contract hire costs of new vans (all 175g/km)	4,765
Contract hire costs of car leased from 1 May 2021 (40g/km)	<u>3,000</u>
Total	13,627

continued overleaf

6. Travel expenses comprise:

	£
Air fares and hotel expenses incurred on business trips to trade fairs	1,750
Meals with potential new suppliers/customers	900
Expenses incurred sending trainee engineers on courses	1,400
Total	4,050

7. Subscriptions and donations comprise:

	£
Subscription to Engineering Monthly	448
Donation to political party – disallowed	500
Total	948

8. Entertainment comprises:

	£
Staff Christmas party	500
Entertaining potential clients and their family in restaurant – disallowed	1,200
Total	1,700

9. General expenses comprise:

	£
Increase in capital provision for replacement of capital assets	50,000
Miscellaneous small allowable items	566
Total	50,566

Requirement

Write a letter to Paul advising him of the correct corporation tax liability for the year ended 31 March 2022. Provide comments on any adjustments necessary to the previously submitted corporation tax computation for the year ended 31 March 2022. All relevant information to do so is provided in Appendix 1 above. Assume that capital allowances have been calculated correctly and that the company has no related 51% group companies.

Question 13.5

Spider Ltd has the following income/payments during the year to 31 March 2022:

	£
Accounting profits (after charging depreciation of £5,000)	96,000
Property income	17,000
Payment to British Red Cross	8,000

Requirement

Calculate the company's taxable total profits for the year ended 31 March 2022.

Question 13.6

Ice Sculptors Ltd received £475,000 of dividend income from Ice Sculptors Ireland Ltd, a non-UK tax resident company. The dividend was received in September 2022 as part of its 31 December 2022 accounting period end. Ice Sculptors Ltd is not a small company for the purpose of the dividend exemption rules.

Ice Sculptors Ltd is a UK resident company and is able to secure control by virtue of powers conferred by the Articles of Association, so that the affairs of Ice Sculptors Ireland Ltd are conducted in accordance with its wishes.

Requirement
Advise your client whether the receipt of the above dividend is subject to UK corporation tax during the accounting period ended 31 December 2022.

Question 13.7

Dragger Ltd, a UK resident company, owns 30% of the ordinary share capital of Dragger GmbH, a company resident in Germany. During the year to 31 December 2022, Dragger Ltd received a dividend from Dragger GmbH of £48,000. Dragger GmbH paid tax on the profits out of which the dividend was paid. Dragger GmbH has 20 employees and gross assets of €5 million.

Requirement
Explain the tax treatment of the dividend in Dragger Ltd.

Corporation Tax Loss Relief

Learning Objectives

After studying this chapter you will understand:

- How to determine and apply trading and non-trading loss reliefs as appropriate.
- How to determine and apply terminal loss relief as appropriate.

14.1 Relief for Trading Losses in a Single Company

Trading losses are computed in the same way as trading income, and the company must prepare its corporation tax computation in the normal way and forward its completed form CT600 (recording chargeable profits as "Nil"), statutory accounts and associated computations to HMRC, in iXBRL format, similar to that required if the company had made a trading profit.

There are a number of options available:

1. carry forward and set against first available trading profit arising from the same trade, subject to the carry-forward loss restriction rule – **only applies to trading losses incurred pre-1 April 2017** (section 45A CTA 2010);
2. carry forward and set against first available total profits, subject to the carry forward loss restriction rule (section 45A CTA 2010);
3. set against total profits in the current chargeable accounting period (section 37(3)(a) CTA 2010); or
4. carry back and set against total profits in the preceding 12 months (section 37(3)(b) CTA 2010. As a temporary measure for companies with accounting periods ending between 1 April 2020 and 31 March 2022, the carry back of trading losses (up to £2,000,000 per 12-month period) can be set against total profits in the preceding 36 months/3 years.

In each of the options 2–4, 'total profits' refers to income and gains before deducting qualifying charitable donations (QCDs).

CTA 2010 requires a formal claim to be made for items 2–4 above, and claims must be made within two years of the end of the accounting period in which the loss occurs.

14.1.1 Loss Restriction Rule – Losses Carried Forward

Companies with profits/chargeable gains in excess of the relevant "deductions allowance" are not able to reduce profits/gains wholly to nil by using relief for carried-forward losses. This rule applies to several different types of losses carried forward, including trading losses, surplus non-trading loan relationship deficits, UK property business losses and capital losses (for accounting periods ending on or after 1 April 2020 only (see **Section 14.7**). Qualifying charitable donations cannot be carried forward.

In addition, because relief for certain types of carried-forward losses can only be set against particular types of profit (pre-1 April 2017 trading losses can only be set against future trading profits under section 45 CTA 2010), the relevant maximum must, in cases using such losses, be computed separately for trading profits and non-trading profits. The company may decide how its deductions allowance should be allocated between trading and non-trading profits.

A company that is not a member of a group has a deductions allowance for each accounting period of £5 million. If, however, the accounting period is less than 12 months, this amount is reduced proportionately. A company that is a member of a group may have a different deductions allowance, however it will never be more than £5 million.

Where a company's taxable profits exceed £5 million, only 50% of the profits above this threshold can be sheltered by carried-forward losses.

Example 14.1

Artic Ltd is a stand-alone company. In its accounting period ending 31 March 2022 the company has £18 million of profits remaining after in-year reliefs. The company has trading losses carried forward from the accounting period ended 31 March 2021 of £20 million and wishes to claim relief for the maximum possible in 2022.

The company will pay corporation tax in 2022 as follows:

	£
Profit	18,000,000
Less: trading loss carried forward	
£5 million deductions allowance plus 50% of remaining £13,000,000)	(11,500,000)
Taxable total profits	6,500,000
Corporation tax @ 19%	1,235,000

Loss Memo

	£
Loss brought forward	20,000,000
Utilised via section 45A claim	(11,500,000)
Loss carried forward	8,500,000

14.1.2   Carry Forward of Trading Losses Arising post-1 April 2017

Trading losses arising after 1 April 2017 can be carried forward, under section 45A CTA 2010, for set-off against **future profits (of any type)**. As this is a carry-forward relief, the loss restriction rule may apply.

Where a company has a trade loss carried forward under section 45A, it will only be relieved if the company makes a claim under section 45A(5). It is not necessary for the loss to be used to the full extent possible; the company can specify the amount of the loss it wants to relieve. Any remainder will be carried forward to the subsequent period.

14.1.3   Carry Forward of Trading Losses Arising pre-1 April 2017

Trading losses arising before 1 April 2017 can only be carried forward, under section 45 CTA 2010, for set-off against **future trading profits of the same trade** only.

While no formal claim is required to carry forward pre-1 April 2017 trading losses (as this relief is given automatically), the company, in its corporation tax return, must state the amount of the loss to be carried forward. As this is also a carry-forward relief, the loss restriction rule may apply. However, a company can claim to prevent automatic relief in this manner where the losses carried forward would be set against profits arising post-1 April 2017.

Pre-1 April 2017 carry-forward losses are set against the first available trading profits from the same trade. If there are not sufficient profits to use up the total losses, the excess is further carried forward to be set against the next available trading profits.

In a scenario where a company has unused trading losses irrespective of the date they were incurred, this could create an issue if the company ceases to trade. This means there would be no future profits/trading profits against which to set the carried-forward losses. Any balance of carried-forward losses would thus be wasted.

There is, however, a special type of relief for trading losses incurred in the last 12 months of trading. Losses in this period are known as 'terminal losses', and can potentially be relieved (see **Section 14.2**).

Example 14.2

ABC Ltd, a UK company with no subsidiaries, has the following results for the year ended 31 March 2022.

	£
Trading income (as adjusted for tax purposes)	55,000
Net credit from loan relationships	2,000
Property income	3,200
Chargeable gains	25,000
Qualifying charitable donations	(3,000)
Trading losses (of same trade) brought forward (Note 1)	(70,000)

Note:

1. Trading losses brought forward are from year ended 31 March 2018 under section 45. There were no trading income/profits from the years ended 31 March 2018 to 31 March 2020 inclusive.

ABC Ltd
Corporation Tax Computation for year ended 31 March 2022

	£	£
Trading income	55,000	
Less: trading losses c/fwd	(55,000)	
		0
Net credit from loan relationships		2,000
Property Income		3,200
Chargeable gains		25,000
Total profits		30,200
Qualifying charitable donations		(3,000)
Taxable total profits (TTP)		27,200

Corporation tax payable:

£27,200 @ 19%	5,168

Corporation tax due on or before 1 January 2023.

Loss Memo

	£
Trading losses brought forward	70,000
Utilised (y/e 31/03/2022)	(55,000)
Carried forward (to set against future trading profits of the same trade)	15,000

continued overleaf

> If the trading profits of ABC Ltd had been greater than £70,000 for the year ended 31 March 2022, all of the losses brought forward would have been utilised.
>
> If ABC Ltd had made no trading profit (i.e. it either broke even or made a loss), then the brought forward trading losses would have been carried forward to the year ended 31 March 2023 to be set against any potential trading profits of that year, provided the same trade was being carried on. This process would be continued until either all of the losses had been utilised or the company ceased trading.

14.1.4 Relief by Set-off Against Total Profits of the Same Accounting Period

Before carrying forward the trading loss of an accounting period, a company with other sources of income can choose to set a current-period trading loss against the total profits of the same accounting period, under section 37(3)(a) CTA 2010. Offset of a trading loss in the current period against other income is **not** subject to the loss restriction rule.

The claim must be for the lower of the available loss or the available profit. In other words, no partial claims are allowed – the claim must either use all of the loss or eliminate all of the available profits.

Example 14.3

Jones Limited has the following income for the year ended 31 March 2022.

	£
Trading income losses	(17,500)
Net credit from loan relationships	5,000
Property income	4,300
Chargeable gains	7,200
Qualifying charitable donations	(2,500)

Solution

	£
Net credit from loan relationships	5,000
Property income	4,300
Chargeable gains	7,200
Profits	16,500
Trading loss of same accounting period (under section 37(3)(a))	(16,500)
Total profits	Nil
Deduct qualifying charitable donations	Nil
Taxable total profits (TTP)	Nil

As the company's trading loss of £17,500 is greater than its total profits, the QCDs of £2,500 cannot be offset and are wasted. The company's remaining loss in 2022 of £1,000 can either be carried forward under section 45A or carried back 12 months (see **Section 14.1.5**).

14.1.5 Relief by Set-off Against Total Profits of the Same Accounting Period Followed by Carry Back Against Total Profits of the Previous 12 Months

Where a company has incurred a trading loss that exceeds the total profits of the same accounting period, and it has made a claim against these total profits under section 37(3)(a) CTA 2010, the company can then elect to carry the "excess" back to set against the total chargeable profits of the previous 12 months (under section 37(3)(b)). To obtain this relief the company must have carried on the same trade in the previous 12 months. The relief for the trading loss must be taken in this strict order (i.e. against profits of the same accounting period first). Any excess losses after in-year offset can either be carried back or forward (as previously described). Offset of a trading loss in the previous 12 months is also **not** subject to the loss restriction rule.

Once again, there is no facility to make a partial claim of the trade losses incurred. If there are no profits in the current period, then it is not possible to make a current-year section 37(3)(a) claim. However, this does not prevent a carry back. Remember that the carry back of a loss is for a full 12-month period. If the previous accounting period is less than 12 months, you can carry back to the period before that one by applying time apportionment to the total profits of the previous period.

Example 14.4

Apple Ltd, a single company, has the following results for the accounting periods ended 31 March 2020 through to 31 March 2022. It has carried on the same trade throughout.

	Year ended 31 March		
	2020	**2021**	**2022**
	£	£	£
Trading income	10,000	(16,500)	7,600
Property income	4,000	2,700	3,850
Chargeable gains	6,750	8,300	–

Outline the various options that are open to Apple Ltd to utilise its trading losses of £16,500 for the accounting period ended 31 March 2021.

Solution

(a) It can first utilise as much of the loss as possible (£11,000) against the company's total profits of the same period and then either carry the balance (£5,500) back to the previous 12-month period to set against the total profits of that period (namely the £20,750 in the year ended 31 March 2020);

or

(b) it could elect to carry forward the remaining £5,500 to set against the future total profits (i.e. the £11,450 in the year ended 31 March 2022) by not choosing to carry back. As the losses being carried forward arose post-1 April 2017, they can be relieved against total profits of any type, rather than future profits of the same trade. There is no restriction here as profits are well below the £5 million threshold.

The company could also choose to carry forward the entire loss to the next accounting period. However, it is unlikely to do this as that would trigger a corporation tax liability in 2021. The company's method of choice will depend on the specifics of the original assessable profits. In commercial terms, the company may more than likely adopt the carry-back option – because the results of the future period may not be known for some considerable time and corporation tax rates are planned to fall in the future. A carry-back would secure a refund of corporation tax with obvious cash flow benefits. It is important to be aware of all potential options available to the company.

A carry-back of trading losses to the previous 12-month period could, in some circumstances, substantially reduce the company's corporation tax liability for that period, and possibly even wipe it out completely. In this situation, a company may decide not to make any payment for that year. However, the company will still be charged **interest** on the unpaid liability from its normal due date until the due date of the loss period.

Example 14.5

Zanny Ltd had an accounting year end of 30 September. Its taxable total profits for the year ended 30 September 2021 were £125,000, and it had a corporation tax liability of £23,750. In the first four months of 2022, the company suffered a major downturn in trading activity and it had projected trading losses for the following year to 30 September 2022 of £180,000. The company had no other income and decided that it would thus not need to make the payment of £23,750 on 1 July 2022.

In due course, the company carried back its 2022 trading losses and wiped out the 2021 profits of £125,000. However, HMRC will still charge interest on the corporation tax liability from 1 July 2022 to 1 July 2023 – the effective date of the loss carry-back.

14.1.6 Relief by Set-off Against Total Profits of the Same Accounting Period Followed by Carry Back Against Total Profits of the Previous 36 Months – Temporary Measure

For accounting periods ending between 1 April 2020 and 31 March 2022, where acompany has incurred a trading loss and that trading loss exceeds the total profits of the same accounting period, **and** it has made a claim against these total profits under section 37(3)(a) CTA 2010, the company can elect to carry the 'excess' back to set against the total profits of the previous three years/ 36 months. Such losses are required to be set against profits of most recent years first before carry back to earlier years.

There is no limit on the amount of losses that can be carried back for12 months (see **Section 14.1.5**), however, for the extended relief, the amount of loss that can be carried back to the earlier two years of the extended period is to be capped for each of those two years. A cap of £2,000,000 of losses applies for all relevant accounting periods ending in the period 1 April 2020 to 31 March 2021 (FY 2020). A separate cap of £2,000,000 applies for all relevant accounting periods ending in the period 1 April 2021 to 31 March 2022 (FY 2021).

Extended loss carry-back claims will be required to bemade in a corporation tax return, however, claims below a *de minimis* limit of £200,000 may be made outside of a return. This means that any company with losses capable of providing relief up to a maximum of £200,000 may make a claim in respect of a relevant accounting period without having to wait to submit the company's corporation tax return. Any company wishing to make a claim exceeding £200,000 will be required to make the claim in its company tax return.

Example 14.6

Lunny Ltd has an accounting year ended 31 March 2022. Lunny Ltd incurred a trading loss of £3,300,000 in the year ended 31 March 2022. Lunny Ltd has no other income or gains for the year ended 31 March 2022. Lunny Ltd had the following results for its previous accounting periods:

	Total Profits
Year ended 31 March 2021	£1,100,000
Year ended 31 March 2020	£1,750,000
Year ended 31 March 2019	£1,250,000

continued overleaf

The relief available for the trading losses incurred in the year ended 31 March 2022 is as follows:
1. Claim £1,100,000 of the loss against the total profits of £1,100,000 for the year ended 31 March 2021. This claim is uncapped.
2. The temporary extended carry-back rules allow for Lunny Ltd to carry back £1,750,000 (limited to the profits of the period) against the total profits of £1,750,000 for the year ended 31 March 2020. As the claim exceeds the *de minimis* amount of £200,000, the claim must be made in the corporation tax return. Only £250,000 remains eligible for claim under the extended loss carry-back rules.
3. The temporary extended carry-back rules allow for Lunny Ltd to carry back the remaining £250,000 (limited to the unused amount of the £2,000,000 losses available for carry back) against the total profits of £1,250,000 for the year ended 31 March 2019. As the claim exceeds the *de minimis* amount of £200,000, the claim must be made in the corporation tax return.

Loss Memo

Trading loss in year ended 31 March 2022	£3,300,000
Trading loss against total profits year ended 31 March 2021	(£1,100,000)
Trading loss against total profits year ended 31 March 2020	(£1,750,000)
Trading loss against total profits year ended 31 March 2019	(£250,000)
Trading losses carried forward at 31 March 2022	£200,000

Example 14.7

Bunny Ltd has an accounting year ended 31 December. In the year ended 31 March 2021 Bunny Ltd incurred a current-year trading loss of £2,125,000. In the year ended 31 March 2022, the company had a current-year trading loss of £5,550,000. Bunny Ltd had the following results for its previous accounting periods:

	Total Profits
Year ended 31 March 2020	£1,100,000
Year ended 31 March 2019	£3,225,000
Year ended 31 March 2018	£1,175,000

Claims – trading loss of £2,125,000 in the year ended 31 March 2021:
1. Claim £1,100,000 of the loss against the total profits of £1,100,000 for the year ended 31 March 2021. This claim is uncapped.
2. The remaining £1,025,000 can be set against the profits of £3,225,000 under the new rules, leaving remaining profits of £2,200,000.

Loss Memo

Trading loss in year ended 31 March 2021	£2,125,000
Trading loss against total profits year ended 31 March 2020	(£1,100,000)
Trading loss against total profits year ended 31 March 2019	(£1,025,000)
Trading losses carried forward at 31 March 2021	Nil

Claims – trading loss of £5,550,000 in the year ended 31 March 2022:
1. No claim can be made against the years ended 31 March 2021 or 31 March 2020 as no total profits exist for offset against.
2. A maximum of £2,000,000 may be relieved under the new rules. This £2,000,000 can be claimed against the total profits for the year ended 31 March 2019 leaving total profits of £200,000 chargeable.

Loss Memo

Trading loss in year ended 31 March 2022	£5,550,000
Trading loss against total profits year ended 31 March 2019	(£2,000,000)
Trading losses carried forward at 31 March 2022	£3,550,000

14.2 Relief for Loss on Cessation (Terminal Losses)

14.2.1 Section 39 CTA 2010 – Relief for Trading Losses in the Final 12 Months

It is possible that a company may have to cease trading as a result of a downturn in its trading activities. Thus, a company may have unused trading losses, and it will obviously not have any future profits against which to set any such losses. It is also unlikely that a company will cease trading exactly on its former accounting year end.

The losses available for relief on cessation are known as 'terminal losses' and may qualify for terminal loss relief.

A terminal loss is the loss relevant to the last 12 months of trading. Where the date of cessation coincides with the company's year end, the terminal loss will be the whole of that period's loss. Where the cessation date is not coterminous with the company's accounting date, the 12-month period will be the last period (if less than 12 months) plus the relevant proportion of the preceding accounting period. Thus, if a company that has always had 30 September as its accounting year-end ceased on 31 March 2022, then the terminal loss would comprise the loss of the six months to 31 March 2021, plus 6/12ths of the loss (if any) of the accounting year ended 30 September 2021.

Instead of the normal carry-back period of 12 months, terminal losses can be carried back for 36 months, provided the same trade was being carried on during that time. The terminal loss can be carried back in full without tailoring against **total** profits arising in the previous 36 months, starting with the later periods first. For example, if a terminal loss arose in the year to 31 December 2021, it could be carried back against profits of the year to 31 December 2020, then to 31 December 2019 and finally to 31 December 2018.

14.2.2 Section 45F CTA 2010 – Relief for Trading Losses Carried Forward

When a trade ceases, the company may also be able to claim terminal loss relief under section 45F CTA 2010 for carried-forward losses of that trade that could not have been relieved in previous years due to the loss restriction rule. This only applies for trade losses carried forward to the period of cessation under section 45 or section 45A CTA 2010.

Where certain conditions are met, section 45F relief allows these losses to be set against profits of the three years **ending** with the end of the period of cessation without being subject to the loss restriction. For example, if a trade ceases in the period ending 31 March 2022, relief will be available under section 45F against the profits of the three years from 1 April 2019 to 31 March 2022. Therefore, the three-year period used for relief under section 45F is not the same as the three-year period for relief under section 39 CTA 2010.

The extent to which losses can be relieved depends on whether they were previously carried forward under section 45 or under section 45A.

- Losses carried forward to the period of cessation under section 45A and which can be set against total profits, can be relieved against total profits in the previous 36 months.
- Losses carried forward to the period of cessation under section 45 can be relieved against profits of the same trade only in the previous 36 months.

Other non-trading losses carried forward cannot be relieved.

Relief is only available for periods beginning on or after 1 April 2017. In addition, relief under section 45F is not available against profits of:

- the period in which the loss to be used was originally sustained; or
- any preceding periods.

That is, relief is only available in periods subsequent to the original loss-making period. Losses relieved under section 45F should always be deducted from profits of a later period first, to the full extent possible, before they are deducted from profits of any earlier periods. Profits of the period of cessation itself should therefore be given priority and relieved to the full amount possible before any profits of the preceding period are relieved. (Terminal loss relief prior to 1 April 2017 is beyond the scope of this textbook.)

14.3 Pre-trading Expenditure

If a company incurs expenditure within seven years of commencing to trade that would otherwise have been allowable if incurred when the trade commenced, then the company may treat the debit as a trading expense in the first accounting period of trading. Note that any interest that a company incurs before trading commences would ordinarily be deemed to be a non-trading deficit. Carry-forward surplus non-trade loan relationship deficits can only be utilised by carry-forward for set-off against future non-trading income.

However, HMRC allows a company to elect, within two years of the end of the accounting period in which the non-trade debit arose, that such interest is not to be treated as a non-trading deficit but rather as a trading expense once trade commences; this is also subject to a seven-year time limit.

If allowable pre-trading expenditure expenses exceed the company's trading income, resulting in a loss, this loss can be used in the usual ways already covered in this chapter.

14.4 Relief for Qualifying Charitable Donations

As outlined in **Chapter 13**, qualifying charitable donations (QCDs) are allowed as a deduction from a company's total profits and are deducted after any other relief from corporation tax. Any excess cannot be relieved by carry-back or carry-forward.

Reliefs, such as trading losses carried back, are given **prior** to any deduction of QCDs, which may result in the company's QCDs being wasted as it is not possible to choose how much of a loss is to be carried back and partial claims are not possible.

14.5 Property Losses

The income from letting of UK land and property is taxed on companies as property income.

If the company has property losses, the utilisation of such losses is not ring-fenced. Property losses must first be set against the company's total profits for the same accounting period, before qualifying charitable donations and in preference to trading losses. Any excess is then carried forward and deemed to be a property loss of the next accounting period and is thus available for set-off against total profits. However, the property trade must still be carried on in the next accounting period. This process is continued until either:

- the property loss is used up; or
- the property business ceases.

Losses from a property business are very flexible. However, they **cannot** be carried back.

14.6 Non-trading Losses

A company can incur non-trading losses in any of the following situations.

14.6.1 Losses from Miscellaneous Income

Such losses are first relieved against other miscellaneous income of the same accounting period, and then against the miscellaneous income of future periods; hence, their use is quite restrictive.

14.6.2 Net Debits on Non-trading Loan Relationships

If a company incurs a deficit on its non-trading loan relationships, then it can be relieved by:

(a) set-off against the total profits of the company in the same accounting period, before QCDs and in preference to trading and property losses;
(b) carry back against surplus non-trading loan relationship credits (if any) for the previous 12 months (an 'all or nothing' claim, and can be carried back even if a current-year claim has not been made); or
(c) carry forward and set against total profits in future accounting periods of the company.

14.7 Capital Losses

As noted in **Chapter 12**, a company is charged to corporation tax on its chargeable gains. The quantum of chargeable gains is reduced by any capital losses of the same period, as well as any unrelieved capital losses brought forward. Capital losses can only be set against chargeable gains of the current period or carried forward to set against future chargeable gains. It is not possible to carry back capital losses or to set such losses against other income, except in certain circumstances. The loss restriction rule (see **Section 14.1.1**) will apply to capital losses carried forward by a company and will have the effect of restricting the amount of chargeable gains that can be relieved with carried-forward capital losses to 50%. The company can decide how much of its £5 million deductions allowance it wants to allocate to chargeable gains, trading and/or non-trading profits.

14.8 Choices regarding Loss Relief and Order of Loss Reliefs

14.8.1 Loss Relief – Considerations

If a company incurs a trading loss, it will have a variety of choices as to how best to relieve this loss. The choice of which loss relief to avail of will depend on a variety of factors including, *inter alia*:

1. for trading losses arising **before** 1 April 2017, the possibility that any offset against future trading profits will be subject to the restriction on the amount of profit that can be relieved by carried-forward losses;

2. for losses arising **after** 1 April 2017, the possibility that relief for these losses against future profits may be subject to the restriction on the amount of profit that can be relieved by carried-forward losses.
3. For companies with trading losses for accounting periods ending between 1 April 2020 and 31 March 2022, the possibility that relief for these losses against the total profits of the previous 36 months. Subject to the £2,000,000 per 12-month period restriction.
4. the rates of corporation tax of the different accounting periods involved (although the 19% rate of corporation tax has applied since FY 2017 and will continue to FY 2022);
5. the possibility that QCDs may be unrelieved;
6. the company's cash flow position;
7. the company's overriding desire to maximise the tax saved as a result of the loss claim; and
8. the level of future projected income of the company.

14.8.2 Order of Loss Reliefs

Certain losses arising in the accounting period can be set-off against other profits of the company, either in the current period or in a future period; this is sometimes known as 'sideways relief '. However, there are specific rules as to the order in which these losses can be utilised. This applies to current-period trading losses and trading losses carried forward pre- and post-1 April 2017 (which may be restricted as outlined earlier).

Where a company makes a trading loss in the current accounting period, 'sideways relief' for that loss is given **after** relief for:

- surplus non-trade debits brought forward (against non-trade profits);
- losses from a UK property business; and
- surplus non-trade debits in the current year.

but **before**:

- relief for surplus non-trade debits carried back; and
- relief for qualifying charitable donations.

14.9 Summary of Loss Reliefs

The table overleaf summarises the various loss reliefs discussed in this chapter.

SUMMARY OF LOSS RELIEFS

Type of Loss	Current Year	Carry Back	Carry Forward	
			Pre-1 April 2017	Post-1 April 2017
Trading loss	• Set off against profits before QCDs. • 'All or nothing' claim – partial claims **not** permitted.	• Carried back against profits of the previous 12 months (or 36 months if trading losses arose in accounting periods ending between 1 April 2020 and 31 March 2022) before QCDs. • A current-year claim must be made before losses are carried back. • 'All or nothing' claim.	Carried forward against future profits of the same trade in the same company.	Carried forward against total profits in the company.
Non-trade loan relationship deficits	Set off against profits before QCDs in preference to trading and property losses – partial claims permitted.	• Carried back against non-trade loan relationship surpluses of previous 12 months. • 'All or nothing' claim. • Losses can be carried back even if a current-year claim not made.	[Beyond scope of this textbook.]	Carried forward against total profits of the company.
UK property losses	Mandatory set off against profits before QCDs in preference to trading losses – partial claims **not** permitted.	Cannot be carried back.	[Beyond scope of this textbook.]	Carried forward against total profits of the company.

Questions

Review Questions

(See Suggested Solutions to Review Questions at the end of this textbook.)

Question 14.1

Using the figures given below for Enya Ltd, show how the property income and trade losses may be used. Enya Ltd is not a member of a group.

Year ending	Property income	Trading profits/(losses)	Income from loan relationships
	£	£	£
31/03/2019	50,000	600,000	100,000
31/03/2020	(40,000)	700,000	50,000
31/03/2021	60,000	(1,300,000)	100,000
31/03/2022	80,000	100,000	35,000

Requirement

Calculate the taxable total profits for each year, showing the loss relief claimed and a loss memorandum showing the loss carried forward at 1 April 2022.

Question 14.2

Hells Bells Ltd shows the following results:

	Year ended 31 March 2022	Nine months ended 31 December 2022
	£	£
Trading profit/(loss)	167,000	(190,000)
Rents	4,000	(4,000)
Chargeable gains/(losses)	(19,000)	10,000
Net credit from loan relationships	10,000	20,000

Requirement

Calculate the corporation tax payable for each accounting period claiming the earliest possible relief for losses.

Question 14.3

Monk Ltd, a manufacturing company, prepares annual accounts to 31 March each year. Recent results were as follows:

	Year Ended 31 March	
	2022	**2023**
	£	**£**
Adjusted trading profit/(loss) (Note 1) (before capital allowances)	360,000	(310,000)
Capital allowances	20,000	90,000
Bank deposit interest	5,000	30,000
Property income	15,000	20,000
Chargeable gains	12,000	126,000

The following additional information is available:

1. Monk Ltd has an agreed unutilised trading loss forward from the year ended 31/03/2017 of £20,000.
2. The company wishes to claim the loss reliefs available so as to maximise the benefit of the losses.

Requirement

Compute the corporation tax payable for each of the above years and indicate the amount (if any) of unutilised losses available for carry forward to year ending 31 March 2024.

Part Three
Capital Gains Tax

15

Introduction, General Principles and Administration

Learning Objectives

After studying this chapter you will understand:

- The application of the general principles for the computation of capital gains tax (CGT) liabilities.
- The payment of CGT and the filing of returns.
- How to identify chargeable and exempt assets for CGT purposes.
- How to determine and apply the appropriate treatment of capital losses, including negligible value claims.
- How to determine the appropriate treatment for assets passing on death.

Chartered Accountants Ireland's *Code of Ethics* applies to all aspects of a Chartered Accountant's professional life, including dealing with CGT issues. As outlined at the beginning of this book, further information regarding the principles in the *Code of Ethics* is set out in **Appendix 2**.

In addition, **Appendix 3** of this book examines the distinction between tax planning, tax avoidance and tax evasion which can arise in relation to all taxes including CGT.

15.1 The Basic Charge to CGT

There are three basic elements that must exist before the provisions relating to the taxation of capital gains come into operation:

1. there must be a **chargeable disposal**,
2. of a **chargeable asset**,
3. by a **chargeable person**.

The Taxation of Chargeable Gains Act (TCGA) 1992, as amended by subsequent Finance Acts, contains the main provisions for the taxation of chargeable gains.

15.2 Disposal

In order for a liability to CGT to arise, a disposal of a chargeable asset must take place or must be deemed to take place. A disposal for these purposes will occur in each of the following situations:

- on the sale of an asset;
- on the sale of part of an asset (part disposal);
- on the gift of the whole or part of an asset;
- on the receipt of a capital sum resulting from the ownership of an asset, e.g. receipt of compensation for damage to assets or the receipt of a capital sum in return for forfeiture or surrender of rights;
- on the receipt of a capital sum as consideration for use or exploitation of assets;
- on the transfer of an asset to a trust or a corporate body;
- on an exchange of assets in a barter transaction.

However, the sale of an asset in the course of a trade (for example, the sale of trading stock) is not a chargeable disposal since any gain arising is taxed as a trading profit.

In respect of **gifts**, the asset is treated as if it were sold for CGT purposes and the consideration is deemed to be its market value even though the transferor receives no consideration. Certain disposals are **exempt** from CGT including gifts to charities and gifts of national heritage property (subject to certain conditions). A list of exempt assets is included below.

As a general rule, CGT is not triggered on **death**. There is, therefore, no chargeable disposal on death, even though the deceased no longer owns the assets. Chargeable assets held on death are, however, revalued to their market value as at the date of death. The market value at the date of death (the probate value) becomes the base cost for the person inheriting the asset.

It is **important** to note that although transfers of assets between **husbands and wives** (and legally recognised civil partnerships) are chargeable disposals for CGT purposes, they are specifically deemed to occur at a value such that neither a chargeable gain nor an allowable loss occurs on the transfer (disposal), i.e. on a no gain/no loss basis.

A **chargeable disposal occurs at the date of the unconditional contract** or the date that the condition is satisfied on a conditional contract. A contract can be written or verbal.

15.3 Chargeable Assets

Chargeable assets for CGT purposes include all forms of property, whether situated in the UK or not, including options, debts and foreign currency. The basic rule is that any capital asset of an individual or company is a chargeable asset unless it is specifically exempt from CGT or corporation tax on chargeable gains. Specifically included is an interest in property, e.g. a lease. As seen in the previous chapters, a company generally calculates its chargeable gains on the same basis as individuals (apart from indexation, which is available for companies up to 31 December 2017, and the fact that there is no annual exemption for companies).

The main **exempt assets** for CGT purposes include:

- motor cars;
- chattels (items of tangible movable property), which are disposed of for gross proceeds of £6,000 or less and where the cost is also £6,000 or less (see **Chapter 16**);
- wasting chattels, which are chattels with a predictable useful life of 50 years or less (unless used in the taxpayer's business and eligible for capital allowances);
- a taxpayer's principal private residence (see **Chapter 17**);
- winnings from betting, lotteries and the pools;
- decorations for valour (unless purchased), life insurance policies (unless purchased from a third party);
- National Savings & Investment Certificates, Premium Bonds and ISAs;

- gilt-edged securities (e.g. Treasury stock) and qualifying corporate bonds;
- foreign currency for private use abroad; and
- damages for personal or professional injury.

15.4   Chargeable Persons

CGT is charged on gains accruing (realised or deemed to be realised) by individuals, business partners, trustees and personal representatives of a deceased person. Companies are also chargeable persons, but are assessed to corporation tax on chargeable gains and not to CGT (see **Chapter 12**). A person is chargeable to CGT in respect of worldwide chargeable gains accruing to them in the year of assessment if during any part of the tax year they are resident in the UK (see **Chapter 1**).

15.5   Rate of Tax, Date of Payment and Returns

15.5.1   Rates of CGT

CGT is charged by reference to fiscal years of assessment for individuals, i.e. year ending 5 April. Individuals must calculate their total taxable income to be able to apply the correct CGT rate. The calculation is as follows:

1. Calculate taxable income by deducting any tax-free allowances (personal allowance for 2021/22 is £12,570) and reliefs that are due.
2. Identify how much of the basic rate band is already being used against taxable income. The maximum basic rate band for 2021/22 is £37,700.
3. Allocate any remaining basic rate band against gains in 2021/22. Gains that fall to be taxed within the basic rate band are charged at 10% (for most taxable gains) or 18% (for residential property). The legislation ensures that an individual can use any remaining basic rate band in the most tax-efficient way.
4. Any remaining gains above the basic rate band are charged at 20% (for most taxable gains) or 28% (for residential properties).

The rates of CGT for gains on residential property are 18% for those in the basic rate band and 28% thereafter. A residential property for these purposes includes both UK and non-UK situs residential properties. The rates of CGT for most other taxable gains are 10% for those in the basic rate band and 20% thereafter.

Trustees and personal representatives pay CGT at 20% on gains, regardless of the level of income. The 28% higher rate applies to residential property disposals.

Example 15.1

Julie's total taxable income in 2021/22, after deducting allowances and reliefs, is £28,915 and her capital gains, after tax-free allowance and reliefs, are £17,000. None of the gains relate to residential property.

The maximum basic rate band for 2021/22 is £37,700. Julie has used £28,915 of this amount against her income, so she has £8,785 remaining.

£8,785 of Julie's gains will fall within the basic rate band and will be taxed at 10%.

The remaining £8,215 gains (£17,000 less £8,785) are taxed at 20%.

Companies pay corporation tax on their chargeable gains at the company's effective tax rate. For the financial year 2021 this is 19% for all companies (see **Chapter 12**).

15.5.2 Date of Payment – Non-residential Property Disposals

The UK self-assessment regime also applies to CGT. CGT due must be paid on or before 31 January following the end of the relevant tax year. For example, the CGT due on a chargeable gain or gains arising during 2021/22 falls due for payment on or before 31 January 2023. The payment of CGT does not impact on the following tax year's payments on account. Where a UK resident individual disposes of UK residential property, a special payment and reporting date applies (see **Section 15.5.4**).

Example 15.2

An individual disposes of a commercial investment property in July 2021, giving rise to a chargeable gain of £10,000; and disposes of a plot of land in November 2021, giving rise to a chargeable gain of £6,200. The individual had a loss forward of £2,700 from the disposal of shares in 2020/21. Their total taxable income for the year (after tax-free allowance and reliefs) was £19,700. CGT is payable by the individual as follows:

CGT rate computation

	£
Basic rate band 2021/22	37,700
Less: total taxable income	(19,700)
Remaining basic rate band	18,000

Total taxable gains (i.e. chargeable gains after capital losses brought forward, annual exemption, etc.) are less than £18,000, so the CGT rate of 10% will be applied to all taxable gains.

CGT computation

	£
Chargeable gains	16,200
Less: capital losses from 2020/21 (see **Section 15.11**)	(2,700)
Less: CGT annual exemption (see **Section 15.6.3**)	(12,300)
Taxable gain	1,200
CGT @ 10%	120

CGT for 2021/22, payable on or before 31 January 2023, is £120.

15.5.3 Payment by Instalments

In a situation where the taxpayer receives the disposal proceeds in instalments over a period of 18 months or more, they may choose to make a claim to pay the CGT liability by way of interest-free instalments. The size and frequency of the instalments are at the discretion of HMRC, but the period over which they are paid must not exceed:

1. an eight-year period; **or**
2. the date on which the last instalment of the consideration is payable.

It is also possible for the taxpayer to elect to pay by instalments where gift relief is not available (see **Chapter 18**). This election for payment by instalment is not interest-free and interest will accrue on outstanding balances.

15.5.4 Date of Payment – UK Residential Property Disposals

From 6 April 2020, UK tax residents will need to report and pay CGT on all UK residential property disposals within 30 days of the date of completion of the disposal (rather than the deadline of 31 January following the end of the tax year in which the sale is made). The transaction must be reported on HMRC's new online service designed specifically to capture details of projected CGT liability on a UK residential property disposal and the related payment on account.

The calculation of the CGT liability will, in some cases, require an estimate of the individual's income and other CGT transactions in order to complete the payment on account return and assess the relevant CGT rate. If the individual is already in the self-assessment system, they will also be required to report the residential property disposal details as part of their self-assessment return for the relevant tax year (see **Section 15.5.5**). If the individual is not part of the self-assessment system, no further reporting will be required beyond the 30-day submission.

Any payment of CGT made will be offset against the individual's CGT and income tax liabilities for the relevant tax year when their self-assessment tax return is completed and submitted to HMRC.

The 30 days reporting and payment requirements will not apply where:

- the residential property that has been sold is located outside the UK; or
- the gain on the residential property disposal is not chargeable to CGT, e.g. where:
  - the gain (including any other chargeable residential property gains in the same tax year) is within the annual exempt amount of £12,300 for 2021/22;
  - the residential property is sold at a loss;
  - capital losses are available and cover the gain;
  - the gain is covered by private residence relief (see **Chapter 17**); or
  - the transaction is a gift between spouses/civil partners on a no gain/no loss basis (see **Section 15.8.3**).

15.5.5 Returns

A return of chargeable gains must be made within the self-assessment income tax return filing deadline for individuals.

By way of reminder, the latest filing date for a personal tax return is:

- 31 October following the end of the tax year for paper returns; and
- 31 January following the end of the tax year for online returns.

Taxpayers are normally **not** required to complete the CGT pages of their tax return if **both** the following conditions are satisfied:

1. the total disposals proceeds from the tax year do not exceed four times the amount of the annual exemption (£49,200 for 2021/22); **and**
2. the total chargeable gains for the tax year do not exceed the annual exemption (£12,300 for 2021/22).

In this case, a statement to this effect, in lieu of the CGT pages, will suffice. For the purposes of these conditions, the total chargeable gains are before deduction of either current year capital losses or capital losses brought forward from previous years.

It should be noted that relief for capital losses cannot be claimed unless they are notified to HMRC within four years from the end of the tax year in which the losses were incurred. So if a loss is made in 2021/22, the deadline for claiming the loss (although not for claiming relief for the loss) is 5 April 2026.

As chargeable gains are reported to HMRC under self-assessment, the self-assessment regime equally applies to CGT (see **Chapter 10**).

15.6 Computation of Gain or Loss

15.6.1 General

In summary, taxable gains are the net chargeable gains (after current year capital losses) of the tax year reduced by unrelieved losses brought forward from previous years and the annual exemption.

The capital gain is the difference between:

1. the consideration for the disposal of the asset, or the deemed consideration (e.g. market value in the case of a gift or disposal between connected persons); and
2. the cost of acquisition of the asset or its market value if not acquired at arm's length (e.g. property acquired by way of inheritance or gift).

If any part of the sales consideration is taken into account in computing income tax or corporation tax profits or losses, it is excluded from the amount under 1 above. Any expenditure that is allowable as a deduction from income tax or corporation tax profits, or which would be allowable if the asset had been employed as a fixed asset of a trade, is excluded from 2 above.

Allowable expenditure for CGT purposes includes the following:

1. The cost of acquiring (or providing) the asset and certain incidental costs of acquisition or disposal, e.g. agent's commission, stamp taxes, valuation costs, cost of transfer or conveyance, auctioneers', accountants' or solicitors' fees and advertising costs.
2. Expenditure incurred for the purposes of enhancing the value of the asset, which is reflected in the nature or state of the asset at the time of disposal, e.g. **improvements to property**. To be allowable, the expenditure must not have been abortive nor must its value have wasted away before the disposal of the asset. Expenditure incurred in establishing, preserving or defending an owner's title or interest in an asset is allowable within this definition. Enhancement expenditure does not include costs of repairs and maintenance, costs of insurance or capital grants expended out of public funds.

A typical CGT computation for an asset sold during 2021/22 might be as follows.

J. Jones – Capital Gains Tax Computation for 2021/22

	£	£
Sales proceeds (or market value)	X	
Less: incidental costs of sale	(X)	
		X
Deduct allowable costs:		
Original cost of asset	X	
Incidental costs of acquisition	X	
Enhancement expenditure	X	
		(X)

continued overleaf

Gain	X
Deduct: loss relief (if any – see **Section 15.11**)	(X)
Deduct: annual exemption (see **Section 15.6.3**)	(X)
Taxable chargeable gain	X
CGT payable: taxable gain at 10%/18%/20%/28% (for individuals)	X

15.6.2 Indexation Allowance

As seen in earlier chapters, indexation allowance is available to increase acquisition and enhancement costs in line with inflation for companies, but only up to and including 31 December 2017 for assets bought before 1 January 2018 and sold on or after that date. Assets bought on or after 1 January 2018, therefore, attract no indexation allowance when sold. There is no indexation allowance for individuals.

15.6.3 Annual Exemption

Every individual is entitled to an annual exemption, which is available for offset against the "taxable" gains of the particular tax year. The annual exemption cannot be carried forward and thus any excess over the taxable gains is lost. Furthermore, the annual exemption cannot be transferred, e.g. between spouses or civil partners.

The annual exemption for 2021/22 is £12,300 (2020/21: £12,300).

The "taxable" gains are usually the chargeable gains accruing to the taxpayer for a year of assessment after deduction of allowable losses. Thus, allowable losses of the current year must be utilised against the chargeable gains arising in that year, even if this means that part or all of the annual exemption will be wasted. However, where capital losses are being carried forward or carried back (applicable only on death), these can be tailored so as not to waste any of the annual exemption. Current-year losses must be claimed in priority to losses brought forward. The offset of current-year losses cannot be tailored to protect the use of the annual exemption.

Both the annual exemption and losses should be used in the most beneficial way possible, i.e. set against any gains taxed at the higher CGT rate of 28%, followed by gains taxed at 20%, then gains taxed at 18% and finally against gains taxed at 10%.

Companies are not entitled to the CGT annual exemption.

Example 15.3

Four taxpayers, John, Paul, George and Matthew, each make chargeable disposals during 2021/22. None of them have any capital losses brought forward from previous years. None of the gains relate to residential property. Calculate their CGT assessable chargeable gains for 2021/22.

(a) John had gains of £2,800 (30 June), £3,600 (15 September) and £5,150 (10 January) and a capital loss of £2,450 (5 May).

(b) Paul had gains of £10,300 (18 May), £3,600 (5 December) and capital losses of £700 (30 April) and £800 (1 February). He has £5,000 of his basic rate band remaining.

(c) George had a gain of £9,600 (5 August) and capital losses of £3,500 (30 November), £2,900 (12 December) and £8,200 (4 March).

(d) Matthew had gains of £6,000 (15 May), £8,600 (10 October) and £9,100 (8 February). He has £10,000 of his basic rate band remaining.

continued overleaf

Solution

(a) John's 'net' position is a net gain of £9,100. This is less than the annual exemption and thus he will have a CGT assessment of nil and the unused part of his annual allowance, £3,200 (£12,300 – £9,100), is lost.

(b) Paul's 'net' position is a net gain of £12,400. Deducting his annual exemption leaves a taxable gain of £100, which is within his surplus basic rate band. Therefore, CGT is payable for 2021/22 at 10% × £100 = £10.

(c) George's 'net' position is a net loss of £5,000 and his CGT assessment for 2021/22 will be nil and all of his annual exemption will be lost. The capital loss will be carried forward and is available for offset against future capital gains.

(d) Matthew's 'net' position is a gain of £11,400 (£23,700 – £12,300) after deducting the annual exemption. £10,000 of this will be taxed at 10% and £1,400 at 20%, resulting in a CGT liability of £1,280.

Example 15.4

Three taxpayers, George, Robert and Denis, have capital losses carried forward from previous years of £3,000, £4,000 and £5,000 respectively. All three had made chargeable gains of £14,800 and a capital loss of £1,400 during 2021/22. Calculate each of their CGT assessments for 2021/22. You can assume that each has used up their basic rate band in full before the gains are taken into account and that none of the gains relate to residential property.

Solution

Each has a 'net' position for 2021/22 (prior to utilisation of their annual exemption and their individual capital losses brought forward) of £13,400. Each taxpayer needs only to utilise sufficient of his carried forward losses to reduce (where possible) the 'net' gain to the level of the annual exemption.

In order to arrive at how much, if any, of the capital losses each taxpayer must use, one has to consider the position after deducting the annual allowance, **before** looking at losses forward. In each case, this would be a figure of £1,100 (£13,400 – £12,300).

Thus, George would use £1,100 of his carried-forward capital losses of £3,000 and leave no taxable gain (after deduction of his annual exemption). He would carry forward the remaining £1,900 of his losses. His CGT assessment for 2021/22 is nil.

Robert would only utilise £1,100 of his capital losses brought forward (i.e. he leaves sufficient 'net' gain to be covered by his annual exemption). He would then have capital losses to carry forward of £2,900 (£4,000 less £1,100 used in 2021/22). His CGT assessment for 2021/22 is nil.

Similarly, Denis would only utilise £1,100 of his brought forward-losses and his carried-forward capital losses would thus be £3,900 (£5,000 less £1,100 used in 2021/22). His CGT assessment for 2021/22 is nil.

Denis – CGT computation

	£
Chargeable gain	14,800
Less: current-year capital losses	(1,400)
	13,400
Less: losses brought forward	(1,100)
	12,300
Less: annual exemption	(12,300)
Net chargeable gain	0
CGT	Nil
Memo of losses carried forward	5,000
Utilised 2021/22	(1,100)
Losses available for carry forward	3,900

Note differences in claiming relief for current-year losses and losses carried forward.

15.6.4 Special Rules Relating to Allowable Deductions

As outlined above, expenditure that is allowable as a deduction when computing the quantum of the chargeable gain is:

1. The costs of acquiring (or providing) the asset, which includes certain incidental costs of acquisition wholly and exclusively incurred for the purposes of the acquisition (such as stamp duty, stamp duty land tax, fees, commission, valuation fees and professional services of estate agents, solicitors, surveyors, etc.) and advertising costs.
2. Enhancement costs for the asset and any costs of establishing, preserving or defending title to an asset.
3. Certain incidental costs of disposals. While the allowable incidental costs of disposal are generally similar to those for incidental costs of acquisition, specifically excluded are the costs associated with resolving valuation disputes with HMRC. As stated above, no deduction is allowable for expenditure which is allowable as a deduction in computing the profits or losses of a trade for income tax or corporation tax purposes.
4. Grants – No deduction is allowed in computing chargeable gains for any expenditure which has been met by the provision of government, public or local authority grants.

15.6.5 Part Disposal

As we have seen above, the partial disposal of an asset is a chargeable event for CGT purposes. Where a portion of an asset is sold, the sale proceeds are easily quantified but it is necessary to calculate **how much of the original cost of the asset is allowable as a deduction** in computing the chargeable gain or allowable loss arising on the part disposal.

The legislation provides that this is calculated as being the proportion of the original cost of the asset which the value of the part being disposed of bears, at the time of disposal, to the market value of the whole asset. The formula is, therefore:

$$\text{Original cost} \times \frac{A}{A + B}$$

where A is the amount of the 'gross' proceeds/market value of the part disposal (i.e. before deducting incidental costs of disposal) and B is the market value of the portion of the asset which is retained.

However, any expenditure incurred wholly in respect of a particular part of an asset should be treated as an allowable deduction in full for that part and not apportioned, e.g. selling costs which are wholly attributable to the part disposed of.

Example 15.5

Assume an asset cost £1,000 on 1 September 2007 and part of the asset was sold for £600 on 6 June 2021. The market value of the remainder of the asset was £700. The chargeable gain in respect of the disposal would be computed as follows (assuming that the annual exemption has been used elsewhere):

	£
Sales proceeds	600
Less: allowable cost:	
$£1,000 \times \dfrac{£600}{£600+£700}$	(462)
Chargeable gain	138

continued overleaf

The base costs for onward disposal of the remaining part of the asset is:

	£
Original cost of asset	1,000
Less: cost of part disposal	(462)
Cost of remaining part	538

Example 15.6

A commercial investment property cost £10,000 on 10 April 1984. Part of the asset was sold on 10 November 2021 for £27,000. The market value of the remainder asset at that date was £50,000. The individual has other income in 2021/22 of £78,000.

Calculate the CGT liability.

	£
Proceeds	27,000
Cost: £10,000 × $\dfrac{£27,000}{£27,000 + £50,000}$	(3,507)
	23,493
Annual exemption	(12,300)
	11,193

CGT payable is £11,193 × 20% = £2,239 (due by 31 January 2023).

Base cost of the remaining part for onward disposal is:

	£
Original cost	10,000
Less: cost of part disposal	(3,507)
Cost of remaining part	6,493

"Small Disposal" Proceeds of Land

Where the proceeds for a part disposal of land are small compared with the value of the land held, then the taxpayer may claim not to be treated as having made a capital disposal, but instead deduct the proceeds from allowable expenditure on a subsequent disposal. This claim can only be made if the proceeds for the part disposal of land are:

1. not more than 20% of the entire holding of the land's market value **and** not more than £20,000, **and** the net aggregate proceeds from the part disposal and any other disposals of land (including buildings) in the same tax year do not exceed £20,000; **or**
2. the land is subject to a compulsory purchase order and the proceeds received are deemed to be small, i.e. 5% or less of the market value of the entire holding, or £3,000 or less (irrespective of whether the 5% test is met).

The claim cannot be made if the allowable expenditure is less than the part disposal proceeds, i.e. a capital loss has arisen.

Example 15.7

An individual bought five acres of land in October 2008 for £10,000 and sold one acre for £5,000 in November 2021. This was their only disposal in 2021/22. The market value of the land prior to sale is £40,000. The disposal costs were £500. What is the CGT position?

Can the taxpayer claim to be treated as if no disposal has been made?

The consideration is £5,000. This is less than 20% of the market value (20% of £40,000 = £8,000) and less than £20,000. As there have been no other disposals in 2021/22, the net aggregate proceeds of all land and buildings disposals are also less than £20,000. As all conditions are met, a claim for part disposal can be made.

Claim small disposal relief:	£
Base cost: cost of five acres	10,000
Deduct net proceeds of part disposal (£5,000 – £500)	(4,500)
Allowable base cost of land retained	5,500

As a claim has been made, no disposal takes place at this time; therefore there is no taxable capital gain. Instead the base cost of the land is reduced by the net proceeds received and the reduced base cost is carried forward to be used in the CGT computation on any future sale of the land.

15.6.6 Application of Market Value

Normally, where a disposal is at arm's length and the consideration is known in money terms, the consideration paid is accepted for CGT purposes. However, in certain circumstances, the market value of an asset is substituted for the actual consideration paid for the disposal. This will occur:

1. where there is a transaction between connected persons (see **Section 15.10**)
2. where a disposal is not made at arm's length (e.g. a gift);
3. where the consideration is not valued in money terms or is a barter transaction;
4. where the asset is acquired or disposed of wholly or partly for a consideration that cannot be valued; or
5. where the asset is acquired by way of a distribution from a company in respect of shares in the company.

In all of the above scenarios, the market value is deemed to be the consideration for the purpose of determining the chargeable gain or allowable loss.

However, the market value rule is overridden when the asset is transferred between husband and wife and between civil partners. In such situations, the transfers are deemed to occur at a value such that there is neither a chargeable gain nor an allowable loss (i.e. on a no gain/no loss basis).

15.7 Time of Disposal

The time of disposal for the purposes of CGT is generally determined by reference to the time a contract is made. Briefly, the rules for the following situations are:

1. In the case of an **unconditional contract**, the date of the contract is the relevant date, irrespective of the date of the conveyance or transfer of the asset (i.e. "the closing date" or "completion date" is not relevant).
2. In the case of a **conditional contract**, the time of the disposal for the purposes of CGT is the date on which the condition is satisfied.

3. In the case of **gifts**, the date of disposal is the date on which the property effectively passes. This rule also applies to gifts into settlements, e.g. in the case of the gift of a chattel, the date that the chattel is delivered is the date of disposal for CGT purposes.
4. In the case of **compulsory purchases**, the date of disposal is the time at which the compensation for the acquisition is agreed or otherwise determined (e.g. by arbitration). Variations in the compensation on appeal are disregarded in determining the date of disposal and acquisition.

15.8 Married Couples and Civil Partners

15.8.1 General

A husband and wife, or each member of a civil partnership, are separate "persons" for CGT purposes and their gains or losses are computed separately. (For the rest of this section references to "couple" or "spouses" should be treated as referring also to civil partnerships and civil partners). Losses made by one spouse cannot be transferred to the other spouse. Each spouse is responsible for making returns of his or her own gains, and for paying the CGT due on those gains. The residence status of each spouse is also considered individually to decide whether or not that person is chargeable to CGT.

15.8.2 Annual Exemption

Each person is entitled to their own annual exemption. For 2021/22, the annual exemption is £12,300 for individuals.

15.8.3 Disposal by One Spouse to the Other

A disposal of an asset from one spouse to the other does not give rise to a CGT liability where the spouses are living together. The asset is deemed to have passed from one to the other at a value which gives rise to a no gain/no loss position. On a subsequent disposal of the asset to a third party, there is a chargeable gain or allowable loss by reference to the whole period of ownership by both spouses. There is no requirement that the spouses should be living together throughout the tax year – it is sufficient for them to have lived together at some time in the year. In addition, it does not matter that one spouse is UK-resident and the other is not.

There is one exception to this important no gain/no loss rule, which is where the asset concerned forms part of the stock in trade of either spouse. In that case, there is a disposal and the consideration is always deemed to be the market value, regardless of the value agreed between the spouses.

15.8.4 Jointly Held Assets

Where a couple disposes of an asset that has been held in their joint names, any chargeable gain arising is apportioned between them in accordance with their respective beneficial interests in the asset at the time of the disposal. If the split of ownership between the spouses is clear, the respective gains should be reported to HMRC on the basis of that split. If the split of ownership is not clear, HMRC normally accepts that the spouses hold the asset in equal proportions.

15.9 Partnerships

An asset owned by all the partners is a "partnership asset". If not all the partners own an asset, then HMRC treat this as simply "other assets". Rollover relief will be available where a partner disposes of a qualifying asset (this is dealt with in **Chapter 18**). Where partners own assets personally, HMRC may allow rollover relief where the owner lets the assets to the partnership in which they are a partner, provided such assets are used for the partnership's business.

Dealings in partnership assets are treated as dealings by the individual partners and not by the firm. Each partner has to be considered to own a fractional share of each partnership asset, rather than an interest in the partnership as a whole. Chargeable gains or allowable losses accruing on the disposal of partnership assets are therefore apportioned among the partners in accordance with their capital profit-sharing ratio. An individual's share of a partnership's allowable capital loss may therefore be set-off against personal (non-partnership) gains, and vice versa. If a partnership makes a part disposal, then the part disposal rules are applied before the gain is divided among the partners.

Example 15.8

A and B are in partnership sharing profits and losses at 60% and 40% respectively. The capital sharing ratio is also 60:40. During 2021/22, the partnership disposed of a building which it had originally acquired for £30,000 in June 1986. It realised £100,000 on disposal.

Computation of gain	£
Sale proceeds	100,000
Deduct: cost	(30,000)
	70,000
Apportioned to A 60% × £70,000	42,000
Apportioned to B 40% × £70,000	28,000
	70,000

Each partner would be entitled to claim any personal capital losses against the above gains and, of course, each would be entitled to claim his or her annual exemption.

Partnership goodwill is a chargeable asset, and consequently a gain on the disposal by a partner of their share of a firm's goodwill is chargeable.

Partners may decide to change their profit shares in the firm, e.g. when a new partner joins the firm or a partner retires. Each partner is treated as acquiring or disposing of an appropriate share in the partnership assets.

A reduction in an individual partner's share of a partnership asset is a disposal for CGT purposes. The actual CGT treatment will depend on whether the consideration is dealt with in the accounts or outside them, and whether the assets have been revalued.

If there is no direct payment outside the partnership, then the consideration for the disposal will be the fraction of the asset's current statement of financial position value that corresponds to the fractional share passing between the partners. Where no revaluation of the asset has taken place on the statement of financial position, the disposal is treated as one on which there is no gain/ no loss.

Example 15.9

James and John are in partnership and share profits and losses in the ratio 70:30. The capital sharing ratio is also 70:30. The only chargeable asset on the statement of financial position is a property, which has not been revalued. They change their profit share to 50:50. In this situation, James has disposed of 20% of his share and John has acquired 20%. If the current statement of financial position value of the property is £100,000, then James's disposal proceeds and John's acquisition cost would both be £20,000.

Since the asset has not been revalued, James's disposal will be on a no gain/no loss basis. However, if there had been a revaluation (upward) in the past, then the two partners would have had the proportional fraction of the increase credited to their respective capital accounts. While there would have

continued overleaf

been no capital gain at the time of revaluation, the change in the profit sharing will mean that John has now effectively realised a proportion of the unrealised gain. A chargeable gain for each partner is now crystallised.

Where a payment is made outside of the partnership accounts on a change of profit-sharing arrangements, a chargeable gain will crystallise on the partner whose profit share has been reduced. The partner who has acquired the additional profit share will treat his payment as an acquisition cost for onward disposal.

The special rules relating to disposals between connected persons (i.e. market value rules) will not apply on disposals and acquisitions between partners where an interest in a partnership asset is transferred between partners on commercial terms and provided that the individuals are not otherwise connected, e.g. father and son.

15.10 Connected Persons

15.10.1 Meaning of Connected Person

Where there is a transaction between "connected persons", the consideration is **deemed to be the open market value** (unless specifically overwritten, as in the case of spousal/civil partner transfers, etc.). Any consideration agreed between the connected persons is ignored for the purposes of computing chargeable gains or allowable losses. The following are connected persons:

1. **Relatives** Relatives include husband, wife, brother, sister, ancestor and lineal descendants but excludes uncle, aunt, niece and nephew.
2. **Trustees** A trustee of a settlement is connected with:
   (a) the settlor;
   (b) any person connected with the settlor; and
   (c) any company connected with the trust.
   A company will be deemed to be connected with the trust if, at any time during the year of assessment, it is a close company and the shareholders include the trustees of, or a beneficiary under, the settlement.
3. **Partners** A person is connected with any person with whom he is in partnership, and with the spouse or civil partner or a relative of any individual with whom he is in partnership. In this case, there is an exception to the market value rule in relation to the acquisition and disposal of partnership assets pursuant to bona fide commercial arrangements.
4. **Company** A company is connected with another person if that person has control of the company or if that person and the persons connected with him together have control of the company. Companies under common control are also connected persons.

15.10.2 Losses

Where a disposal to a connected person results in an allowable loss, that loss may only be set-off against chargeable gains on disposals to the same connected person.

15.10.3 Treatment of a Series of Transactions between Connected Persons

Where a person disposes of assets by means of a series of transactions to one or more connected person(s) (as defined in **Section 15.10.1**) through a series of linked transactions (rather than in one transaction), and:

■ the aggregate market value of the asset acquired as a whole is greater than the combined total of their separate values when acquired singly; then

■ all of the acquisitions are treated as if they were acquired in one single transaction for a consideration equal to their aggregate market value (when acquired in a single transaction); and

■ that revised aggregate market value is then apportioned rateably to each transaction for the purposes of determining the consideration for which each disposal is deemed to have taken place.

Transactions are linked if they occur within six years of each other.

Example 15.10

George and Jimmy are brothers. George has three sets of rare Cuban stamps. He gifts them to Jimmy in three separate transactions as follows:

Date of gift		£
01/05/2018	Set 1 market value (on individual basis)	5,000
01/06/2019	Set 2 market value (on individual basis)	10,000
01/07/2021	Set 3 market value (on individual basis)	15,000
		30,000

The market value of the three sets, if disposed of together, is £40,000.

For the purpose of computing George's CGT liability (if any) on the disposals, the aggregate £40,000 market value will be apportioned rateably to the three transactions as follows:

Revised consideration: £

Set 1: $\dfrac{£5,000}{£30,000} \times £40,000$ 6,667

Set 2: $\dfrac{£10,000}{£30,000} \times £40,000$ 13,333

Set 3: $\dfrac{£15,000}{£30,000} \times £40,000$ 20,000

            40,000

George's liability to CGT would then be computed by reference to the increased consideration for each of the three disposals separately.

15.11 Losses

15.11.1 General

Losses are computed in the same manner as gains. An allowable loss may arise in certain circumstances, even where the asset is not disposed of, e.g. a loss arising from the value of an asset becoming negligible (see **Section 15.12**). Note that, when computing a company's chargeable gains position, **indexation allowance cannot create or increase a loss**, i.e. the indexation allowance is limited to the amount required to reduce the gain to nil. However the indexation allowance for companies is only available up to and including 31 December 2017 for assets bought before 1 January 2018 but sold on or after that date. Assets bought on or after 1 January 2018, therefore, attract no indexation allowance when sold.

Subject to certain specific exemptions, **allowable losses may not be carried back** prior to the year of assessment in which they are incurred (see **Section 15.11.2**).

In general, a loss is an allowable loss if, had there been a gain on the disposal of the assets, the gain would have been a chargeable gain.

Current-year Capital Losses

Allowable losses arising must be set-off against chargeable gains accruing in the same year of assessment, insofar as this is possible, even if this wastes all or part of the annual exemption. Current-year capital losses may be set against gains in any way in order to maximise tax relief. To the extent that there is an unutilised balance, the capital losses unutilised must be carried forward and set-off against chargeable gains arising in subsequent years.

Capital Losses Carried Forward

As seen at **Section 15.6.3**, the taxpayer does not have to use all of the losses brought forward. The taxpayer may 'restrict' the quantum of the brought forward loss (or not use it at all) in order to ensure that the full benefit of that year's annual exemption is preserved.

Note: good tax planning would be to reduce the chargeable gain with enough losses brought forward to bring the chargeable gain down to the level of the annual exemption, and then carry forward any excess capital losses.

Example 15.11

An individual has the following gains/losses for 2021/22:

		£
Asset 1	Gain	6,000
Asset 2	Gain	2,000
Asset 3	Loss	(4,000)
Asset 4	Gain	1,000

The individual also has allowable losses forward of £2,000 from 2020/21. Loss relief will be claimed as follows:

	£
Chargeable gains	9,000
Deduct: 2021/22 current-year capital losses	(4,000)
Brought forward losses not utilised (gain already covered by annual exemption)	5,000
Deduct: annual exemption	(5,000)
Net taxable gains after loss/annual exemption	Nil

£7,300 of annual exemption is lost. Carry forward capital losses of £2,000 remain.

15.11.2 Carry Back of Losses

The general rule is that capital losses cannot be carried back to earlier years. An exception to this rule is made in the case of losses which accrue to an individual in the tax year in which they die. These losses may be carried back and set against gains of the three years of assessment preceding the year of assessment in which the individual died, with these losses set-off against the later years first.

As with capital losses carried forward, capital losses carried back are set against the net gains only to the extent that those net gains exceed the annual exemption for the year in which they arise.

Example 15.12

Mr X dies on 31 August 2021. In the period 6 April to 31 August 2021, Mr X made disposals of assets and realised allowable losses of £15,000.

The losses of £15,000 will first be available for set-off against any chargeable gains assessed on Mr X in 2021/22, with any residue against any chargeable gains in 2020/21, then against net gains in 2019/20 and, finally, against any net chargeable gains in the tax year 2018/19. Any overpaid tax will be repaid to his estate by HMRC.

Example 15.13

Patricia died on 30 December 2021. She had made a capital loss of £8,500 in 2021/22 prior to her death. Patricia had net gains in the previous three years of £13,200 (2020/21), £8,600 (2019/20) and £11,800 (2018/19).

Given that the annual exemption for each year was £12,300 (2020/21), £12,000 (2019/20) and £11,700 (2018/19) show the amount assessable to CGT for each tax year.

Solution
2021/22: Losses in this tax year, so nil assessable and £12,300 of annual exemption is wasted.

2020/21: Net gains exceed the annual exemption of £12,300 by £900. Hence, only £900 of carried-back losses will be utilised, leaving the excess of £7,600 available to carry back to earlier years.

2019/20: Gain of £8,600 can be covered by the annual exemption (£3,400 of which is wasted). No utilisation of carried-back losses required.

2018/19: Net gain exceeds the then annual exemption of £11,700 by £100, so taxpayer can utilise loss of £100. The remainder of the carried-back losses of £7,500 (£7,600 − £100) **cannot be relieved**.

The assessable amounts for each of the years are thus NIL and the taxpayer's estate or personal representatives will be entitled to a repayment of the CGT already paid in the tax years 2018/19 and 2020/21.

15.11.3 Losses on Chattels

We will see in **Chapter 16** that, where a chargeable chattel is disposed of for gross proceeds of £6,000 or less and its original cost was also £6,000 or less, it is **exempt** from CGT. As it is exempt, a capital loss cannot therefore arise.

15.11.4 Losses between Connected Persons

Losses realised by a person on the disposal of an asset to another person with whom they are connected may **only** be set-off against any chargeable gains realised by them on the disposal of an asset to the **same connected person**.

15.11.5 General Restriction on Loss Relief

The following general rules apply in relation to relief for capital losses:

1. Losses may not be set-off against gains of an earlier year of assessment except in the case of losses accruing to an individual in the year of death.
2. Relief may not be given more than once in respect of any loss.

15.11.6 Personal Representatives

Personal representatives are treated as having the deceased's residence and domicile at the date of death. They are liable to CGT on any disposal made by them during the administration period of the estate. They are entitled to the annual exemption for the year of death and the following two years.

15.11.7 Losses on Assets Qualifying for Capital Allowances

In general, expenditure allowable as a deduction in computing trading profits is not deductible in computing chargeable gains. There is no general exclusion of expenditure for which a "capital allowance" is made. However, if a capital loss accrues on the disposal of such an asset (e.g. machinery used in a business), it may be restricted with reference to any capital allowances claimed. This would have the effect of reducing the capital loss to nil, but it can never turn a loss into a gain. Where a gain arises on the disposal of such an asset, no account is taken of capital allowances claimed and the normal rules apply.

Example 15.14

Patricia purchased a machine with a useful life of 15 years for use in her business for £115,000 on 6 April 2018. The machine was eligible for capital allowances (no first year allowances or annual investment allowances were claimed). She sold the machine in May 2021 for £65,000. Compute her chargeable gain/loss on this sale. The accounting date of the business is 31 March.

Solution

As capital allowances have been claimed on the cost of the asset, the capital loss arising of £50,000 is restricted by the capital allowances claimed. This is necessary as otherwise double tax relief would be obtained on the asset. Therefore, any loss arising on the sale of the asset will not be allowable for CGT purposes as it will have been effectively relieved already for income tax purposes.

Capital allowances after any balancing adjustment is £50,000 (£115,000 – £65,000). To confirm:

	£	£
Cost	115,000	
Capital allowances claimed to date: 3 yrs (W1)	(51,593)	51,593
TWDV	63,407	
Entry in pool (lower of cost and proceeds)	(65,000)	
Balancing charge adjustment to pool in yr of sale	(1,593)	(1,593)
Total allowances claimed		50,000

CGT Computation

	£
Gross proceeds	65,000
Cost	(115,000)
Gain/(Loss)	(50,000)
Reduced by relief obtained for capital allowances against income tax	50,000
Capital loss	0

continued overleaf

Working 1		Allowances	
	£	£	
Purchase price	115,000		
Less: 18% WDA 2018/19	(20,700)	20,700	
TWDV c/f to 2019/20	94,300		
Less: 18% WDA 2019/20	(16,974)	16,974	
TWDV c/f to 2020/21	77,326		
Less: 18% WDA 2020/21	(13,919)	13,919	
TWDV c/f to 2021/22	63,407		
Total capital allowances claimed		51,593	

15.12 Negligible Value Claims

Where an asset becomes worthless, a negligible value claim can be made to crystallise a capital loss. Where a claim is made, a disposal is deemed to take place and the asset immediately reacquired for consideration equal to the value specified in the claim. The effect of a claim is to trigger a capital loss, even though a disposal has not actually taken place.

15.12.1 Method of Relief

Ordinarily, a loss cannot be carried back against gains in earlier periods. However, in this instance, the loss can be claimed in that year, or in either of the two preceding tax years provided that the asset was of negligible value in the relevant year also. Once allocated to a year, it is treated as a capital loss for that year.

There is no requirement to make a claim within a specified time of the asset having become of negligible value.

If the value of the asset subsequently increases in value, the subsequent gain (as compared with the capital loss arising on its negligible value) is not chargeable until the asset is actually disposed of.

Negligible value relief triggers a capital loss.

15.13 Value at 31 March 1982

For disposals after 6 April 2008 of assets acquired before 31 March 1982, the gain or loss arising is **always** calculated with reference to the market value as at 31 March 1982 (this is called rebasing).

Thus, all acquisition and enhancement costs incurred on or before 31 March 1982 are irrelevant for CGT purposes for individuals as they will be replaced by the asset's market value as at 31 March 1982.

It is important to note that this rule does **not apply** to companies. A company should always carry out two calculations of the chargeable gain – one using the 31 March 1982 value, and one using the original base cost. The lowest gain or highest capital loss is then chosen.

Questions

Review Questions
(See Suggested Solutions to Review Questions at the end of this textbook.)

Question 15.1

1. Maurice purchased a holiday home for £20,000 on 2 February 1989 and subsequently sold it on 30 November 2021 for £80,600. Incidental legal costs on purchase amounted to £300 and £750 on sale. Maurice's taxable income for the year, after all deductions and allowances, was £36,315.
2. Vincent bought shares in a plc in December 1973 for £800. He sold the shares for £9,500 on 30 April 2021. The market value of the shares on 31 March 1982 was £1,200. Vincent's taxable income for the year, after all deductions and allowances, was £25,765.

Requirement
Compute the CGT due or allowable losses in each case. (Assume that the individuals had no other realised gains or losses during the year or brought forward from previous years.)

Question 15.2

(a) James acquired a commercial property in July 1969 for £160,000. Additional capital expenditure was incurred as follows:

	£
July 1973	8,000
July 1996	10,000

James sold the property on 31 May 2021 for £650,600. The market value of the asset at 31 March 1982 was £230,000.

James had no other capital gains during 2021/22 and no capital losses brought forward. He had **other taxable income in the year (after personal allowance and other reliefs) of £58,000.**

Requirement (a)
Compute the CGT payable by James.

(b) Declan purchased a residential property, which he never lived in, on 6 April 1972 for £15,000. Additional expenditure was incurred as follows:

	£
Additional 5 June 1974	5,000
Additional 6 August 1985	20,000
Additional 1 February 2004	39,250

The market value of the property at 31 March 1982 was £55,000.

Declan sold the property for £400,900 on 1 July 2021.

Declan had no other capital gains during 2021/22 and no capital losses brought forward. He had other taxable income in the year (after personal allowance and other reliefs) of £32,700.

Requirement (b)

Compute the CGT payable by Declan on the sale.

Question 15.3

Paulette owns a five-acre plot of land that she acquired as an investment in August 1997 for £18,000. On 25 March 2022, she sold two acres of it for £80,000, from which selling costs totalling £2,600 were deducted. The remaining three acres were valued at £145,000 on 25 March 2022.

Paulette had taxable income for 2021/22 of £30,915 and made no other disposals during the year.

Requirement

Calculate Paulette's capital gains tax liability for 2021/22 and state when the capital gains tax liability falls due for payment.

16

Chattels and Wasting Assets

Learning Objectives

After studying this chapter you will understand:

■ The appropriate CGT treatment of wasting and non-wasting chattels.
■ The appropriate CGT treatment of wasting assets (excluding leases).

16.1 Chattels

A chattel is an item of "tangible movable property". Movable is not defined in the legislation. If an asset is attached to land or any building, it is usually regarded as part of that land or building and, therefore, is not movable, so the chattel rules will not apply. As you will see below, a wasting chattel is an asset with a remaining life of less than 50 years and such assets are generally exempt from CGT. A non-wasting chattel has a remaining life of more than 50 years and is not generally exempt from CGT.

16.1.1 Non-wasting Chattels – Rules

There are three special rules to be aware of for non-wasting chattels:

1. **Exemption relief** If a chattel is sold for gross proceeds of £6,000 or less and the original cost was £6,000 or less, then **any gain** will be exempt from CGT (even if capital allowances have been, or could have been, claimed). Any loss arising is not an allowable capital loss. This is a very practical relief and can prove to be very beneficial.

   The £6,000 limit relates to the gross proceeds, prior to the deduction of any incidental costs of sale such as commission costs, etc.

Example 16.1
A work of art is bought for £1,000 and later sold for £3,500. The chargeable gain on disposal of £2,500 is exempt from CGT. There is no chargeable gain as the asset is a non-wasting chattel sold for less than £6,000 and its original cost was also less than £6,000, therefore the exemption rule applies.

If the work of art had instead been bought for £3,500 and sold for £1,000, a loss of £2,500 would have arisen – however this loss would not be allowable.

---

2. **Restricted loss relief** If the disposal consideration is less than £6,000 and the base cost is also less than £6,000, there is no tax charge on any chargeable gain arising, even if a loss occurs. However, if a loss arises and the base cost exceeds £6,000, any loss relief claim is restricted. So, where a chattel is sold for less than £6,000, any capital loss arising is restricted. In preparing the CGT computation, the actual proceeds are replaced by deemed proceeds of £6,000, which has the effect of reducing the allowable capital loss. This rule cannot turn a loss into a gain, instead the loss would be reduced to nil and there is neither a gain nor a loss.

Example 16.2

Geraldine purchased an antique table in January 2008 for £9,700. She sells this table for £6,400 in August 2021 (selling costs £200). Compute the allowable loss.

Since the gross proceeds exceed £6,000, the disposal of the chattel is not exempt.

	£
Gross proceeds	6,400
Less: disposal costs	(200)
Net proceeds	6,200
Cost	(9,700)
Allowable loss	(3,500)

The special rules at 1, 2 above (and 3 below) do not apply.

What would Angela's loss be if the gross sales proceeds had instead been £5,100?

In this instance, the gross proceeds are less than £6,000 (namely £5,100) and the cost is in excess of £6,000, so rule 2 above applies, and the loss is restricted by deeming the gross proceeds to be £6,000.

	£
Gross proceeds	5,100
Notional gross proceeds	6,000
Less: disposal costs	(200)
Net proceeds	5,800
Cost	(9,700)
Allowable loss (restricted)	(3,900)

Without this rule, the loss would have been £4,800.

---

3. **Marginal relief** Where the gross proceeds exceed £6,000 but the asset originally cost less than £6,000, an individual is able to avail of "marginal relief " in that the chargeable gain is restricted to the **lower of**
   (a) the gain itself, and
   (b) 5/3rds of the excess of the gross disposal proceeds over £6,000 (5/3 × (gross proceeds − £6,000)).

Example 16.3
Angela purchased a watercolour painting in May 2008 for £5,250. She sold the painting in June 2021 for £5,940, having incurred commission costs of 10% of the selling price. Calculate her chargeable gain.

	£
Gross sale proceeds (£5,940 × 100/90)	6,600
Incidental costs of sale (commission at 10%)	(660)
Cost	5,940
Chargeable gain	(5,250)
Gain is the lower of:	690

(i) actual gain, £690 or
(ii) 5/3 × (£6,600 − £6,000) = £1,000

So the taxable gain is £690.

What would her gain have been if the cost in 2008 had been £4,600?

	£
Gross sale proceeds	6,600
Incidental costs of sale (commission at 10%)	(660)
	5,940
Cost	(4,600)
Chargeable gain	1,340

Gain is the lower of:
(i) actual gain of £1,340; or
(ii) 5/3 × (£6,600 − £6,000) = £1,000.

So the gain is restricted to £1,000.

16.2 Wasting Chattels

Chattels which have an effective useful life of 50 years or less are referred to as "wasting chattels" and are generally exempt from CGT, with the disposal normally giving rise to neither a chargeable gain nor an allowable loss. Wasting chattels include, for example, racehorses, leases with a useful life of less than 50 years and movable plant and machinery (however, see below). Plant and machinery will always have a useful life of less than 50 years and so are wasting chattels (unless fixed to premises and immovable, in which case they are not chattels). Machinery includes motor vehicles (except cars, which are exempt under general rules), railway and traction engines, engine-powered boats, clocks and watches.

As noted above, certain wasting chattels are exempt from CGT. Gains arising from the disposal of assets used as plant or machinery, and where capital allowances could not be claimed, is one such case.

Where capital allowances can be claimed the asset is treated under the non-wasting chattels rules outlined above.

16.2.1 Wasting Chattels and Capital Allowances

There is an exception to the general rule that wasting chattels are exempt from CGT. Movable plant and machinery used in a business and eligible for capital allowances is **not exempt**. In this case, the wasting chattels are treated as non-wasting chattels and the normal chattel rules above apply. Therefore, the gain will only be exempt if the gross proceeds are less than £6,000 and the cost is also less than £6,000.

Thus a calculation of the potential chargeable gain must be carried out under the normal chattel rules. One slight nuance is where a capital loss arises and the sales proceeds are actually less than the original cost. In this case, the allowable loss will be reduced by any capital allowances (including balancing adjustments) claimed. This effectively reduces the capital loss to nil and the result is a no gain/no loss disposal.

If the gross proceeds are less than £6,000 and the cost is also less than £6,000, any gain arising will be exempt under the exemption relief explained above. However, if the gross proceeds exceed the original cost (and £6,000), the subsequent chargeable gain will, as for chattels, qualify for marginal relief and be restricted to the lower of the gain and 5/3rds of the excess over £6,000.

Example 16.4

Andrew purchased a machine used in his business for £5,200 in May 2011. The machine was eligible for capital allowances. He sold the machine in July 2021 for £7,900. Compute his chargeable gain on this sale.

Solution

The machine is a wasting asset; however capital allowances have been claimed. Therefore, we apply the normal non-wasting chattel rules.

	£
Gross proceeds	7,900
Cost	(5,200)
Gain	2,700

The gain is not restricted to 5/3 × (£7,900 – £6,000), i.e. £3,167, as this is higher.

Example 16.5

Louise purchased a machine used in her business for £125,000 on 30 April 2016. The machine was eligible for capital allowances (no annual investment allowance (AIA) or first year allowance (FYA) were claimed). She sold the machine in May 2021 for £80,000. Compute her chargeable gain/loss on this sale. The accounting date of the business is 31 March.

Solution

Though the machine is a wasting asset, capital allowances have been claimed, so we must apply the normal chattel rules. As capital allowances have been claimed on the cost of the asset, the loss arising is restricted by the capital allowances claimed. This is necessary as otherwise double tax relief would be obtained on the same asset. As such, any loss arising on the sale of the asset will not be allowable for CGT purposes, as it will have been effectively relieved for income tax purposes already.

Capital allowances after any balancing adjustment are £45,000 (£125,000 – £80,000). To confirm:

continued overleaf

	£	£
Cost	125,000	
Capital allowances claimed to date (W1)	(78,658)	78,658
TWDV	46,342	
Entry in pool (lower of cost and proceeds)	(80,000)	
Balancing adjustment in pool in year of sale	(33,658)	(33,658)
		45,000

CGT Computation

	£
Gross proceeds	80,000
Cost	(125,000)
Loss	(45,000)
Reduced by income tax relief claimed as capital allowances	45,000
Capital loss	0

Working 1	£	*Allowances*
Purchase price:	125,000	
Less: WDA @ 18% 2016/17	(22,500)	22,500
TWDV c/f to 2017/18	102,500	
Less: WDA @ 18% 2017/18	(18,450)	18,450
TWDV c/f to 2018/19	84,050	
Less: WDA @ 18% 2018/19	(15,129)	15,129
TWDV c/f to 2019/20	68,921	
Less: WDA @ 18% 2019/20	(12,406)	12,406
TWDV c/f to 2020/21	56,515	
Less: WDA @ 18% 2020/21	(10,173)	10,173
TWDV c/f to 2021/22	46,342	
Total capital allowances claimed		78,658

16.3 Wasting Assets (Not Chattels)

If a wasting asset is not a chattel, then it is not exempt from CGT. The main types of non-chattel wasting assets are intangible assets (as they are neither tangible nor movable), fixed plant and machinery (as it is not movable) and leases (as they are neither tangible nor movable).

As its name implies, the original cost of the asset "wastes away" over time. Generally, the allowable cost is reduced on a straight-line basis in proportion to the total length of ownership. The chargeable gain is calculated by comparing the disposal proceeds with the unexpired part of the asset's cost at the disposal date. Note that assets eligible for capital allowances and used throughout the period of ownership in a business do not have their allowable expenditure wasted away.

Example 16.6
Deborah acquired a 30-year patent for £24,000 in December 2012. In December 2021 she sold the patent for £41,000. Compute her chargeable gain.

Solution
The patent had 22 years unexpired life when Deborah sold it, having had a 30-year life when she acquired it.

	£
Sale proceeds	41,000
Allowable cost = 22/30 × £24,000	(17,600)
Gain	23,400

Note: the treatment of leases and options under the wasting assets rules is beyond the scope of this textbook.

Questions

Review Questions
(See Suggested Solutions to Review Questions at the end of this textbook.)

Question 16.1

Shauna Quinn made the following disposals in 2021/22:

1. A painting at auction for gross proceeds of £50,000 on 12 January 2022. The auctioneer's costs of sale were 1% of the gross proceeds. Shauna had inherited the painting from her great aunt Margaret on 31 March 1982. Its value at this time was £2,500.
2. An antique vase on 2 March 2022 for £4,000. This vase was purchased for £14,000 in May 2003.
3. A commercial unit on 2 March 2022 for £185,600. The unit was purchased by Shauna's husband on 1 August 2006 for £55,000. Darren transferred the unit to Shauna on 30 June 2021 when it was worth £75,000. The unit was let out to a local engineering company throughout the period that it was owned by Shauna and Darren. On sale the legal fees were £2,250 and the estate agent's fee was £1,850.
4. Sale of four acres of land on 30 November 2021 for proceeds of £80,000. This was part of a 10-acre plot of land acquired as an investment by Shauna on 1 May 2004 for £40,000. The remaining six acres were valued at £48,000 on 30 November 2021.
5. Sale of her cherished vintage 1963 MGB Roadster car for £13,250 on 5 November 2021. Shauna bought the car in January 2005 for £11,250.

Requirement
Calculate Shauna's capital gains tax liability for the tax year 2021/22. Shauna's only other source of income for this tax year was employment income of £29,500. She has capital losses carried forward at the start of the year of £210,000.

Question 16.2

John Smith is a new client of your office, and at a recent meeting in July 2021 he was interested in a number of capital gains issues, as he owns several capital gains assets. However, he has never taken capital gains tax advice and therefore would like some general UK capital gains tax advice on what would happen if he sold a number of his assets. John is a wealthy man who earns in excess of £100,000 of income each year.

Requirement

Write a memo to John dealing with the following issues, with reference to the 2021/22 tax year:

(a) Rate of capital gains tax payable.
(b) Date that any capital gains tax will be due.
(c) How any significant capital gains are declared to HMRC.
(d) Amount of gains that can be realised in a tax year without a tax charge arising.
(e) John has heard that some countries give an "inflationary allowance" to deductible costs when a capital gains asset is sold. Clarify the position in the UK.
(f) What types of expenditure qualify as deductible from the sales proceeds received when he sells a capital asset?
(g) John thinks that he might have capital losses of about £15,000 carried forward from a sale of a painting many years ago. How can these capital losses be used?
(h) Would the answer to requirement (g) be different if the asset had been sold to his brother?
(i) John inherited a rental property from his grandmother on her death in February 2010, and wants to know what the capital gains base cost will be on a future sale.
(j) What would the capital gains base cost of the property have been in his hands if his grandmother had gifted it to him the day before she died?

17

Principal Private Residence Relief and Lettings Relief

Learning Objectives

After studying this chapter you will understand:

■ The application of principal private residence relief.
■ The application of lettings relief.

17.1 Principal Private Residence Relief

17.1.1 The Relief

Principal private residence (PPR) relief is one of the CGT reliefs that can potentially have an impact on the majority of individuals.

Provided certain conditions are met any gain on the disposal by an individual of their PPR is exempt. Note, this is an exemption relief and not a deferral relief. PPR relief is deducted from the chargeable gain arising on the disposal.

	£
Gain on property	X
Less: PPR relief	(X)
Chargeable gain	X

What is a PPR?
A PPR is an individual's only or main principal private residence. It includes:

1. a **dwelling house** or part of a dwelling house which is, or has been at any time during the period of ownership, an individual's only or main residence; and
2. **surrounding land**, which the individual has for their own occupation and enjoyment with that residence as its garden or grounds up to an area (inclusive of the site of the dwelling house) of half a hectare (approx. 1.24 acres) or such larger area as, having regard to the size and character of the dwelling house, is required for the reasonable enjoyment of the property as a residence. If the house does not warrant grounds in excess of half a hectare, PPR relief will not apply to the excess grounds.

A dwelling house includes relevant buildings within the curtilage of the main house, e.g. garage, outhouses, etc. There is extensive case law on this area, which is beyond the scope of this textbook.

It is important to note that:

1. A taxpayer may have only one PPR at any given time.
2. It is not sufficient to simply own the property as the taxpayer must have occupied the property as a residence (i.e. not merely as temporary accommodation). Therefore, there must be a degree of permanency in the individual's occupation of the property.
3. As the relief prevents qualifying gains from becoming chargeable, it also prevents losses from being allowable.
4. A married couple or civil partners who live together may only have one PPR between them.
5. If a taxpayer owns and actually resides in two (or more) properties, they must elect which of the properties is to be treated as their PPR (see **Section 17.3**).
6. There is no PPR relief available where a property (or interest therein) was purchased with a view to resale to make a gain. This restriction also extends to expenditure subsequently incurred wholly or partly for the purposes of realising a gain on the disposal.

17.1.2 Full Exemption

A chargeable gain arising on the disposal of a PPR will be wholly exempt if the owner has occupied the whole of the residence throughout the entire period of ownership as their only or main residence.

Where the residence has been occupied for only part of the period, or only part of the property has been occupied as a residence (e.g. part has been used for business purposes), then the relief available is diluted.

17.1.3 Partial Exemption

If occupation of the PPR has been for only part of the period of ownership, the proportion of the gain which is exempt from CGT is given by the formula:

$$\frac{\text{Period of occupation post} - 31 \text{ March } 1982}{\text{Total period of ownership post} - 31 \text{ March } 1982} \times \text{Total gain}$$

Note: it is only the period of occupation and period of ownership since 31 March 1982 which is taken into account.

The above formula is further adjusted if only part of the property has been occupied as the owner's PPR (see below). For ease of calculation, the periods are normally calculated to the nearest month.

17.2   Deemed Periods of Occupation

For the purposes of determining the availability of the relief there are two types of periods of occupation:

- actual occupation where the individual resides in the property as their only or main residence; and
- deemed occupation where the legislation treats periods of absence as periods of occupation for the purposes of the formula above.

Deemed periods of occupation include the following:

1. If an individual has resided in a property as their only or main residence at some point in time during the ownership period, then **the last nine months will always be treated as a period of occupation**. This is the case even if, during those last 9 months, the taxpayer has another property that has been elected as a new PPR. This includes occupation pre-31 March 1982.

    The final-period exemption is 36 months if, at the time of the disposal, one of the two following conditions is met:
    (a) the individual is a disabled person or a long-term resident in a care home and does not have any other relevant right in relation to a private residence.
    (b) the individual's spouse or civil partner is a disabled person or a long-term resident in a care home, and neither the individual nor the individual's spouse or partner has any other relevant right in relation to a private residence.

Example 17.1

Jane bought a house in April 1982 for £25,000. She lived in this property until she purchased a new home on 1 April 2017. She immediately moved into this new property and elected for it to be her PPR. Jane sold her former home on 31 December 2021 for £310,000. The 31 March 1982 value of the property was £70,000.

Solution

The total period of ownership (ignoring the period prior to 31 March 1982) is 38 years 9 months (465 months). Jane actually resided in the property for 34 years. The last 9 months are also deemed to be a period of residence (since she lived in the property as her PPR at some point). Thus her period of residence is 34 years and 9 months (417 months).

	£
Proceeds	310,000
Market value 1982	(70,000)
Gain	240,000
PPR exemption (417/465 × £240,000)	(215,226)
Chargeable gain (after PPR) (before AE)	24,775

Jane is effectively taxed on that proportion of the gain (48 months) when she was not residing in her former home and which did not relate to the last 9 months of deemed occupation. If Jane's annual exemption has not already been utilised in tax year 2021/22, then this will reduce the above chargeable gain to £12,475.

---

2. Certain other periods of absence are regarded as deemed periods of occupation provided that:
    (a) the taxpayer had no other exempt PPR at the time; and
    (b) there is a period of actual physical occupation both at some time before and after the period of absence. For these purposes, **deemed** occupation of the last nine months **does not** count as actual occupation. It is not necessary for the periods of occupation to immediately precede and follow the periods of absence. It is enough that there was occupation at some time before and after periods of absence.

    It is not possible to claim PPR on one property and also relief for another property for the same period under the absence relief rules, save for the last nine months.

Hence, subject to (a) and (b) above, the "**deemed periods of occupation**" are:

(i) any period (or periods taken together) of absence, for **any reason**, up to a total of **36 months**;

(ii) **any periods of absence** during which the taxpayer is required by their employment to live **abroad**;* and

(iii) a total of up to **four years** of absence during which the taxpayer is **working elsewhere in the UK** (either employed or self-employed) such that they could not occupy their PPR.*

Note: these three periods of absence can apply cumulatively. In addition, it does not matter if the PPR was let during the period of absence.

* Legislation waives the requirement that the taxpayer must reside in the property at some time after the period of absence where their absence is work-related (i.e. (ii) and (iii) above) and they are unable to resume residence in their home because the terms of their employment require them to work elsewhere.

Example 17.2

John purchased a house in Omagh on 31 March 1997 for £45,000. He lived in this house as his PPR until 30 September 2004 when he went abroad to work for his employer for three years, returning to live in the house again on 1 October 2007. John's job meant that he had to move to Belfast on 30 September 2016 and he lived in rented accommodation from then on. John sold his former home in Omagh for £275,000 on 30 June 2021.

Compute the chargeable gain.

Solution

	£
Sale proceeds	275,000
Cost	(45,000)
Chargeable gain (before PPR)	230,000

John's period of ownership of the house in Omagh is a total of 24 years 3 months (291 months) and can be broken down as follows:

Dates	Period	Residence	Absence	Actual Occupation	Deemed Occupation
01/04/1997 to 30/09/2004	90 mths	Actual		90 mths	
01/10/2004 to 30/09/2007	36 mths	Employment abroad			36 mths
01/10/2007 to 30/09/2016	108 mths	Actual		108 mths	
01/10/2016 to 30/06/2021	57 mths	Up to 48 mths working elsewhere in UK (by concession) plus the last 9 mths			57 mths
Total	291 mths		0 mths	198 mths	93 mths

Hence all of the gain is exempt.

	£
Gain as above	230,000
Less: PPR 291/291 × £230,000	(230,000)
Chargeable gain	0

Example 17.3

Celine bought a semi-detached house in Portrush on 1 March 2000 and lived in it from purchase. In March 2001, she relocated to Milton Keynes for employment, where she lived in an apartment which she leased until the end of February 2010. She returned to Portrush and lived in her house until the end of February 2014, at which point she moved to Belfast to reside with her mother. Celine never returned to the house after this date. She sold the house in Portrush on 28 February 2022, making a gain of £200,000.

What is the chargeable gain on the sale of the house?

Solution

Dates	Period	Residence	Absence	Actual Occupation	Deemed Occupation
Mar 2000 to Feb 2001	12 mths	Actual		12 mths	
Mar 2001 to Feb 2010	108 mths	Working elsewhere in UK (36 deemed "any" reason and 48 deemed "employment elsewhere")	24 mths		84 mths
Mar 2010 to Feb 2014	48 mths	Actual		48 mths	
Mar 2014 to Feb 2022	96 mths	Elsewhere in UK (last 9 mths deemed)	87 mths		9 mths
Total	264 mths		111 mths	60 mths	93 mths

	£
Gain as above	200,000
Less: PPR 153/264 × £200,000	(115,909)
Chargeable gain (before AE)	84,091

17.2.1 Delay in Moving In

Where there is a delay in a taxpayer taking up residence because of the completion of construction, renovation, redecoration or alteration of the residence, or because of the continuing occupation of the previous residence while arrangements are made to sell it, the period of non-occupation between the acquisition and occupation will be treated as a period of occupation, provided that the period does not exceed two years and no other person has used the property as a residence during that time.

17.3 More than One Residence

17.3.1 Election

Where a person has more than one residence (owned or rented), they may elect for one of the properties to be regarded as their main or sole residence by giving notice to HMRC within two years of commencing occupation of the second residence. It should be noted that, for the election to be valid, the individual must actually reside in both properties.

An election is not required if the second residence is being treated as a residence by means of the "delay in moving in rule" discussed above.

In the absence of an election, HMRC will impose a ruling as to which residence is to be treated as the PPR of an individual with more than one residence.

Example 17.4

Applying the facts of **Example 17.2** above, if John had purchased another property on 1 October 2016 when his job located him in Belfast and elected this new property to be his PPR from that date, would the CGT position dffer?

Solution

If he had elected for his second new home to be his PPR then the 48 months from 1 October 2016 up to 30 September 2020 (the commencement of the last 9 months), would not have been a deemed period of occupation, as John was claiming another property as his PPR during that time. The last nine months would still have qualified as deemed occupation as John lived in the house at some point as his PPR.

The chargeable gain would be as follows:

	£
Gain as above	230,000
Less: PPR 243/291 × £230,000	(192,062)
Chargeable gain (before AE)	37,938

17.4 Married Couples/Civil Partnerships

Where a husband and wife or civil partners live together, only one residence may qualify as the main residence for PPR. Where they each owned one property before the marriage/registration of the civil partnership, a new two-year period for electing which property is to be treated as their main residence commences on their marriage/registration.

On a marriage breakdown, provided one spouse disposes of their interest to the other spouse, the departing spouse will, by concession, be treated as continuing to be resident in the house for CGT purposes provided that they have not claimed another house as their PPR and the remaining spouse has continued to reside in the former matrimonial home.

Where a residence passes from one spouse/civil partner to the other (e.g. on death) the recipient also inherits the previous spouse/civil partner's periods of ownership and occupation for PPR purposes.

17.5 Business Use

As stated above, where part of a residence is used **exclusively** for business purposes throughout the period of ownership, PPR relief will not be available on the portion of the gain relating to this part of the property. Note that it is the use throughout that period of ownership which is considered and not just the use at the date of disposal. In addition, the last nine months (36 months in some cases) of deemed occupation will not apply to this portion.

Example 17.5

Denise acquired a property in June 2013 and sold it in May 2021 making a gain of £350,000. The house contains seven rooms. From the date of purchase, four of the seven rooms in the property were used exclusively as Denise's main residence; one room was used partly for her hairdressing business and partly as her residence. The remaining two rooms were used wholly for her business. It is assumed that all the rooms are of equal size.

		Proportion used exclusively for business (2/7ths)	Remaining proportion (5/7ths)
	£	£	£
Chargeable gain	350,000	100,000	250,000
Deduct: PPR		(0)	(250,000)
Chargeable gain (annual exemption)		100,000	Nil

The total gain before annual exemption is £100,000. If a room is not used exclusively for business, then PPR should be available.

The part used for trade purposes may qualify for relief as the replacement of a business asset (see rollover relief in **Chapter 18**).

An apportionment between business and residential use must be undertaken on a just and reasonable basis, e.g. number of rooms in use, floor area, etc. Each case would be judged on its own merits.

17.6   Lettings Relief

PPR relief is extended to a gain accruing, up to a certain limit, while the property is let to tenants as residential accommodation. This extended relief is known as "lettings relief". PPR relief should be deducted from the gain first and takes priority over lettings relief.

The exemption will apply where part of the property has been used as a residence, whilst the other part has been let to tenants as residential accommodation (e.g. there are three floors of a property, with two floors used as the owner's residence and the top floor is let out to tenants). The absence from the let part cannot be deemed a period of occupation as the owner has another PPR at the same time (namely the rest of the property). However, the let part will qualify for the last nine months (36 months in some cases) of deemed occupation if the let part formed part of the only or main residence at some point in time.

For lettings relief to be available, the letting must have been for residential purposes only.

Lettings relief may be available to cover some or all of the gain which is not covered by PPR. Relief will normally be given where the let accommodation forms part of the owner's dwelling and the owner previously resided in the whole premises. It will not be available if the let accommodation is a dwelling which is entirely separate from the owner's residence.

Lettings relief is restricted to the **lower** of:

1. the amount of PPR relief due in respect of the disposal; or
2. £40,000; or
3. the amount of the chargeable gain made while letting out part of the home.

Example 17.6

Christopher purchased a house on 1 June 2001 for £100,000 and occupied the entire house up to 31 July 2010 when he rented part of the top floor (comprising one-quarter of the house) to residential tenants. Christopher continued to reside in the remainder of the house. On 1 January 2022, he sold the house for £585,000. Compute the chargeable gain.

Dates	Period	Residence	Let	Actual	Deemed
01/06/2001 to 31/07/2010	110 mths	Actual		110 mths	
01/08/2010 to 31/12/2021	137 mths	3/4 actual 1/4 let last 9 months	32 mths	96 mths	9 mths
Total	247 mths		32 mths	206 mths	9 mths

	£
Sales proceeds	585,000
Cost	(100,000)
Chargeable gain (prior to PPR exemption and letting relief)	485,000

The total period of ownership was 20 years 7 months (247 months). He resided in the whole property for 9 years 2 months (110 months) and the last 9 months, a total of 119 months. Christopher resided in three-quarters of the property for the remaining 128 months, so three-quarters of the gain arising in this period will also be exempt.

Lettings relief will be available on any residue.

	£
Gain (as above)	485,000
Less: PPR exemption (206 + 9 = 215)	
215/247 × £485,000 (Note 2)	(422,166)
	62,834
Less: letting exemption – restricted (Note 1)	(40,000)
Net chargeable gain (before AE)	22,834

Notes

1. Letting relief, being the lowest of:

    (i) PPR relief: £422,166; or
    (ii) £40,000; or
    (iii) 32/247 × £485,000 = £62,834

2. PPR – could alternatively have been calculated as follows:

	£
119/247 × £485,000	233,664
128/247 × £485,000 × ¾	188,502
Total	422,166

Where the letting consists of taking in a lodger who shares the taxpayer's living accommodation and has their meals with the family, HMRC does not consider that the taxpayer has ceased to occupy any part of the property as their only or main residence, therefore there is no restriction on the exemption. HMRC takes this view only where a taxpayer takes a single lodger into their home, not where a taxpayer runs a lodging house as a business. Where an individual lets a room under the "rent a room" scheme, PPR should still be available in full on the subsequent sale of the property.

Questions

Review Questions
(See Suggested Solutions to Review Questions at the end of this textbook.)

Question 17.1

James sold a house in the 2021/22 tax year and realised a gain, before any available reliefs, as follows:

Proceeds	£2,000,000
Original cost	£1,200,000
Gain arising	£800,000

James owned the house for a total of 10 years. He lived in it for the first three years on his own, and then let half of it for five years while he resided in rest of the house. He then lived in the whole house, by himself, for the last two years of ownership.

Requirement
Calculate, with appropriate explanations, the capital gains tax, if any, that is due for 2021/22. James has not made any other asset disposals in 2021/22, he is an additional rate taxpayer and it was the only house he owned in that 10 years.

Question 17.2

Jack Bates, a widower with no children, is currently living in a rented apartment in London. His only investment in property to date is his residence in Belfast.

Jack has recently been offered a sum of £1.3 million for his Belfast property by developers who wish to incorporate the property into a large commercial development.

After acquiring the property on 1 September 1997 for its residential value of £65,000, Jack resided there until 1 January 2005, when he was transferred by his employer to their London office. During his period in London, Jack let his residence at a rental of £400 per month.

On 30 April 2013, Jack was transferred back to his employer's head office in Belfast, where he remained until his retirement on 31 January 2019. On 1 February 2019 Jack immediately moved to London. While in Belfast between 2013 and 2019, Jack lived in his Belfast residence, but on retiring to London in 2019 this property has again been let.

Requirement

Write a letter to Jack outlining the following:

(a) How principal private residence relief operates and the consequences of absences from the property.

(b) The capital gains tax implications for Jack if he sells the Belfast property to the developer for £1.3 million on 1 July 2021, supported with a computation of the capital gains tax payable (if any). Jack is an additional rate taxpayer.

Capital Gains Tax Reliefs

Learning Objectives

After studying this chapter you will understand:

■ How to determine and apply appropriate CGT reliefs, including:
  ● rollover relief for business assets; and
  ● holdover/gift relief.

18.1 Rollover Relief and Depreciating Assets

18.1.1 Rollover Relief

If an individual disposes of a business asset, a chargeable gain will crystallise. Where the individual reinvests **the proceeds** into a replacement asset within a fixed timeframe, they may make a claim to defer the CGT charge on the gain until a future date.

Rollover relief is relief for **the replacement of business assets** used in a trade. It is available for individuals as well as companies, but it cannot be claimed by an investment business.

Provided certain conditions are met, an individual may claim that a chargeable gain arising on the disposal of a business asset (the "old asset") may be "rolled over" against the cost of acquiring a replacement business asset (the "new asset").

In this scenario, the disposal of the old asset is deemed to give rise to neither a gain nor a loss and the cost of the new asset is reduced by the gain that would have arisen but for the "rollover" relief. In essence, the chargeable gain is "deferred" until such time as the new asset is disposed of (subject to the possibility of a further rollover claim being available).

The Relief
On a claim, full or partial relief is available depending on the circumstances. This relief is a deferral relief. The gain will therefore become taxable at some time in the future. In line with general CGT principles, as death does not trigger a CGT charge a gain rolled over is not triggered on death.

Full rollover relief is only available provided all of the disposal **proceeds** (not just the chargeable gain) are applied in acquiring the new asset.

Partial rollover relief is where any proceeds not reinvested fall to be taxed immediately. In this instance, the cost of the new asset is reduced by the amount of the gain that was not immediately chargeable.

No rollover relief is available where the amount retained (i.e. proceeds not reinvested) exceeds the chargeable gain.

The relief may be claimed by a person who carries on more than one trade, either consecutively or concurrently, on the basis that they are treated as a single trade. The relief is only available where the new assets are acquired by the same individual taxpayer who made the gain on the old assets.

The **conditions** that must be met before a rollover claim can be made are:

1. Both the old and the new asset must be within one of the specified classes of assets (see below). However, it is not necessary that they should both be within the same class.
2. The old asset must have been used only **for trade purposes** throughout the period of ownership and the new asset must be taken into and **used immediately in the trade**.
3. The new asset must be acquired during the specified period beginning **12 months** before and ending **36 months** after the date of disposal of the old asset.

The **class of assets** referred to above include:

- land, buildings and fixed plant and machinery;
- ships, hovercraft, aircraft, satellites, space stations and spacecraft;
- milk, potato and fish quotas and certain other EU quotas;
- goodwill.

Note: shares are not a qualifying asset for rollover relief as they cannot be used for the purposes of the trade.

It is generally accepted that it is the disposal consideration net of incidental costs of disposal that should be compared with the total costs of acquisition including incidental costs of acquisition.

Example 18.1

On 1 January 2021, a farmer sells land for £40,000. The expenses of sale are £3,000. On 1 October 2020, the farmer buys land for use in the trade at a cost of £35,000 plus expenses of £4,000. For the purposes of a claim, the disposal consideration is £37,000 and the amount applied in acquiring new assets is £39,000. Full relief is therefore due.

Claims for Rollover Relief

Claims for the relief must be made within four years after the end of the tax year (or accounting period for companies) in which the later of the disposal of the old asset or the acquisition of the new asset took place. Where the disposal of the old asset takes place in 2019/20 and the acquisition of the new asset is made in 2021/22, the claim must be made on or before 5 April 2026.

It is possible to make provisional claims for rollover relief if it is intended that a purchase of a qualifying asset will take place within the specified period.

It may be preferred not to claim rollover relief on business assets where sufficient capital losses and annual exemption are available for claim. Remember, a company cannot claim the annual exemption on any chargeable gains.

Note: it is not possible to specify the amount of rollover relief to be claimed. Either full relief will be available where the full proceeds are reinvested, or partial relief in circumstances where the full proceeds have not been reinvested.

Example 18.2

On 1 July 2006, John Smith acquired freehold trade premises for £100,000. The business expanded and, during December 2021, new premises were acquired for £200,000 and the old premises were sold on 1 November 2021 for £160,000. John's full basic rate band is utilised against other income.

In the absence of a claim for rollover relief, there would be chargeable gains as follows:

Sale of old premises – without rollover relief	£
Disposal proceeds	160,000
Deduct: Allowable cost	(100,000)
Chargeable gain	60,000
Less: annual exemption	(12,300)
Taxable chargeable gain	47,700
CGT @ 20%	9,540

Where rollover relief is claimed, the position is as follows:

Sale of old premises – with rollover relief	£
Disposal proceeds	160,000
Deduct: Allowable cost	(100,000)
Chargeable gain	60,000
Less: rollover relief	(60,000)
Taxable chargeable gain	0

Base cost of new asset:

Purchase of new asset:	
Cost	200,000
Deduct: rollover relief	(60,000)
Revised base cost	140,000

Where rollover relief is claimed, John's annual exemption is wasted as rollover relief is an 'all or nothing' claim.

Example 18.3

Beth purchased a property for £80,000 in July 2005 for use in her business. In June 2021, she purchased another property for use in her business and two months later sold the original property for £175,000. Beth wishes to claim rollover relief on the sale of the original property.

Compute her chargeable gain if the cost of the replacement property was respectively (assuming both the old and new asset are within the relevant class of assets):

(i) £190,000 (ii) £150,000 and (iii) £70,000

The chargeable gain on the disposal of the original property is:

	£
Proceeds	175,000
Cost	(80,000)
Gain	95,000

continued overleaf

The quantum of the gain which can be rolled over will depend on the amount reinvested:

1. If the new property was purchased for £190,000, all of the sale proceeds have been reinvested and, thus, all of the gain of £95,000 can be rolled over into the cost of the new asset. The base cost for CGT purposes of the new asset is £95,000 (being £190,000 – £95,000 (rolled over)). In essence, the gain of £95,000 is deferred until the new asset is sold (subject to any potential further rollover claim).
2. In this situation, £25,000 of the disposal proceeds have not been reinvested and thus become **immediately** chargeable. The residue of the gain, namely £70,000 (£95,000 – £25,000) can be rolled over into the cost of the new property and the CGT base cost of the new asset will be £80,000 (being £150,000 – £70,000 (rolled over)).
3. In this situation, the amount of the proceeds **not** reinvested is £105,000, which exceeds the actual chargeable gain of £95,000. Thus, all of the gain of £95,000 is immediately chargeable and rollover relief does not apply.

18.1.2 Companies and Rollover Relief

For companies, unlike individuals, rollover relief is generally only claimed in respect of land, buildings and fixed plant and machinery.

18.1.3 Mixed Use (Business and Non-business Use)

In order to qualify for full relief, the old asset must have been used only for the purposes of the business throughout the whole period of ownership and the new asset must, on acquisition, be taken into use and used only for business purposes. However, where this is not the case, then the business portion and non-business portion must be treated as separate assets. There are two situations in which partial relief may be given when these conditions are not met.

1. If the old asset was not wholly used for business purposes, it is treated as two separate assets in calculating the rollover relief. The disposal proceeds are apportioned between the business use and the non-business use. Only the part of the overall gain applicable to the business use qualifies for rollover relief.

   A similar apportionment is made where the new asset not used wholly for business purposes. Any gain can only be rolled over into the expenditure arising on business use of the new asset. This scenario can therefore apply to the old asset, the new asset or to both.
2. If the claimant did not use the old asset for business purposes for the entire ownership period (excluding any period before 31 March 1982), the asset is treated as two separate assets in calculating the rollover relief. Expenditure on acquisition and disposal are apportioned between business use and non-business use. Only the part of the overall gain that relates to business use qualifies for rollover relief.

The apportionment is to be made on a just and reasonable basis.

Example 18.4
Richard Moss, trading in fireplace manufacturing, acquired a building on 1 November 2002 for £110,000. 40% of the building was used as business offices and the remainder was let on leases to unconnected parties. On 1 November 2021, the building was sold for £400,000 and a new building acquired for £500,000, of which 25% was used for business.

continued overleaf

The calculation of the gain on the old building before rollover relief is:

	Total	40% Business asset	60% Non-business asset
	£	£	£
Disposal proceeds	400,000	160,000	240,000
Deduct: cost	(110,000)	(44,000)	(66,000)
Net gain	290,000	116,000	174,000

The business element in the new building is £125,000 (25% of £500,000); therefore, £35,000 of the proceeds of the £160,000 business disposal has not been reinvested. The amount not reinvested is less than the gain of £116,000; therefore, rollover relief is permitted for £81,000 of the gain. £35,000 is assessed to CGT immediately. The gain on the disposal chargeable to tax is:

	£
Gain on non-business asset	174,000
Gain on business asset: proceeds not reinvested	35,000
Chargeable gain	209,000

The deemed cost of the business element in the new building is £44,000 (£125,000 less gain rolled over of £81,000).

18.1.4 Depreciating Assets

A depreciating asset is fixed plant and machinery not forming part of a building, or an asset that has a predictable useful life not exceeding 60 years from the time it is acquired. Another example of a depreciating asset is a short-term lease.

Where the new replacement asset is a "depreciating asset", the chargeable gain arising on the disposal of the old asset **cannot** be rolled over and is **not** deducted from the base cost of the new asset. Instead, the chargeable gain is "frozen" or "temporarily parked" until it becomes chargeable (crystallises) on the **earliest** of the following three dates:

1. the date on which the new depreciating asset is disposed of;
2. the date on which the new depreciating asset ceases to be used in the trade; or
3. the tenth anniversary of the acquisition of the new depreciating asset.

If a taxpayer purchases a non-depreciating asset (within the relevant class – see **Section 18.1.1**) prior to the earliest of the above three dates expiring, then it could "convert" the temporarily "frozen" gain into a "rolled over" gain. This effectively widens the window of opportunity for the taxpayer to reinvest the original proceeds into the relevant class of assets.

In effect, the taxpayer can "park" the gain against the purchase of a depreciating asset until such time as a qualifying asset for rollover relief is purchased and a claim for the relief can be made.

Example 18.5

Michelle bought business premises in September 2010 for £115,000. She sold the premises for £150,000 on 1 October 2015. On 15 September 2015, she bought some fixed plant and machinery to use in her business costing £140,000. These were sold for £155,000 on 30 June 2021. What is Michelle's CGT liability?

The gain on the premises may be deferred by parking the gain against the purchase of the depreciating asset. Note that the gain on the premises is frozen; it is not rolled over into the cost of the depreciating asset. When the depreciating asset is sold, then as well as the gain on this sale being taxable, the gain on the frozen sale of the premises also crystallises.

continued overleaf

	£
2015/16 Sale of premises	
Proceeds	150,000
Cost	(115,000)
Gain	35,000
Less: gain frozen on purchase of fixed P&M	(25,000)
Chargeable gain (proceeds not reinvested)	10,000
2021/22 Sale of fixed P&M	
Proceeds	155,000
Cost	(140,000)
Gain	15,000
2021/22: Total gain chargeable on sale of fixed P&M	
Gain on sale of fixed P&M	15,000
Crystallised gain	25,000
Total chargeable gain	40,000

18.2   Gift Relief/Holdover Relief

18.2.1 Section 165 Gift Relief – Business Assets

When a qualifying business asset is gifted for nil consideration, the transferor receives no proceeds from the transaction. For CGT purposes, the disposal is treated as a disposal at market value as the transaction is not at arm's length. This is the case even if the parties are unconnected. A chargeable gain will therefore crystallise, which means that the taxpayer, in the absence of any "gift relief", could find themselves in a difficult financial position, having to pay CGT in respect of the gift but not having received any proceeds with which to fund it. This is known as a 'dry' tax charge.

Section 165 relief is a form of deferral relief for business assets. Where a gain arises on a gift or a sale at an undervalue of a **business asset**, the gain may be "held over" until such time as the transferee disposes of the asset(s) concerned. Both the transferor and transferee must jointly elect for the gain on the gift to be held over. Where gift relief is claimed, the taxable capital gain is deferred by deducting the gain from the base cost of the asset in the hands of the transferee/recipient.

Example 18.6
A gifts an asset to B. The market value of the asset is £100,000 at the time of the gift. The chargeable gain on disposal of the asset is £40,000. A and B jointly elect to claim gift relief.

A has no CGT liability as the capital gain of £40,000 is reduced by the claim for gift relief. The base cost of this asset for B going forward is £60,000 (£100,000 – £40,000). B sells the asset for £130,000. B makes a gain of £70,000 (£130,000 – £60,000).

Claims must be made within four years from the end of the tax year of disposal, e.g. in respect of disposals made in 2021/22, claims must be made on or before 5 April 2026.

For the purposes of section 165 gift relief, gifts must be business assets. So what is a business asset for gift relief purposes? The gifted asset must be one of the following:

1. An asset used in the business carried on by the transferor or by the transferor's "**personal trading company**" (a trading company in which the transferor can exercise at least 5% of the voting rights). A holding company of a trading group also qualifies if the holding company is the transferor's personal company. A trading company is defined as a company carrying on trading activities which do not include, to a substantial extent, non-trading activities. If HMRC can show that there is a "substantial" element of non-trading activities in a company or group, gift relief will not be available. "Substantial" is generally taken to be 20% and can relate to a percentage of turnover, assets or management time.
2. Shares/securities of trading companies or holding companies of trading groups where:
   (a) the shares are unlisted (i.e. not listed on a recognised stock exchange) (AIM listed shares are not listed shares for these purposes); or
   (b) the shares are in the transferor's **personal trading company** (provided the transferee is not a company).
3. Agricultural land and buildings used for a farming trade that would qualify for inheritance tax agricultural property relief (beyond the scope of this textbook).

An individual may decide not to claim gift relief if the gain is such that it is covered by the annual exemption and/or capital losses.

18.2.2 Section 165 Gift Relief – Restricted Cases

There are two instances where gift relief will be restricted: sales at undervalue, and gifts of shares in a personal trading company.

Sales at Undervalue
Gift relief can also apply where qualifying assets are 'sold' at an undervalue, i.e. for less than their market value. For example, transfers to a connected person may be at an undervalue. The rule in this instance is that the "excess proceeds", i.e. **the amount of the proceeds exceeding the original cost** of the asset, fall to be taxed immediately and only the residue is available to be "held over" and deferred.

Example 18.7
In December 2021, Gordon gifts a property (used in his business) to his son Tony when its market value is £210,000. The property was purchased in June 2003 by Gordon for £95,000. Gordon and Tony jointly elect for the chargeable gain to be 'held over' under section 165. Calculate the quantum of gain which may be held over and indicate what effect, if any, there would be if the son were to pay £100,000 for the property.

Solution
(a) Outright gift

Chargeable gain for Gordon	£
Proceeds	210,000
Cost	(95,000)
Gain (available to be held over)	115,000
Less: gift relief	(115,000)
Chargeable gain	0

Tony's CGT base cost would thus be £95,000 (being the market value of £210,000 less held over gain of £115,000).

continued overleaf

(b) Sale at an undervalue

If Tony paid £100,000 for the property, then the excess proceeds of £5,000 (the excess of the amount paid over the original cost) would become immediately chargeable and the held over gain would be reduced to £110,000 (being £115,000 less the £5,000 which is immediately chargeable).

Tony's CGT base cost in this situation would be £100,000 (being the market value of £210,000 less the held over gain of £110,000). This makes sense as this is the financial cost to Tony of buying the property.

Chargeable gain for Gordon	£
Proceeds	210,000
Cost	(95,000)
Gain (available to be held over)	115,000
Less: gift relief	(110,000)
Chargeable gain	5,000

Gifts of Shares in a Personal Trading Company

If the gift is of shares in a personal trading company, and the company has any non-business assets (such as investments) at the date of the gift, the gain eligible for gift relief is restricted. Gift relief is only available on that part of the gain represented by the proportion of chargeable business assets (CBA) to total chargeable assets (CA).

$$\text{Qualifying gain} = \frac{\text{Market value of CBA}}{\text{Market value of CA}} \times \text{Share gain}$$

Market values of the assets as per the statement of financial position at the date of the gift are used for these purposes.

CBAs are assets that are typically used in the business, e.g. goodwill, factory premises, plant and machinery, etc. However, goodwill will be neither a CBA nor a chargeable asset if it was acquired or created on or after 1 April 2002, as in those cases goodwill is treated as an intangible fixed asset under the corporate intangibles regime (which is beyond the scope of this textbook).

Chargeable assets are CBAs plus any non-business chargeable assets (e.g. investments). This would include, for example, rental properties and quoted shares held as investments. Stock, debtors and cash are not chargeable assets and do not form part of this calculation.

Example 18.8
In December 2021, Gemma gave her daughter Lily shares in her personal company. The shares cost Gemma £40,000 when acquired in March 1998 and their market value is £300,000 in December 2021. The gain on the shares is £260,000. The company owned assets with the following values at December 2021:

	£
Freehold business offices	100,000
Plant and machinery (cost £50,000)*	30,000
Goodwill (created pre-1 April 2002)	80,000
Trade receivables	40,000
Cash	20,000
Shares held as investments	50,000
Sundry net assets (all non-chargeable)	30,000

*Comprises one single item of plant and machinery

continued overleaf

Chargeable assets and chargeable business assets are as follows:

	Chargeable assets	Chargeable business assets
	£	£
Freehold business offices	100,000	100,000
Plant and machinery	30,000	30,000
Shares held as investments	50,000	
Goodwill	80,000	80,000
	260,000	210,000

Gift relief is, therefore, restricted to the fraction 210,000/260,000.

	£
Gain on shares	260,000
Deduct: held over gain = £260,000 × 210,000/260,000	210,000
Chargeable gain	50,000

The base cost of the shares now held by Lily is £90,000 (i.e. £300,000 less the £210,000 held over gain).

18.2.3 Mixed Use (Business and Non-business Use)

As for rollover relief, gains on assets (other than shares) with mixed use must be apportioned, i.e.:

- an asset used partly for business and partly for non-business use; or
- an asset only used for business purposes for part of the ownership period.

Only the gain relating to the business portion may qualify for gift relief. It is therefore necessary to treat the business and non-business portions as separate assets

18.2.4 Instalment Payments

For certain assets gifted where gift relief is not available (i.e. non-business assets), CGT may be payable in 10 equal annual instalments, if elected. The CGT instalment option is available for land and buildings, shares in unquoted companies (e.g. investment companies) and shares in quoted companies where the donor has control before the gift. Note, such instalments are interest-bearing.

In certain circumstances, any outstanding CGT liability becomes due for payment if the asset is sold.

Questions

Review Questions
(See Suggested Solutions to Review Questions at the end of this textbook.)

Question 18.1

Sarah owns 10% of the shares in Rathdiner Ltd, which she purchased in December 1998 for £50,000. Sarah has worked in this company since its commencement. She gave the shares to her 22-year-old daughter Emily as a gift on 1 February 2022.

The market value of Rathdiner Ltd as at 1 February 2022 is £1,050,000, as below:

	Market values
	£
Goodwill (created pre-1 April 2002)	410,000
Land and buildings	470,000
Plant and machinery*	2,500
Motor vehicle	4,000
Trade receivables	40,000
Inventory	3,000
Cash	500
Rental property	120,000
Total	1,050,000

* The cost of each individual item of plant and machinery is less than £6,000 and no individual item has a market value in excess of this amount.

Requirement

(a) Calculate the capital gain arising to Sarah if she jointly claims gift/holdover relief under section 165 TCGA 1992 with her daughter.
(b) What is the base cost for Emily once a claim is made under (a)?
(c) Calculate the capital gain arising to Sarah if she and her daughter do not claim gift/holdover relief.
(d) Under (c), what would be the base cost for Emily?

Question 18.2

It is mid-November 2021 and you are working on the file of your client, Áine Taylor, who runs a manufacturing business as a sole trader. The factory used in the business was acquired in November 2000 for £500,000, but due to recent growth in orders is now too small to cope with demand, even though the business has been working night shifts as well as day shifts.

Áine has therefore been considering her options and has decided to sell the factory and move to new premises. An offer of £1,500,000 was accepted from a local property developer for the existing factory on 8 November 2021.

She has recently been to see you to discuss her options. She is open to whether the business will lease new factory premises or purchase new factory premises. Áine is very keen to ensure that she takes advantage of any available reliefs to reduce/defer any tax liability arising on sale of the factory.

Áine has not made any other capital disposals in the 2021/22 tax year and is an additional rate taxpayer.

Requirement
Write a letter to Áine that covers the following topics:

(a) Calculate the tax payable on sale of the factory, state the date that the tax is due and the type of tax that is payable.
(b) Explain rollover relief and how it could be used to defer any tax payable on the sale of the factory.

Part Four

Value-Added Tax

Value-Added Tax (VAT): An Introduction

Learning Objectives

After studying this chapter you will be able to:

- Recognise and advise on straightforward ethical dilemmas that can arise when dealing with VAT issues.
- Explain and determine the registration requirements of VAT.
- Explain and determine VAT rates.
- Explain and determine the amount on which VAT is chargeable.
- Explain what is a supply of goods and determine the place of supply for goods.
- Explain what is a supply of services and determine the place of supply for services.
- Explain and determine what is deductible and non-deductible VAT.
- Explain the reliefs available for bad debts.
- Explain and determine the:
  - records to be maintained;
  - accountable persons; and
  - payment of tax
- Apply the general principles of VAT in order to compute the VAT liability arising for an individual or business for a VAT period.
- List the information that must be included in VAT invoices, discount notes and credit notes.
- Explain the operation of the cash accounting scheme, flat rate scheme and annual accounting scheme.

The Chartered Accountants Ireland *Code of Ethics* applies to all aspects of a Chartered Accountant's professional life, including dealing with VAT issues. As outlined at the beginning of this book, further information regarding the principles in the *Code of Ethics* is set out in **Appendix 2**.

This chapter introduces the general principles of value-added tax (VAT) for **UK-only vatable supplies**: who is chargeable to VAT and what goods and services are liable to VAT and at what rate. The requirements of VAT registration (and de-registration) are critical to understanding how the VAT system works so these are discussed in detail (**Section 19.3**) before looking at the various tax rates in operation in the UK and the types of supply under each category (**Section 19.4**). Consideration is then given to the amount on which VAT is chargeable (**Section 19.5**) and an outline of the basic concepts around the supply of goods and services (**Sections 19.6–19.8**). For businesses an important consideration in terms of VAT is the recovery of VAT that has been paid on purchases. **Section 19.9** covers this aspect in detail, including deductible and non-deductible VAT, and VAT relief on bad debts. **Section 19.10** deals with the administrative requirements, including the VAT return cycle, the VAT records to be maintained by a VAT-registered business and the penalties that a trader may be exposed to if they do not administer their VAT correctly. The chapter concludes with a discussion of some special VAT schemes that have been introduced to help certain types of business, depending on their size and sector.

19.1 Introduction

VAT is a tax on consumer spending. The basic principle of VAT is that it is charged at each stage in the supply of goods and services. This type of VAT, i.e. one that is charged on sales, is referred to as **output VAT**. If the customer is VAT-registered and uses the supplies for business purposes, a credit will be received for the VAT charged to them. This type of VAT is referred to as **input VAT**, i.e. VAT that is charged on purchases. As VAT-registered businesses can deduct their input VAT from their output VAT to establish if they have an overall VAT liability to pay to HMRC, the effect of VAT is not felt by VAT-registered businesses but is instead borne by the final customer.

The terms 'output VAT' and 'input VAT' will be referred to frequently throughout this chapter as they are central to understanding the operation of VAT. The subject of VAT also has its own specific terminology. Two key terms that are also referred to frequently are "taxable supplies" and "taxable person". "Taxable person", for VAT purposes, refers to an individual, partnership, company or other trading entity that is either registered for VAT or is required to be registered for VAT (see **Section 19.3**).

"Taxable supplies" are goods or services that are liable to VAT, whether at the standard rate, reduced rate or zero rate (see **Section 19.4**). Supplies that are exempt are **not** considered as taxable supplies. Examples of taxable supplies include:

- the sale of goods (including capital items);
- the sale of services;
- charges between associated businesses (such as management charges);
- the leasing or renting of goods or services;
- royalties from copyright;
- the sale of land and buildings; and
- recharging the salaries of staff, etc.

19.1.1 European Union Directives, UK Legislation and Case Law

Prior to 'Brexit', VAT was the only tax where the operational rules were decided by the EU. The UK and each other Member State were permitted to set the rates of VAT (within certain parameters) within their own territories, but the rules in relation to the operation of the system and the categorisation of goods and services for VAT-charging purposes were set by the EU. From 1 January 2021, the date the UK left the European Union, the UK continues to levy VAT and the rules relating to UK domestic transactions continue to apply to businesses as they did prior to Brexit. From 1 January 2021, VAT procedures on the whole remain as those prior to 31 December 2020, but there have been some changes to the VAT rules and to the procedures for transactions between the UK and EU Member States. Such transactions are beyond the scope of this textbook.

The UK VAT legislation is consolidated in the Value Added Tax Act 1994 (VATA 1994).

19.2 General Principles of VAT

Registered traders collect VAT on the **supply of goods and services** to their customers. Each trader in the chain of supply, from manufacturer through to retailer, will **charge VAT on their sales**, i.e. on their output on behalf of HMRC. The trader is entitled to **deduct** from this amount the **VAT paid on purchases**, i.e. on their inputs, before paying the net VAT over to HMRC. The effect of offsetting purchases against sales is to impose the tax on the **value added** at each stage of production – hence value-added tax. It is the final consumer, who is usually not registered for VAT, who absorbs VAT as part of the purchase price. This can be illustrated by way of a simple example.

Consider a wardrobe. The timber merchant sells the raw material to the manufacturer for £100 plus VAT at 20%, i.e. £120. The timber merchant keeps £100 and £20 is paid to HMRC.

The manufacturer uses the raw material to produce a wardrobe and sells the wardrobe to a retailer for £150 plus VAT at 20%, i.e. £180. The manufacturer keeps £150 and pays the VAT charged of £30, less the VAT of £20 (paid previously to HMRC) suffered on the purchase of the raw material. Therefore HMRC receives £10 at this stage.

The retailer sells the wardrobe to the final consumer for £200 plus VAT at 20%, i.e. £240. Similarly, the retailer pays the VAT charged (£40) less the VAT suffered on the purchase of the wardrobe from the manufacturer (£30) to HMRC. HMRC, therefore, receives £10 at this stage.

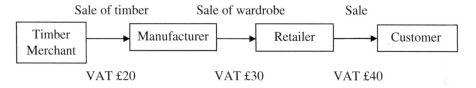

The final consumer is not registered for VAT and so cannot claim a deduction for VAT paid. The consumer has suffered VAT of £40. The total VAT received by HMRC through these transactions is also £40 (£20 + £10 + £10).

The combined effect of the transactions is that at each stage in the transaction a portion of the VAT due has been collected and paid over to HMRC, but the whole amount has been paid, in effect, by the **final consumer**.

19.3 VAT Registration and De-registration

Broadly, registration for VAT is compulsory if you make:

(a) taxable supplies,
(b) as a taxable person,
(c) "in the course or furtherance of any business carried on".

Taxable supplies are standard rated (20%), reduced rate (5%) or zero-rated (0%) supplies, **not** exempt supplies. A **taxable person** is an individual, partnership, company or other trading entity that is either registered for VAT. A taxable person also includes someone who should have registered for VAT but has not yet notified HMRC.

The phrase "in the course or furtherance of any business carried on" is deliberately broad and vague as it is intended to be all-embracing. However, an individual can make a sale that is not part of their business. For instance, a furniture salesperson could sell a piece of their own, private furniture and, unless it was on the shop floor, the sale would not be part of their "business".

Section 94 Value Added Tax Act 1994 (VATA 1994) states that the word "business" includes any trade, profession or vocation (see **Chapter 3**).

19.3.1 Registration Thresholds

For 2021/22, the VAT registration limit is £85,000. Registration for VAT is necessary if:

1. a trader's taxable supplies (excluding VAT), which include zero-rated sales, have exceeded the registration limit in the previous 12 calendar months (**the historical test**) – unless the trader can satisfy HMRC that their taxable supplies (excluding VAT) in the following 12 months will not exceed the de-registration limit (see **Section 19.3.4**);
2. there are reasonable grounds for thinking that the trader's taxable supplies (excluding VAT) in the next 30 days alone will exceed the limit, i.e. the trader will make a sale or sales within the next 30 days that will exceed £85,000 (**the future test**); or
3. a trader takes over another business and either 1. or 2. above applies.

Hence a trader should check the cumulative total turnover at the end of each calendar month to determine if registration is necessary.

In all cases, the trader must notify HMRC:

- within 30 days of the end of the relevant month (where the threshold is exceeded as a result of past sales); or
- within 30 days (in the case of expected sales, i.e. where the trader believes that the taxable supplies in the next 30 days alone will exceed the registration threshold).

Notification to register is made on Form VAT1. See **Section 19.10** for more details on the administration and procedures around VAT. Once notification has been submitted the trader will be registered from either:

1. the **end of the month after that in which the annual limit was exceeded** (as a result of past sales); or
2. from the **beginning of the 30-day period** (for expected sales).

19.3.2 Voluntary Registration

A person can choose to register for VAT even if their taxable turnover falls below the registration limit. There can be many reasons for voluntary registration of VAT, for example:

- they may wish to recover input tax on purchases.
- it may depend on the status of his or her customers, i.e. if they are VAT-registered or not;
- the status of his or her outputs (i.e. are they exempt, zero-rated or standard rated?); or
- the business image that the trader wants to portray.

If the majority of a trader's customers are private individuals, the trader may prefer not to register if not compulsorily required to do so.

Registration for VAT can also be applied for when an individual intends to trade; evidence of the intention is required.

19.3.3 Specific Requirements by Business Type

The type of business in operation affects the VAT registration requirements.

Sole Trader

Sole traders can only have one VAT registration for **all** the "business" activities they own. If they have a number of businesses, VAT registration affects each business of the sole trader. It is the person(s) or the entity that is VAT-registered. Form VAT1 is used to register a business for VAT.

Partnerships

Each partnership must register separately for VAT if the partners are different. Hence, if a father and mother were one partnership, father and son another partnership and father and daughter another, the father would be required to make three separate VAT registrations.

When registering, partnerships must also complete Form VAT2 (in addition to Form VAT1). Form VAT2 requires the details of all partners.

Limited Liability Partnership

An ordinary partnership is not the same as a limited liability partnership (LLP). The partners in an LLP are not personally liable for debts the business cannot pay. Each partner's liability is limited to the amount of money they invest in the business. Each LLP must have its own separate registration. However, if the partners of the LLP have control over a limited company (or companies), then the LLP can be grouped with it.

Limited Company

A limited company must register for VAT on its own unless it is part of a VAT group. (The concept of group registration for VAT is beyond the scope of this textbook.)

Other Organisations

Other kinds of organisations, such as clubs, societies and charities, are also potentially liable to register. It does not matter what you do, who you are or whether you make a profit, the overriding criteria is that you **must register for VAT if you make taxable supplies in the course or furtherance of your business where the taxable supplies exceed the registration limit in force**.

19.3.4 De-registration

A person is eligible for **voluntary de-registration** if, in the upcoming 12 months, the taxable supplies (net of VAT and excluding capital assets) is not expected to exceed £83,000 (for 2021/22).

Also, traders may be **compulsorily de-registered**. De-registration is compulsory if, for example, the trader stops making taxable supplies, the business is sold, the business joins a VAT group, etc. Failure to notify a requirement to de-register within 30 days may lead to a penalty (see **Section 19.10**). There may also be a clawback of input VAT if de-registration is late.

Changes in legal status also cause de-registration, e.g. incorporation of a sole trader to a limited company, although the trader can request to keep his or her existing VAT registration number.

On de-registration, VAT is chargeable on all stocks and capital assets on which input VAT has been claimed and which are held at the date of de-registration. If VAT due is less than £1,000, it is disregarded. However, if it is £1,000 or more it must be paid to HMRC in line with the final VAT return.

19.4   VAT Rates

VAT rates depend on the type of goods or services in question. In the UK there are three rates:

	VAT rate*	VAT fraction**
Standard rate	20%	1/6
Reduced rate	5%	1/21
Zero rate	0%	0

* Used where the value of the supply/sale is quoted exclusive of VAT.
** Used where the value of the supply/sale is quoted inclusive of VAT.

In addition, goods or services can be categorised as exempt supplies, meaning they are not liable to VAT. **It is important not to confuse the two concepts of zero-rated and exempt supplies**, as a business that makes only exempt supplies is not eligible to register for VAT. Whereas, a business that makes only zero-rated supplies can register for VAT.

19.4.1 Standard Rate

The standard rate of UK VAT is currently 20%. Standard-rated supplies are those that do not fall into the other categories, i.e. are not zero-rated, reduced rate or exempt.
     The VAT portion for standard-rated supplies can be quickly calculated by:

Value of supply + VAT =	"gross consideration"
Rate of VAT 20%:	£100 + £20 = £120
VAT fraction	20/120 = 1/6
Quick calculation:	£120 × 1/6 = £20

19.4.2 Zero Rate

No VAT needs to be charged on zero-rated supplies (so that they are not more expensive to the end consumer). It is very important to recognise zero-rated supplies as they are still "taxable supplies", just with a 0% VAT rate. A trader making zero-rated supplies can register for VAT and recover VAT incurred on making the zero-rated supplies, i.e. input VAT (see **Section 19.9**). Businesses that make zero-rated supplies will therefore always be in a VAT recovery/refund position.
     Table 19.1 overleaf lists some examples of zero-rated supplies.

19.4.3 Reduced Rate

The VAT portion for reduced-rate supplies can be quickly calculated by:

Value of supply + VAT =	"gross consideration"
Rate of VAT 5%:	£100 + £5 = £105
VAT fraction	5/105 = 1/21
Quick calculation:	£105 × 1/21 = £5

VAT is charged on the VAT-exclusive price.
     Table 19.2 overleaf lists some examples of reduced rate supplies.

TABLE 19.1: EXAMPLES OF ZERO-RATED SUPPLIES

Zero Rate (0%)	Notes/Exceptions
Food and drink for human consumption	Food and drink is, in general, zero-rated. "Luxury" items, however, such as alcoholic drinks, confectionery, crisps, savoury snacks, food for catering or hot takeaways, ice- cream, soft drinks and mineral water are all standard rated.
Baby and children's clothes and footwear	
Equipment for blind, partially sighted and disabled people	
Construction of buildings	Construction and sale of new residential buildings (NB: not commercial); construction and sale of new buildings for charitable purposes.
International services	Intra-EU supplies (where supplier and customer are VAT registered).
Transport	Passenger transport that carries not less than 10 passengers.
Brochures, leaflets and pamphlets	Includes books, children's painting and picture books, maps, charts, magazines, newspapers, printed/copied music and publications generally (though online revisions are standard rated).

TABLE 19.2: EXAMPLES OF REDUCED RATE SUPPLIES

Reduced Rate (5%)	Notes/Exceptions
Electricity, gas, heating oil and solid fuel	For domestic and residential use. (Where the supply is to a business the standard rate applies.)
Energy-saving material installed in residential premises	Air- and ground-source heat pumps, wood-fuelled boilers, insulation, solar panels, water and wind turbines, etc.
Smoking cessation products	
Women's sanitary products	
Renovating living accommodation	Renovation of an empty residential building.
Children's safety seats	Including booster seats.

19.4.4 Exempt Supplies

No VAT is chargeable on exempt supplies. A trader making only exempt supplies cannot register for VAT. Therefore, such a trader will not be able to recover VAT on the costs associated with making the exempt supplies, i.e. no input VAT is recoverable (see **Section 19.9**).

Table 19.3 lists some examples of exempt supplies.

TABLE 19.3: EXAMPLES OF EXEMPT SUPPLIES

Exempt	Notes/Exceptions
Physical education and sports activities	
Betting and lotteries and bingo	
Burial and cremation services	
Health and welfare	Medical services generally, e.g. services by doctors, dentists, opticians, pharmacists, etc.
Education, training or other services	Provided by an eligible body, like a school or college.
Financial services and investments	Loans and credit facilities; insurance services.
Cultural services	Admission to museums, galleries, theatrical and musical performances.
Investment gold	

As noted above, it is important to understand the distinction between a trader making zero-rated supplies and one making exempt supplies. If a trader makes exempt supplies only, they are unable to recover any of the input VAT that is charged on those purchases that relate to the exempt sales.

> **Example 19.1**
> The fees charged by a university are exempt for VAT. However, the university will incur VAT on various costs that it needs to operate, for example, heat and light in the lecture theatres. The university will have to pay the reduced rate of VAT on its electricity and heating bills (either oil or gas).
>
> A university making only exempt supplies will not be able to register for VAT and so it will not be able to recover the VAT it is charged on its heating and light costs.

19.4.5 Supplies Outside the Scope of UK VAT

Finally, as well as supplies that are exempt, there are other sales that are deemed to be outside the scope of UK VAT. For example, sales/services for which the place of supply is treated as being outside the UK.

19.5 Amount on which VAT is Chargeable

The general rule for the supply of goods or services is that the amount on which VAT is chargeable is normally the **total sum** paid or payable for the supply of the goods or services, including all taxes, commissions, costs and charges, but **not including** the VAT chargeable in respect of the transaction.

> **Example 19.2**
> Clive is a Chartered Accountant and is registered for VAT. He bills his client £1,000 for his annual income tax return, £1,500 for the cost incurred in preparing his annual accounts and £500 for a meeting at his client's premises to discuss the controls in his business.
>
> Clive's total fee will be £3,000 plus VAT of £600, i.e. a total fee of £3,600.

In some instances HMRC may determine that the **value** on which VAT is charged in relation to certain transactions **between connected persons** is the **open market value**. Where, for example, the actual amount charged is below market value because the supplier and the purchaser are connected.

19.5.1 Specific Rules

Credit Card Transactions
In the case of credit card transactions, the amount chargeable to VAT is the total amount actually charged to the customer by the trader. Any amount withheld by the credit card companies from their settlement with the trader forms part of the taxable amount.

Packaging and Containers
When goods are supplied packaged for sale and **no separate charge** is made for the packaging in which the goods are contained, the rate of VAT chargeable is that **applying to the goods**. If containers are charged for **separately** from the goods (e.g. where the goods and the container for transportation are billed for separately), the transaction is regarded as consisting of separate sales of goods and of packages and **each** such **separate sale** is chargeable at the appropriate rate.

Where containers are returnable and a separate charge in the nature of a deposit is included on an invoice (e.g. once the container is returned the deposit will be repaid), the containers are regarded as being the property of the supplier and the **deposit** is **not** subject to VAT. VAT **is** payable on the value of containers that are **not returned** to the supplier. This VAT may be accounted for at the time when the containers account is being balanced and a charge is being raised by the supplier against the customer for the value of containers not returned.

Mixed and Composite Supplies
Different goods and services are sometimes invoiced together at an inclusive price (a **mixed supply**). Some items may be chargeable at the standard rate and some at the zero rate, in which case the supplier must account for VAT separately by splitting the total amount payable in a fair proportion between the standard- and zero-rated elements; VAT is charged on each at the appropriate rate; there is no special way of making this apportionment (i.e. HMRC do not dictate any specific method).

If a mixed supply cannot be split into different elements it is a **composite supply**, e.g. when one element of the supply is merely incidental to the main element. A composite supply must have a single VAT rate applied. For example, normal and necessary packaging (such as tins, bottles and jars) is treated as part of the goods that it contains, so that if the contents are zero-rated, then zero-rating also applies to the packaging (composite supply). If, however, the packaging is more than is normal and necessary, e.g. storage containers that could be sold separately from the contents, then it is a mixed supply and VAT is charged on the constituent elements at the appropriate rate.

19.6 Supply of Goods or Services

19.6.1 Supply of Goods

A taxable **supply of goods** means the **normal transfer of ownership** of goods from one person to another and includes the supply of zero-rated goods. A taxable supply of goods includes:

- the transfer of ownership of goods by agreement;
- the supply of any form of power, heat, refrigeration or ventilation or of water;

■ taking goods permanently out of the business for the non-business use of a taxable person (see below: **Self-supply of Goods**) or for other private purposes, including the supply of goods by an employer to an employee for his private use; and

■ transfers under an agreement contemplating a transfer of ownership, such as a hire-purchase agreement.

Gifts of Goods

Gifts of goods are normally treated as sales at cost. VAT will therefore be due. However, business gifts are not supplies of goods if:

1. the total cost of gifts made to the same person does not exceed £50 in any 12-month period. If exceeded, output VAT is due on the full amount; or
2. the gift is a sample.

Self-supply of Goods

Where goods are **permanently** removed from the business for non-business purposes for no consideration, VAT must be accounted on their **market value** at that time.

If goods are loaned out **temporarily** to the proprietor personally, then a supply of services has been made for no consideration and not a supply of goods. VAT, in this instance, is due on the cost to the business of lending the goods out.

Example 19.3

One of the non-current assets of a business, a mini-digger, was loaned out for 40 days for private use to the proprietor.

The cost to the business of the mini-digger is the annual depreciation. If the annual depreciation is £2,000, then VAT is due at 40/365 × £2,000 = £220. Therefore the cost of the supply is £220, which attracts VAT at 20%.

VAT of £44 is due.

19.6.2 Supply of Services

For VAT purposes, a "service" is any commercial activity, **other than** a supply of goods (apart from a few specific examples), which is carried out in return for consideration. Consideration is any form of payment, in money or in kind, including anything which is itself a supply.

Typical services include:

■ caterers, mechanics, plumbers, accountants, solicitors, consultants, etc.;
■ hiring or leasing of goods;
■ restaurants – regarded as a supply of services not goods; and

Services also include the granting or surrendering of a right. A supply of services also takes place if:

■ goods are lent to someone outside the business;
■ goods are hired to someone; and
■ services that were bought for business purposes are used for private purposes.

Certain services, including agents, banking agents and certain related agents, are **exempt** from VAT.

Self-supply of services are those services purchased for business use but put to private use instead. If that happens, then VAT must be accounted on the **cost to the business** of making the services available for private use. Such services could be computer software or building services, for example.

19.7   Time of Supply of Goods or Services

VAT becomes due, or a liability for VAT arises, at the time when a **supply of goods or services takes place**. This is called the **tax point**. VAT must normally be accounted for in the VAT period in which the tax point occurs and at the rate of VAT in force at that time (unless the cash accounting scheme is being used, see **Section 19.11.2**).

19.7.1   Basic Tax Point

The basic tax point for a **supply of goods** is the date the goods are removed, i.e. dispatched to or collected by the customer. If the goods are not removed, it is the date they are made available for the customer's use.

The basic tax point for a **supply of services** is the date the services are performed or completed. The basic tax point is the default position that will apply if the 'actual tax point' is not used.

19.7.2   Actual Tax Point

In the case of both goods and services, where a VAT invoice is raised or payment is made before the basic tax point, there is an **earlier actual tax point** at the time the invoice is issued or payment is received, whichever occurs first.

In practice, there is usually a later tax point as the basic tax point is extended to the date the invoice is issued, if this is within 14 days (30 days at HMRC's discretion) after the basic tax point. However, this is subject to the overriding rule noted above regarding the actual tax points. If an invoice is not issued within the 14 days (30 days at HMRC's discretion) of the basic tax point, then the basic tax point rule applies. An actual tax point takes priority over a basic tax point.

Other specific rules apply for continuous supplies of services.

19.8   Place of Supply of Goods or Services

The place of supply rules are very important for VAT as goods and services are liable to VAT **in the place where they are supplied**, or are deemed to be supplied. For example, if a supply is in the UK, the UK rates of VAT apply. If instead the supply is in France, then no UK VAT would arise because it is outside the scope of UK VAT.

The general rules with regard to the place of supply of goods are outlined below.

19.8.1   Place of Supply of Goods

The place of supply of goods is deemed to be as follows:

1. If the supply requires the transportation of goods, the place where the transportation begins is deemed to be the place of supply.
2. In all other cases, the location of the goods at the time of supply determines the place of supply.

Generally, when goods leave the UK the place of supply will be treated as the UK. Conversely, where goods arrive from outside the UK, then the place of supply will typically be the supplier's country.

The supply of goods internationally will usually fall under one of two categories:

1. exports (where goods are sold to a customer outside the UK);
2. imports (where goods arrive in the UK from a non-UK supplier).

The VAT treatment and regulations of the international supply of goods are beyond the scope of this textbook.

19.8.2 Place of Supply of Services

The general rule for the place of supply of services is (subject to some exceptions) deemed to be:

1. (If the recipient is in business) in the country where the recipient of the service is located. These are known as business-to-business (B2B) supplies.
2. (If the recipient is not in business) in the country where the supplier is located. These are known as business-to-consumer (B2C) supplies.

There are some exceptions to the above general rule outlined above. For example, services relating to land are always treated as being supplied in the country where the land is located.

19.9 Recovery of VAT

19.9.1 Deductible VAT – Input VAT

In computing the amount of VAT payable in respect of a taxable period, a registered person may **deduct** the VAT paid by them on the purchase of goods and services, which are used for the purposes of the **taxable business**. To be entitled to the deduction, the trader must have a proper VAT invoice or relevant customs receipt as appropriate.

While a deduction of VAT is allowable only on purchases that are for the purposes of a taxable business, a situation may arise where a **portion** of a trader's purchases may be for the purposes of the taxable business and the remaining portion for the trader's **private use** (e.g. electricity, telephone charges, heating expenses, etc. where the business is carried on from his private residence). It may also arise that inputs may be used for **both taxable and non-taxable** activities. **In such cases, only the amount of VAT that is attributable to the taxable business is deductible**.

Similarly, where a trader engages in both taxable and exempt activities, it will be necessary to **apportion** the input VAT on a "just and reasonable" basis.

There is no distinction between capital and revenue expenditure for VAT. This is in contrast to the position for income tax as outlined in **Chapter 3**.

19.9.2 Non-deductible VAT

No deduction is allowed in respect of VAT paid on expenditure on any of the following:

- VAT on expenses incurred on business **entertaining** where the cost of the entertaining is not a tax-deductible trading expense.
- VAT on **motor cars** not used wholly for business purposes. VAT is never reclaimable unless the car is acquired new for resale, the car is a pool car (see **Section 5.4.3**) or is acquired for use in a taxi business, a self-drive car hire business or a driving school.
- VAT on expenses incurred on domestic accommodation for directors/proprietors of a business.
- VAT on non-business items passed through the business accounts.
- VAT that does not relate to the making of supplies by the buyer in the course of a business (i.e. for VAT to be deductible, it must be incurred in respect of a cost that relates to the vatable supplies of the business).

Where input VAT is not recoverable, it forms part of the cost of the asset for income tax, CGT, corporation tax and capital allowance purposes.

Fuel
A VAT reclaim is permitted on business fuel only. If fuel is supplied for private purposes, all input VAT incurred on the fuel may be allowed to be claimed, but only if the trader accounts for output VAT using a set of scale charges **per VAT return** based on the CO_2 emissions of the car (CO_2 emissions are rounded down to the nearest 5%.). Scale charges are provided inclusive of VAT. See **Example 19.4** below for the inclusion of deemed output VAT in respect of the private fuel adjustment required in line with the VAT fuel scale charges.

Example 19.4
Adrian operates as a sole trader and is registered for VAT. All of his supplies are taxable. The following information is relevant to his VAT return for the quarter ended 31 March 2021:

1. Invoiced sales of £40,000 (excluding VAT). Sales were invoiced to customers in the UK and were standard rated.
2. Invoiced sales of £10,000 (excluding VAT). Sales were invoiced to customers in the UK and were for zero-rated items.
3. Purchases of standard-rated stock in the amount of £12,000 (VAT exclusive), of which £600 was used by Adrian personally.
4. Payment of £200 (VAT inclusive) on a meal to entertain new clients.
5. Purchase of a new computer for the business at £1,800 (VAT inclusive).
6. Adrian uses his car for the business. Overall the car usage is 80% business and 20% personal. Adrian charges all of his petrol costs (£150 per month VAT inclusive) to the business. The car emits 150g/km of CO_2.
7. Adrian had an outstanding debtor of £1,500 (including VAT). The invoice was due for payment on 31 March 2020. Adrian received £750 in November 2020 as partial settlement and, in January 2021, he wrote off the remainder of the debt as irrecoverable.

Calculate the VAT payable to/repayable from HMRC in respect of the quarter ended 31 March 2021.

(Note: VAT scale charge for a car with CO_2 emissions of 150g/km is: £1,170 (12 months, inclusive of VAT); £292 (3 months, inclusive of VAT).)

continued overleaf

Output VAT	£
Standard-rated sales (£40,000 × 20%)	8,000
Zero-rated sales	0.00
Petrol: fuel scale charge (£292 × 1/6) (Note 1)	48.67
Input VAT	
Stock ((£12,000 – £600) × 20%) (Note 2)	(2,280)
Meal (Note 3)	0.00
Computer equipment (£1,800 × 1/6) (Note 4)	(300)
Petrol (£150 × 1/6 × 3 months) (Note 5)	(75)
Bad debt relief (£750 × 1/6) (Note 6)	(125)
Total VAT payable to HMRC (£8,049.33 – £2,780)	5,268.67

Notes:
1. This can be avoided if Adrian does not reclaim the input VAT on fuel.
2. Cannot reclaim VAT on items for personal use.
3. Cannot reclaim VAT on entertaining customers.
4. Input VAT reclaimed regardless of whether items are revenue or capital in nature.
5. A fuel scale charge is added to output VAT as a direct result of reclaiming the input VAT on petrol where there is private use.
6. Debt is over six months old and has been written off in the accounts.

19.9.3 Pre-registration Input Tax

VAT incurred on **goods** purchased in the four years prior to VAT registration can be reclaimed in the first VAT return, provided they were still held at the date of registration.

VAT incurred on **services** purchased for the businesses in the six months prior to VAT registration can be reclaimed in the first VAT return.

19.9.4 Reclaiming Overpaid VAT

There is a four-year limit on the right to reclaim overpaid VAT. HMRC can refuse a repayment if it would unjustly enrich the claimant.

19.9.5 Bad Debts

Relief for VAT on bad debts is allowed where the debt is over six months old (measured from when payment is due) and has been written off in the trader's account. This means that VAT that has previously been paid to HMRC on an invoice basis (see **Section 19.2**) can be reclaimed through the VAT return, provided the above conditions are met. To reclaim the bad debt VAT amount, that amount is added to the input VAT being claimed for the current period.

Bad debt claims must be made within four years from the time the debt became eligible for relief.

A business that has claimed input tax on a supply, but which has not paid the supplier of the goods or services within six months of the date of the supply, must repay the input tax, irrespective of whether the supplier has made a claim for bad debt relief.

Bad debt relief does not apply to cash accounting recording (see **Section 19.11.2**) of VAT. Under the cash accounting scheme, cash is never received from a customer, hence no output tax needs to be accounted for – effectively bad debt relief is already given.

19.9.6 VAT and the Construction Industry Scheme

Where a subcontractor supplies certain construction services that fall within the CIS, the domestic reverse charge for VAT will apply. This effectively means that the contractor (the customer), rather than the supplier (the subcontractor), will be required to account for any VAT due.

The key conditions for the reverse charge to apply are:

- The supply for VAT consists of construction services and materials.
- It is made at a standard or reduced rate of VAT.
- Both the supplier and the customer are UK VAT-registered.
- Both the supplier and the customer are registered for the CIS.
- The customer intends to make an ongoing supply of construction services to another party.
- The supplier and customer are not connected.

The aim of the measure is to reduce VAT fraud in the construction sector.

Example 19.5

John is a VAT-registered subcontractor who provides carpentry services and supplies materials (all standard rated) to a VAT-registered contractor. The contractor, in turn, is supplying construction services to a VAT-registered developer. The subcontractor has gross payment status.

John will invoice the contractor for £100,000. His invoice will state that "CIS reverse charge applies" and that the applicable rate of VAT is 20%. The contractor will pay John the net £100,000 fee. The contractor will then account for output and input VAT of £20,000 on the supply on its own VAT return. John does not account for output VAT in his VAT return as he has invoiced only his fee £100,000.

19.10 Administration of VAT

VAT is a self-assessed tax. The onus is therefore on a trader to recognise when they need to register for VAT and to report their VAT position to HMRC by making regular VAT returns. The records of the calculations and back-up documents used in the preparation of VAT returns must be retained in case HMRC need to verify the calculations.

19.10.1 Registering for VAT

A trader can register for VAT by using either a paper Form VAT1 or through the HMRC's VAT Online service.

The information required on the VAT registration form (both paper and online) includes:

- business turnover;
- business activity; and
- business bank details.

Once HMRC have processed the registration, the trader's VAT number will be received in writing (regardless of the method of registration).

19.10.2 VAT Returns and Payment of VAT

All VAT-registered businesses are required to submit their VAT returns and to pay any VAT amounts due to HMRC online. HMRC recognises limited exemptions whereby a business does not have to submit their VAT return online or pay their VAT electronically, namely:

- if the business is subject to an insolvency procedure; or
- HMRC is satisfied that the business is run entirely by practising members of a religious society whose beliefs prevent them from using computers; or
- where it is "not reasonably practicable" for the business owner to use the online system.

A VAT-registered person normally accounts for VAT on a quarterly basis.

VAT returns submitted online must be filed, and any VAT due paid, within one month and seven days of the end of the relevant quarter, e.g. a return for the quarter ended 31 March 2021 is due by 7 May 2021. Where a trader is constantly in a VAT refund situation, they may instead elect for monthly VAT returns so that their refund is processed quicker.

Where the taxpayer pays by direct debit, it is stated that the direct debit will not be claimed by HMRC until three working days after the return is due – in essence, 10 days after the relevant month end. This provides the taxpayer with a cash-flow benefit.

19.10.3 VAT Records

Records to be Maintained

A VAT-registered trader must keep **full records** of all transactions that affect his liability to VAT. The records must be kept up to date and be sufficiently detailed to enable a trader to accurately calculate liability or repayment and also to enable HMRC to check the calculations, if necessary.

Purchases and Sales Records

The recording of purchases should include:

- VAT invoices, credit notes and debit notes received;
- a summary of supplies received;
- details of any goods taken for non-business use; and
- records of goods received from EU Member States or imports from outside the EU.

The sales records should include:

- copies of VAT invoices, credit notes and debit notes issued;
- a summary of supplies made; and
- records of goods sent to other EU Member States or exports sent to outside the EU.

Retention of Records

A taxable person **must retain** all books, records and documents relevant to the business, including invoices, credit and debit notes, receipts, accounts, cash register tally rolls, vouchers, stamped copies of customs entries and other import documents and bank statements. These business records must be retained for **six years** from the date of the latest transaction to which they refer, unless written permission from HMRC has been obtained for their retention for a shorter period.

Information to be Included on VAT Invoices/Credit Notes

HMRC imposes strict requirements on the information given on invoices and credit notes. This information establishes the VAT **liability** of the supplier of goods or services and the **entitlement** of the customer to an **input deduction** for the VAT charged.

Form of VAT Invoice/Credit Note

A taxable person who supplies taxable goods or services to **another taxable person** is obliged to issue a VAT invoice showing the following:

- name and address of the trader issuing the invoice;
- trader's VAT registration number;
- name and address of the customer;
- date of issue of the invoice;
- date of supply of the goods or services (tax point);
- full description of the goods or services;
- quantity or volume and unit price of the goods or services supplied;
- the amount charged, **exclusive** of VAT (expressed in any currency);
- the rate (including zero rate) and amount of VAT at each rate;
- the total invoice/credit note amount exclusive of VAT (in Sterling);
- the rate of any cash discount; and
- the total amount of VAT chargeable (expressed in Sterling).

A less detailed invoice may be issued by retailers where the invoice is for a total, including VAT, of up to £250.

Allowances, Discounts, etc.

When the amount of VAT payable as shown on an invoice is reduced because of an allowance or discount, the trader who issued the VAT invoice must issue a credit note stating the amount of the reduction in the price and the appropriate VAT. This trader may then reduce his VAT liability by the amount credited in the accounting period in which the credit note is issued. Likewise, the customer or recipient of the credit note must increase his VAT liability by the same amount. All credit notes must contain a reference to the corresponding invoices.

Where a VAT-registered supplier and a VAT-registered customer **agree** in respect of a transaction **not to make any change** in the VAT shown on the original invoice, even though the price charged may subsequently be reduced, there is **no obligation** to issue a credit note in respect of the VAT. Such a practice saves trouble for both seller and purchaser.

Alternatively, in the case of a prompt payment discount, if the supplier does not want to issue a credit note but wants to account to HMRC for the VAT on the amount he or she actually receives, the supplier must ensure that the invoice includes the terms of any prompt payment discount as well as a statement that the customer can only recover as input tax the VAT paid to the supplier.

Making Tax Digital (MTD)

Making Tax Digital (MTD) is a Government initiative to implement a fully digital tax system that aims to make tax administration more effective, more efficient and easier for taxpayers. MTD for VAT has been in place since 1 April 2019.

Businesses with a turnover above the VAT threshold (currently £85,000) must keep their VAT records digitally and provide their VAT return information to HMRC through MTD-compatible software.

Examples of VAT records that must be kept digitally within the MTD-compatible software include:

- business name, address, VAT registration number and details of any VAT accounting schemes used;
- for each supply/sale:
  - the time of supply (tax point);
  - the net value excluding VAT; and
  - the rate of VAT charged;

■ for each supply received/purchased:
  ● the time of supply (tax point);
  ● the value of the supply; and
  ● the amount of input tax claimed.

MTD for VAT is available, on a voluntary basis, to other businesses.

19.10.4 Penalties

Late Registration Penalty
The total penalty depends on how late the registration is, how much VAT is due and whether the disclosure was prompted or unprompted. The biggest reduction to the penalty will be given if the taxpayer makes an "unprompted disclosure", i.e. where the taxpayer informs HMRC about the failure when they have no reason to believe that HMRC has discovered it or is about to discover it. Anything else is a "prompted disclosure". If an unprompted disclosure is made within 12 months of the date the VAT is due, the penalty may be reduced to nil.

The new penalty regime levies the penalty according to the behaviour of the individual (see **Table 19.4**).

TABLE 19.4: PENALTIES – LATE REGISTRATION FOR VAT

Behaviour	Maximum Penalty	Minimum penalty – unprompted disclosure	Minimum penalty – prompted disclosure
Careless	30%	>12 months 10% <12 months 0%	>12 months 20% <12 months 15%
Deliberate but not concealed	70%	20%	35%
Deliberate and concealed	100%	30%	50%

Penalties and Interest on Late Payments of VAT
HMRC record a 'default' for VAT if:

1. a VAT return is not received by the deadline; or
2. full payment for the VAT due on a VAT return is not paid by the deadline.

Surcharges
Where a trader has defaulted, they may enter a 12-month "surcharge period". If the trader defaults again during this time:

■ the surcharge period is extended for a further 12 months; and
■ the trader may have to pay an extra amount (a surcharge) in addition to the VAT owed.

The surcharge is a percentage of the VAT outstanding on the due date for the accounting period that is in default. The surcharge rate increases every time the trader defaults again in a surcharge period. No surcharge is payable on a first default.

Table 19.5 shows the surcharge rates in a 12-month surcharge period.

TABLE 19.5: VAT SURCHARGE RATES

Number of defaults within 12 months	Surcharge if annual turnover is less than £150,000	Surcharge if annual turnover is £150,000 or more
2	No surcharge	2% (no surcharge if it is less than £400)
3	2% (no surcharge if it is less than £400)	5% (no surcharge if it is less than £400)
4	5% (no surcharge if it is less than £400)	10% or £30 (whichever is the greater)
5	10% or £30 (whichever is the greater)	15% or £30 (whichever is the greater)
6 or more	15% or £30 (whichever is greater)	15% or £30 (whichever is the greater)

A trader will not be subject to a surcharge where a VAT return is submitted late and:

- the VAT is paid in full by the due date;
- no VAT is due;
- or where a VAT repayment is due.

In addition to a surcharge, HMRC may also charge a penalty of up to:

- 100% of any VAT under-stated or over-claimed if a return contains a careless or deliberate inaccuracy;
- 30% of an assessment if HMRC issues an under-assessment and the taxpayer does not inform HMRC it is wrong within 30 days; or
- £400 if a trader submits a paper VAT return, unless HMRC has advised that this is acceptable.

Example 19.6

Amanda's VAT return for the quarter ended 30 September 2021 was submitted late. The VAT due of £10,000 was paid on 20 November 2021.

Her return for the following quarter to 31 December 2021 was also submitted late – the VAT due of £15,000 was paid on 26 February 2022. Amanda's annual turnover is in excess of £150,000.

Outline the consequences arising from the late submission of the VAT returns.

1. Quarter ended 30 September 2021 – first default: surcharge liabilities notice issued. Surcharge period runs from the date of the notice to 30 September 2022.
2. (a) Quarter ended 31 December 2021 – second default (falls within surcharge period): surcharge period extended to 31 December 2022.
   (b) Surcharge penalty of £300 (i.e. 2% × £15,000) is due, but as this is below £400 an assessment will not be issued.

The position is slightly different for **small businesses**. A small business is one with a turnover below £150,000. When a small business is late submitting a VAT return or paying VAT, it will receive a letter from HMRC offering help. No penalty will be charged. A surcharge liability notice will be issued if there is a second default within 12 months of the letter offering help, again without penalty. However, on the issue of a third letter, a 2% penalty will apply, which increases to 15% on the issue of a sixth subsequent default.

HMRC may charge interest if the correct amount of VAT is not reported and paid. HMRC may also pay interest to a trader who has overpaid VAT. The rate of interest charged on late or unpaid VAT by HMRC is 2.60%. The repayment rate of interest HMRC will pay out to a trader who has overpaid is 0.5%.

New VAT penalty and interest rules will apply from 1 April 2022 for those who fail to submit returns on time or who fail to pay on time.

Amending Errors

Errors can be corrected on the VAT return if the net value of errors found in the relevant period is **less** than the **greater** of £10,000 or 1% of turnover (excluding VAT) (subject to a maximum of £50,000). Errors above this limit must be disclosed separately in writing to HMRC.

HMRC can only raise an assessment to correct errors retrospectively for four years. The four-year cap works both ways. Although one cannot correct an overpayment made more than four years ago, in general one would not have to correct underpayments made more than four years ago either.

19.11   Special VAT Schemes

HMRC operates special schemes in relation to specific business size, industries or sectors.

19.11.1   *Flat Rate Scheme*

A trader can choose to avail of the flat rate scheme, in which VAT is charged at a flat percentage of turnover, with the percentage being aligned to the particular sector in which the trader operates. There are various conditions that apply before a business can join the scheme, the main one being that the expected taxable turnover in the next 12 months will not exceed £150,000 (net of VAT).

The purpose of the scheme is to ease administration for small businesses, and HMRC promote it on the basis that it is quicker, easier and less onerous for small businesses. However, the scheme is not simple and may not be beneficial for all small businesses. For example, the scheme is not suitable for traders who regularly receive VAT repayments, or for traders who make mainly zero-rated supplies.

The scheme works by enabling businesses to calculate VAT due by simply applying a flat-rate percentage to their **VAT-inclusive** turnover, including zero-rated and exempt supplies. Different sectors have different flat rates, fixed by HMRC. For example, the accounting services flat rate is 14.5%, whereas for hairdressing or other beauty treatment services the flat rate is 13%. However, under the scheme a trader cannot reclaim the VAT on purchases, except for certain capital assets over £2,000.

If the total value of the trade's tax-inclusive supplies (excluding sales of capital assets) is more than £230,000, the business must leave the scheme. However, if a business using the flat rate scheme exceeds the annual exit threshold as a result of a one-off transaction, but in the subsequent year expects its tax-inclusive annual flat-rate turnover to be less than £191,500, it may remain in the scheme with the agreement of HMRC.

A 1% reduction off the flat-rate percentage can be made by businesses in their first year of VAT registration. Note, invoices raised will show VAT at the normal rate and not at the flat rate.

Example 19.7

An accountant makes total supplies of £75,000, including VAT at 20%, in the VAT year. The flat-rate percentage is 14.5%. Assume the rate of VAT is 20% throughout the VAT year.

The VAT due to HMRC under the flat rate scheme will be 14.5% × £75,000 = £10,875. Under normal VAT accounting rules, the output tax would be £12,500 (£75,000 × 1/6).

Under the flat rate scheme no input VAT can be reclaimed.

19.11.2   Cash Accounting Scheme

VAT-registered traders normally become liable for VAT at the time of the **issue** of the invoice to their customers, **regardless** of whether they have received payment for the supplies made. For example, a trader must include in their VAT return for quarter ended 31 March 2021 all invoices issued during January, February and March 2021. This is known as the **invoice basis of accounting** for VAT.

Alternatively, small businesses can operate a cash receipts basis when accounting for VAT, whereby traders **do not** become liable for VAT until they have actually **received payment for goods or services supplied**. Likewise, they can only claim input VAT **when payment has been made for purchases** and not, as under the invoice basis, when the invoice for purchases is received.

The scheme can only be used by a trader whose annual taxable turnover (exclusive of VAT) does not exceed £1,350,000. If the value of taxable supplies exceeds £1,600,000 in the 12 months to the end of a VAT period, a trader must leave the scheme.

A trader who opts for the cash receipts basis of accounting is liable for VAT at the **rate in effect at the time the supply is made** rather than the rate in effect at the time payment is received.

Traders who opt for the cash receipts basis of accounting must **issue credit notes** for all discounts given to suppliers to ensure that a greater amount of VAT is not claimed by the purchaser than has been paid by the supplier.

The advantages of the cash receipts basis are that output VAT is not due until payment is received; in addition, there will be no VAT payable on bad debts (see **Section 19.9.5**). The disadvantages are that there will be no input VAT recovery until the trader pays the supplier. The business's accounting system may need to be modified to ensure that VAT (both input and output) is recorded only on payments or receipts.

19.11.3   Annual Accounting Scheme

Small businesses can choose to submit one return annually. In the meantime, they pay fixed sums to HMRC based on their previous year's VAT liability.

To be eligible to join the annual accounting scheme, the taxable turnover limit (excluding VAT) must not be expected to exceed £1,350,000 per annum over the following 12 months, and the taxpayer must leave the scheme if the taxable turnover is expected to exceed £1,600,000 per annum.

Under the annual accounting scheme, the taxpayer makes nine interim payments at monthly intervals or three quarterly interim payments based on the previous year's actual payments or, if newly registered, what is expected to be paid over the next 12 months. The first of these consecutive payments is made on the last working day of the fourth month of the scheme's accounting year. That is, 90% of the total payment is paid in nine equal instalments on the last day of months 4, 5, 6, 7, 8, 9, 10, 11 and 12 of the VAT year. The final payment is made when the annual return is submitted, which must be within two months of the end of the scheme's accounting year. Only one annual return is required.

A claim can be made to reduce the interim payments if the taxpayer believes that the annual VAT due in the current year will be less than in the previous year (obviously there can be many potential reasons for this).

Questions

Review Questions
(See Suggested Solutions to Review Questions at the end of this textbook.)

Question 19.1

Outline:

(a) the criteria for determining when a person making taxable supplies needs to register for VAT;
(b) how to register for VAT and the requirements regarding the payment of VAT due; and
(c) the VAT records to be maintained.

Question 19.2

Stephen has just started to trade as a seller of fine furniture. He has the following sales:

	£
May 2021	2,000
June 2021	6,500
July 2021	6,000
August 2021	8,000
September 2021	8,000
October 2021	15,000
November 2021	14,000
December 2021	23,000
January 2021	5,000
February 2022	70,000
March 2022	5,000

Requirement
(a) When is Stephen required to register for VAT, and when should he start to charge VAT?
(b) Would the answer to (a) be different if Stephen had thought he would make sales of £82,000 by September 2021 when he started trading?

Question 19.3

Outline the VAT rules for determining the tax point or time when a supply of goods or services is treated as taking place.

Question 19.4

What information must be included on a VAT invoice in order for it to be a valid VAT invoice on which input VAT can be reclaimed? (Assume the rules for simplified VAT invoices do not apply.)

Question 19.5

Michael, a friend of yours, has recently set up business in Bangor, Co. Down, selling computers. He has already registered for VAT.

Requirement
What penalties will arise if Michael does not consistently file his VAT returns on time?

Question 19.6

Mr Byte supplies computers to business and retail outlets. You are given the following information in connection with his VAT return for the period July/August/September 2021. All figures are exclusive of VAT. He is not using the cash receipts basis of VAT accounting.

	£
Invoiced sales	100,000
Cash received	75,000
Purchase invoices received	42,000
Purchase invoices paid	50,000
Other expenses:	
Stationery	6,000
Wages	20,000
Electricity	10,000
Entertaining	1,000

Requirement
Compute Mr Byte's VAT liability for the period July/August/September 2021.

Question 19.7

Joe, who is a baker, supplies you with the following information from his books for the months of May, June and July 2021 (all figures are exclusive of VAT):

	May	June and July
	£	**£**
Gross sales of bread	10,000	8,000
Cash discounts given	500	400
Purchase of ingredients	5,000	2,000
Stationery	1,000	1,000
Accountancy fees	2,000	2,000
Bank interest	400	400

Requirement

Compute Joe's VAT liability for the period in question.

Question 19.8

What type of person/business would apply for voluntary registration for VAT? Discuss the reasons why they would choose to apply for voluntary registration.

Question 19.9

Discuss the place where goods and services are deemed to be supplied for VAT purposes.

Question 19.10

Andrew opened a coffee shop on 17 March 2021 and the transactions undertaken during the first VAT period, March–May 2021, were as follows:

Sales and Receipts

1. Net receipts in respect of sales of goods and services to sit-in customers amounted to £2,000.
2. Net receipts in respect of sales of cold food (not cakes) to take away amounted to £4,000.

Purchases and Payments

1. Purchases of food for re-sale: £588 inclusive of VAT at 20%
2. Purchase of stock for re-sale: £334 at zero-rated VAT
3. Purchase of tables and chairs: £440 plus VAT
4. Purchases of second-hand cash register on three months' credit. The invoice, dated 3 March 2021, was for £690 in total and included VAT at 20%.
5. Payment of £200 plus VAT at 20% to the tiler on 16 March 2021.
6. Payment of £750 on account to a solicitor for legal fees on foot of a bill received for £1,728 inclusive of VAT.
7. Purchase, for the business, of a commercial van for £10,350 inclusive of VAT. All invoices relating to the above transactions have been received unless otherwise stated. Assume that Andrew was registered for VAT prior to incurring any expenditure.

Requirement

Calculate the VAT liability/refund for the VAT period March–May 2021 (round amounts to the nearest £ for the purpose of the question). Andrew registered for VAT immediately when he commenced to trade.

Appendix 1

Taxation Reference Material for Tax Year 2021/22 (Finance Act 2021)

Table of Contents

GENERAL

Beneficial Loans

Official rate of interest is 2%.

HMRC Late Payment and Repayment Interest Rates

The current late payment and repayment interest rates applied to income tax, national insurance, VAT, corporation tax* and inheritance tax are:

■ Underpayments: late payment interest rate – 2.60%

■ Overpayments: repayment interest rate – 0.5%

*Only applies to companies not paying corporation tax in instalments.

INCOME TAX

Income Tax Rates*

	Rate%
Starting rate for non-dividend savings income up to £5,000	0
First £37,700	20 (Basic rate)
£37,701–£150,000	40 (Higher rate)
Over £150,000	45 (Additional rate)
Basic rate for dividends	7.5
Higher rate for dividends	32.5
Additional rate for dividends	38.1

Income Tax Allowances*

	£
Personal allowance (1)	12,570
Income limit for personal allowance (1)	100,000
Marriage allowance (2)	1,260
Blind person's allowance	2,520
Dividend allowance (3)	2,000
Personal savings allowance (4):	
Basic rate taxpayers	1,000
Higher rate taxpayers	500
Property allowance (5)	1,000
Trading allowance (5)	1,000

* The rates and allowances in Scotland and Wales may differ.

(1) All individuals are entitled to the same personal allowance, regardless of the individuals' date of birth. This allowance is subject to the £100,000 income limit, which applies regardless of the individual's date of birth. The individual's personal allowance is reduced where their income is above this limit. The allowance is reduced by £1 for every £2 above the limit.

(2) A spouse or civil partner who is not liable to income tax; or not liable at the higher or additional rate, can claim to transfer this amount of their personal allowance to their spouse or civil

partner. The recipient must not be liable to income tax at the higher or additional rate. The relief for this allowance is given at 20%.

(3) The dividend allowance means that individuals do not have to pay tax on the first £2,000 (2020/21: £2,000) of dividend income they receive.

(4) The personal savings allowance means that basic rate taxpayers do not have to pay tax on the first £1,000 of savings income they receive and higher rate taxpayers will not have tax to pay on their first £500 of savings income.

(5) The first £1,000 of trading income is not subject to income tax. The trading allowance also applies to certain miscellaneous income from providing assets or services. A £1,000 allowance is also available for property income.

Car Benefits Charges

Car Benefit Percentage

The percentage rates applying to petrol and electric cars (first registered **before 6 April 2020**) with CO_2 emissions up to 55g/km:

0g/km	1%
1–50g/km (electric range >130 miles)	2%
1–50g/km (electric range 70–129 miles)	5%
1–50g/km (electric range 40–69 miles)	8%
1–50g/km (electric range 30–39 miles)	12%
1–50g/km (electric range <30 miles)	14%
51–54g/km	15%
55g/km	16%

For each 5g/km that a car is above 55g/km, an additional 1% is added to the percentage rate.

The percentage rates applying to petrol and electric cars (first registered on or **after 6 April 2020**) with CO_2 emissions up to 55g/km:

0g/km	1%
1–50g/km (electric range >130 miles)	1%
1–50g/km (electric range 70–129 miles)	4%
1–50g/km (electric range 40–69 miles)	7%
1–50g/km (electric range 30-39 miles)	11%
1–50g/km (electric range <30 miles)	13%
51–54g/km	14%
55g/km	15%

For each 5g/km that a car is above 55g/km, an additional 1% is added to the percentage rate.

For diesel cars, a 4% diesel supplement is added. Diesel cars that meet the Real Driving Emissions test are exempt from the supplement.

The maximum percentage charge is 37% and applies to petrol cars that have CO_2 emissions of 165g/km or more and diesel cars with emissions of 145g/km or more.

Fuel Benefit Charge

The same percentage figure used to calculate the car benefit charge, as above, is used to calculate the fuel benefit charge. The relevant percentage figure is multiplied by £24,600 for 2021/22 (£24,500 in 2020/21).

Van Benefits Charges

Van benefit	£3,500
Fuel benefit	£669

The charges will not apply if a "restricted private use condition" is met throughout the year. There is no van benefit charge for zero-emission vans (for 2020/21 the van benefit charge was 80% of the main rate).

Authorised Mileage Allowance Rates

Use of own vehicle:

Vehicle	Flat rate per mile with simplified expenses
Cars and goods vehicles – first 10,000 miles	45p
Cars and goods vehicles – after 10,000 miles	25p
Motorcycles (all miles)	24p
Bicycles (all miles)	20p

Use of company car (rates from 1 June 2021):

Engine size	Petrol	LPG
1400cc or less	11p	8p
1401cc to 2000cc	13p	9p
Over 2000cc	19p	14p

Engine size	Diesel
1600cc or less	9p
1601cc to 2000cc	11p
Over 2000cc	13p

Simplified Expenses

Motor Expenses

Vehicle	Flat rate per mile
Cars and goods vehicles:	
first 10,000 miles	45p
after 10,000 miles	25p
Motorcycles	24p

Working from Home

Hours of business use per month	Flat rate per month
25 to 50	£10
51 to 100	£18
101 and more	£26

Living at Business Premises

Number of people	Flat rate per month
1	£350
2	£500
3+	£650

Pension Scheme Limits

Annual allowance	£40,000*
Lifetime allowance	£1,073,100
Maximum contribution without earnings	£3,600
Lifetime allowance charge – if excess drawn as cash	55%
Lifetime allowance charge – if excess drawn as income	25%
Annual allowance charge on excess – linked to individual's marginal tax rate	20%/40%/45%

* The annual allowance for certain high earners is reduced on a tapering basis. For every £2 of adjusted income over £240,000 an individual's annual allowance will reduce by £1 but is not reduced below £4,000 (also £4,000 in 2020/21).

Individual Savings Accounts (ISAs)

Overall annual investment limit: 2021/22   £20,000
(split any way between cash and stocks/shares)

High-income Child Benefit Charge

Where income is between £50,000 and £60,000, the charge is 1% of the amount of child benefit received for every £100 of income over £50,000.

Capital Allowances

	2021/22 %	2020/21 %
Main pool (Note 1)	18	18
Motor cars – CO_2 emissions:		
0g/km (2021/22); < 50g/km (2020/21)	100	100
1–50g/km (2021/22); 51–110g/km (2020/21) (Note)	18	18
>50g/km (2021/22); >10g/km (2020/21) (Note)	6	6
New and unused zero-emission goods vehicles	100	100
Special rate pool (long-life assets and integral features of a building) (Note)	6	6
Research and development	100	100
Structures and buildings allowance	3%	3%

Note: Allowances are given on a writing down allowance reducing balance basis.

From 1 January 2019 to 31 December 2021, there is a 100% annual investment allowance on the first £1,000,0000 tranche per annum of capital expenditure incurred per group of companies or related entities on plant and machinery, including long-life assets and integral features but excluding cars. The limit is £200,000 from 1 January 2022.

Super-deduction and Special Rate Allowance

From 1 April 2021 to 31 March 2023, where a company incurs qualifying expenditure on new plant or machinery it may be able to claim the super-deduction and special rate first-year allowance (SR allowance).

The super-deduction provides an allowance equal to 130% of the qualifying spend and applies to new plant or machinery that would ordinarily qualify for the 18% main rate writing down allowance.

The SR allowance provides a first-year allowance of 50% on new plant or machinery that would ordinarily qualify for the 6% rate writing down allowance.

The two reliefs are not available to unincorporated businesses (such as sole traders or partnerships).

NATIONAL INSURANCE CONTRIBUTIONS

Limit/Threshold	Frequency	£
Lower earnings limit:	Weekly	120
	Monthly	520
	Yearly	6,240
Upper earnings limit:	Weekly	967
	Monthly	4,189
	Yearly	50,270
Primary threshold (employee):	Weekly	184
	Monthly	797
	Yearly	9,568
Secondary threshold (employer):	Weekly	170
	Monthly	737
	Yearly	8,840
Upper secondary threshold (under 21) (employer):	Weekly	967
	Monthly	4,189
	Yearly	50,270
Upper secondary threshold (apprentice under 25) (employer):	Weekly	967
	Monthly	4,189
	Yearly	50,270

Employee's Contributions

▨ Rate:
  ● on weekly earnings between £184 and £967   12%
  ● on weekly earnings above £967   2%

Employer's Contributions

▨ Rate: on weekly earnings over £170   13.8%
▨ Employer's allowance   £4,000

Other Classes

Classes 1A and 1B   13.8%
Class 2:
  Self-employed per week   £3.05
  Small profits threshold   £6,515
Class 3:
  Voluntary per week   £15.40
Class 4:
  Self-employment (rate on profits):
          on annual profits between £9,568 and £50,270   9%
          on annual profits above £50,270   2%

CORPORATION TAX

	Main rate
1 April 2020–31 March 2021	19%
1 April 2021–31 March 2022	19%

CAPITAL GAINS TAX

Annual Exemption

Annual exemption for individuals..£12,300
Annual exemption for trustees...£6,150

Rates

General

The following rates apply to gains (except for residential land and property gains):

▨ 10% for individual basic rate taxpayers*
▨ 20% for individual higher rate/additional rate taxpayers.

Gains on residential land and property disposals are taxed as follows:

▨ 18% for individual basic rate taxpayers and
▨ 28% for individual higher rate/additional rate taxpayers.

*Personal representatives of deceased taxpayers are not entitled to the basic rate of CGT.

Non-resident Capital Gains Tax on Direct Disposals of UK Land and Property

The following rates apply to gains on non-residential land and property disposals:

- 10% for individual basic rate taxpayers
- 20% for individual higher rate taxpayers
- 20% for personal representatives of a non-resident who has died.

Gains on residential land and property are taxed as follows:

- 18% for basic rate taxpayers
- 28% for higher rate/additional rate taxpayers
- 28% for personal representatives of someone who has died.

Non-resident Capital Gains Tax on Indirect Disposals of UK Land and Property

The following rates apply:

- 10% for individual basic rate taxpayers
- 20% for individual higher rate taxpayers
- 20% for personal representatives of a non-resident who has died

VAT

Registration and Deregistration Limits

	Annual value of taxable supplies
Registration limit for years 2019, 2020 and 2021 (from 1 April)	£85,000
Deregistration limit for years 2019, 2020 and 2021 (from 1 April)	£83,000

Rates

Rate	Examples
Exempt	<ul><li>Insurance</li><li>Postal services</li><li>Finance</li><li>Education</li><li>Health and welfare</li><li>Professional subscriptions</li></ul>
Zero rate (0%)	<ul><li>Food</li><li>Water and sewage services</li><li>Books (printed) and certain electronic publications</li><li>Transport</li><li>Charities</li><li>Children's clothing</li><li>International services</li><li>Women's sanitary products</li></ul>

Standard rate (20%)	All supplies of goods and services by taxable persons that are not exempt, zero rated or subject to reduced rate. Includes:
	■ Adult clothing and footwear
	■ Office equipment and stationery
	■ Drinks and certain foods
Reduced rate (5%)	■ Domestic fuel or power
	■ Installation of energy-saving materials for residential properties
	■ Children's car seats

UK Retail Price Indices (as adjusted to base 100 in January 1987)

	1982	1983	1984	1985	1986	1987	1988	1989	1990	1991	1992	1993	1994	1995	1996	1997	1998	1999	2000
January	-	82.6	86.8	91.2	96.2	100.0	103.3	111.0	119.5	130.2	135.6	137.9	141.3	146.3	150.2	154.4	159.5	163.4	166.6
February	-	83.0	87.2	91.9	96.6	100.4	103.7	111.8	120.2	130.9	136.3	138.8	142.1	146.9	150.9	155.0	160.3	163.7	167.5
March	79.4	83.1	87.5	92.8	96.7	100.6	104.1	112.3	121.4	131.4	136.7	139.3	142.5	147.5	151.5	155.4	160.8	164.4	168.4
April	81.0	84.3	88.6	94.8	97.7	101.8	105.8	114.3	125.1	133.1	138.8	140.6	144.2	149.0	152.6	156.3	162.6	165.2	170.1
May	81.6	84.6	89.0	95.2	97.8	101.9	106.2	115.0	126.2	133.5	139.3	141.1	144.7	149.6	152.9	156.9	163.5	165.6	170.7
June	81.9	84.8	89.2	95.4	97.8	101.9	106.6	115.4	126.7	134.1	139.3	141.0	144.7	149.8	153.0	157.5	163.4	165.6	170.7
July	81.9	85.3	89.1	95.2	97.5	101.8	106.7	115.5	126.8	133.8	138.8	140.7	144.0	149.1	152.4	157.5	163.0	165.1	170.5
August	81.9	85.7	89.9	95.5	97.8	102.4	107.9	115.8	128.1	134.1	138.9	141.3	144.7	149.9	153.1	158.5	163.7	165.5	170.5
September	81.9	86.1	90.1	95.4	98.3	102.4	108.4	116.6	129.3	134.6	139.4	141.9	145.0	150.6	153.8	159.3	164.4	166.2	171.7
October	82.3	86.4	90.7	95.6	98.5	102.9	109.5	117.5	130.3	135.1	139.9	141.8	145.2	149.8	153.8	159.5	164.5	166.5	171.6
November	82.7	86.7	91.0	95.9	99.3	103.4	110.0	118.5	130.0	135.6	139.7	141.6	145.3	149.8	153.9	159.6	164.4	166.7	172.1
December	82.5	86.9	90.9	96.0	99.6	103.3	110.3	118.8	129.9	135.7	139.2	141.9	146.0	150.7	154.4	160.0	164.4	167.3	172.2

	2001	2002	2003	2004	2005	2006	2007	2008	2009	2010	2011	2012	2013	2014	2015	2016	2017
January	171.1	173.3	178.4	183.1	188.9	193.4	201.6	209.8	210.1	217.9	229.0	238.0	245.8	252.6	255.4	258.8	265.5
February	172.0	173.8	179.3	183.8	189.6	194.2	203.1	211.4	211.4	219.2	231.3	239.9	247.6	254.2	256.7	260.0	268.4
March	172.2	174.5	179.9	184.6	190.5	195.0	204.4	212.1	211.3	220.7	232.5	240.8	248.7	254.8	257.1	261.1	269.3
April	173.1	175.7	181.2	185.7	191.6	196.5	205.4	214.0	211.5	222.8	234.4	242.1	249.5	255.7	258.0	261.4	270.6
May	174.2	176.2	181.5	186.5	192.0	197.7	206.2	215.1	212.8	223.6	235.2	242.4	250.0	255.9	258.5	262.1	271.7
June	174.4	176.2	181.3	186.8	192.2	198.5	207.3	216.8	213.4	224.1	235.2	241.8	249.7	256.3	258.9	263.1	272.3
July	173.3	175.9	181.3	186.8	192.2	198.5	206.1	216.5	213.4	223.6	234.7	242.1	249.7	256.0	258.6	263.4	272.9
August	174.0	176.4	181.6	187.4	192.6	199.2	207.3	217.2	214.4	224.5	236.1	243.0	251.0	257.0	259.8	264.4	274.7
September	174.6	177.6	182.5	188.1	193.1	200.1	208.0	218.4	215.3	225.3	237.9	244.2	251.9	257.6	259.6	264.9	275.1
October	174.3	177.9	182.6	188.6	193.3	200.4	208.9	217.7	216.0	225.8	238.0	245.6	251.9	257.7	259.5	264.8	275.3
November	173.6	178.2	182.7	189.0	193.3	201.1	209.7	216.0	216.6	226.8	238.5	245.6	252.1	257.1	259.8	265.5	275.8
December	173.4	178.5	183.5	189.9	194.1	202.7	210.9	212.9	218.0	228.4	239.4	246.8	253.4	257.5	260.6	267.1	278.1

Appendix 2

Taxation and the *Code of Ethics*

Under Chartered Accountants Ireland's *Code of Ethics*, a Chartered Accountant shall comply with the following fundamental principles:

(a) **Integrity** – to be straightforward and honest in all professional and business relationships.
(b) **Objectivity** – to not compromise professional or business judgements because of bias, conflict of interest or undue influence of others.
(c) **Professional Competence and Due Care** – to attain and maintain professional knowledge and skill at the level required to ensure that a client or employing organisation receives competent professional service based on current technical and professional standards and relevant legislation; and act diligently and in accordance with applicable technical and professional standards.
(d) **Confidentiality** – to respect the confidentiality of information acquired as a result of professional and business relationships and, therefore, not disclose any such information to third parties without proper and specific authority, unless there is a legal or professional right or duty to disclose, nor use the information for the personal advantage of the Chartered Accountant or third parties.
(e) **Professional Behaviour** – to comply with relevant laws and regulations and avoid any conduct that the professional accountant knows or should know might discredit the profession.

The Institute's "Five Fundamental Principles, Five Practical Steps" is a useful resource for members and students and is available at www.charteredaccountants.ie. As a Chartered Accountant, you will have to ensure that your dealings with the tax aspects of your professional life are also in compliance with these fundamental principles. You may be asked to define or list the principles, as well as be able to identify where these ethical issues arise and how you would deal with them.

Examples of situations that could arise where these principles are challenged in the context of tax are outlined below.

Example 1
You are working in the tax department of ABC & Co. and your manager is Jack Wilson. He comes over to your desk after his meeting with Peter Foley. He gives you all the papers that Peter has left with him. He asks you to draft Peter's tax return. You know who Peter is as you are now living in a house that your friend Ann leased from Peter. As you complete the return, you note that there is no information regarding rental income. What should you do?

Action
As a person with integrity, you should explain to your manager that your friend Ann has leased property from Peter and that he has forgotten to send details of his rental income and expenses. As Peter sent the information to Jack, it is appropriate for Jack to contact Peter for details regarding rental income and related expenses.

Example 2

You are working in the tax department of the Irish subsidiary of a US-owned multinational. You are preparing the corporation tax computation, including the R&D tax credit due. You have not received some information from your colleagues dealing with R&D and cannot finalise the claim for R&D tax credit until you receive this information. Your manager is under pressure and tells you to just file the claim on the basis of what will maximise the claim. He says, "It is self-assessment, and the chance of this ever being audited or enquired into is zero." What should you do?

Action

You should act in a professional and objective manner. This means that you cannot do as your manager wants. You should explain to him that you will contact the person in R&D again and finalise the claim as quickly as possible.

Example 3

Anna O'Shea, financial controller of Great Client Ltd, rings you regarding a VAT issue. You have great respect for Anna and are delighted that she is ringing you directly instead of your manager. She says that it is a very straightforward query. However, as you listen to her, you realise that you are pretty sure of the answer but would need to check a point before answering. What should you do?

Action

Where you do not know the answer, it is professionally competent to explain that you need to check a point before you give an answer. If you like, you can explain which aspect you need to check. Your client will appreciate you acting professionally rather than giving incorrect information or advice.

Example 4

The phone rings, and it is Darren O'Brien, your best friend, who works for Just-do-it Ltd. After discussing the match you both watched on the television last night, Darren explains why he is ringing you. He has heard that Success Ltd, a client of your tax department, has made R&D tax credit claims. Therefore, you must have details regarding its R&D. Darren's relationship with his boss is not great at present, and he knows that if he could get certain data about Success Ltd, his relationship with his boss would improve. He explains that he does not want any financial information, just some small details regarding R&D. What should you do?

Action

You should not give him the information. No matter how good a friend he is, it is unethical to give confidential information about your client to him.

Example 5

It is the Friday morning before a bank holiday weekend, and you are due to travel from Dublin to west Cork after work for the weekend. Your manager has been on annual leave for the last week. He left you work to do for the week, including researching a tax issue for a client. He had advised you that you were to have an answer to the issue by the time he returned, no matter how long it took. It actually took you a very short time and you have it all documented for him.

Your friend who is travelling with you asks if you could leave at 11am to beat the traffic and have a longer weekend. You have no annual leave left, so you cannot take leave. You know that if you leave, nobody will notice, but you have to complete a timesheet. Your friend reminds you that the research for the client could have taken a lot longer and that you could code the five hours to the client. What should you do?

Action

It would be unprofessional behaviour and would show a lack of integrity if you were to charge your client for those five hours.

Example 6

You act as tax agent for a friend of yours, John Smyth, who owns and runs his own sole-trade business. John's business has been doing well in recent times and he hints that, when the tax return is being prepared, it would be good if he could pay less tax or claim more business expenses and asks for your help as a long-time friend.

Action

It would be unethical to falsify business records or to underpay tax. You must explain to John that the tax return must accurately reflect the results of the business and highlight that if you were found to be providing false information, you could be prosecuted by HMRC under the legislation for 'dishonest conduct by tax agents' and charged a penalty of between £5,000 and £50,000.

Appendix 3

Tax Planning, Tax Avoidance and Tax Evasion

The global financial and economic crash of 2008 and the ensuing worldwide recession led to a fall in tax collected by many governments and pushed tax and tax transparency higher up the agenda. Subsequent events further increased the focus and attention of the wider public – as well as governments – on both tax avoidance and evasion of taxes: the revelations in the 'Paradise Papers' and the 'Panama Papers', the EU's state aid decision against Ireland and Apple Inc., coupled with the 'tax-shaming' of many multinational brand names and famous people has led to tax, and tax ethics, appearing in media headlines almost on a daily basis. As a result, a number of international and domestic initiatives have dramatically changed the tax planning and tax compliance landscape and brought tax transparency to the fore in many businesses and boardrooms.

The tax liability of an individual, partnership, trust or company can be reduced by tax planning, tax avoidance or tax evasion. Although the overriding objective of each is to reduce the taxpayer's tax bill, the method each adopts to do so is different. Each is also vastly different from an ethical and technical perspective.

Tax receipts are used to fund public services such as education, hospitals and roads. Individuals and businesses in a country benefit from these services directly and indirectly and it is therefore seen as a social and ethical responsibility for them to pay their fair share of taxes. Evading or avoiding paying your taxes is viewed as unacceptable as a result.

Tax Planning

Tax planning is used by taxpayers to reduce their tax bill by making use of provisions within domestic tax legislation. For example, any company with good tax governance will seek to minimise its tax liability by using the tools and mechanisms – allowances, deductions, reliefs and exemptions for example – made available to them by the government.

Planning can also take the form of simple decisions, such as delaying sales when a fall in the rate of corporation tax is expected so that the company pays a lower rate of corporation tax on its taxable profits. Or a taxpayer may consider what type of assets to buy to maximise capital allowances. Any tax planning decision should work, not just from a tax planning and legislative perspective, but it should also be commercially feasible.

The UK government accepts that all taxpayers are entitled to organise their affairs in such a way as to mitigate their tax liability – as long as they do so within the law and within the spirit in which Parliament intended when setting the law. Tax planning is both legally and ethically acceptable.

Tax Avoidance

Tax avoidance is often viewed as a grey area because it is regularly confused with tax planning. Tax avoidance is the use of loopholes within tax legislation to reduce the taxpayer's tax liability. Although tax avoidance may seem similar to tax planning, as the taxpayer is using tax law to reduce their overall tax burden, the taxpayer is using tax legislation in a way not intended, or anticipated, by Parliament.

In 2004, the UK government launched the Disclosure of Tax Avoidance Schemes (DOTAS) regime, which covers most taxes in the UK including income tax, national insurance, VAT, capital gains tax, corporation tax, inheritance tax and stamp duty land tax. DOTAS was designed to provide early information to HMRC about tax avoidance schemes that had been developed and the users of those schemes.

The regime has been amended a number of times to ensure it remains up to date and that it identifies tax avoidance schemes as the tax avoidance market changes. The DOTAS requires schemes that contain certain 'hallmarks' of tax avoidance to be notified to HMRC. HMRC then take action to close down the scheme, usually by legislation as part of the annual Budget process.

The users of such schemes are also required to notify HMRC that they have used a particular scheme by including the scheme notification number on the relevant tax return or submission made to HMRC. HMRC will thereafter pursue the scheme user by opening an enquiry that challenges the avoidance scheme.

Avoidance behaviour is also challenged by the UK's General Anti-Abuse Rule (GAAR), which took effect from 17 July 2013 and is intended to counteract "tax advantages arising from tax arrangements that are abusive" and applies across a number of taxes.

Tax arrangements exist where obtaining a tax advantage is "one of the main purposes". To date, the opinions given by the GAAR advisory panel have all been in HMRC's favour. The GAAR counteracts the abusive behaviour and in effect reverses the tax saving.

The *Ramsay* principle (or doctrine) refers to an approach to statutory interpretation developed by the courts in cases involving tax avoidance. It began with the landmark decision by the House of Lords in *W. T. Ramsay Ltd. v. Inland Revenue Commissioners* (1981). The *Ramsay* principle can be summarised as:

1. look at the legislation – what did Parliament intend when it chose those words?
2. look at the particular facts of the transaction – should an individual transaction be considered in a wider context?
3. in light of 1. and 2., how does the law apply to these facts?

While tax avoidance is arguably legal, it is generally viewed as ethically unacceptable behaviour. Tax avoidance behaviour that is successfully challenged by HMRC will lead to the original tax saving being paid, in addition to penalties and interest on the error.

Tax Evasion

At the extreme end of the spectrum is tax evasion. Tax evasion involves breaking the law deliberately and either not paying any of the taxes that fall due or underpaying the taxes that fall due when the law clearly states that they must be paid. Tax evaders intend to deliberately break rules surrounding their tax position in order to avoid paying the correct amount of tax they owe.

A tax evader illegally reduces their tax burden, either by a misrepresentation to HMRC or by not filing tax returns at all, thereby concealing the true state of their tax affairs. Tax evasion can include onshore (within the UK) and offshore deliberate behaviour.

Examples of tax evasion include, *inter alia*:

- failure to file a tax return and pay the relevant tax arising;
- failure to declare the correct income;
- deliberately inflating expenses, which reduces taxable profits or increases a loss;
- hiding taxable assets;
- wrongly claiming a tax refund or repayment by being dishonest;
- not telling HMRC about a source of income;
- not operating a PAYE scheme for employees/pensioners;
- not registering for VAT when required to do so; and
- deliberate submission of incorrect or false information.

In all cases the Exchequer suffers a loss of tax. This is known as tax fraud. Tax evasion, and the tax fraud that flows from this behavior, is a criminal offence prosecutable by HMRC. It is viewed as ethically unacceptable behaviour. The error will generally fall into the deliberate behaviour with concealment category (the HMRC's penalty regime is beyond the scope of this textbook).

As Chartered Accountants, we must be cognisant of the activities of clients and potential clients, particularly in cases of tax avoidance and tax evasion.

Suggested Solutions to Review Questions

Chapter 1

Question 1.1

(a) A paper income tax return is due on or before 31 October after the end of the tax year.
(b) An online return is due on or before 31 January after the end of the tax year.
(c) Payment of self-assessed income tax must reach HMRC by 31 January and 31 July after the end of the tax year. For example, for the 2021/22 tax year, income tax payments will be due as follows:
- first payment on account by 31 January 2022;
- second payment on account by 31 July 2022; and
- balancing, or final, payment by 31 January 2023.

Question 1.2

Under Chartered Accountants Ireland's *Code of Ethics*, a Chartered Accountant shall follow the principle of confidentiality. This principle requires a Chartered Accountant to respect the confidentiality of information acquired as a result of professional and business relationships.

If Emma provides such confidential information about a client to Jack, she would be in breach of this principle. She should not provide the information to Jack.

Chapter 2

Question 2.1

Income tax computation for Pat for income tax year 2021/22

	Non-savings £
Income from employment	15,920
Total income	15,920
Less: personal allowance	(12,570)
Taxable income	3,350

continued overleaf

Tax payable:

£3,350 @ 20%	670
Less: tax deducted at source	(3,000)
Tax refund due for 2021/22	(2,330)

Income tax computation for Una for income tax year 2021/22

	Savings
	£
UK interest income	40,920
Total income	40,920
Less: personal allowance	(12,570)
Taxable income	28,350
Tax payable:	
£5,000 @ 0% (savings starting limit)	0
£1,000 @ 0% (personal savings allowance)	0
£22,350 @ 20%	4,470
Tax due for 2021/22	4,470

Question 2.2

Income tax computations for Paul for income tax year 2021/22

	Non-savings Income	Savings Income	Total
	£	£	£
Income from employment (Note 1)	29,000		29,000
UK property business	47,850		47,850
Interest income (Note 2)		300	300
Total income	76,850	300	77,150
Less: personal allowance	(12,570)		(12,570)
Taxable income	64,280	300	64,580
Tax payable:			
Non-savings income			
£37,700 @ 20%			7,540
£26,880 @ 40%			10,752
Savings income			
£300 @ 0% (personal savings allowance: £500 available)			0
Total tax liability			18,292
Less: tax deducted at source:			
PAYE			(5,000)
Tax due for 2021/22			13,292

continued overleaf

Notes:

1. Grossed-up employment income is £24,000 net + £5,000 PAYE deducted at source.
2. Interest earned from a joint account is shared equally between the individuals. Paul's (and Jean's) share is thus £300 each.

Income tax computations for Jean for income tax year 2021/22

	Non-savings Income	Savings Income	Total
	£	£	£
Self-employment income	41,850		41,850
Bank interest	_____	300	300
Total income	41,850	300	42,150
Less: personal allowance	(12,570)	____	(12,570)
Taxable income	29,280	300	29,580
Tax payable:			
Non-savings income			
£29,280 @ 20%			5,856
Savings income			
£300 @ 0% (personal savings allowance: £1,000 available)			0
Total tax liability			5,856
Tax due for 2021/22			5,856

Explanatory Note

▦ The £50 Jean received from their neighbour for cutting his grass can be ignored as it is an exempt amount (less than £100).

Question 2.3

Income tax computations for M. Smyth for income tax year 2021/22

	Non-savings Income	Savings Income	Dividend Income	Total
	£	£	£	£
Income from employment	27,500			27,500
UK property business	10,350			10,350
Savings interest income		20,000		20,000
Dividend income	_____	_____	6,000	6,000
Total income	37,850	20,000	6,000	63,850
Less: personal allowance	(12,570)	_____	_____	(12,570)
Taxable income	25,280	20,000	6,000	51,280

continued overleaf

Tax payable:

Non-savings income

£25,280 @ 20%	5,056

Savings income £

£500 @ 0% (personal savings allowance)	0
£11,920 @ 20%	2,384
£7,580 @ 40%	3,032

Dividend income

£2,000 @ 0% (dividend allowance)	0
£4,000 @ 32.5%	1,300
Total tax liability	11,772
Less: tax deducted at source: PAYE	(4,000)
Tax due for 2021/22	7,772

Chapter 3

Question 3.1

Year of Assessment	Basis
2019/20	**First year**: actual profits arising on time-apportioned basis from start of trading to the end of the tax year. Thus, from 1 June 2019 to 5 April 2020 = 10/12 of £48,000 = £40,000
2020/21	**Second year**: there is a 12-month accounting date ending in the tax year and so the basis period is the 12 months to that accounting date. Therefore, taxable profits for the year are those arising in the 12 months ended 31 May 2020: = £48,000 There is an overlap period from 1 June 2018 to 5 April 2019, giving rise to overlap profits of £40,000 (10 months) – these profits have been taxed in both 2019/20 and 2020/21.
2021/22	**Third year**: there was an accounting date falling in the previous tax year. Therefore, the taxable profits for the 2021/22 tax year are £39,000 (as the basis period is the period of account ending in this tax year – i.e. the period to 31 May 2021).
2022/23	**Fourth year**: the trade did not cease in this year, so the period of account is the year ended 31 May 2022. Therefore, the taxable profits for the 2022/23 tax year are £37,200 (as the basis period is the period of account ending in this tax year – i.e. the one to 31 May 2022).

Question 3.2

Year of Assessment	Basis
2020/21	**First year**: actual profits arising on time-apportioned basis from start of trading to the end of the tax year. Thus, from 1 May 2020 to 31 October 2020 = £44,800.

However, 31 October 2020 is not the end of the tax year, so we must time-apportion profits arising in the year ended 31 October 2021 to the period from 1 November 2020 to 5 April 2021:

= 5/12 × £54,400 = £22,667

Taxable profits for tax year 2020/21 = £44,800 + £22,667

= £67,467

2021/22	**Second year**: there is a 12-month accounting date ending in the tax year and so the basis period is 12 months to that accounting date.

Therefore, taxable profits for year are those arising in the 12 months ended 31 October 2021, i.e. £54,400.

There is an overlap period from 1 November 2020 to 5 April 2021, giving rise to overlap profits of £22,667.

2022/23	**Third year**: there was an accounting date falling in the previous tax year, and a 12-month accounting period ending in this tax year.

Therefore, the taxable profits for this tax year are £53,600 (as the basis period is the period of account ending in this tax year, i.e. the one to 31 October 2022).

2023/24	**Fourth year:** the trade did not cease in this year, so the basis period is the year ended 31 October 2023 (as this is the 12-month accounting period ending in this tax year).

Therefore, the taxable profits for the 2023/24 tax year are £46,400.

Question 3.3

(a)

Year of Assessment	Basis
2020/21	**First year**: actual profits arising on time-apportioned basis from start of trading to the end of the tax year, i.e. 1 May 2020 to 5 April 2021:

= 11/12 × £48,000

= £44,000

2021/22	**Second year**: there is a 12-month accounting date ending in the tax year and so the basis period is the 12 months to that accounting date.

Therefore, taxable profits for year are those arising in the 12 months ended 30 April 2021, i.e. £48,000.

continued overleaf

There is an overlap period from 1 May 2020 to 5 April 2021, giving rise to overlap profits of £44,000.

2022/23   **Third year**: there was an accounting date falling in the previous tax year.

Therefore, the taxable profits for this tax year are £60,000 (as the basis period is the period of account ending in this tax year – i.e. the year ended 30 April 2022).

2023/24   **Fourth year**: the trade did not cease in this year, so the basis period is the year ended 30 April 2023.

Therefore, the taxable profits for this tax year are £9,600.

(b) As Jim is a solicitor, this income arises from a profession.

Question 3.4

(a)

2020/21   No taxable profits arise. See letter below for explanation.

2021/22   The £10,000 profit on the job lot is a trading transaction – see below. It is therefore taxable in the 2021/22 year. This is also the year of commencement for her trade. Thus taxable profits are time-apportioned to 5 April 2021, i.e. for the period 1 September 2021 to 5 April 2022:

= 7/12 × £79,400 = £46,317

Taxable total profits in 2021/22:

= £46,317 + £10,000 = £56,317

2022/23   This is the second year and there is a 12-month accounting period ending in the tax year. This is the basis period and taxable profits are therefore £79,400.

There is an overlap period from 1 September 2021 to 5 April 2022, giving rise to overlap profits of £46,317. (Note: the initial profit made in June 2021 is not included in this calculation as it was not included in the accounts prepared for the year ended 31 August 2022.)

Income tax computations for D. Ross

	2021/22	2022/23
	£	£
Trading income	56,317	79,400
Total income	56,317	79,400
Less: personal allowance	(12,570)	(12,570)
Taxable income	43,747	66,830
Tax payable:		
£37,700 @ 20%	7,540	7,540
£6,047 @ 40%	2,419	–
£29,130 @ 40%	–	11,652
Total tax due	9,959	19,192

(b)
Ms Ross
2 Belfast Road
Belfast

1 May 2023
Re: Taxable income from eBay

Dear Donna,
I refer to our meeting last week.

Badges of Trade

In arriving at the above tax liabilities, it has been necessary to consider whether your eBay activities represent taxable income. This will generally only be the case if they arise from "an adventure in the nature of a trade".

The rules for deciding whether or not you were trading are governed by considerations called the "badges of trade" – of which there are six. These are outlined below, along with a brief narrative on how the fact pattern of your eBay activities fits into these badges.

The conclusion is that your eBay activity from 1 September 2021, together with the sale of the job lot of children's clothes in June 2021, is taxable as a trade. However, the initial sales of surplus items from your house are not taxable as trading income (they were probably sold for less than you purchased them) and, therefore, the £5,000 you received in 2020/21 does not represent taxable income.

Badges of Trade	Your Circumstances
Subject matter (if ownership does not give income or personal enjoyment, then sales indicate trading)	As your initial sales were of items bought originally for your enjoyment, this is not indicative of trading. However, later items were not bought for personal use.
Length of ownership (short indicates trading)	Initial sale items had been owned for quite a while until surplus to everyday needs. The 2021 job lot purchase and sale had a very quick turnaround, indicating trading.
Frequency (more over a long period indicates trading)	The initial transactions appear infrequent and opportunistic, not indicative of trading. However, the purchase and sale of the job lot, with subsequent focused trading, suggests trading.
Supplementary work indicates trading	As you didn't have a formal eBay shop until 2021, there is no indication of a concerted effort to obtain customers prior to this. Organised effort to obtain profit began with the job lot.
Circumstances, if opportunistic or unsolicited, refute trading	Until sale of job lot, sales had been opportunistic and, because the items sold were personal in nature, would counteract trading suggestion.
Profit motive	The evidence suggests the activity was merely to realise small amounts of cash until the sale of the job lot, at which case a clear profit motive was present.

In deciding if a trade is being carried on, all rules are evaluated and the whole picture is taken into account. The overriding evidence in your case suggests that no trading took place until the job lot was purchased for onward sale.

Overlap Profits

Due to the way the tax rules operate, profits of £46,317 apportioned to the period from 1 September 2021 to 5 April 2022 will be taxed twice. However, relief will be available for this amount either:

1. when you change your accounting date from 31 August to a date later in the tax year; or
2. when you cease your eBay trade.

I hope the above is helpful; however, please give me a call if you have any queries.

Yours sincerely

Question 3.5

2020/21

There is only one accounting period ending in this tax year and it is a 12-month period. The trade did not cease in the tax year. The basis period for this tax year is, therefore, the 12 months ended 31 May 2020.

  Taxable profits are therefore £72,000.

2021/22

The trade ceased in this tax year. The basis period thus runs from the end of the basis period in the previous tax year to the date of cessation, i.e. from 1 June 2020 to 31 December 2021. Taxable profits are therefore:

	£
£9,600 + £12,000	21,600
Less: overlap relief of £5,000	(5,000)
Taxable profits	16,600

Question 3.6

2020/21	here was an accounting date falling in the previous tax year. Thus, the basis period for this year is the year ended 31 October 2020.
	Therefore taxable profits = £64,000
2021/22	The accounting date in the year is less than 12 months after the end of the previous basis period. The basis period is therefore the 12 months ending on the new accounting date.
	These 12 months are the 11 months ended on 30 September 2021, plus the month of October 2020.
	Therefore taxable profits = £24,000 + (£64,000 × 1/12) = £29,333

The profits for October 2020 have therefore been taxed twice. Thus, additional overlap profits of £5,333 arise, giving total overlap profits carried forward from 2021/22 of £20,333.

Question 3.7

Computation of taxable trading profit for Joseph Murphy y/e 31 December 2021

	£	£
Profit per accounts		9,874
Add:		
Drawings (Note 1)	8,500	
Interest on VAT (Note 2)	1,121	
Interest on PAYE (Note 2)	1,238	
Depreciation (Note 3)	13,793	
Subscriptions (political, football, old folks, sports) (Note 4)	525	
Repairs (£6,480 – £2,335) (Note 5)	4,145	
Bad debts – increase in general provision (Note 6)	2,875	
Legal fees (Note 7)	1,009	33,206
		43,080
Deduct:		
Dividend from URNO Co. (Note 8)	2,813	
National loan interest (Note 8)	2,250	
Deposit interest (Note 8)	170	
Profit on fixed assets (Note 9)	5,063	(10,296)
Trading profit		32,784

Notes:
1. Disallow Mr Murphy's salary of £7,500 and the £1,000 holiday trip – these are drawings.
2. Interest on late payment of tax specifically disallowed.
3. Depreciation on assets not acquired under a finance lease is always added back – capital allowances are given instead.
4. Donations to political parties are never tax deductible.

   In accordance with the tax legislation, in order for donations to be tax deductible as a trading deduction, it must be shown that the donations were provided for the purposes of the business's trade. In practice, these circumstances will be limited. An example could be where a donation is provided to a local football club in return for recognition in an article in the football club's monthly magazine.

   It is possible, therefore, that the £50 to the football club, £150 to the old folks' home and £250 to the sports club could be claimed as a deduction under the above legislation. However, it has been assumed that this is not the case here. Full marks would be awarded for either approach, provided the student explained the basis of their answer. Subscriptions to traders' associations and for trade papers are wholly and exclusively business expenses and are therefore deductible.

   Note: it is possible that even where donations have been disallowed as trading deductions, relief may still be available personally to the individual under the gift aid scheme (provided a gift aid declaration has been made).

5. The £3,000 on the new extension is capital expenditure and is therefore not tax deductible. The general provisions in the repairs account do not conform to IAS 37 and so are also not tax deductible. The only allowable repairs expense is the £2,335 for repairs expenditure during the period. The only amount to be added back is £3,000 (re. the new extension) + £1,145 (the increase in the repairs provision).
6. Only specific impairment provisions for bad debts are allowable for tax purposes.
7. Related to a capital item (freehold) and so disallowed.
8. Taxed as investment income and not trading income, so removed from computation of trading profit.
9. Capital and so disallowed – dealt with under capital allowances regime.

Question 3.8

Computation of taxable trading profit for Ann Reilly y/e 31 December 2021

	£
Net profit before taxation	49,560
Add: disallowed expenses:	
Motor vehicles (Note 1)	2,978
Depreciation – Equipment	2,500
– Motor vehicles	3,000
– Office equipment	900
Construction of garages (capital)	3,150
General bad debt provision	275
Drawings	10,000
Entertainment (Note 2) – Holiday	120
– Tickets	30
– Customer business meals	120
Taxable trading profits	72,633

Notes:	£	£
1. Total expenses for Andy Reilly's car		4,000
Disallow lease element 15% × £4,000	600	
Disallow personal element 60% (£4,000 – £600)	2,040	2,640

Disallowance for sales rep's cars as CO_2 emissions are greater than 110g/km (they are 150g/km) = £2,250 × 15% = £338 to be added back. Therefore, total add back for motor vehicles is £2,640 + £338 = £2,978

2. Staff entertainment is allowable, although PAYE issues may arise if not within prescribed limits. Business entertaining is specifically disallowed.

Explanatory Note
■ Defalcations by Andy would clearly not be tax deductible. However, those by an employee are tax deductible.

Question 3.9

(a) Computation of adjusted trading profits for the 15 months ended 31 December 2021 and the 12 months ended 31 December 2022.

	15 months ended 31/12/2021		12 months ended 31/12/2022	
	£	£	£	£
Net loss per accounts		(4,350)		(7,400)
Add: disallowed expenses:				
Depreciation	3,000		2,400	
General provision for bad debts	2,500			
Entertaining	1,500		700	
Political donations	100			
Charitable donations	50			
Interest on late payment of VAT	250			
Drawings	15,000	22,400	12,000	15,100
		18,050		7,700
General provision bad debts				(500)
Adjusted profit		18,050		7,200

(b) Tony's taxable trading profit for 2021/22:

2021/22 is Tony's second tax year of trading. An accounting period for a period in excess of 12 months ends in the tax year – namely, the 15-month period ending 31 December 2021. Thus, Tony's basis period will be the 12 months ending on 31 December 2021. Taxable trading profits for 2021/22 are, therefore, the time-apportioned profits from the accounting period ending in the tax year, i.e. £18,050 × 12/15 = £14,440.

Question 3.10

Computation of taxable trading profits for John Smith for the 12 months ended 30 April 2021

	Notes	£	£
Profit per accounts			2,820
Add:			
Drawings (wages to self)		5,200	
Own NICs		200	
Depreciation		1,250	
Motor expenses	1	924	
Leasing charges	2	1,372	
Extension	3	1,500	
Provision for repairs	4	1,000	

continued overleaf

Interest on late payment of tax	5	120	
Donation to church	6	970	
Life assurance	7	460	12,996
Less: interest received			(390)
Adjusted trading profits			15,426

Notes:

	Add back	
	£	£
1. Motor expenses	1,860	
Less: parking fine	(100)	100
	1,760	
Add: car insurance	300	
	2,060	
Less: private element 40%	(824)	824
	1,236	
		924
2. Lease charges on car	2,800	
Less: 15% disallowance	(420)	420
	2,380	
Less: private element 40%	(952)	952
	1,428	1,372
	(allowable)	(add back)

3. Extension to store is capital expenditure and, therefore, not tax deductible
4. General provisions do not conform to IAS 37, so add back. Note, if painting the premises was required to make them suitable for trading, may also be disallowed. However, no further details are given in the question, so it is reasonable to assume that this cost is tax deductible, as normal painting costs are a repair and thus tax deductible.
5. Personal liability and so not allowed.
6. This charitable donation is not deductible against trading profits, but John should obtain tax relief for it personally if made under the gift aid scheme.
7. On the basis that these are for John personally, they are not tax deductible. If they were for an employee, then it is possible that they may be deductible.

Explanatory Notes
- An accrued bonus that is not paid within nine months of the accounting period end must be disallowed. The accrued bonus paid on 1 July 2021 was paid within this timeframe, therefore no adjustment is required.
- Sometimes the practice is to disallow key person insurance contributions on agreement with HMRC that the associated income, if received, would not be taxable. If a deduction is taken for the premiums, then the income paid out under the policy would be taxable.

Question 3.11

Computation of tax-adjusted profit for Polly Styrene for the year ended 31 December 2021

	£	£
Profit per accounts		2,500
Add back:		
Wages to self	8,000	
Light, heat and telephone (5/6 × 1,500) (Note 1)	1,250	
Repairs and renewals (Note 2)	3,400	
Legal and professional fees (Note 3)	300	
Bad debts (Note 4)	(600)	
Travel and entertainment (Note 5)	1,100	
Depreciation (Note 6)	5,000	
Sundries (Note 7)	1,549	19,999
Taxable trading profits 2021/22		22,499

Notes:
1. Non-business element disallowed.
2. Extension (capital) and general provision (not conforming to IAS 37) disallowed.
3. Surveyor's fees disallowed – related to capital purchase.
4. General provision decreases are not taxable.
5. Private use re. car expenses disallowed – £500 – as are customer entertaining costs of £600.
6. A trading deduction is available for interest payments on finance lease assets. However, they do not qualify for capital allowances; rather, a tax deduction is available for the accounting depreciation charge on finance lease assets (but not on operating lease assets). Thus the depreciation restriction is £20,000 – £15,000 = £5,000.
7. Political party subscription disallowed, parking fines disallowed (would be allowed if incurred by employees while performing their duties – not made clear here, so disallowed), charitable donation not allowed as trading expense, but Polly should obtain tax relief personally if it were made under gift aid.

Explanatory Note
- Trade-related royalties are tax deductible on a gross basis, therefore no adjustment is required when computing taxable trading profits.

Question 3.12

Distribution of profits

	Total	Partner A	Partner B	Partner C
	£	£	£	£
Year ended 30/09/2017	20,000	10,000	10,000	Nil
Year ended 30/09/2018	25,000	10,000	10,000	5,000

continued overleaf

Year ended 30/09/2019	30,000	12,000	12,000	6,000
Year ended 30/09/2020	30,000	Nil	15,000	15,000
Year ended 30/09/2021	35,000	Nil	17,500	17,500

Once the profits of a partnership have been allocated to each partner, then each partner is treated for tax purposes as a sole trader and the income is taxed using the basis period rules in exactly the same way. For instance, the year you become a partner, the commencement rules apply. The year you cease to be a partner, the cessation rules apply (unless you are the only partner left and are continuing the trade as a sole trader). Overlap profits are calculated and relieved by reference to each partner's individual circumstances, as if they were a sole trader.

Taxable profits for A, B and C are as follows:

Partner A A's basis period for 2017/18 is the year ended 30 September 2017 and so taxable profits for that year are £10,000.

A's basis period for 2018/19 is the year ended 30 September 2018 and so taxable profits for that year are £10,000.

A ceases to be a partner in 2019/20. A's basis period is from 1 October 2019 (end of previous basis period) to the date A ceased to be a partner, i.e. 30 September 2019.

A's taxable profits for 2019/20 are, therefore, £12,000 (less any available overlap relief).

Partner B B has never left the partnership, so B's basis period for each of the 2017/18 to 2021/22 tax years is the normal accounting period. Therefore, B's taxable profits are:

2017/18	£10,000
2018/19	£10,000
2019/20	£12,000
2020/21	£15,000
2022/23	£17,500

Partner C C commenced to trade on 1 October 2017. C's taxable profits are calculated as follows:

2017/18 **First year**: basis period is from date of commencement to end of the tax year. Therefore, taxable profits are actual profits arising on time-apportioned basis for the period, i.e. 1 October 2017 to 5 April 2018:

$$= 6/12 \times £5,000$$
$$= £2,500$$

2018/19 **Second year**: there is a 12-month accounting date ending in the tax year and so the basis period is 12 months to that accounting date. Therefore, taxable profits for the year are those arising in the 12 months ended 30 September 2017 = £5,000

There is an overlap period of 1 October 2017 to 5 April 2018, giving rise to overlap profits of £2,500.

2019/20 **Third year**: there was an accounting date falling in the previous tax year, and the accounting date in this year is 12 months from end of previous basis period.

Thus the taxable profits for this tax year = £6,000.

C's basis period for each of the 2020/21 and 2021/22 tax years is the normal accounting period. Thus C's taxable profits are:

2020/21	£15,000
2021/22	£17,500

Question 3.13

	£	£
Net profit y/e 30/04/2021		46,000
Disallowed expenses	26,000	
Partners' salaries	41,000	
Partners' interest	13,000	80,000
Assessable profit		126,000

	Total	**Jack**	**John**
	£	£	£
Salaries	41,000	20,000	21,000
Interest	13,000	6,000	7,000
Balance (50:50 share)	72,000	36,000	36,000
Total	126,000	62,000	64,000
Taxable trading profits for 2021/22		62,000	64,000

Chapter 4

Question 4.1

	AIA	**Main Pool**	**Allowances Claimed**
	£	£	£
TWDV b/fwd at 06/04/2021		20,000	
Additions (Note 1)		11,500	
Disposals		–	
		31,500	
Additions qualifying for AIA (Note 2)	12,100		
Allowances 100%	(12,100)		12,100

continued overleaf

Remaining TWDV to main pool	–	–	
Allowances @18%		(5,670)	5,670
TWDV c/fwd at 05/04/2022		25,830	
Total capital allowances claim			17,770

Notes:

1. Cars with CO_2 emissions of 50g/km or less with no private use are treated as additions to the main pool, with WDA at 18%.
2. The maximum AIA for the year ended 6 April 2022 is £800,000 ((9/12 × £1,000,000) + (3/12 × £200,000)).

Explanatory Note

■ Capital allowances are available on the filing cabinets as they were paid for before the year-end – even though they were not delivered until after the year-end. On the other hand, if they had been delivered before the year-end and not paid for until more than four months after the year-end, then the cost would only have qualified for capital allowances in the accounting period in which the bill was paid.

Question 4.2

	Special Rate Pool	AIA/FYA Pool	Main Pool	Allowances Claimed
		£	£	£
TWDV b/fwd at 1 September 2020			100,000	
Additions	40,000		10,000	
Disposals			–	
			110,000	
Allowances @ 6%	(2,400)			2,400
Additions qualifying for AIA		13,900		
AIA		(13,900)		13,900
Remaining TWDV to main pool		0	0	
Allowances @ 18%			(19,800)	19,800
TWDV c/fwd at 31 August 2021	37,600		90,200	
Total capital allowances claim				36,100

Notes:

1. AIAs or FYAs are not available on cars. Cars with CO_2 emissions more than 50g/km go to the special rate pool, with WDA for year ended 31 August 2021 of 6%.
2. The maximum potential AIA for the year ended 31 August 2021 is £1,000,000.

Question 4.3

	AIA/FYA	Main Pool 18%	Allowances Claimed
	£	£	£
TWDV b/fwd at 1 September 2020		120,000	
Additions qualifying for AIA	155,000		
Other additions (no AIA) – car		20,000	
Disposals		–	
		140,000	
AIA	(155,000)		155,000
T/F to main pool/special rate pool	Nil	0	
		140,000	
WDA @ 18%		(25,200)	25,200
TWDV c/fwd at 31 August 2021		114,800	
Total capital allowances claim			180,200

Explanatory Notes

- While the printing press (£110,000) is a special rate pool item, being a long-life asset > 25 years, it would normally qualify for WDA at 6% per annum. However, it and the van (£15,000) and the miscellaneous plant and machinery (£30,000) all fall within the limits available on which AIA can be claimed.
- The maximum AIA for the year ended 31 August 2021 is £1,000,000.
- Vans qualify for AIA and do not have to be kept in a separate pool, unlike expensive cars.
- Cars do not qualify for AIA.

Question 4.4

	AIA/FYA	Main Pool 18%	Allowances Claimed
	£	£	£
TWDV b/fwd at 6 April 2021		20,000	
Additions		–	
Disposals (Note 1)		(15,000)	
		5,000	
Additions qualifying for AIA	10,000		
AIA (max. £800,000) (Note 2)	(10,000)		10,000
Excess to main pool (Note 3)	0	0	
Allowances @ 18%		(900)	900
TWDV c/fwd at 5 April 2022		4,100	
Total capital allowances claim			10,900

Notes:

1. Profit on disposal of the fixed assets will be disallowed in calculating the taxable trading profits for the period. However, the proceeds received on assets that have previously qualified for capital allowances must be included in the main pool. As the NBV was £10,000 and the profit £5,000, proceeds received are £15,000, and are deducted from the TWDV b/fwd before calculating the allowances due.
2. Maximum AIA: $(9/12 \times £1,000,000) + (3/12 \times £200,000) = £800,000$.
3. No excess as additions are less than the available AIA of £1,000,000.

Question 4.5

	Single Asset Pool – Car	Private Use Adjustment (25%)	Allowances Claimed
	£	£	£
2019/20			
TWDV b/fwd at 1 January 2019	–		
Additions	26,000		
Disposals	–		
Allowances @ 6.5% ((3/12 × 8%) + (9/12 × 6%))	(1,690)	423	1,267
TWDV c/fwd at 31 December 2019	24,310		
2020/21			
TWDV b/fwd at 1 January 2020	24,310		
Additions	–		
Disposals	–		
Allowances @ 6%	(1,459)	365	1,094
TWDV c/fwd at 31 December 2020	22,851		
2021/22			
TWDV b/fwd at 1 January 2021	22,851		
Additions	–		
Disposals	–		
Allowances @ 6%	(1,371)	343	1,028
TWDV c/fwd at 31 December 2021	21,480		

Question 4.6

	Single Asset Pool – Car	Private Use Adjustment (1/3rd)	Allowances Claimed
	£	£	£
2019/20			
TWDV b/fwd at 6 April 2019	–		
Additions 2019/20	13,000		
Disposals	–		
Allowances @ 6.5% (3/12 × 8% + 9/12 × 6%)	(845)	282	563
TWDV c/fwd at 5 April 2020	12,155		
2020/21			
TWDV b/fwd at 6 April 2020	12,155		
Additions	–		
Disposals	–		
Allowances @ 6%	(729)	243	486
TWDV c/fwd at 5 April 2021	11,426		
2021/22			
TWDV b/fwd at 6 April 2021	11,426		
Additions	–		
Disposals	–		
Allowances @ 6% (Note 1)	(686)	229	457
TWDV c/fwd at 5 April 2022	10,740		

Notes:

1. Car acquired on 10 November 2019 and its CO_2 emissions exceed 50g/km. The car is a special rate pool asset with a WDA of 8% (reduced to 6% from 6 April 2021). As a result of the private use, a single asset pool must be created.
2. The tax-deductible allowances in 2019/20 (and each of the years) are only two-thirds, as only two-thirds of the use of the car relates to business use. However, the TWDV carried forward is reduced by the full annual allowance each year.

Question 4.7

	AIA	Main Pool (18%)	Allowances Claimed
Period ended 30 September 2021	£	£	£
TWDV b/fwd at 1 January 2021		–	
Additions (Note 1)		11,000	
Disposals		–	
		11,000	
Additions qualifying for AIA (Note 3)	22,400		
AIA £1,000,000 × 9/12 = £750,000	(22,400)		22,400
Transfer to main pool	0	0	
Allowances @ 18% × 9/12 (Note 2)		(1,485)	1,485
TWDV c/fwd at 30 September 2021		9,515	
Total claim			23,885
Year ended 30 September 2022			
TWDV b/fwd at 1 October 2021		9,515	
Additions		–	
Disposals		–	
		9,515	
Additions qualifying for AIA	3,500		
AIA (max. £400,000, i.e. (3/12 × £1,000,000) + (9/12 × £200,000))	(3,500)		3,500
Transfer to main pool	0	0	
Allowances @ 18%		(1,713)	1,713
TWDV c/fwd at 30 September 2022		7,802	
Total claim			5,213

Notes:

1. The car has CO_2 emissions of 50g/km or less and no private use is indicated, so it is added to the main pool. Cars do not qualify for AIA.
2. Accounting period is only nine months long. Therefore, the AIA and main pool allowances are restricted to nine months' worth.
3. Additions qualifying for AIA are less than the AIA available and so no excess to transfer to the main pool.

Question 4.8

	Main Pool	Claim
	£	£
TWDV b/fwd	10,000	
Additions	–	
Disposals	(35,000)	
Balancing charge	(25,000)	(25,000)

No capital allowances are available in the period. Rather, taxable profits will be increased by the £25,000 balancing charge that arises when the assets are sold. This is taxable income.

The £35,000 proceeds are calculated as follows:

NBV of assets sold £10,000. Profit on sale £30,000. Thus proceeds are £40,000. However, the proceeds that go to the main pool on sale of an asset are **limited** to the cost of that asset – which was £35,000.

If plant was sold for £3,000 in the 2022/23 period, and no plant was purchased, the TWDV brought forward on the main pool would be £Nil, but proceeds of £3,000 would have been received. As such, a balancing charge of £3,000 would arise in 2022/23.

Question 4.9

	AIA	Main Pool (18%)	Special Rate Pool (6%)	Allowances Claimed
	£	£	£	£
Additions (Note 1)		11,000		
Disposals		–		
Additions qualifying for AIA	232,000			
AIA	(232,000)			232,000
Transfer to special rate pool	0		0	
	–	11,000		
Allowances @ 18%		(1,980)		1,980
Allowances @ 6%				
TWDV c/fwd at 31 December 2022		9,020	0	
Total capital allowances claim				233,980

Note:

1. Car has CO_2 emissions of 50g/km or less and no private use indicated, so an addition to main pool WDA @ 18% (cars do not qualify for AIA).

Explanatory Notes

- Included are long-life asset (£200,000), van (£14,000), partition walls (£5,000), toilets (£4,000), desk (£1,000) and portable toilets (£8,000). Partition walls are qualifying plant and machinery if they serve a purpose of being moved to change the available space to reflect changing staff numbers or working patterns. Doors may be allowed if they serve a particular function, but none is specified here so they should be disallowed. The portacabin provided the setting for the business rather than serving a function for the business and so is not qualifying plant and machinery. When answering a question you should state your reasons for determining whether an asset is qualifying plant if there is any doubt.

- The maximum AIA is £1,000,000.

Question 4.10

(a) Joe Bloggs's taxable trading income for 2021/22 is £11,223 – £6,256 = £4,967.

(b) Capital allowances claim for 2021/22 is £6,256.

Taxable trading profit for the year ended 31 March 2022

	£	£
Loss per accounts to 31 March 2022		(310)
Add back:		
Wages to self	5,200	
Motor expenses 1/4 × £1,750	438	
Light and heat 1/4 × £1,200	300	
Christmas gifts	300	
Depreciation	900	
Charitable donation (Note 1)	105	
Cash register	380	
Shelving	2,920	
Display freezer	600	
Flat contents insurance	100	
Notional rent	2,000	13,243
		12,933
Deduct:		
Building society interest received	210	
Sale proceeds of equipment	1,500	(1,710)
Adjusted profits		11,223

Note:

1. Not a trading expense unless some form of trading benefit is obtained as a result of making it (not specified), but Joe will obtain tax relief through his personal tax computation if paid under gift aid.

Capital allowances computation 2021/22

	AIA	Main Pool	Single Asset Pool – Car	Private Use Adjustment (25%)	Claim
	£	£	£	£	£
TWDV b/fwd at 1 April 2021 (Note 1)		12,750	7,347		
Additions					
Disposals (Note 2)		(1,500)	–		
		11,250			
Addition qualifying for AIA (Note 3)	3,900				
AIA	(3,900)	–			3,900
Transfer to pool	0	0			
Allowances @ 18%		(2,025)	(1,322)	331	3,016
TWDV c/fwd at 31 March 2022		9,225	6,025		
Total claim					6,916

Notes:

1. Capital allowances to date on car:

Purchased 2020/21	£8,960
WDA 2020/21 = £8,960 × 18%	£1,613
TWDV b/f 2021/22 = £8,960 – £1,613	£7,347
WDA 2021/22 = £7,347 × 18%	£1,322
TWDV b/f 2022/23 = £7,347 – £1,322	£6,025

2. Sale proceeds of old equipment; assume proceeds are less than cost.
3. Cash register (£380), shelving (£2,920), display freezer (£600) = £3,900.

Question 4.11

	£
Trading profits	–
Employment income	80,000
Total income	80,000
Less: current year loss relief against total income	(50,000)
Net income	30,000
Less: personal allowance	(12,570)
Taxable income	17,430

Question 4.12

	£
Trading profits	–
Investment income	25,000
Employment income	50,000
Total income	75,000
Less: current year loss relief against total income	(30,000)
Net income	45,000
Less: personal allowance	(12,570)
Taxable income	32,430

When calculating the tax due, the loss can be set-off by the taxpayer in the most advantageous way possible, i.e. against income taxed at the highest rate.

Question 4.13

	£
Profit	20,000
Less: capital allowances	(37,000)
	(17,000)
Add: balancing charge	10,000
Loss for 2021/22	(7,000)

This loss can be relieved in the same manner as other current year losses.

Question 4.14

(a) John's net income for 2019/20, 2020/21 and 2021/22

	2019/20	2020/21	2021/22
	£	£	£
UK property business	20,000	30,000	25,000
Investment income	1,000	1,200	1,200
Trading income	30,000	0	45,000
	51,000	31,200	71,200
Loss relief	(51,000)	(31,200)	(45,000)
Taxable income	0	0	26,200

(b) *Loss Memorandum*

	£
Loss arising 2020/21	187,000
Set against other income 2020/21 section 64 ITA 2007	(31,200)
	155,800
Carry back 2019/20 section 64 ITA 2007	(51,000)
	104,800
Carry forward 2021/22 section 83 ITA 2007	(45,000)
Loss to carry forward	59,800

The losses carried forward can only be set against income of the same trade, so taxable income arises in 2021/22 even though there are still unused trading losses from 2020/21. These unused losses shall be carried forward to set against future profits from the **same** trade.

Question 4.15

	2019/20	2020/21	2021/22
	£	£	£
Trading income	Nil	7,000	30,000
Less: loss relief		(7,000)	(1,000)
Taxable income	Nil	Nil	29,000

Jim is obliged to take relief for the loss forward in the first year in which trading profits from the same trade are available. This occurs in 2020/21 and results in a waste of his personal allowances for that year. Jim would have preferred to defer relief for some of the loss until 2021/22 to avoid wasting his 2020/21 allowances. Unfortunately, this is not permitted.

Question 4.16

	2019/20	2020/21	2021/22
	£	£	£
UK property business	20,000	30,000	25,000
Investment income	1,000	1,200	1,200
Trading profits	80,000	–	45,000
	101,000	31,200	71,200
Less: loss relief	(37,000)	–	–
Taxable income	64,000	31,200	71,200

It is best to carry back the losses as this gives tax relief as soon as possible, and against income taxed at 40%. It also avoids wasting the personal allowance in 2020/21.

Chapter 5

Question 5.1

Income tax computation for Dermot O'Donnell for tax year 2021/22

	£
Salary (Super McBurgers) (Note 1)	37,000
Salary (Burger Palace) (Note 2)	18,200
Total income	55,200
Less: personal allowance	(12,570)
Taxable income	42,630
Tax payable:	
£37,700 @ 20%	7,540
£4,930 @ 40%	1,972
Total tax liability	9,512
Less: tax deducted at source	
PAYE (Burger Palace)	(2,900)
PAYE (Super McBurgers)	(9,500)
Tax refund for 2021/22	(2,888)

Notes:

1. The provision of a work mobile phone is a tax-free BIK – even if the company pays for all the personal calls that are made by the employee.
2. The £4,000 payment to join Burger Palace is taxable as an inducement payment. Therefore, his total salary from Burger Palace is £14,200 + £4,000 = £18,200.

Question 5.2

Calculation of taxable benefits in kind – Sid Harvey

1. Round sum allowance of £100 a month – taxable income as there are no receipts to support the expenditure. If Sid were able to show receipts for genuine expenses, it would be possible to claim a deduction for these expenses in his tax return.
    Taxable BIK: £1,200
2. Company car – the starting point is the list price of the car when new. This will not always be the amount that was paid for the car by Sid's employer.
    The list price is £36,000/0.9 = £40,000 (before discount). It was first registered before 6 April 2020.
    The relevant % = 30% (125 – 55 = 70; 70/5 = 14; 16% + 14% = 30%)
    Basic charge is therefore £40,000 × 30% = £12,000
    However, a deduction is also available for employee contributions – £1,200 in this case.
    Taxable BIK: £10,800
3. Company car: fuel – no BIK arises as the full cost, including private use, is reimbursed to the company. (NB: HMRC has stated that it is almost impossible to confirm that all private fuel has been reimbursed, so very good records would need to be maintained to provide as evidence; otherwise HMRC may impose a fuel BIK.)
4. Household expenses – all treated as a BIK as these are private living costs.
    Taxable BIK: £890
    Apartment – normally it is the cost of providing the accommodation that is used to calculate the BIK that arises. However, as the company has owned the property for more than six years at the date it was first made available to Sid, the market value of the property when it was first made available to Sid is used instead of the cost of providing the accommodation when calculating the BIK.

Annual rateable value	£600
Additional taxable rent (£80,000 – £75,000) × 2%	£100

    Taxable BIK: £700
5. Staff canteen – available to all staff, therefore no BIK arises.
6. Preferential loan – a taxable benefit will arise on the waiver of an employee loan. It does not have to be a beneficial loan or amount to £10,000 to be a BIK here.
    Taxable BIK: £1,000
    Total BIK: £14,590

Income tax computation for Sid for tax year 2021/22

	£
Salary	40,500
BIK	14,590
Total income	55,090
Less: personal allowance	(12,570)
Taxable income	42,520

continued overleaf

Tax payable:

£37,700 @ 20%	£7,540	
£4,820 @ 40%	£1,928	
Total tax liability		9,468
Less: tax deducted at source (PAYE)		(13,900)
Tax refund due for 2021/22		(4,432)

Question 5.3

(a) Calculation of benefits in kind

1. Company car: the starting point is the list price of the car when new. This will not always be the amount that was paid for the car by the employer.
    The list price is £30,000. CO_2 emissions are 127g/km. This is rounded down to 125g/km.
    $125 – 55 = 70$, $70/5 = 14$; $16\% + 14\% = 30\%$.
    As the car is a diesel car, an additional 4% is added to the 34%.
    Basic charge is, therefore, £30,000 × 34% = £10,200.
2. The BIK on the fuel is £24,600 × 34% = £8,364; total benefit on car and fuel is £18,564.
3. BIK on golf club membership is £3,500.
4. Loan interest BIK:

	£
£125,000 × (2% – 2%) – no beneficial rate	0
£4,000 × 2% to give taxable benefit on golf club loan	80
Total BIK on loans	80
Total BIK £22,144	

(b)

Income tax computation for Terry for tax year 2021/22

	Old	New
	£	£
Salary	75,500	70,500
BIK	0	22,433
Total income	75,500	92,933
Less: personal allowance	(12,570)	(12,570)
Taxable income	62,930	80,363

continued overleaf

Tax payable:

£37,700 @ 20%	7,540	7,540
Remainder @ 40%	10,092	17,065
Total tax liability	17,632	24,605
Net pay	57,886	45,895
Less costs: mortgage interest	(6,875)	(2,500)
Car	(10,500)	
Net cash in hand (new job leaves him better off)	40,493	43,395

Question 5.4

(a)

Income tax computation for Philip Stodge for tax year 2021/22

	£
Salary (Note 1)	50,100
BIK (Notes 2 and 3)	0
Total income	50,100
Less: deductions (Notes 4 and 5)	(5,360)
Less: personal allowance	(12,570)
Taxable income	32,170

Tax payable:

£32,170 @ 20%	6,434
Total tax liability	6,434
Less: tax deducted at source: PAYE	(7,900)
Tax refund due for 2021/22	(1,466)

Notes:

1. Despite the fact that the sales commission is paid directly to his wife, it is taxable on Philip as it is earned by him. The employer's pension contributions are a tax-free benefit, so salary taxable is £43,600 + £6,500 = £50,100.
2. No taxable BIK arises from provision of a parking space at or near work for you by your employer, even if they have to pay for it.
3. Employers can pay up to £5 a night to employees to cover incidental costs arising when they are away from home without a taxable income arising.
4. If an employer does not reimburse an employee business mileage, the employee can claim a deduction of £0.45 per mile in their tax return for up to 10,000 business miles, and the remainder at £0.25 a mile. If the employer pays the employee less than these rates, the employee can claim the difference in their tax return. If the employee is paid more than these rates, the excess is taxable. Philip can, therefore, claim £0.45 × 10,000 = £4,500.

5. The cost of the suit is never allowed as a deduction from employment income. However, professional subscriptions and genuine expenses "wholly exclusively and necessarily incurred in the course of your work" can be claimed – thus phone, train and course are allowable. Deduction claimed = £4,500 + £400 + £180 + £150 + £130 = £5,360.

(b) You should advise your manager of the disposal by your client so that your manager can liaise with the client to establish whether there was some explanation for the omission. In line with the Chartered Accountants Ireland's *Code of Ethics*, a fundamental principle a Chartered Accountant should follow is professional competence and due care. The client should be advised of the need to return details of the additional income to HMRC and pay the tax due (if any). The likely penalties and interest that HMRC will charge if they discover the omission should be made clear to Philip.

Question 5.5

Income tax computation for Frank for tax year 2021/22

	£
Salary	49,000
Car BIK (Note 1)	42,550
Fuel BIK (Note 2)	9,102
Total income	100,652
Less: deductions (Note 3)	(800)
	99,852
Less: personal allowance	(12,570)
Taxable income	87,282
Tax payable:	
£37,700 @ 20%	7,540
£49,852 @ 40%	19,833
Total tax liability	27,373

Notes:
1. The list price is £120,000.
    However, a deduction is available for any capital contributions made by the employee. The available tax deduction is capped at £5,000.
    The cost of the car is therefore £115,000 (£120,000 less capital contribution £5,000 restricted). The relevant % = 37%.
    The car benefit is therefore £115,000 × 37% = £42,550.
2. Fuel benefit = £24,600 × 37% = £9,102.
3. Professional subscriptions are generally allowable as a deduction against employment income, provided the organisation to which they are made appears on the approved HMRC list (available on HMRC's website).

Chapter 6

Question 6.1

Income tax computation 2021/22

	Non-savings income	Savings income	Total
	£	£	£
Rental income	15,620		15,620
Building society interest		11,760	11,760
Total income			27,380
Less: personal allowance	(12,570)		(12,570)
Taxable income	3,050	11,760	14,810

Income tax due:					
Non-savings income					
Basic rate	£3,050	@	20%		610
Savings income					
Starting rate (£5,000 – £3,050)	£1,950	@	0%		0
PSA	£1,000	@	0%		0
Basic rate	£8,810	@	20%		1,762
	£14,810				
Tax payable					2,372

Question 6.2

Income tax computation 2021/22

	Non-savings income	Dividend income	Total
	£	£	£
Business profits	30,630		30,630
Property income	750		750
Dividends		115,100	115,100
Total income			146,480
Less: personal allowance	0		0
Taxable income	31,380	115,100	146,480

continued overleaf

Income tax due:

Non-savings income

Basic rate	£31,380	@	20%	6,276

Dividend income

Dividend allowance	£2,000	@	0%	0
Basic rate	£4,320	@	7.5%	324
Higher rate	<u>£108,780</u>	@	32.5%	35,354
	<u>£146,480</u>			
Tax payable				<u>41,954</u>

Personal allowance not available due to size of adjusted net income.

Question 6.3

Income tax computation 2021/22

	Non-savings income £	Savings income £	Dividend income £	Total £
Trading income	10,350			10,350
Debenture interest		6,200		6,200
ISA interest (exempt)		0		0
Dividends			14,000	14,000
Total income				30,550
Less: personal allowance	(10,350)	(2,220)		(12,570)
Taxable income	0	3,980	14,000	17,980

Income tax due:

Non-savings income

Basic rate	£0	@	20%	0

Savings income

PSA	£1,000	@	0%	0
Basic rate	<u>£2,980</u>	@	20%	596
	<u>£3,980</u>			

Dividend income

Dividend allowance	£2,000	@	0%	0
Basic rate	£12,000	@	7.5%	<u>900</u>
Tax payable				<u>1,496</u>

Question 6.4

Income tax computation for Maeve for tax year 2021/22

	Non-savings income £	Savings income £	Dividend income £	Total £
NSB interest		6,800		6,800
Credit union		1,550		1,550
Pension	7,800			7,800
Dividend income			21,244	21,244
Total income	7,800	8,350	21,244	37,394
Less: personal allowance	(7,800)	(4,770)		(12,570)
Taxable income	0	3,580	21,244	24,824

Tax payable:
Non-savings income:
£0 @ 20%   0
Savings income:
£1,000 @ 0% (personal savings allowance)   0
£2,580 @ 20%   516
Dividend income:
£2,000 @ 0% (dividend allowance)   0
£19,244 @ 7.5%   1,443
Total   1,959

Remember: ISA interest is tax-free.

Question 6.5

Income tax computations for David Lee for tax year 2021/22

	Non-savings Income £	Savings Income £	Total £
Bank interest		625	625
Salary	42,500		42,500
Government loan interest		1,130	1,130
Building society interest		175	175
Total income	42,500	1,930	44,430

continued overleaf

Less: personal allowance	(12,570)	————	(12,570)
Taxable income	29,930	1,930	31,860

£

Tax payable:

Non-savings income:

£29,930 @ 20%	5,986

Savings income:

£1,000 @ 0% (personal savings allowance)	0
£930 @ 20%	186
Total	6,172
Less: tax deducted at source:	
PAYE (Note 1)	(4,900)
Tax due for 2021/22	1,272

Note:
1. NICs are not deductible expenses for income tax purposes.

Explanatory Notes

■ Lottery winnings, interest from National Savings certificates and premium bond payouts are specifically exempt from tax under section 692 ITTOIA 2005.
Note: National Savings certificates are different from National Savings accounts, interest on which is taxable.

■ A gift from a neighbour for a one-off job will not be subject to income tax. If David had done the shopping every week for a set amount, that income would then be taxable.

Chapter 7

Question 7.1

As rental receipts do not exceed £150,000, the cash basis of accounting will apply (not the accruals basis).

	Properties			
	A	**B**	**C**	**D**
	£	£	£	£
Rent receivable (Note 1)	6,000	9,000	4,250	52
Premium on lease	–	6,000	–	–
	6,000	15,000	4,250	52
Less: allowable expenses (Note 2)				
Bank interest	–	(7,200)	–	–
Storm damage	–	(1,400)	–	–

continued overleaf

Advertising	–	–	(130)	–
Roof repairs	–	–	–	(1,600)
Blocked drains and painting	–	–	(790)	–
Net rent (Note 3)	6,000	6,400	3,330	(1,548)

Summary	**£**
Property A	6,000
Property B	6,400
Property C	3,330
Property D	0
UK property business	15,730

Notes:

1. Property B
   Let from 1 August 2021, i.e. 9 months @ £1,000 p.m. = £9,000
   Assessable portion of premium:
   $$£10,000 - (£10,000 \times (21 - 1)/50) = £6,000$$

Property C	£	
£6,000 × 1/12	500	(one month to 30/04/2020)
£9,000 × 5/12	3,750	(five months to March 2021)
	4,250	

2. Allowable Expenses

   Property A
   As this is a residential letting, none of the mortgage interest on the loan to acquire/renovate the property (i.e. its finance costs) is deductible from rental income. A basic rate tax reduction may be available in respect of the finance costs when calculating the income tax liability for the year.

   Property B
   Expenses incurred to get the property into a fit state for letting prior to a first letting are not allowable (i.e. dry rot and windows). There is an argument for these repair costs being either deductible or non-deductible and the available marks would be given for student rationale in assessing the information. Repairs would not be deductible if they were required for the house to be fit for letting; however, if the house was in a fit state and available for letting and the repairs were undertaken when the house was vacant, then a tax deduction should be available for the repairs (*Odeon Associated Theatres Ltd v. Jones* (see **Section 3.3.5**)).
   As a property business is already in place, the bank interest cost of £7,200 p.a. is fully deductible.

   Property C
   Although the property was vacant when the expenditure was incurred, this was only a temporary cessation and the expenditure is allowed in full.

3. Relief for losses on Property D

In general, losses on one UK property may be offset against the net rental profits arising on other UK properties. However, the loss arising on property D is ignored for tax purposes as it arises on a non-commercial rent charged to a connected party (favoured lease).

Question 7.2

As rental receipts exceed £150,000, the accruals basis of accounting will apply (not the cash basis).
UK property business income assessable 2021/22

	Prop. 1	Prop. 2	Prop. 3	Prop. 4	Prop. 5	Total
	£	£	£	£	£	£
Gross rents (Note 1)	160,000	8,000	8,800	6,750	120	
Expenses	(4,300)	(1,200)	(800)	–	(10)	
Interest	–	–	(1,400)	–	–	
Net rents (Note 2)	155,700	6,800	6,600	6,750	110	175,960

Notes:

1. The taxable rent for the year is £6,750 (£2,250 × 3 payments on 30 September 2020, 31 December 2020 and 31 March 2021).
2. The profits on Property 5 are taxable, even though it is rented to a connected party. However, if a loss was incurred as a result of higher expenses (say, £150 of expenses would lead to a £30 loss), the loss would not be allowed as it is a favoured letting (compare with the solution to **Question 7.1**. See Note 3 to the solution specifically).

Question 7.3

As rental receipts do not exceed £150,000, the cash basis of accounting will apply (not the accruals basis). Josephine's property income and income tax liability for 2021/22 is:

	£
Property income calculation	
Rental income	14,375
Finance costs	–
Other allowable expenses	(7,000)
Property income profits	7,375
Income tax computation	
Trading income	40,000
Property income	7,375
Total/net income	47,375
Less: personal allowance	(12,570)
Taxable income	34,805

continued overleaf

Income tax

£34,805 @ 20%	6,961
Less: 20% tax reduction (Note)	(1,475)
Income tax liability	5,486

Note:

Tax reduction is calculated as 20% of the lower of:

(a) finance costs not deducted = £22,500

(b) property profits = £7,375

(c) adjusted total income (exceeding Personal Allowance) = £34,805

The lowest amount is calculated at (b), therefore £1,475 (£7,375 × 20%) is the tax reduction. The £15,125 finance costs (£22,500 – £7,375) that have not been used to calculate Jospehine's basic rate tax reduction are carried forward to calculate her basic rate tax reduction in the following year.

Chapter 8

Question 8.1

Income tax computation for John for income tax year 2021/22:

	£
Total income	20,500
Less: personal allowance	(12,570)
Taxable income	7,930
Tax payable:	
£7,930 @ 20%	1,586
Less:	
Marriage allowance – full £1,260 @ 20%	(252)
Tax due for 2021/22	1,334

Question 8.2

Mr Smith is entitled to a personal allowance of £12,570. He is not entitled to any marriage allowance as his spouse's income is in excess of the £12,570 personal allowance.

Income tax computation for Mr Smith for income tax year 2021/22:

	£
Total income	34,400
Less: personal allowance	(12,570)
Taxable income	21,830
Tax payable:	
£21,830 @ 20%	4,366

Question 8.3

Income tax computation for Joe for income tax year 2021/22:

	£
Employment income	51,975
Less: relief for deductions	(1,000)
Net income	50,975
Less: personal allowance	(12,570)
Taxable income	38,405
Tax payable:	
£38,405 @ 20%	7,681
Total tax liability	7,681

Note:

1. The gift aid payment operates to increase the basic rate band by £780/0.80 = £975. Note, the charity can reclaim the £195 direct from HMRC. All of Joe's income will be taxed at 20% because of the extension to the basic rate band available as a result of the gift aid donation. Basic rate band of £37,700 is extended by £975 to £38,675.

Question 8.4

Income tax computation for Rachel for income tax year 2021/22:

	Non-savings Income £	Dividend Income £	Total £
Non-savings income (Note 1)	60,500		60,500
Dividend income		600	600
Total income	60,500	600	61,100
Less: personal allowance	(12,570)	—	(12,570)
Taxable income	47,930	600	48,530

Tax payable:	
£37,700 @ 20%	7,540
£10,230 @ 40%	4,092
£600 @ 0% (covered by dividend allowance)	0
Total tax liability	11,632

Note:
1. Rachel cannot claim any marriage allowance as she is a higher rate taxpayer.

Question 8.5

Income tax computation for Mr Frost for 2021/22:

	£
Non-savings income	30,500
Less: deductions	(780)
Net income	29,720
Less: personal allowance	(12,570)
Taxable income	17,150
Tax payable:	
£17,150 @ 20%	3,430
Less: tax deducted at source: PAYE	(5,000)
Tax repayment due for 2021/22	(1,570)

The tax reclaimable by Action Cancer is £195. This arises only on the cash gift of £780. Action Cancer cannot reclaim any gift aid on the gift of quoted shares as this is treated as a deduction from income, and the taxpayer gets relief as a deduction from total income.

Note that as the taxpayer does not have any income at the higher rate or additional rate band, there is no need to increase the basic rate or higher rate band by the amount of the gross cash gift to Action Cancer. If net income had been in the higher rate band, then the basic rate band would have increased from £37,700 to £38,675 and, if an additional rate taxpayer, then in addition to the basic rate band being extended to £38,675, the higher rate band would also have increased from £150,000 to £150,975.

The gift of shares would not increase the basic rate or higher rate band.

Question 8.6

Donations made under gift aid are made net of basic rate tax at 20% – as they are made by the taxpayer out of after-tax income. The charity receiving the gift reclaims the basic rate tax that has been paid on the gift.

If the taxpayer has not paid sufficient income tax to cover the income tax reclaimed by the charity, the taxpayer must pay it over to HMRC on their tax return.

If the taxpayer is a higher rate taxpayer, the basic rate band is increased by the gross gift, i.e. gift/0.80, so that the higher rate tax relief is obtained on the gift; if they are an additional rate taxpayer, the higher rate band is also increased by the gross gift.

Donations made under the payroll giving scheme are deducted by the employer from gross earnings of the employee before tax is applied. The employer will pay the amount withheld from the employee's salary to the relevant charity. Tax relief is therefore given at the taxpayer's marginal rate at the time of the donation.

Question 8.7

(a) £3,600 – anyone can make a gross pension contribution of up to £3,600 a year. They pay an amount net of basic rate tax (so a net contribution of £2,880 would be required to make a gross contribution of £3,600) and the government pays the balance into the pension fund – even if the individual has no taxable income.

(b) £40,000 – the upper limit on pension contributions in 2021/22.

(c) £40,000 – property income is not counted as relevant earnings for pension purposes.

(d) £40,000 – the upper limit on pension contributions in 2021/22. Both trading and employment income are treated as relevant earnings for pension purposes.

Question 8.8

Income tax computation for Sarah for income tax year 2021/22:

	£
Trading income	50,000
Less: deductions	(1,000)
Net income	49,000
Less: personal allowance	(12,570)
Taxable income	36,430
Tax payable:	
£36,430 @ 20%	7,286
Total tax liability	7,286

Explanatory Note

Increased basic rate band due to pension contribution. The maximum potential increase in the basic rate band is £20,000; however, there is not enough income to utilise this, so some higher rate relief on the pension is lost.

The £20,000 would be paid into the pension pot as follows:

Sarah would pay £16,000 to the pension company. The pension company would then reclaim £4,000 from HMRC. Total would be £20,000. This is because the payment is made net of basic rate tax and HMRC then pays the basic rate tax over to the pension fund.

Question 8.9

Income tax computations for Irwin for income tax year 2021/22

	Non-savings Income £	Dividend Income £	Total £
Employment income	32,000		32,000
UK property business	5,500		5,500
Dividends		9,000	9,000
Total income	37,500	9,000	46,500
Less: deductions	(18,000)	0	(18,000)
Net income	19,500	9,000	28,500
Less: personal allowance	(12,570)		(12,570)
Taxable income	6,930	9,000	15,930

continued overleaf

Tax payable:

Non-savings income:

£6,930 @ 20%	1,386

Dividend income:

£2,000 @ 0% (dividend allowance)	0
£7,000 @ 7.5%	<u>525</u>
Total tax liability	1,911
Less: tax deducted at source: PAYE	<u>(7,000)</u>
Tax refund due for 2021/22	(5,089)

Chapter 9

Question 9.1

	£
Personal allowance for 2021/22	12,570
Less: BIK	<u>(400)</u>
Net allowances	12,170
Tax code: 1217L	

The tax code is arrived at by taking the net allowances and removing the last digit. The L suffix merely indicates that Mary is a normal taxpayer and therefore not entitled to any special allowances.

Question 9.2

	£
Personal allowance for 2021/22	12,570
Less: BIK	<u>(750)</u>
Net allowances	11,820
Tax code: 1182L	

Question 9.3

	£
Personal allowance for 2021/22	12,570
Less: BIK	(4,169)
Impact of underpayment	<u>(5,000)</u>
Net allowances	3,401
Tax code: 340L	

Value of benefit of van is £3,500 flat rate. Van fuel benefit is £669.

In general, small over- or under-payments of PAYE from previous tax year will be collected through the PAYE system, via adjustment of the notice of coding.

Thus we need to adjust the notice of coding to take into account the fact that additional tax of £1,000 needs to be collected. As Sean is a basic rate taxpayer, this is done by dividing £1,000 by 0.20 and deducting the answer (£5,000) from his allowances remaining after deducting the impact of a BIK.

Question 9.4

	£
Personal allowance for 2020/21	12,570
Less: BIK	(500)
Impact of overpayment	375
Net allowances	12,445
Tax code: 1245L	

The mobile phone is not a taxable benefit but the medical insurance is. The benefit is the amount of the gross premium.

As Alison is a higher rate taxpayer, we divide the £150 (her 2020/21 overpayment for which she is due credit) by 0.40 to determine the adjustment to her tax code.

The £375 is added to her personal allowance, less benefit deduction, to give the net allowances.

Question 9.5

	£
Cumulative pay to date (Note 1)	6,933
Less: 2/12ths of annual tax-free amount (Note 2)	(600)
Taxable pay	6,333
Tax payable (Note 3):	
£6,283 @ 20%	1,257
£50 @ 40%	20
Tax liability for year to date	1,277
Less: tax paid to date	(500)
PAYE due in month to 5 June 2021	777

Notes:

1. £2,500 for April (i.e. month to 5 May), plus £4,433 for May (i.e. month to 5 June).
2. Tax code of 360L indicates annual tax-free amount of £3,600. As we are in the second tax month of the year, he is due 2/12ths of this amount at the time of this payment: £3,600 × 2/12 = £600.
3. To determine the rates at which tax is payable, we take 2/12ths of the annual basic rate, i.e. £37,700 × 2/12 = £6,283. Paul's taxable pay exceeds this amount by £50. Therefore £6,283 is taxed at the basic rate and £50 is taxed at the higher rate.

Question 9.6

(a) PAYE deductions for David for month to 5 October 2021

	£
Cumulative pay to date (Note 1)	20,000
Plus: 6/12ths of annual tax-addition amount (Note 2)	600
Taxable pay	20,600
Tax payable (Note 3):	
£18,850 @ 20%	3,770
£1,750 @ 40%	700
Tax liability year to date	4,770
Tax paid to date	(3,600)
PAYE due in month to 5 October 2021	870

Notes:

1. £17,000 for year to date plus £3,000 for this month.
2. September, i.e. month to 5 October, is the sixth month in the tax year and so 6/12ths of David's annual tax addition amount (as is the case where there is a K code) of £1,200 should be credited by this month.
3. To determine the rates at which tax is payable, we take 6/12ths of the annual basic rate, i.e. £37,700 × 6/12 = £18,850. David's taxable pay exceeds this amount by £1,750. Therefore, £18,850 is taxed at the basic rate and £1,750 is taxed at the higher rate.

(b) Change to PAYE deducted to date of £2,900

	£
Cumulative pay to date	20,000
Plus: 6/12ths of annual tax-addition amount	600
Taxable pay	20,600
Tax payable:	
£18,850 @ 20%	3,770
£1,750 @ 40%	700
Tax liability year to date	4,470
Tax paid to date	(2,900)
	1,570
PAYE due in month to 5 October 2021 (Note 1)	1,500

Note:

1. When a K code is in operation, tax deducted in each payment period is limited to 50% of the gross pay in that period. As £1,570 exceeds 50% of the gross salary of £3,000, actual PAYE deducted is £1,500.

Question 9.7

NIC works on an earnings period basis. As the earnings period in this case is one month, the NICs are calculated as follows:

■ 12% Class 1 primary NICs payable on earnings between £797 and £4,167
   = (£4,167 – £797) × 12%
   = £404.40

Question 9.8

No Class 1 primary NICs will be due by Jonathan as he is over 66 years of age. No NICs are payable by employees who are over State pension age. However, Class 1 secondary NICs will be still be payable in respect of these earnings.

Question 9.9

Sarah's earnings from employment were paid in 12 equal instalments, therefore we can calculate the Class 1 NICs on an annual basis, as follows:

■ 12% Class 1 primary NICs payable on earnings over £9,568 (Sarah's earnings fall well below the annual upper earnings level of £50,270)
   = (£12,000 – £9,568) × 12%
   = £291.84

Sarah is also self-employed and so is required to pay Class 2 and Class 4 NICs on these earnings, as follows:

■ Class 2 NICs are payable (Sarah's earnings exceed the small earnings exception of £6,515 in the tax year) at £3.05 per week:
   = £3.05 × 52
   = £158.60
■ 9% Class 4 NICs on earnings over £9,568 (Sarah's earnings fall well below the upper earnings limit of £50,270):
   = (£22,000 – £9,568) × 9%
   = £1,118.88

Total NICs payable by Sarah for 2020/21:

Class 1	£291.84
Class 2	£158.60
Class 4	£1,118.88
Total NICs	£1,569.32

Question 9.10

Income tax computation for Frank for tax year 2021/22

	£
Car BIK (Note 1)	5,550
Fuel BIK (Note 2)	9,102
Golf subscription BIK	800
Total BIKs	15,452

Class 1A NICs	
£15,452 × 13.8%	2,132.38

Notes:

1. The list price is £20,000.
   The relevant % capped at 37%. The car benefit is therefore £15,000 × 37% = £5,550.
2. Fuel benefit = £24,600 × 37% = £9,102.

Chapter 10

Question 10.1

Mr Murphy
3 High Street
Banbridge

19 August 2021

Re: Self-assessment

Dear Mr Murphy,

I refer to your letter requesting information regarding the HMRC system of self-assessment. I have outlined below the main features of HMRC's self-assessment system.

Notice of liability
It is the taxpayer's responsibility to submit a tax return if he has uncollected tax or national insurance contributions (NICs) for a tax year. For example, uncollected tax and NICs may arise where an individual's tax/NICs are not paid in full under PAYE or otherwise deducted at source. This would be the case where a taxpayer has income from other sources such as property. This is the case whether or not they have been issued with a tax return by HMRC – it is the taxpayer's obligation to notify HMRC if they are in receipt of income that is liable to tax.

In your case, you must register as self-employed with HMRC before 5 October 2022.
The first year for which you will be required to complete a self-assessment tax return (SA100) will be the tax year ended 5 April 2022. If you want to file a paper return, it must be filed by 31 October 2022 or, if HMRC issued the return after that date, three months after the date it was issued.

You can also file your return online, the deadline for which is 31 January 2022, or three months after the date HMRC notified you that you must complete a tax return. You may wish to appoint a tax agent to look after your tax affairs with HMRC.

Record-keeping

A taxpayer must keep sufficient records to enable them to complete their tax return. These records must be retained once the tax return has been filed in case HMRC requests to see them during an enquiry into the return.

Your new business must keep a copy of all receipts of income, all expenses and all supporting documents relating to business transactions, i.e. contracts, purchases, VAT returns, bank statements, how you calculate your closing stock, etc. These records must be kept for five years after 31 January following the end of the tax year to which they relate.

HMRC can charge you a penalty of up to £3,000 if you fail to keep proper records.

Late filing penalties

If you do not submit your tax return by the required date, as outlined above, you may be liable to a late filing penalty. The penalties for late filing are as follows:

- Initial penalty of £100 for failure to submit the return on time.
- A daily penalty of £10 per day for a maximum of 90 days can be imposed if the return is more than three months late.
- If six months late, the penalty will be the greater of £300 or 5% of the tax due.
- If 12 months late, the penalty will be the greater of £300 or 5% of the tax due.

Tax payments and interest

All taxpayers within the self-assessment system are required to pay their income tax liability by 31 January after the end of the tax year. Payments on account are paid before the income tax return is submitted and before the tax liability for the year is finalised. Payments on account are usually based on the previous tax year's liability. The balancing amount of tax is the difference between the tax due for the tax year per the final tax return and the payments on account already made in respect of the tax year.

However, payments on account on 31 January in the tax year and 31 July after the end of the tax year are required, if, in the previous tax year:

(i) less than 80% of the income tax liability was collected by deduction at source; and
(ii) the amount not collected was more than £1,000.

Each payment on account will be 50% of the amount not collected at source in the previous tax year. In your case, no payments on account will be required for 2021/22 as you only commenced your sole trade in that period. However, they are likely to be required for 2022/23.

The balancing amount of tax for any tax year is then due on 31 January after the end of the tax year. Any amount of tax that has not been paid 30 days after the end of the due date is subject to a late payment penalty of 5% of the unpaid tax. Interest is also charged on late payments. If any amount of tax is unpaid after 31 July, a further penalty of 5% of the amount of unpaid tax is due and a further 5% penalty if any tax is unpaid by the following 31 January.

If your payments on account exceed your tax liability for the year, HMRC will refund the overpaid amount. HMRC may also pay interest on the refund that you are due. It is possible to elect to reduce your payments on account – however this should only be done if you are reasonably sure that the tax due for the year will be lower than the tax liability for the previous tax year, as interest will be payable on any amounts underpaid. HMRC may also impose penalties if it considers payments on account have been reduced without good reason.

If you require any further information, please do not hesitate to contact me.

Yours sincerely,

Question 10.2

Income tax computation for Cian Connors for tax year 2021/22

	Non-savings Income	Savings Income	Total
	£	£	£
Non-savings income	48,000		48,000
Investment income		920	920
Total income	48,000	920	48,920
Less: personal allowance	(12,570)		(12,570)
Taxable income	35,430	920	36,350
Tax payable:			
£35,430 @ 20%			7,086
£920 @ 0% (personal savings allowance of £1,000 available)			0
Total tax liability			7,086
NIC Class 4:			
(£48,000 – £9,568) @ 9%			3,459
Total self-assessment liability for 2021/22			10,545

Payments on account for 2022/23 of £5,272.50 each will be due for payment on 31 January 2023 and 31 July 2023.

Question 10.3

Income tax computation for Mark Johnston for tax year 2021/22

	Non-savings Income	Savings Income	Total
	£	£	£
Non-savings income	50,000		50,000
Investment income		10,500	10,500
Total income	50,000	10,500	60,500
Less: personal allowance	(12,570)		(12,570)
Taxable income	37,430	10,500	47,930

continued overleaf

Tax payable:

£37,430 @ 20%	7,486
£500 @ 0% (personal savings allowance)	0
£10,000@ 40%	4,000
Total tax liability	11,486
Tax deducted at source	(11,000)
Tax due	486

Payments on account are not required as the amount of tax due is less than £1,000.

Question 10.4

If Tom markets or sells this tax planning scheme to a number of his clients, then he will potentially be in breach of a number of Chartered Accountants Ireland's *Code of Ethics*. Namely: integrity; professional competence and due care and professional behaviour.

Tom will be in breach of the principle of integrity as the scheme will be seen as misleading if his clients pay him to put the scheme in place and it turns out to be deemed a tax-avoidance scheme, which HMRC will then counteract to remove the tax advantage.

Tom will be in breach of the professional competence principle as he is going to market and sell the scheme, despite not fully understanding how the scheme operates.

Finally, Tom will be in breach of the principle of professional behaviour as he is marketing and selling a scheme that may be viewed as not complying with the relevant tax laws and regulations. As a Chartered Accountant, Tom's involvement in the scheme could also have a damaging impact on the profession as the scheme does not apply the tax laws in an appropriate manner and it is likely that the scheme could be deemed an abusive tax-avoidance scheme by HMRC.

Chapter 11

Question 11.1

Calculation of CIS deduction and payment to subcontractor:

	£
Total payment	4,600
Less: cost of materials (inclusive of VAT) (Note 1)	(900)
Amount liable to CIS deduction	3,700
Amount deducted @ 20% (standard rate)	740
Net payment to subcontractor (£4,600 – £740)	3,860

Note:

1. The cost of materials is the VAT-inclusive amount because the subcontractor is not VAT-registered. If the subcontractor was VAT-registered, then they would not suffer the VAT cost as this would be deemed input VAT (see **Chapter 19**), i.e. the amount deducted would be £750 £900 – £150) rather than £900.

Question 11.2

Calculation of CIS deduction and payment to subcontractors:

	Contractor A	Contractor B	Contractor C
	£	£	£
Total payment	8,500	12,000	3,500
Less: materials	(3,500)	(2,000)	(1,500)
Amount liable to CIS deduction	5,000	10,000	2,000
Amount deducted	Nil	2,000	600
Payments to the subcontractors	8,500	10,000	2,900

Total monthly payment by the contractor for the period ended 5 February 2022 is £2,600. This amount should be paid online to HMRC by 22 February 2022.

Chapter 12

Question 12.1

Venus Ltd

Venus Ltd will pay in instalments for the year ended 31 December 2022, if it:

- was "large" in the previous year (31 December 2021); and
- it is "large" in the current year – year ended 31 December 2022.

Year ended 31 December 2021
In year ended 31 December 2021 Venus had two related 51% group companies during the period. Saturn Ltd was not an associate because it was not under the control of Venus (as the shareholding is only 40%). So the upper relevant maximum amount of £1.5 million is divided by three, i.e. £500,000. Therefore Venus Ltd was "large" in the previous period as its augmented profits were £550,000.

Year ended 31 December 2022
In order to determine whether the company is "large" for 2022, the £1.5 million upper relevant maximum amount must be divided by the number of related 51% group companies at the end of the previous accounting period.

Venus Ltd, once again, had two related 51% group companies in the year to 31 December 2022. The upper relevant maximum amount was, again, £500,000 (£1.5 million divided by three). Therefore the company, having augmented profits of £505,000, is a "large" company for instalments purposes. This is because we are required to include the £80,000 dividend expected to be received from Saturn Ltd, which is a non-group company, so this dividend is franked investment income. The £80,000 dividend is added to the TTP of £425,000 to give augmented profits of £505,000. Venus Ltd may have the opportunity to waive part of its dividend entitlement so that its augmented profits are below £500,000 and it is not exposed to instalment payments.

Energy Ltd

Where the company has a short period of account the limits are pro-rated. As profits are expected to exceed £1,125,000 (£1.5 million × 9/12) it looks like Energy Ltd is required to pay in instalments for the nine months ending 31 December 2022, as its projected profits are £1,200,000.

However, it was not a large company in the year ended 31 March 2022 and therefore, because projected profits are not expected to exceed £10 million × 9/12 (£7,500,000) in the nine months to 31 December 2022, instalment payments are not required.

Question 12.2

	£
Credits: Interest received	15,000
Loan written off by bank	20,000
	35,000
Less: Debits	
Legal fees incurred re: loan write-off	(1,500)
Net loan relationship credit	33,500

Question 12.3

(a) A loan relationship is any transaction for the borrowing or lending of money in relation to a money debt. Loan relationships cover all loans made both by and to the company. These will either be trading or non-trading.

(b) Examples include: bank overdrafts and loans, mortgages, employee loans, interest on underpaid and overpaid corporation tax, corporate bonds, interest on savings.

(c) All non-trading debits and credits, calculated in line with generally accepted accounting principles, are aggregated separately and the overall debit or credit is included in the corporation tax computation. Trading debits are deductible in calculating trading profits. Excess non-trading credits are taxable and included in the calculation of TTP. Non-trade debits are relievable in various ways.

Question 12.4

	£
Non-trade interest received	
Bank deposit interest	6,233
Bond held with local council	775
	7,008
Less: Non-trade interest paid	
Mortgage on rental property	(3,178)
Bank loan for shares	(555)
Net non-trade loan relationship credit	3,275

All of the remaining sources of interest received and paid are trade-related.

Question 12.5

■ Interest on corporation tax paid late is allowable as a non-trading loan relationship debit, therefore it should be added back to the adjustment of trading profits and relieved later as a non-trade debit.

■ The loan to buy equipment is for a trading purpose and so interest is allowable as a deduction against trading income on an accruals basis, i.e. £2,200 is deductible.

■ The mortgage interest is an allowable trading deduction.

Question 12.6

	£
Debenture interest receivable	7,000
Bank overdraft interest payable (trading related)	–
Property loan interest (2/4 × £12,000)	(6,000)
Incidental costs of loan finance (2/4 × £2,500)	(1,250)
Non-trading loan relationship debit	(250)

This can be offset against total profits of the same accounting period or carried back and set against surplus non-trading loan relationship credits for the previous twelve months. Alternatively it can be carried forward against non-trading profits of future accounting periods.

Chapter 13

Question 13.1

TELESTAR LTD
Corporation Tax Computation
for the 12-month Accounting Period Ended 31 March 2022

	£	£
Profit (pre-tax)		117,000
Add: Depreciation	15,389	
Motor expenses (Note 1)	–	
Entertainment (Note 2)	1,050	
Finance lease depreciation (Note 3)	–	
Legal fees (Note 4)	2,400	18,839
		135,839
Less: Grant for extension of premises (Note 5)	10,000	
Employment grant (Note 6)	–	
Patent royalty (Note 7)	1,600	
Dividends from UK company (Note 8)	1,300	

continued overleaf

Profit on sale of van (Note 9)	1,000	
Profit on sale of shares (Note 10)	3,000	
Bank deposit interest (Note 11)	600	
Capital allowances	<u>7,272</u>	<u>(24,772)</u>
Trading income		<u>111,067</u>
Loan relationships – bank interest		600
Miscellaneous income:		

$$\text{Patent royalty (gross)} = 1,600 \times \frac{100}{80} \qquad\qquad 2,000$$

Chargeable gain (Note 12)	<u>1,632</u>
Taxable total profits (TTP)	<u>115,299</u>

Corporation tax payable:	
£115,299 @ 19%	21,906.81
Less: income tax suffered on patent royalty £2,000 @ 20%	<u>(400.00)</u>
Corporation tax payable	<u>21,506.81</u>

Corporation tax is due on or before 1 January 2023 as the company is not "large" for instalment purposes, its TTP being less than £1,500,000.

Notes

1. It is assumed that motor expenses are wholly allowable, therefore there is no add-back.
2. Entertainment costs are disallowed as follows:

	£
Christmas gifts for suppliers	150
Entertainment costs incurred by MD	350
General customer entertainment	<u>550</u>
	1,050

Costs incurred for benefit of staff, i.e. Christmas party and prizes, are deductible.

3. As depreciation on finance lease assets is deductible, no adjustment is required.
4. Legal fees are of a capital nature and, therefore, are disallowed.
5. Grant for extension of premises is a capital receipt and is not liable to corporation tax.
6. Employment grant is taxable as a revenue receipt relating to the trade.
7. Patent royalty is not taxable as trading income as it relates to non-trading activities. The gross amount is taxable as miscellaneous income. However, the income tax suffered can be set-off against the corporation tax chargeable. As only the net amount (i.e. the amount after deduction of standard rate income tax) has been credited in the statement of comprehensive income, then this is the correct amount to deduct.

8. The dividend from the UK company is exempt from corporation tax under the exemption in section 931B CTA 2009 for "small" companies.
9. Profit on sale of van is a capital profit and not a trading receipt and so is adjusted through capital allowances.
10. Profit on sale of shares is a capital profit and not a trading receipt and so it is taxable as a chargeable asset (see Note 12).
11. Bank deposit interest is taxable as income from a non-trading loan relationship.
12. Chargeable gain:

	£	£
Proceeds		6,000
Cost	3,000	
Indexation	1,368	
Indexed cost		(4,368)
Chargeable gain		1,632

Question 13.2

Zaco Ltd
Corporation Tax Computation
for year ended 30 September 2021

	£	£
Profit per accounts		379,900
Add: Disallowed repairs	5,200	
Disallowed professional fees	300	
Political donations	750	
Entertainment	600	
Depreciation	13,000	19,850
		399,750
Less: Dividends (Note 2)	3,600	
Profit on sale of fixed assets	15,200	
Bank interest receivable	1,200	
Property income	4,300	(24,300)
		375,450
Less: Capital allowances		(9,846)
Tax-adjusted trading profits		365,604
Loan relationships		1,200
Property income		4,300
Total income		371,104

continued overleaf

Add: Chargeable gains (Note 1)		Nil
Taxable total profits (TTP)		**371,104**
Corporation tax payable:		
£371,104 @ 19%		70,510

The corporation tax liability is due on or before 1 July 2022.

Notes

1. Chargeable gain on sale of building

	£	£
Proceeds		215,200
Cost	200,000	
Indexation (£200,000 × 0.035)	7,000	(207,000)
Gain		8,200
Less: capital loss forward (restricted)		(8,200)
Chargeable gain		NIL
Capital loss carried forward		(1,800)

2. The foreign dividend is exempt from UK tax.

Question 13.3

ALPHA LTD
Corporation Tax Computation Year Ended 31 March 2022

	£	£
Profit per accounts		424,605
Add: Repairs	15,000	
Insurance	350	
Loss on sale of investments	600	
Legal expenses	2,000	
Depreciation	13,260	
Subscriptions (Note 1)	1,815	
Motor expenses (Note 2)	3,169	
Sundry (Note 3)	2,201	
Entertainment	1,191	39,586
		464,191

Less: UK dividends	7,000	
Gain on sale of fixed assets	1,000	
Amortisation of grant	240	
Interest on tax overpaid	475	
Rents received	6,000	
Deposit interest	<u>1,500</u>	<u>(16,215)</u>
		447,976
Capital allowances		<u>(46,006)</u>
Trading income for period		401,970
Net credit from loan relationships (£475 + £1,500)		1,975
Property income:		
Gross rents	6,000	
Less: Insurance	<u>(350)</u>	
Net property income		<u>5,650</u>

Taxable total profits (TTP)   **409,595**

Corporation tax payable @ 19% = £77,823 and is due on or before 1 January 2023.

Notes

1. Subscriptions: Political: £1,815
2. Motor expenses: Leasing charges: disallowable £21,126 × 15%* = £3,169
   * As the CO_2 emissions exceed 110g/km, the limit which applies for leases entered into on or after 1 April 2018.
3. Sundry:

	£
Interest on late payment of VAT	1,630
Health and safety fines	30
Gifts to customers	<u>541</u>
	2,201

4. Profit on sale – excluded from calculation of taxable total profits.
5. The capital loss of £189 carried forward from 31 March 2021 remains unused and is increased by a further capital loss of £600 on the share disposal. The total capital loss carried forward is therefore £789.

Question 13.4

Anytown Tax Advisors
Anytown

Mr Paul Morrisey
Classic Engineering Consultancy Ltd

11 July 2023

Amended corporation tax computation – 31 March 2022

Dear Paul,

Further to your recent instructions, I have set out below the information and advice you requested. I have enclosed with this letter the amended corporation tax computation for the accounting period ended 31 March 2022.

In summary, there were a number of errors identified in the computation. Including those identified on Appendix 1, the corporation tax rate originally applied to the adjusted trading profits was also not correct – the rate was 19% for the 2021 financial year. Despite the company's taxable profits being in excess of £1,500,000 in 2022, quarterly instalments were not required because it would appear that this was the first period where taxable profits exceeded £1,500,000, and, as they did not exceed £10,000,000, the company did not qualify as "large". Therefore, the corporation tax liability was due on 1 January 2023.

Unfortunately, the corporation tax liability for 2021 has been underpaid by £38,861.98. As a result of this, interest of 2.60% per annum for late payment is payable from the original due date of 1 January 2023.

You should also note that a £100 late filing penalty will also arise – it is irrelevant that this is the first time the company has filed a late corporation tax return.

If we can be of further assistance in this regard, or if you have any questions, please do not hesitate to contact me.

Yours sincerely,

CLASSIC ENGINEERING CONSULTANCY LTD
Amended Corporation Tax Computation
for the accounting period ended 31 March 2022

	Workings	£	£
Adjusted trading profit per original computation			1,598,328
Less: profit on sale of machine	W1		(22,800)
Add: Disallowed repairs and renewals	W2	50,400	
Disallowed legal fees	W3	13,225	
Depreciation	W4	28,289	
Disallowed motor expenses	W5	400	
Disallowed travel expenses	W6	900	
Capital provision	W7	50,000	143,214
Amended adjusted profit			1,718,742

continued overleaf

Corporation tax payable:	£
Revised corporation tax payable @ 19%	326,560.98
Corporation tax per original computation submitted	287,699.00
Underpayment	**38,861.98**

Workings

W1 These were added back instead of being deducted, hence we need to deduct twice.

W2 The building extension costs of £50,400 are capital in nature and should have been added back in the original computation.

W3 The planning appeal fees of £13,225 are also capital in nature and should have been added back.

W4 Depreciation on the assets under hire purchase is also disallowable.

W5 Speeding fines of £400 are disallowed.
No add-back needed of contract hire on car costs as the CO_2 emission is < 50g/km, the limit for contracts taken out on or after 1 April 2021.

W6 Add back meals with potential new suppliers/customers.

W7 The increase in a capital provision should have been added back as it is capital in nature.

All other items in the computation submitted appear correct.

Question 13.5

	£
Profit	96,000
Add: depreciation	5,000
Trade profit	101,000
UK property business	17,000
Total profits	118,000
Less: qualifying charitable donation	(8,000)
Taxable total profits	110,000

Question 13.6

The dividend is exempt from corporation tax as Ice Sculptors Ireland Ltd can be controlled by Ice Sculptors Ltd and therefore (as we have no further information to the contrary) the dividend falls with section 931E CTA 2009 as an exempt distribution from a controlled company.

Question 13.7

The dividend is exempt from corporation tax as Dragger GmbH qualifies as a small company as it has less than 50 employees and gross assets of less than £10 million therefore (as we have no further information to the contrary) the dividend falls with section 931B CTA 2009 as an exempt distribution from a small company. Therefore the dividend receipt is not taxable.

Chapter 14

Question 14.1

ENYA LIMITED

	£
31/03/2019	
Trading income	600,000
Net credit from loan relationships	100,000
Property income	50,000
Taxable total profits	750,000
Less: losses claim	(430,000)
Taxable total profits	320,000
31/03/2020	
Trading income	700,000
Net credit from loan relationships	50,000
Property loss	(40,000)
Taxable total profits	710,000
Less: section 37(3)(b) claim	(710,000)
Taxable total profits	Nil
31/03/2021	
Trading income	—
Net credit from loan relationships	100,000
Property income	60,000
Total profits	160,000
Less: section 37(3)(a) claim	(160,000)
Taxable total profits	Nil
31/03/2022	
Trading income	100,000
Net credit from loan relationships	35,000
Property income	80,000
Taxable total profits	215,000

Loss Memo

	£
Relevant trading loss for y/e 31/03/2021	1,300,000
Utilised against y/e 31/03/2021	(160,000)
Utilised against y/e 31/03/2020	(710,000)
Utilised against y/e 31/03/2019	(430,000)
Loss carried forward at 31/03/2022	Nil

Question 14.2

HELLS BELLS LTD

	£
Year ended 31 March 2022	
Trading income	167,000
Property income	4,000
Net credit from loan relationships	<u>10,000</u>
Total profits	181,000
Less: section 37(3)(b) claim	<u>(174,000)</u>
Taxable total profits	<u>7,000</u>
Tax payable £7,000 @ 19%	1,330
9 months ended 31 December 2022	
Trading income	–
Property income (Note 1)	(4,000)
Net credit from loan relationships	20,000
Chargeable gains (Note 2)	<u>–</u>
Total profits	16,000
Less: section 37(3)(a) claim	<u>(16,000)</u>
Taxable total profits	<u>Nil</u>

Notes

1. Property income – A property loss must be set against other profits in the current accounting period.
2. Chargeable gains:

	£
Gain	10,000
Less: capital loss forward	<u>(19,000)</u>
Loss forward	<u>(9,000)</u>

Loss Memo

	£
Relevant trading loss for p/e 31/12/2022	190,000
Utilised by way of section 37(3)(a) p/e 31/12/2022	(16,000)
Utilised by way of section 37(3)(b) y/e 31/03/2022	<u>(174,000)</u>
Loss forward to 2022	<u>Nil</u>

Question 14.3

MONK LTD

	£	£
Year ended 31 March 2023		
Trading income		–
Net credit from loan relationships		30,000
Property income		20,000
Chargeable gain		<u>126,000</u>
Taxable profits		176,000
Less: section 37(3)(a) claim		<u>(176,000)</u>
Taxable total profits		<u>Nil</u>
Year ended 31 March 2022		
Trading income	360,000	
Less: capital allowances	<u>(20,000)</u>	340,000
Less: section 45 – loss carried forward*		<u>(20,000)</u>
Trading income		320,000
Net credit from loan relationships		5,000
Property income		15,000
Chargeable gain		<u>12,000</u>
Taxable profits		352,000
Less: section 37(3)(b) claim		<u>(224,000)</u>
Taxable total profits		<u>128,000</u>
Tax:		
£128,000 @ 19%		<u>24,320</u>

Loss Memo

	£
Relevant trading loss for y/e 31/03/2023 (£310,000 + £90,000)	400,000
Utilised by way of section 37(3)(a) against y/e 31/03/2023	(176,000)
Utilised by way of section 37(3)(b) against y/e 31/03/2022	<u>(224,000)</u>
Loss forward to 2023	<u>Nil</u>

* Section 45A claims are subject to the restriction rule. However, the company's deduction allowance for losses carried forward is £5 million, meaning 100% relief is available for these losses.

Chapter 15

Question 15.1

1. Maurice – CGT Computation 2021/22

	£	£
Sale proceeds		80,600
Incidental costs of disposal		(750)
Net proceeds		79,850
Deduct: Base cost	20,000	
Costs of acquisition	300	
		(20,300)
Chargeable gain		59,550
Less: annual exemption		(12,300)
Taxable gain		47,250

CGT liability:

£37,700 – £36,315 = £1,385 @ 18%	249.30
£47,250 – £1,385 = £45,865 @ 28%	12,842.20
Total	13,091.50

As the holiday home is residential property, the gain does not attract the 10% or 20% rate of CGT.

2. Vincent – CGT Computation 2021/22

	£	£
Sale proceeds		9,500
Deduct: allowable cost: market value at 31 March 1982	1,200	
		(1,200)
Chargeable gain		8,300
Less: annual exemption		(8,300)
Taxable gain		Nil

£4,000 of annual exemption is wasted.

Question 15.2

(a) James – CGT Computation 2021/22

	£	£
Sale proceeds		650,600
Deduct: allowable costs:		
Market value at 31 March 1982	230,000	
Enhancement expenditure – July 1996	10,000	(240,000)
Chargeable gain		410,600
Less: annual exemption		(12,300)
Taxable gain		398,300
CGT @ 20%		79,660

Note: the gain is taxable at 20% as the level of James's taxable income for 2021/22 exceeded the basic rate band threshold and the asset disposed of is not residential property.

(b) Declan – CGT Computation 2021/22

	£	£
Sale proceeds		400,900
Deduct: allowable costs:		
Market value at 31 March 1982	55,000	
Expenditure August 1985	20,000	
Expenditure February 2005	39,250	(114,250)
Chargeable gain		286,650
Deduct: annual exemption		(12,300)
Taxable gain		274,350
CGT £5,000 @ 18% (i.e. £37,700 – £32,700)		900
CGT £269,350 @ 28% (i.e. £274,350 – £5,000)		75,418
Total CGT payable on 31 January 2023		76,318

Question 15.3

Capital Gains Tax Computation 2021/22

	£
Sale proceeds	80,000
Less: selling costs	(2,600)
	77,400
Less: cost:	
$\dfrac{£80,000}{£80,000 + £145,000} \times £18,000$	(6,400)
Chargeable gain	71,000
Less: annual exempt amount	(12,300)
Taxable gain	58,700
Taxable as follows:	
£37,700 – £30,915 = £6,785 @ 10%	679
£58,700 – £6,785 = £51,915 @ 20%	10,383
CGT liability	11,062

The above liability falls due for payment on 31 January 2023. The base cost of the remaining land is £11,600 for any future disposal. The disposal does not qualify as a small part disposal of land as the various conditions are not met.

Chapter 16

Question 16.1

Shauna Quinn – CGT 2021/22

	Painting £	Vase £	Shop £	Land £	Total £
Chargeable gains	47,000	0	126,500	55,000	228,500
Capital losses current year					(8,000)
Capital losses c/fwd					(208,200)
Net chargeable gains					12,300
Annual exemption					(12,300)
Chargeable gains					Nil

	£
Capital losses b/fwd	210,000
Used against 2021/22 gains	208,200
Capital losses c/fwd	1,800

Workings

1. Painting

	£
Proceeds	50,000
Less: costs of sale	(500)
Net proceeds of sale	49,500
Less: cost	(2,500)
Chargeable gain	47,000

2. Antique vase

	£
Proceeds	4,000
Deem gross proceeds to be £6,000	6,000
Less: costs	(14,000)
Loss	(8,000)

3. Freehold shop – the transfer from Darren to Shauna is a no gain/no loss transfer. The base cost for Shauna is therefore £55,000. The value of the unit at the date of the transfer is irrelevant.

	£
Proceeds	185,600
Less: costs of sale: Legal fees	(2,250)
Estate agents fee	(1,850)
Net proceeds of sale	181,500
Less: cost	(55,000)
Gain	126,500

4. Land

	£
Proceeds	80,000
Less: costs	
$£40,000 \times \dfrac{£80,000}{£80,000 + £48,000}$	(25,000)
Gain	55,000

The small disposal rules do not apply.

5. Car – exempt from capital gains tax.

6. Capital losses – the current-year capital losses must be used in their entirety against any available current-year gains and in priority to any capital losses carried forward. However, the capital losses carried forward can be tailored in how they are used so as not to waste any of Shauna's annual exempt amount. Only £208,200 of the capital losses carried forward is used and Shauna will have capital losses carried forward to 2021/22 of £1,800.

Question 16.2

MEMO

From:	An Accountant
To:	John Smith
Date:	3 July 2021
Subject:	Outline of UK capital gains tax system

As discussed in our recent meeting, I have outlined below the basic principles of the UK capital gains tax system. Please do not hesitate to contact me if you have any queries in relation to this memo.

(a) Capital gains tax is payable in the UK at a flat rate of 10% on chargeable gains in the available basic rate band (£37,700 in 2021/22) with 20% charged on gains in excess of the basic rate band. As you have income in excess of £100,000, any chargeable gains would be taxed at 20%. Note that gains on residential property are taxed at 18% within the basic rate band and 28% thereafter.

(b) Any capital gains tax due for the year ended 5 April 2022 will be due for payment by 31 January 2023 unless the property disposed of is a UK residential property. From 6 April 2021, UK tax residents will need to report and pay CGT on all UK residential property disposals within 30 days of the date of completion of the disposal (rather than the deadline of 31 January following the end of the tax year in which the sale is made).

(c) Generally, the capital gains should be declared to HMRC by filing in the relevant sections in your self-assessment tax return for the 2021/22 tax year. However, in respect of UK residential property disposals, if the individual is in the self-assessment tax system prior to the disposal of UK residential property, they will also be required to report any UK residential property disposal details as part of their self-assessment tax return. If the individual is not part of the self-assessment tax return system but they have returned details of the UK residential property disposal online within 30 days, then no further reporting to HMRC will be required beyond the 30-day online submission and payment.

(d) Each individual has an annual exempt amount for each tax year which can be set against gains in that year. For 2021/22 the annual exempt amount is £12,300. This can be set against gains arising in the most beneficial way, i.e. against gains arising at 28% first, followed by gains at 20%, then those at 18% and finally against gains at 10%.

(e) Indexation allowance is generally not available to individuals. Note that companies still receive indexation on capital assets they sell from the month of acquisition to the month of sale, but up to 31 December 2017 only.

(f) The following types of expenditure qualify as deductible for capital gains purposes:
- Consideration given wholly and exclusively for acquisition of the asset.
- Incidental costs of acquisition and incidental costs of disposal. These are limited to stamp taxes and professional fees directly related to the acquisition and/or sale.
- Expenditure incurred on enhancing the value of the asset that is reflected in the state and nature of the asset at the date of sale and expenditure in preserving or defending title to the asset.

(g) Unused capital losses are carried forward to set against capital gains arising in future periods. They cannot be carried back. However, as the capital losses will be used in periods after the period in which they arose, they can be partially set against gains arising to bring them down to the level of the annual exemption so that this is not wasted (rather than being used to reduce the gain to below the annual exemption or £Nil).

(h) If the asset had been sold to your brother, this would be a sale to a connected person. Therefore the capital loss would be 'ring-fenced' and could only be used against a capital gain arising on a sale of a capital asset to your brother either in the same tax year that the loss arose or in a future tax year. Such a loss could therefore not be used against general gains on sale of capital assets.

(i) The capital gains base cost of the rental property will be the probate value of the property. This is likely to be the market value of the property at the date of your grandmother's death.

(j) As you are 'connected' with your grandmother under the capital gains tax legislation, then the gift of the property to you would be deemed to occur at the market value of the property at the date of gift – which would then be your capital gains base cost.

Chapter 17

Question 17.1

The house will have been James's principal private residence (PPR) as it was the only house he owned when he purchased it and he lived in it as a residence on acquisition. Therefore the periods of qualifying ownership for PPR exemption are as follows:

- Actual occupation – first three years plus last two years = 5 years; and
- Five years when he resided in one half of the house as his PPR and let the remaining half to a residential tenant = 2.5 year PPR.

Therefore, 7.5 years of ownership count as occupation and 2.5 years do not. The gain subject to tax is therefore £800,000 × 2.5/10 = £200,000.

However, as half of the property was let for residential purposes while James resided there also, lettings relief is available to further reduce the chargeable gain that arises.

The lettings relief is the **lower** of:

- the gain exempt under the PPR provisions – this is £600,000; or
- £40,000; or
- the gain made while letting out part of the home – this is £200,000 (£800,000 × 2.5/10).

Thus, an additional £40,000 of the gain is exempt. The tax due is then calculated as follows:

	£
Gain after PPR relief	200,000
Less: lettings relief	(40,000)
	160,000
Less: annual exemption	(12,300)
Chargeable gain	147,700
CGT @ 28%	41,356

Question 17.2

Dear Jack,

Further to our recent conversation, I have set out below responses to your queries regarding capital gains tax in relation to your UK property.

Principal private residence (PPR) relief

The general rule is that a gain on the disposal of an individual's only or main residence is exempt from capital gains tax. Grounds of up to half a hectare (approx. 1.24 acres) including the dwelling house, or larger areas that are appropriate to the size of the house, also qualify for the relief.

Full exemption applies where the owner has occupied the house throughout his entire period of ownership. Where occupation of the house has been only for part of the period of ownership, the exempt part of the gain is the proportion given by the following formula:

$$\frac{\text{(Period of ownership post} - 31 \text{ March 1982)}}{\text{(Total period of ownership post} - 31 \text{ March 1982)}} \times \text{Chargeable gain}$$

Where there is a delay of up to a year in taking up residence of a property (e.g. complicated sale, house built, redecoration, etc.) then the period of non-residence will count as a period of residence. Providing a property has been an individual's only or main residence at some time during his total ownership (whether before or after 31 March 1982), the last nine months automatically count as a period of residence (this is 36 months in some specific cases).

Certain other absences also count as residence, if preceded and followed (not necessarily immediately before and after) by a period of actual residence and provided that relief is not being claimed for another main residence during the absence. These are:

- Up to three years for any reason.
- Any absence throughout which the individual is employed abroad.
- A total of up to four years of absence during which the taxpayer is working elsewhere in the UK (either employed or self-employed) such that they could not occupy their PPR.

There is further relief for owner-occupiers who, at any time during their period of ownership, have let part of the property as residential accommodation. This is known as "lettings relief". However, lettings relief is not available in this case, as it will only be available where the owner has shared occupancy with the tenant. In other words, part of the residence must still be Jack's main residence, while another part is being let out by him as residential accommodation. As Jack let the entire property, lettings relief is not available.

CGT consequences of potential sale

I attach the capital gains tax calculation associated with the proposed sale of your Belfast property. You will note from same that the potential capital gain arising on disposal is £64,591, which would be taxed at 28% as you are an additional rate taxpayer.

Should you have any further queries in connection with the above, please do not hesitate to contact me.

Yours sincerely,

ABC & Co.
Chartered Accountants

JACK BATES
CGT Calculation – Sale of Apartment

	£
Sale proceeds – July 2021	1,300,000
Cost	(65,000)
	1,235,000
Less: Exempt element of gain:	
250/286 × £1,235,000	(1,079,545)
Chargeable gain	155,455
Annual exemption	(12,300)
	143,155
CGT @ 28%	40,083

Workings

Total duration of ownership: 01/09/1997–01/07/2021 = 286 months, being as follows:

	No. of Months	
01/09/1997–01/01/2005	88	
01/01/2005–30/04/2013	100	Let 100%
30/04/2013–31/01/2019	69	
31/01/2019–01/07/2021	29	Let 100%
	286	
Exempt proportion:		
Owner-occupied	88	
Deemed owner-occupied	48	Maximum
	36	For any reason
Owner-occupied	69	
Last 18 months deemed owner-occupied	9	
Total exempt portion	250	

Chapter 18

Question 18.1

This is Sarah's personal company as she owns at least 5% of the company and its voting rights. The assets are broken down between chargeable business assets and chargeable assets as follows:

	MV 2021	**Chargeable business assets**	**Chargeable assets**
	£	£	£
Goodwill	410,000	410,000	410,000
Land and buildings	470,000	470,000	470,000
Plant and machinery	2,500	Exempt	Exempt

Market value	4,000	Exempt	Exempt
Trade receivables	40,000	n/a	n/a
Inventory	3,000	n/a	n/a
Cash	500	n/a	n/a
Rental property	120,000	n/a	120,000
	1,050,000	880,000	1,000,000

(a) Proceeds – deemed

	£
Proceeds	1,050,000
Less: cost	(50,000)
Gain	1,000,000
Less: gift relief	
£1,000,000 × $\dfrac{£880,000}{£1,000,000}$	(880,000)
Taxable gain	120,000
Annual exemption	(12,300)
	107,700

(b) Base cost for Emily under (a):

	£
Market value	1,050,000
Less: gift relief	(880,000)
Base cost	170,000

(c)

	£
Gain	1,000,000
Annual exemption	(12,300)
Taxable gain	987,700

(d) Base cost for Emily under (c):

	£
Base cost = Market value	1,050,000

Question 18.2

Dear Áine,

I refer to our recent meeting in relation to the proposed factory disposal. I have outlined the information requested below.

(a) Tax due

UK capital gains tax will be payable on the sale of the factory. The calculation below indicates that, in the absence of suitable reliefs, capital gains tax of £197,600 will be payable.

As you are trading as a sole trader, this tax will be payable by you personally. As the disposal will be made in the 2021/22 tax year, the capital gains tax will be payable on or before 31 January

2023. As you are an additional rate taxpayer, the rate of capital gains tax is 20% before any reliefs. This is calculated as follows

	£
Proceeds	1,500,000
Less: base cost	(500,000)
Taxable gain	1,000,000
Less: annual exemption	(12,300)
Taxable gain	987,700
Tax @ 20%	197,540

(b) Rollover relief

Rollover relief is available when a sole trader, such as you, sells a capital asset which is in their trade and uses the sales proceeds to acquire one of a number of specified assets that is immediately brought into use in the trade.

Qualifying assets include:

- Land and buildings.
- Goodwill.
- Fixed plant and machinery.
- Ships, aircraft, hovercraft, satellites, space stations, spacecraft, milk/potato/fish/ewe quotas, suckler cow premiums and payment entitlements under the new agricultural subsidy Basic Payment Scheme.

However, the asset acquired does not have to be the same as the asset sold.

Rollover relief is only available if the new asset is acquired in the period twelve months before and three years after the date the factory is sold. If you are unsure when the new investment will be made, as long as it is within the three years from disposal (i.e. by 8 November 2024) a provisional claim for relief can be made. In addition, it would be recommended that you review expenditure in the year prior to disposal (i.e. from 9 November 2020 to 8 November 2021) to check if any qualifying spend was incurred in that period.

However, in order for full rollover relief to be available, the entire proceeds of sale of the first asset must be reinvested in the second asset.

If all of the proceeds on the sale of the factory (i.e. £1,500,000) are not fully reinvested, a gain equal to the lower of:

- the full gain (i.e. £1,000,000); or
- the cash retained

is left chargeable. If the amount of cash retained exceeds £1,000,000, then no rollover relief may be claimed. So for every £1 of cash that is not reinvested (up to £1,000,000 not reinvested), £1 of the gain is subject to capital gains tax. Therefore, rollover relief will only be available in respect of every pound reinvested over £500,000.

The gain rolled over reduces the capital gains base cost of the new asset by the amount of that gain.

Rollover relief must be claimed in writing to HMRC within four years after the **later** of:

- the end of the tax year in which disposal of the old asset took place (i.e. by 5 April 2026); or
- the end of the tax year in which acquisition of the new asset took place.

In your case, if reinvestment did not occur until 8 November 2024, the date for the claim for relief would be 5 April 2029. The earliest date a claim would be due will always be 5 April 2026 even if you had reinvested in sufficient qualifying assets in the period 9 November 2020–8 November 2021.

You should note that holdover relief is another form of deferral relief that may be available should you decide instead to lease property instead of purchasing a freehold investment.

I hope this is helpful. However, if you have any queries please give me a call.

Yours sincerely,

A.N. Accountant

Chapter 19

Question 19.1

(a) **Obligation to register**
If you are operating a business that is making taxable supplies, i.e. selling goods that are within the charge to VAT, then you must register with HRMC if at any time the total value of taxable supplies made in the previous 12 months exceeds the registration threshold – currently £85,000. This is the historical test.

There is also a second test: if you believe that in the next 30 days alone (i.e. without regard to a previous period) your taxable supplies will exceed the registration threshold (£85,000), you must notify HMRC. This is the future test.

The two tests interact, such that the test that gives the earliest date is the one that applies.

Under the historical test, you must notify HMRC within 30 days of the end of the month in which you exceeded the limit; with the future test you must notify HMRC within 30 days of the date you anticipate exceeding the limit. If you are required to register under the historical test, you will then be registered for VAT from the first day of the second month after the month in which you exceed the £85,000 limit. Under the future test, you must start charging VAT immediately from the start of the month the threshold will be exceeded.

(b) **How to register and make payment**
If a new trader is required to register for VAT (or if they voluntarily wish to do so) they must submit Form VAT1 to HMRC, either in paper format or online using HMRC's VAT Online service.

VAT due to HMRC must be paid electronically seven days after the end of the month following the VAT quarter-end. Very severe penalties can be imposed for repeated failure to file returns on time and failures to file online. For example, for the VAT quarter ended 31 December 2021, the return will need to be filed and payment made by 7 February 2022.

(c) **Records and information**
A taxable person must keep full and true records of all business transactions that affect, or may affect, their liability to VAT. The records must be kept up to date and must be sufficiently detailed to enable the trader to accurately calculate the VAT liability or repayment and, if necessary, for HMRC to check.

Under VAT legislation, there are specifically noted records that must be kept (for at least six years):

- business and accounting records;
- VAT account documentation;

- copies of all VAT invoices issued;
- copies of all VAT invoices received;
- all certificates prepared that relate to the acquisition or disposal of goods or services to or from other EU Member States;
- copy documentation in relation to imports or exports to or from non-EU Member States; and
- copies of all credit notes issued and received.

Question 19.2

(a) January 2022 is the first period in which sales within the previous 12-month period exceed £85,000. Thus, Stephen will have to register with HMRC by 28 February 2022 and start to charge VAT on 1 March 2022.

(b) No – the second test would only apply if he had thought he would make sales of more than £85,000 within 30 days of starting to trade.

Question 19.3

Initially, we must determine the basic tax point. For goods, this is the time that they leave the vendor and go to the buyer. For services it is when the service has been completed, e.g. when an accountant finishes preparing an income tax return and any associated work.

The basic tax point can be adjusted in a number of circumstances. For example, if a payment is received or if an invoice is issued before the basic tax point is reached, the tax point moves forward to either the date the payment is received or the date the invoice is issued. Also, if an invoice is instead issued within 14 days (30 days at HMRC's discretion) of the work being completed (i.e. after the basic tax point), then the actual tax point will move to the date the invoice is issued.

This is important as it may move the sale on to a different VAT return and so to a later, or earlier, VAT payment date.

Question 19.4

A valid VAT invoice must contain the following information:

1. An identifying invoice number.
2. The date of the supply.
3. The date of issue of the document.
4. The name, address and VAT registration number of the supplier.
5. The name and address of the person to whom the goods and/or services are being supplied.
6. Description sufficient to identify the goods and/or services supplied.
7. For each item so described, the quantity of the goods or extent of the services, the rate of VAT charged and the amount payable (excluding VAT).
8. The gross amount payable, excluding VAT.
9. The rate of any cash discount offered.
10. The total amount of VAT chargeable in Sterling.
11. The unit price if the goods are sold in units.

Question 19.5

Michael will need to be careful to file his VAT returns on time because if he does not the penalties that can arise can be very punitive.

The first time he files a late return, HMRC will issue a warning notice to him. This will advise him that if another default (i.e. a late filing) occurs in the next 12 months, he will be liable to a penalty. If Michael subsequently defaults in this 12-month period, he will be liable to a penalty of 2% of the unpaid tax due on the late return. Thus, if the tax is nil or a repayment is due, no penalty will be due.

However, a further consequence of the second late return is that the 12-month "on notice period" is extended to 12 months from the end of the VAT quarter in which the second VAT default occurred. This extension will continue to occur on subsequent defaults until Michael reaches the end of the extended period without another later return. However, the amount due as a penalty continues to rise as further defaults occur in the extended period, as follows:

Third default – 5% of unpaid VAT
Fourth default – 10% of unpaid VAT
Rest of defaults – 15% of unpaid VAT

Thus the penalties can be very large. Penalties can also arise for failure to file online.

The position is slightly different for small businesses – one with a turnover below £150,000. When a small business is late submitting a VAT return or paying VAT, it will receive a letter from HMRC offering help. No penalty will be charged. A surcharge liability notice will be issued if there is a second default within 12 months of the letter, again offering help without penalty. However, on the issue of a third letter, a 2% penalty will apply, which increases to 15% on the issue of a sixth, subsequent default.

New VAT penalty rules will apply from 1 April 2022 for those who fail to submit returns on time or who fail to pay on time.

Question 19.6

VAT liability of Mr Byte for the period July/August/September 2021:

	£	£
VAT charged (Note 1)		20,000
Total input credits		
Purchases (Note 2)	8,400	
Stationery	1,200	
Electricity	2,000	
Claimable input VAT	11,600	(11,600)
VAT due		8,400

Notes:

1. As Mr Byte is not using the cash receipts basis, the sales in the period will be the relevant amount for calculating the output VAT that he has to charge.
2. Based on the tax point being the date of invoice, the £42,000 purchases figure is the relevant one when determining the recoverable input VAT on purchases.

Explanatory Notes

▧ No input VAT is reclaimable on client entertaining costs.
▧ No VAT is charged on wages, so none is recoverable.

Question 19.7

	£	£
VAT charged (Notes 1 and 4)		0
Total input credits		
Purchases (Note 2)	0	
Stationery (Note 3)	400	
Accountancy fees (Note 3)	800	
Claimable input VAT	1,200	(1,200)
VAT due		(1,200)

Notes:

1. Since Joe supplies goods at the zero rate of VAT, he will be in a permanent VAT-repayment position.
2. Joe's purchases of ingredients will also be zero-rated, so he will not be entitled to recover any input VAT on these ingredients.
3. Joe will be able to recover input VAT suffered on the stationery and on the accountancy fees.
4. Cash discounts are irrelevant here as the sales are zero-rated.

Explanatory Notes
■ No VAT is suffered on interest received, so none is recoverable.

Question 19.8

Persons who are not required to register for VAT (due to their turnover not exceeding the registration threshold) may consider voluntary registration. In general, a person might choose to voluntarily register their business for VAT if:

1. They are a small supplier with total sales under the registration threshold, and do not want their customers to realise how small their business is – a VAT registration can give the impression of a larger and more reputable business to customers.
2. They are a start-up business whose sales have not yet exceeded the registration threshold – again, this would help to give the impression to customers that they are a more established business, which may enable them to gain a wider range of customers.
3. They purchase a lot of goods or services from VAT-registered persons, but make zero-rated supplies, or supplies to other registered persons. This will enable them to claim input credits on purchases.
4. They have not actually commenced supplying taxable goods or services, but will soon become a taxable person. This will enable them to obtain credit for VAT on purchases made before trading commences.
5. They are in a net VAT-repayable position even though they are making standard-rated supplies below the registration threshold (generally would apply only if they were making losses in early years).
6. Their customers are all or mostly all VAT-registered.

Question 19.9

The place of supply of goods is deemed to be:

1. in a case where it is a condition of supply that the goods are transported, it is the place where such transportation starts; and
2. in all other cases, it is where they are located at the time of supply, i.e. when ownership is transferred.

The basic rule for supplies of services to non-business customers is that the place of supply is where the supplier is established. For business-to-business supplies of services, the place of supply is where the customer belongs. There are exceptions to this general rule. For example, land-related services are deemed to be supplied where the land is situated.

Question 19.10

	£	£
VAT charged (Note 1)		400
Total input credits		
Food for resale (Note 2)	98	
Tables and chairs (Note 3)	88	
Cash register (Note 4)	115	
Tiler (Note 6)	40	
Solicitor	288	
Van	1,725	
Claimable input VAT	2,354	(2,354)
VAT due		(1,954)

Notes:

1. VAT is not due on most foodstuffs (essentials) taken away cold to eat off the premises, so no output VAT would be charged on the £4,000 receipts in respect of sales of cold food.
2. £588 × 1/6 = £98.
3. Businesses can recover VAT on capital items in the same way as they can on revenue items.
4. The tax point is used to determine when input VAT can be recovered. Thus, even though he has not paid for some items to date, he can recover the input VAT. If he delays paying for over six months, then bad debt relief will apply and he will have to charge himself the VAT he recovered, and claim it back in the VAT period in which he actually pays it.
5. Stock is zero-rated, therefore no VAT to reclaim.
6. A standard-rated VAT invoice was received from the tiler for the amount paid.

Index

![Chartered Accountants Ireland logo] CHARTERED ACCOUNTANTS IRELAND

THANKS FOR JOINING US

We hope that you are finding your course of study with Chartered Accountants Ireland a rewarding experience. We know you've got the will to succeed and are willing to put in the extra effort. You may well know like-minded people in your network who are interested in a career in business, finance or accountancy and are currently assessing their study options. As a current student, your endorsement matters greatly in helping them decide on a career in Chartered Accountancy.

HOW CAN YOU HELP?

If you have an opportunity to explain to a friend or colleague why you chose Chartered Accountancy as your professional qualification, please do so.

Anyone interested in the profession can visit www.charteredaccountants.ie/prospective-student where they'll find lots of information and advice on starting out.

Like us on Facebook, follow us on Twitter.

Email us at info@charteredaccountants.ie

We can all help in promoting Chartered Accountancy, and the next generation to secure their success, and in doing so strengthen our qualification and community. We really appreciate your support.